UNIVERSAL ACCESS THROUGH INCLUSIVE INSTRUCTIONAL DESIGN

Universal Access Through Inclusive Instructional Design explores the ways that educators around the world reduce barriers for students with disabilities and other challenges by planning and implementing accessible, equitable, high-quality curricula. Incorporating key frameworks such as Universal Design for Learning, these dynamic contributions highlight essential supports for flexibility in student engagement, representation of content, and learner action and expression. This comprehensive resource—rich with coverage of foundations, policies, technology applications, accessibility challenges, case studies, and more—leads the way to design and delivery of instruction that meets the needs of learners in varying contexts, from early childhood through adulthood.

Susie L. Gronseth is Clinical Associate Professor of Learning, Design, and Technology in the College of Education at the University of Houston, USA.

Elizabeth M. Dalton is Adjunct Professor of Communicative Disorders at the University of Rhode Island, USA, Senior Consultant for Dalton Educational Services International (DESI), and Director Emeritus of Development and Research at TechACCESS of RI, a statewide assistive technology center in Rhode Island, USA.

UNIVERSAL ACCESS THROUGH INCLUSIVE INSTRUCTIONAL DESIGN

International Perspectives on UDL

Edited by Susie L. Gronseth and Elizabeth M. Dalton

Routledge
Taylor & Francis Group
NEW YORK AND LONDON

First published 2020
by Routledge
52 Vanderbilt Avenue, New York, NY 10017

and by Routledge
2 Park Square, Milton Park, Abingdon, Oxon, OX14 4RN

Routledge is an imprint of the Taylor & Francis Group, an informa business

© 2020 Taylor & Francis

The right of Susie L. Gronseth and Elizabeth M. Dalton to be identified as author of this work has been asserted by them in accordance with sections 77 and 78 of the Copyright, Designs and Patents Act 1988.

All rights reserved. No part of this book may be reprinted or reproduced or utilised in any form or by any electronic, mechanical, or other means, now known or hereafter invented, including photocopying and recording, or in any information storage or retrieval system, without permission in writing from the publishers.

Trademark notice: Product or corporate names may be trademarks or registered trademarks, and are used only for identification and explanation without intent to infringe.

Library of Congress Cataloging-in-Publication Data
A catalog record for this book has been requested

ISBN: 978-1-138-35107-3 (hbk)
ISBN: 978-1-138-35108-0 (pbk)
ISBN: 978-0-429-43551-5 (ebk)

Typeset in Bembo
by Apex CoVantage, LLC

To Grandmother, Elsie Cooper Brown, who has inspired me to continue to expand my borders and embrace the diversity of people, places, and ideas. -SG

To my parents, Robert and Louise Minchin—two dedicated New Jersey high school teachers throughout their professional lives, who instilled within me two very important gifts . . . tenacity and an everlasting love of learning. -ED

CONTENTS

Foreword   xiv
David Rose
Preface   xvi
Susie L. Gronseth and Elizabeth M. Dalton
Acknowledgements   xxii

SECTION 1
Foundations of Universal Design for Learning, Accessibility, and Curricular Quality   1

1 UDL and Connected Laws, Theories, and Frameworks   3
 Elizabeth M. Dalton

2 Conceptual Frameworks for Design and Accessibility: The Design of an Online Learning System   17
 Nantanoot Suwannawut

3 Snapshot—Intersections of Race, Disability, Class, and Gender in Special/Inclusive Education: The Case of Sweden   25
 Girma Berhanu

4 Snapshot—Proactive Design to Ensure Accessibility   30
 Lesley Casarez, David Hooks, Gina Shipley, and Dallas Swafford

SECTION 2
Policies and Structures for Reducing Learning Barriers 33

5 The Prospects of Universal Design for Learning in South
   Africa to Facilitate the Inclusion of All Learners 35
   Marcia Lyner-Cleophas

6 The Global UDL Virtual Classroom: A Model for
   International Collaboration and Learning 46
   Frances Smith and Serra De Arment

7 Decaffeinated UDL: Chile in Quest of Inclusive Education 59
   Boris Alvarez, Paola Andrea Vergara, and Irma Iglesias

8 Universal Design for Learning in China 68
   Haoyue Zhang and George Zhao

9 Snapshot—Reducing Learning Barriers Through the Use
   of the FACE Program 76
   Radhike Khanna and Elizabeth M. Dalton

10 Snapshot—A District's Journey to Measure Universal
   Design for Learning (UDL) 81
   Katie Novak and Laura Chesson

SECTION 3
Inclusive Classroom Design and Instructional Strategies 83

11 Access to the Curriculum for Students With Disabilities:
   Moving Closer to the Promise of UDL in Inclusive US
   Classrooms 85
   Rita Brusca-Vega and Anastasia Trekles

12 Balancing Requirements, Options and Choice in UDL:
   Smorgasbord or Nutritious Diet? 95
   Britt Tatman Ferguson

13 UDL Practices in India: Paving a Path From Equality to
   Equity in Learning 103
   Aashna Khurana

14 UDL-Inspired Pedagogical Practices and a Case Study in
    Regular Japanese Classes   111
    Kiyoji Koreeda

15 Low-Tech Solutions for Utilizing the UDL Framework
    in the Inclusive Mathematics Classroom   120
    Marla J. Lohmann, Ruby L. Owiny, and Kathleen A. Boothe

16 Snapshot—Science for All Through UDL: Using UDL as
    a Framework for Science Education for the
    English Learner   132
    Heather Pacheco-Guffrey and Jeanne Carey Ingle

17 Snapshot—Reconstructing Asynchronous Online
    Learning With UDL   135
    Kathryn Nieves

SECTION 4
Technology Innovations for Inclusive Learning   139

18 SAMR Strategies for the Integration of Technology
    Through UDL   141
    *Debra K. Bauder, Katherine M. Cooper and
    Thomas J. Simmons*

19 Engagement, Representation, and Expression in Online
    Mind Mapping Activities   153
    Rosa Cendros Araujo and George Gadanidis

20 Handcrafted Customized Content and School Activities
    With Newly Developed Technologies   164
    Shigeru Ikuta and Yumi Hisatsune

21 Connecting the World in a Disconnected Classroom   173
    Vivian B. Intatano

22 Snapshot—Wearable Assistive Technology: An Illuminated
    Glove Project With Conductive Thread and LilyPad
    Technology   179
    Cindy L. Anderson and Kevin M. Anderson

23 Snapshot—Aquatic Adventures: Deep Dive Investigation
of UDL Through a Pond Keepers Project 182
Juliet Boone

SECTION 5
Issues in the Design of Accessible Instructional Materials 185

24 Universal Access in Online Distance Education:
A Case Study From the Philippines 187
Melinda dela Peña Bandalaria

25 Applying UDL Principles in an Inclusive Design Project
Based on MOOCs Reviews 197
Francisco Iniesto, Covadonga Rodrigo, and Garron Hillaire

26 General Accessibility Guidelines for Online Course
Content Creation 208
Kathleen Bastedo and Nancy Swenson

27 Snapshot—Creating UDL Learning and Teaching
Strategies to Address the Underrepresentation of
Present-Day Indigenous Perspectives 218
Kerry Armstrong, Brenda Boreham, and Terri Mack

28 Snapshot—Using the YouTube Automated Captioning
Tool for Video Lectures 221
Sandra A. Rogers

29 Snapshot—A Fully Mobile Professional Development
Course for Teachers in Israel 224
Shir Boim-Shwartz and Eran Adi Cioban

30 Snapshot—Examining the Integration of
Digital and Multimodal Resources in
Online Courses Using a Universal Design
Framework 227
Peggy Semingson and Kathryn Pole

SECTION 6
Current Research and Evaluation in Inclusive Learning Around the World   231

31   The Intersection of Chinese Philosophical Traditions and UDL: Exploring Current Practice in Chinese Early Childhood Classrooms   233
Janet Arndt and Nili Luo

32   Promoting Inclusion Education and Intercultural Competence in International Service-Learning Project-Based Course in Ecuador   242
Maria De Freece Lawrence

33   Designing an Online Graduate Orientation Program: Informed by UDL and Studied by Design-Based Research   250
Jennifer Lock, Carol Johnson, Jane Hanson, Yang Liu, and Alicia Adlington

34   Developing Inclusive Education in Ireland: The Case for UDL in Initial Teacher Education   258
Ellen Reynor

35   Snapshot—Understanding How UDL Can Serve as a Framework for Instructional Decisions   267
Lisa Harris and Lindsay Yearta

36   Snapshot—Importance of Classroom Atmosphere in Elementary Schools to Improve the Inclusive Education System in Japan   269
Honami Okabe and Masayoshi Tsuge

SECTION 7
Inclusive Instructional Design Cases   273

37   Innovative Approach: Using Legos in a Hands-On Activity to Teach Educators the Foundations of UDL   275
Amir Bar and Betty Shrieber

38 Spreading the Word About Assistive Technology and
Universal Design for Learning: A Model for Professional
Teacher Learning 284
Jennifer Edge-Savage and Mike Marotta

39 Universal Design for Learning in Augmented and
Virtual Reality Trainings 294
Katharina Menke, Jennifer Beckmann, and Peter Weber

40 Raising the Bar With UDL: A Case for Change 305
Leanne Woodley

41 Snapshot—Designing for Open Educational
Environments: Balancing Access, Equity, and Engagement 315
Elizabeth Childs and Jo Axe

42 Snapshot—Support for Students With Developmental
Disabilities in a Regular Elementary School Class in Japan 318
Shintaro Nagayama and Masayoshi Tsuge

SECTION 8
Future Directions 321

43 The Potential Evolution of Universal Design for Learning
(UDL) Through the Lens of Technology Innovation 323
David Banes and Kirk Behnke

44 Universal Design for Learning and the Landfill of
Revolutionary Educational Innovations 332
Dave L. Edyburn

45 Snapshot—The Precarious Promise of Emergent Tech
and Universal Design for Learning: A Pivotal Point 343
Susan Molnar

46 Snapshot—A Vision for Pre-Service and In-Service
Learner-Centered Teaching Through the Arts 346
Susan Trostle Brand and Laurie J. DeRosa

47 Epilogue: Learning From Diverse Perspectives on
   Inclusive Instructional Design and Next Steps 351
   Susie L. Gronseth

List of Contributors *358*
Index *371*

FOREWORD

One of the fundamental ideas at the heart of UDL is the recognition that personal abilities and disabilities are context-dependent. Whether someone appears to be "gifted" or "handicapped" depends not only on their individual strengths and weaknesses, but on the affordances and barriers in their learning environment.

The reality of context-dependency is fundamental not only to the field of education but also to almost any field of scientific study. How molecules behave, how solar systems behave, how cultures behave: all of these are significantly determined by the context in which they are observed.

To offer a personal example, I sometimes have trouble breathing; I "have" asthma. But my ability to breathe easily is not determined primarily by the status of my lungs but by the status of the environment. My asthma strikes in environments where there is pollen, dust, ragweed, etc., while in most other environments I have no breathing problems at all. And, there are environments where almost *everyone* has trouble breathing. On Mt. Everest, for example, everyone (who gets that far) has severe breathing problems, sometimes fatal breathing problems. Like every aspect of complex biological systems, successful breathing is context-dependent. Life depends not just on our personal biology but on the specific challenges and supports in the environments that surround us.

What is important about this wonderful book, and all of its varied chapters, is that it invites us to explore and learn about the context-dependency of UDL itself.

Whether UDL will be successful in any environment will certainly depend upon the adequacy of the principles and practices it proposes. But its success will also just as certainly depend upon the capability of UDL to "breathe" in highly different contexts or environments. This book signals an important development in the field of UDL, a more advanced stage where we begin to understand the effects of context on the success or failure of UDL itself. This book makes it apparent that we need to understand not only what works and for whom, but under what conditions. Context matters.

Moreover, this book exposes the breadth and depth of what we must mean by context. At first glance, this book is about international cultural differences. Indeed, the rich collection of chapters in this book provides a wonderful view of how the principles and practices of UDL are, or should be, expressed in varied cultures. How well do the tenets of UDL apply in cultures as different as China, South Africa, Germany, or Chile?

But that is just the beginning of understanding context. From the outset, the editors of this book emphasize that there are many important contextual variables that will undoubtedly affect the success of UDL, in any culture. Importantly, they, and the authors of each of the individual chapters, explore how UDL fits within, and/or disrupts, a wide variety of educational theories, frameworks, practices, and technologies. They remind us that the future of UDL will depend upon adequately understanding the intersection of UDL with settings shaped by everything from Confucianism to multiple intelligences, from behavior modification to mastery learning, from Bloom's taxonomy to TPACK, from service learning to online learning, from environmental ecology to virtual reality.

The benefit of examining UDL in all these contexts is not only to learn how to apply its principles and practices optimally, but also to learn how to make UDL itself more truly universal. The chapters in this volume make it clear that the principles and practices of UDL will have to adapt and accommodate to more diverse contexts in the years ahead. Only by doing that will we be assured that UDL itself will be flexible and powerful enough to meet the challenge of the diversity that actually lies ahead. That will be a very good thing.

Since the early days of UDL, we have been saying that "The Future is in the Margins." This book brings those margins into much sharper focus and thus points the way to the future of UDL.

Dr. David H. Rose
CAST Co-Founder and
Chief Education Officer, Emeritus

PREFACE

Providing universal access to education through the implementation of instructional strategies, materials, and systems that can effectively address the needs of widely differing learners, essentially building systems that are fully *inclusive*, is a worldwide priority. As such, countries are at differing development points in this important process, and resources are often lacking. In the spring of 2018, following our Society for Information Technology in Teacher Education (SITE) conference in Alexandria, Virginia, we began to discuss the possibility of developing a book that could bring together the many varied viewpoints and iterations of inclusive instructional design and Universal Design for Learning (UDL) that we knew existed around the world but had not yet been shared with the wider professional community. We have been fortunate to spend time living and traveling internationally and have worked with educational professionals in Qatar, UAE, South Africa, Namibia, the USA, Canada, Brunei, Japan, Denmark, New Zealand, Australia, and beyond. We have learned about many great ideas and efforts that are being used to address the differing needs of students in order to achieve educational access and equity, and we have seen how educators globally are striving to develop inclusive instruction and materials to offer ALL students the same rich opportunities to learn. We are excited to see various systems being developed in different parts of the world that acknowledge and embrace learner variation and address such variation proactively, through innovative design of curriculum and instruction. We wanted to give rise to a book that would provide a representative glimpse of the work that we knew was happening around the world. And so began this book project.

We thought of our immediate contacts through our work with the Inclusive Learning Network (and particularly, the International Committee) of the International Society for Technology in Education (ISTE), our contacts through SITE and other organizations, and the professional connections made over years through consulting and connecting with those who share our interest in design approaches that can provide educational opportunities for all learners. We created a list of these as part of our book proposal. Though our initial list began with professional friends and acquaintances that we already knew, we expanded our horizon of contacts as well through searching professional networks, tools such as LinkedIn, and conference presentations for others who were doing work in this area. We also had a broad call for chapters that provided an opportunity for others to submit proposals to share what they were doing and for us to consider how their work might fit within the scope of the book.

We were initially overwhelmed by the reception of this proposed book and the interest from authors around the world to contribute to it. It became clear that there is expansive work being done by educators globally to address challenges of accessibility and curricular equity and quality in their course design, delivery, and environments. We had so many excellent proposals for chapters that it was difficult to select those that would be carried through to full chapters. There were many that we were not able to include in this first volume, and we may consider pursuing a second volume in some time. Nonetheless, those that we ultimately selected to be developed as either full chapters or shorter chapter snapshots were chosen with purposeful intent to provide broad representation of diverse perspectives from different parts of the world and varied educational settings. The book has 85 contributors from more than 15 countries who discuss projects in Jamaica, Ecuador, Chile, Spain, England, Ireland, Sweden, Germany, Israel, South Africa, India, Thailand, Philippines, China, Japan, Australia, Canada, and the USA. Thus, this book has enabled us to become acquainted with a host of new inclusive learning colleagues. We have engaged closely with them over the past year, working together toward a final copy that enabled their individual views, experiences, and ideas to shine through, and their work continually inspired and strengthened our resolve to bring this book into reality. We deeply appreciate how the many different voices that speak about inclusive instructional design and UDL have come together through the pages of this book.

As co-editors, we devoted much time and thought to how the book should be organized. Typically, books in the education field are structured to address specific levels of education, such as early childhood, K-12, higher education, etc. While we discussed this as a possibility, we came to realize that we sought a structure that would resonate equally with educators around the world and would ensure that all of the thematic areas in which UDL and inclusive instructional design are being applied toward the goal of universal access would be clearly understood by the varied readership. To this end, we organized the chapters into eight themed sections:

1. *Foundations of Universal Design for Learning, Accessibility, and Curricular Quality*
    This section provides a strong foundation on the UDL design framework and similar inclusive instructional design approaches and the theoretical concepts on which they are based. It connects these concepts and design

frameworks to issues of accessibility and curricular quality for supporting learners with differing needs and abilities. Chapters explore foundational laws, theories and frameworks upon which inclusive instructional design is built (Dalton, USA); conceptual frameworks for design and accessibility relevant to online learning systems (Suwannawut, Thailand); perspectives on issues of race, disability, class, and gender in one country's special and inclusive education system (Berhanu, Sweden); and approaches to ensure accessibility through proactive design (Casarez, Hooks, Shipley, and Swafford, USA).

2. *Policies and Structures for Reducing Learning Barriers*

   Chapters in this section identify, explain, and explore the impact of existing educational policies around the world that relate to inclusion and how these policies (or lack thereof) frame international structures that support educational equity for diverse populations. It introduces policies and prospects of UDL in South Africa to facilitate inclusion within higher education (Lyner-Cleophas, South Africa); a model for a global UDL virtual classroom for professional collaboration and learning introduced in Jamaica (Smith and De Arment, USA); concerns about the "decaffeination" of UDL implementation in Chile (Alvarez, Vergara, and Iglesias, Chile); an analysis of inclusive educational policies and practices in China (Zhang and Zhao, USA); a unique program model of education, vocational preparation, and support for persons with developmental disabilities in Mumbai (Khanna and Dalton, India/USA); and the journey of two school administrators to measure UDL in their district (Novak and Chesson, USA).

3. *Inclusive Classroom Design and Instructional Strategies*

   The purpose of this section is to share examples from around the world of how UDL and inclusive design approaches are being applied to change the way that physical and instructional environments address learner variation, support accessibility, and enable teachers to be more effective in achieving inclusion. The experiences shared include a practical model for analyzing the learning environment and implementing needed adaptations to inclusively support students with differing needs and/or disabilities (Brusca-Vega and Trekles, USA); a perspective on balancing requirements, options, and choice in UDL (Tatman Ferguson, USA); an introduction to UDL practices in India, from equality to equity in learning (Khurana, India); a case study of UDL-inspired Japanese pedagogical classroom practices (Koreeda, Japan); low-tech ideas for inclusive, UDL-grounded math strategies inspired by work in several least developed countries (Lohmann, Owiny, and Boothe, USA); use of the UDL framework in science education for English language learners (Pacheco-Guffrey and Ingle, USA); and the re-envisioning of asynchronous online learning through UDL in the middle grades (Nieves, USA).

4. *Technology Innovations for Inclusive Learning*

   This section highlights and explains specific examples of how technology is being used in educational settings around the world to reduce educational barriers, achieve more equitable access, and increase engagement and motivation for learning. The chapters and snapshots represent diverse subject areas, technology applications, and geographic locations, including the following: strategies for applying the SAMR model in conjunction with UDL to integrate technology in K-12 and higher education settings (Bauder, Cooper, and Simmons, USA); online mind-mapping applications in a mathematics education program to address multiple means of engagement, representation, and expression (Cendros Araujo and Gadanidis, Canada); technologically handcrafted original teaching materials using multimedia dot codes that are being used to expand access in general and special needs schools (Ikuta and Hisatsune, Japan); perspectives on the integration of information and communication technologies (ICT) in high school classroom instruction (Intatano, Philippines); development of wearable assistive technology as exemplified through an illuminated glove project (Anderson and Anderson, USA); and examples from an educational science initiative adapted for a high school class of students with a range of developmental disabilities (Boone, USA).

5. *Issues in the Design of Accessible Instructional Materials*

   Chapters in this section speak to the problem of material inaccessibility by describing examples from various countries and identifying and sharing resources that can help students and educators to develop or acquire accessible instructional materials. Initiatives presented in this section include the Open Distance eLearning (ODeL) framework for universal access for adult learners (dela Peña Bandalaria, Philippines); a recommender system that supports user review of MOOCs through the lens of accessibility (Iniesto, Rodrigo, and Hillaire, UK/Spain); best practices and strategies related to the development of accessible online course materials (Bastedo and Swenson, USA); UDL principles as embedded in books developed to represent present-day Indigenous perspectives (Armstrong, Boreham, and Mack, Canada); implementation of YouTube automated captioning for university course lecture videos (Rogers, USA); a fully mobile professional development (PD) course for teachers with flexibility in formats and assignments to address varied learner needs (Boim-Shwartz and Cioban, Israel); and a multimodal design approach for online courses that supports flexibility and high-engagement (Semingson and Pole, USA).

6. *Current Research and Evaluation in Inclusive Learning Around the World*

   This section provides a sampling of exemplary research that explores issues of inclusive educational practice and applied strategies and frameworks in different parts of the world. Results and recommendations applicable to implementing inclusive instructional design are discussed. Chapters describe how early childhood teachers in China build upon the philosophical influence of Confucius in their applications of UDL principles (Arndt and Luo, USA); an international service-learning course in Ecuador that was grounded in UDL and supported the development of intercultural competencies (De Freece Lawrence, USA); design-based research on an online orientation program aligned to the UDL principles (Lock, Johnson, Hanson, Liu, and Adlington, Canada/Australia); reflective inquiry into guidance of undergraduate teacher candidates to use UDL principles in lesson planning and teaching (Reynor, Ireland); exploration through a longitudinal study of the extent to which teacher candidates integrate technology and content during internship (Harris and Yearta, USA); and inquiry into elements of the classroom atmosphere that impact attitudes and understanding in inclusive elementary school classrooms (Okabe and Tsuge, Japan).

7. *Inclusive Instructional Design Cases*

The purpose of this section is to provide representative case study examples of inclusive instructional practices for readers to consider as they look to apply the information and strategies from earlier chapters to their own countries and educational environments. Cases include an innovative approach for motivating teachers to apply UDL through the incorporation of Lego building blocks (Bar and Shrieber, Israel); a blended course model for professional teacher learning in UDL and assistive technology (AT) (Edge-Savage and Marotta, USA); the use and interrelationship of AR/VR learning and UDL as implemented through a vocational training curriculum (Menke, Beckmann, and Weber, Germany); action research in an alternative education school for disengaged, at-risk youth that explores the impact of UDL training and support on teacher practices, student engagement, and attendance (Woodley, Australia); faculty and student perceptions of openness in blended, online, and face-to-face learning informed by principles of UD and UDL (Childs and Axe, Canada); and techniques for supporting students with developmental disabilities in regular education classes (Nagayama and Tsuge, Japan).

8. *Future Directions*

This final section looks ahead and considers inclusive learning issues globally and projects how the concepts presented in this book can leverage change in educational systems and their components in order to move toward universal access to learning for all. Chapters explore emerging technologies and their potential impact on inclusive learning and UDL (Banes and Behnke, UK/USA); critically consider whether UDL is a fad or research-based educational innovation (Edyburn, USA); discuss issues of emergent technology access, equity, and segregation for populations with diverse abilities (Molnar, USA); offer a vision for arts-integrated teaching and curricula through multiple intelligences, UDL, and learner-centered projects (Trostle Brand and DeRosa, USA); and identify themes across chapters in order to help readers consider how to bring inclusive instructional design and UDL integration to the next level of worldwide implementation (Gronseth, USA).

With this being our first book published together as co-editors, we have drawn from and applied our unique experiences and backgrounds in the field of education to its development and completion. Dr. Susie L. Gronseth provided technical and research expertise from experience as clinical faculty in instructional technology and her extensive background in instructional design theories and practices and supporting diverse learners through online learning course development and pedagogy. Dr. Elizabeth (Betsy) Dalton's background lies in many years of teaching in special education, curriculum development, assistive technology, and more recently in Universal Design for Learning, having spent a year as a post-doctoral fellow working with CAST, Inc. and Boston College in UDL. Together, we found that our complementary strengths served to broaden both the perspectives shared in this book as well as the ways in which we were able to look at and review the chapter manuscripts, considering them from many different angles. We are thrilled with the final product and hope that you will enjoy your journey through *Universal Access Through Inclusive Instructional Design: International Perspectives on UDL*.

Susie L. Gronseth, Ph.D.

Elizabeth M. Dalton, Ph.D.

ACKNOWLEDGEMENTS

The editors, Susie L. Gronseth and Elizabeth M. Dalton, would like to acknowledge the chapter authors for contributing their unique perspectives and actively participating in the writing and revising work of this book. Many of the chapter authors also contributed their time to peer-review other chapters, and we are grateful to them for sharing their expertise and feedback. We thank Dr. Kimberly Coy for providing peer-review of chapters as well. We are grateful to the professional organizations who provided networks through which we were able to reach such a wide range of educational scholars and practitioners around the world, including the International Association of Special Education (IASE), the International Committee and the Inclusive Learning Network (ILN) of the International Society for Technology in Education (ISTE), and the Universal Design for Learning Special Interest Group (UDL-SIG) of the Society for Information Technology and Teacher Education (SITE). We recognize Dr. David Rose and Dr. Anne Meyer for their visionary development of UDL, as well as others in the field whose ideas have led the way toward a more inclusive conceptualization of curriculum and instruction. We appreciate the guiding role that CAST, Inc. has played through its leadership in UDL, as well as providing inspiration for this book. We thank Dr. Curt Bonk at Indiana University for his mentorship and insights into the process of developing this internationally focused project. We thank Daniel Schwartz and the editorial team at Routledge for investing in this project and seeing it to completion. We are grateful to our families and friends for their consideration and support for us during this project, particularly during the long hours of editing and finalizing the book draft. Thank you to Elizabeth's sons, John and Martin Dalton, for all of the love and support they continue to provide to their crazy mom who never seems to stop working. Thank you to Susie's husband, Matt, and sons, Cade and Zane Gronseth, for sharing in many international adventures. We look forward to continuing to explore the world together!

SECTION 1

Foundations of Universal Design for Learning, Accessibility, and Curricular Quality

1

UDL AND CONNECTED LAWS, THEORIES, AND FRAMEWORKS

Elizabeth M. Dalton

Background

Universal Design for Learning (UDL) first appeared in professional educational practice in the mid-1990s. It is a curriculum design framework that has its foundation in both neuroscience research and in the earlier work of universal design (UD). The principles of UD were developed in 1988 by Ron Mace and colleagues at North Carolina State University (Center for Universal Design, 2008). UD is a set of architectural guidelines for developing physical environments that are maximally accessible for all users, including those with physical limitations or disabilities. Being aware of the principles of UD through their early assistive technology work, the staff of the Center for Applied Special Technology (CAST) applied UD in their work with individuals who had varying types and degrees of disability to support their access to learning through various means, including technology (CAST, 2018a). In the early 1990s, CAST began to consider how UD might be effectively applied beyond just physical environments to educational environments as well. They looked to the research in neuroscience for insight as to how the brain learned. Through this research, CAST developed the core principles of Universal Design for Learning (Rose, Meyer, Strangman, & Rappolt, 2002).

According to UDL, the *standard* learner does not exist. Rather, it is learner variation that is standard, and the UDL framework offers principles and guidelines to design instruction that addresses this wide range of learners. The three core principles of UDL are Multiple Means of Engagement, Multiple Means of Representation, and Multiple Means of Action and Expression. Each principle is further explained through specific guidelines and checkpoints that assist the user in applying the principles to any learning environment and using them to assist all learners in becoming purposeful, knowledgeable, strategic, and effective learners (CAST, 2018b).

Rationale

The author participated as a post-doctoral fellow in UDL in 2010 with CAST and Boston College. Through this experience and previous UDL-related projects at Rhode Island College in Providence, RI, the author developed a deep understanding of how the UDL framework can be applied in K-12 and adult learning settings, including both adult education and higher education venues. Her work in UDL as a consultant and instructor has influenced teacher candidates and education professionals in the US and many other countries. The author views UDL as an *umbrella concept* that helps educators to implement many other inclusive instructional design theories, frameworks, and laws relating to equity of access to education through the elegant simplicity of its three core principles. In the sections to follow, the author will explain many of these laws, theories, and frameworks, and how each may apply to the educator's practice. Finally, the author will discuss how UDL can provide support to educators to expand their instruction in order to achieve equity of access to learning for students with widely varied needs and/or disabilities.

Main Concepts

Key US Laws Regarding Inclusion

In 1973, the US Rehabilitation Act, and more specifically Section 504 of this act, was the first legislation of its kind to ensure the civil rights of persons with disabilities by prohibiting discrimination in programs receiving federal financial assistance, including public school programs at grades K-12 and higher education levels (Disability Rights Education & Defense Fund, 2018). This law laid the groundwork for further disability rights laws that would impact US public education systems and broader community access. In 1975, the Education for All Handicapped Children Act, also known as Public Law 94–142, was passed by the US Congress to guarantee free and appropriate public education for all children with disabilities, assure that the rights of children with disabilities and their parents/guardians are protected, assist states in providing such education, and assess and ensure the effectiveness of these efforts (US Department of Education, 2010). This legislation remains in force today as the Individuals with Disabilities Education Act (IDEA); it has been reauthorized several times and expanded in its scope and clarification of rights and services for children with disabilities (IDEA, 2018). IDEA currently works in coordination with a new, comprehensive law for US public education known as the Every Student Succeeds Act (ESSA), passed by the US congress in 2015. ESSA supports students with disabilities and their teachers by disaggregating data on student progress to ensure appropriate accommodations, increases local school and team control of individualized programs, supports early intervention programs, requires appropriate assessment accommodations for all students, and articulates parent/guardian rights to opt-out of statewide assessments for their children (Alverez, 2016). Finally, Section 504, as well as the Civil Rights Act of 1964 that prohibits discrimination based on race, color, religion, sex, or national origin, laid groundwork for development and passage of the landmark Americans with Disabilities Act (ADA) in 1990. The ADA is comprehensive civil rights legislation that "guarantees that people with disabilities have the same opportunities as everyone else to participate in the mainstream of American life—to enjoy employment opportunities, to purchase goods and services, and to participate in State and local government programs and services" (US Department of Justice, 2018). Each of these laws has played a vital role in framing the development of inclusive systems of education and community access for both adults and children with disabilities in the US.

Key Laws Regarding Inclusion Around the World

It was quite a number of years after the passage of initial US laws protecting individuals with disabilities from discrimination that world organizations began to discuss and frame guidelines for equity of access to education for persons with disabilities. The first official statement came from the United Nations (UN) through its office concerned with education, science, and culture—UNESCO. UNESCO was established to build peace through international cooperation in the three designated areas (UNESCO, 2018). In 1990, the Office of the United Nations High Commissioner for Human Rights (OHCHR) spearheaded development of the World Declaration on Education for All. It states: "Every person—child, youth and adult—shall be able to benefit from educational opportunities designed to meet their basic learning needs," and it was adopted by the World Conference on Education for All in March, 1990 in Jomtien, Thailand (OHCHR, 2018). Following this, at the World Conference on Special Education Needs organized by the Government of Spain in cooperation with UNESCO, 92 governments and 25 international organizations gathered in Salamanca, developing and adopting the Salamanca Statement on Principles, Policy and Practice in Special Needs Education and a Framework for Action (UNESCO, 1994). This statement affirms the fundamental right of *every* child to education, the uniqueness of every child's abilities and needs, the importance of designing education systems to address diversity, and the recognition that children with special educational needs must have access to regular schools, preferably those with inclusive orientations that combat discriminatory attitudes. The Salamanca Statement serves as a major guiding document for inclusive education initiatives around the world. The world push toward inclusive education was further supported by the Dakar Framework for Action, which outlines six global goals for achieving education for all (UNESCO, 2000):

Goal 1: Expand early childhood care and education
Goal 2: Provide free and compulsory primary education for all
Goal 3: Promote learning and life skills for young people and adults
Goal 4: Increase adult literacy by 50%, by 2015
Goal 5: Achieve gender parity by 2005, gender equality by 2015
Goal 6: Improve the quality of education

As a step toward addressing the implementation of inclusive education around the world, UNESCO developed specific policy guidelines to "serve as a resource for policymakers, teachers and learners, community leaders and members of civil society in their efforts to promote more effective strategies for reaching [Education for All] goals" (UNESCO, 2009, p. 4).

Clearly, a strong legal foundation has been laid in the United States and internationally that supports equal and inclusive education for all children. The challenge remains as to how to bring these desired goals into reality.

Theories

To understand the implementation possibilities of these laws, educators must consider how their own views on learning and the proven theories support learning strategies and frameworks. Next, four key learning theories will be introduced in order to ground such an understanding.

Multisensory Instruction

The first learning theory is that of psychologist Grace Fernald, Multisensory Instruction (Fernald, 1943). The "Fernald method" has guided generations of special educators. Developed as a multisensory whole-word approach (Fernald & Keller, 1921) to teach reading to those with severe learning disabilities initially, it was soon found to have relevance far beyond just the teaching of reading. Often referred to as "VAKT," the acronym stands for Visual-Auditory-Kinesthetic-Tactile, which describes each of the modalities that teachers need to consider applying in their instructional methods and materials to support the learner's primary mode of taking in information and to build other weaker modalities by linking stronger learning paths with weaker learning paths. For example, if the student shows greater strength in learning through their visual modality, new content would include information that has many visual pictures and supports, so that the concepts can be best acquired. At the same time, these visual materials would be linked with other audio, kinesthetic, and/or tactile materials for the same content, to try to strengthen these weaker paths through the connection with the stronger visual learning methods and materials—hence, the Fernald method of multisensory instruction (Cooke, 1997).

Multiple Intelligences

Moving beyond VAKT, Harvard psychologist Howard Gardner wrote a seminal book, *Frames of Mind*, which first introduced and then expanded his theory of human multiple intelligences. Gardner explains that the multiple intelligences, or competencies, that people have relate to their own unique set of aptitudes and, therefore, how they might prefer to learn and demonstrate their knowledge. Gardner's original core set of seven intelligences was initially published in *Frames of Mind* (1983), with two more intelligences added in his book, *Intelligence Reframed* (1999). The nine multiple intelligences are as follows:

1. Verbal-linguistic intelligence (well-developed verbal skills and sensitivity to the sounds, meanings, and rhythms of words)
2. Logical-mathematical intelligence (ability to think conceptually and abstractly, and capacity to discern logical and numerical patterns)
3. Spatial-visual intelligence (capacity to think in images and pictures, to visualize accurately and abstractly)
4. Bodily-kinesthetic intelligence (ability to control one's body movements and to handle objects skillfully)
5. Musical intelligence (ability to produce and appreciate rhythm, pitch, and timbre)
6. Interpersonal intelligence (capacity to detect and respond appropriately to the moods, motivations, and desires of others)
7. Intrapersonal (capacity to be self-aware and in tune with inner feelings, values, beliefs, and thinking processes)
8. Naturalist intelligence (ability to recognize and categorize plants, animals, and other objects in nature)
9. Existential intelligence (sensitivity and capacity to tackle deep questions about human existence such as: What is the meaning of life? Why do we die? How did we get here?)

According to Gardner, each person has each of these nine intelligences within themselves, but the mixture of intelligences—more of one and less of another—is unique for each person. Therefore, it is Gardner's concept that instruction and learning environments should afford opportunities for each person to maximize their own learning by being able to choose to pursue learning through their preferred intelligences. This concept fits well with Universal Design for Learning (UDL). An example of this is Gardner's intrapersonal intelligence, which connects directly with the UDL guideline of self-regulation within the principle of multiple means of engagement. Self-regulation develops as the individual is more aware of his/her own motivations, beliefs, and coping skills, and can reflect upon these through the process of self-assessment (CAST, 2018b).

Taxonomy of Learning

When considering theories that provide real ideas as to how to support effective learning for a widely varied body of students, the work of Benjamin Bloom and colleagues is certainly on the "A" list (Bloom, 1956). Their taxonomy of educational objectives for use in the classification of educational goals, commonly referred to as "Bloom's Taxonomy," has been part of foundational courses in psychology and education for decades (Seaman, 2011). The original taxonomy consisted of six categories for learning objectives—knowledge, comprehension, application, analysis, synthesis, and evaluation; and it identified three domains for educational activities to support learning in these categories—cognitive, affective, and psychomotor. Figure 1.1 depicts a recent iteration of the taxonomy from Vanderbilt University Center of Teaching. Educators continue to use Bloom's Taxonomy to ensure that their lessons cover the many levels and domains of learning needed for balanced instruction.

Conditions of Learning

The fourth theory addressed here was developed and published by Robert Gagne in 1965 in his book, *Conditions of Learning*. He states that there are two primary conditions of learning—internal (involving attention, motivation, and recall) and external (involving factors relating to behavior, such as arrangement and timing of

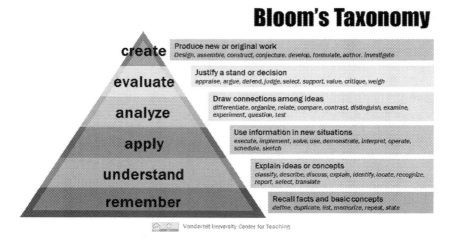

FIGURE 1.1 Bloom's Taxonomy of Educational Objectives

events). Gagne also identifies four phases of the learning process: I. Receiving the stimulus situation, II. Stage of acquisition, III. Storage, and IV. Retrieval (Gagne, 1985). Gagne espouses that these phases need to be present for any learning event to occur. In addition, Gagne outlines five main categories of human capabilities that must be considered when developing learning outcomes or objectives—verbal information, intellectual skills, cognitive strategies, attitudes, and motor skills (ibid). Gagne's theory extends to describe a sequence of nine instructional events, connected with human learning processes, that need to be addressed in the design of instruction. These events include: 1. Gaining attention, 2. Informing learner of the objective(s), 3. Stimulating recall of prerequisite learning, 4. Presenting the stimulus material, 5. Providing learning guidance, 6. Eliciting the performance, 7. Providing feedback about performance, 8. Assessing performance, and 9. Enhancing retention and transfer (ibid). Gagne's theory on the conditions of learning has been integrated throughout educational preparation programs and education systems as a basic structure for the development of well-organized lesson plans, as it serves as a point-by-point guide to make sure that plans follow a logical order and address specific learning outcomes (Driscoll, 2013).

Frameworks

Differentiated Instruction

The curriculum framework for differentiated instruction (DI) is most commonly associated with author and educator Carol Tomlinson, who describes DI as "ensuring that what a student learns, how he or she learns it, and how the student demonstrates what he or she has learned is a match for that student's readiness level, interests, and preferred mode of learning" (Ellis, Gable, Greg, & Rock, 2008, p. 32). In 1999, Tomlinson wrote *The Differentiated Classroom: Responding to the Needs of All Learners*, where she described the four key ways that teachers can differentiate their instruction, through content, process, product, and learning environment (Tomlinson, 1999). By varying these four domains, teachers can extend their instruction to reach a wider range of students. Some of the instructional approaches used to differentiate instruction include layered curriculum with layers of basic knowledge, application, and critical thinking (Nunley, 1998); tiered instruction, featuring core instruction, group interventions, and intensive interventions (RTI Action Network, 2018); and inquiry-based and project-based instruction (Boss & Larmer, 2018).

Mastery Learning

In addition to authoring his taxonomy, Benjamin Bloom is the originator of the mastery learning approach. From Bloom's first publication on the concept (Bloom, 1968), he proposed that mastery learning could positively adjust the curve of how many students could become successful achievers. The two key parameters of mastery learning are the quality and appropriateness of instruction for the learner and the lack of time limitations on learning. Bloom believed and demonstrated that when instruction matches the individual needs and interests of each student and when students have as much time as they need to interact with, understand, and respond to the lesson materials, then more than 90% of students in any classroom can achieve mastery. Some common instructional techniques that support mastery learning include individualized instruction and flipped instruction (Bergmann & Simms, 2012).

TPACK

Matthew Koehler describes the Technological Pedagogical Content Knowledge (TPACK) framework as "a way of thinking about what teachers need to know about technology" (Koehler, 2010). TPACK is based on the early work of Lee Shulman, who wrote prolifically about knowledge growth in teaching. Shulman identified two primary areas of knowledge that all teachers need—content knowledge and pedagogical knowledge (Shulman, 1986). From this foundation, Mishra and Koehler expanded these concepts to integrate technological knowledge, forming the integrated design model of TPACK (Figure 1.2). In the TPACK model, all areas of knowledge must be informed by the other knowledge areas in order for educators to design and deliver instruction competently and effectively.

In addition to the necessary areas of content, pedagogical, and technological knowledge for teachers, Misha and Koehler identify three additional areas of knowledge in the TPACK model, emerging from the overlaps of the original three areas of knowledge:

1. Pedagogical Content Knowledge (PCK): The knowledge that teachers need to have about their content and about how to teach that specific content
2. Technological Pedagogical Knowledge (TPK): The skills and knowledge necessary to identify the best technology to support a particular pedagogical approach; and
3. Technological Content Knowledge (TCK): The skills and knowledge necessary to identify the best technologies to support students as they learn content (Mishra & Koehler, 2006)

The center of the model reveals the place where all of the knowledge areas overlap—this is TPACK, the core knowledge that all teachers need in order to be successful. Since the TPACK model was first developed, it has been studied, researched, and applied in teacher preparation programs internationally. In 2018, a search in the online Learning and Technology Library of the Association for the Advancement of Computing in Education (AACE) yielded more than one

UDL and Connected Laws, Theories, Frameworks   11

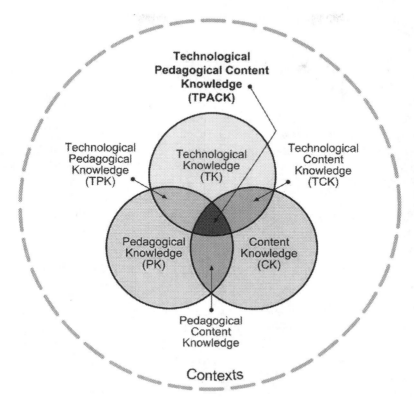

FIGURE 1.2 The TPACK Model (Mishra & Koehler, 2006)
Source: Reproduced by permission of the publisher, © 2012 by tpack.org

thousand papers relating to TPACK. Additional information and resources relating to the TPACK model can be found at the official TPACK website, http://tpack.org/.

SAMR

In 2006, as a consultant to the Maine Department of Education, Dr. Ruben Puentedura gave a presentation to the Maine School Superintendents Association entitled "Transformation, Technology, and Education." In this presentation, Dr. Puentedura shared his recently developed framework for integrating technology into educational practice. The framework has come to be known as SAMR, standing for the following four components (Puentedura, 2006, 2009):

- Substitution: Technology acts as a direct tool substitute, with no functional change.

- Augmentation: Technology acts as a direct tool substitute, with functional improvement.
- Modification: Technology allows for significant task redesign.
- Redefinition: Technology allows for the creation of new tasks, previously inconceivable.

The components of substitution and augmentation provide enhancement of content knowledge through technology, while the components of modification and redefinition provide transformation of this knowledge through the creative opportunities offered through the integration of technology into the learning processes (ibid). The SAMR model for technology integration can be used effectively in many ways, one of which is to provide a means for implementing the different areas of knowledge identified in the previously discussed TPACK model. Information about SAMR may be found at Dr. Puentedura's website at www.hippasus.com/.

UDL

As introduced in the beginning of this chapter, the basic concepts of UDL grew from the principles of UD developed by Ron Mace and colleagues at North Carolina State University (Story, Mueller, & Mace, 1998), outlining how physical buildings and environments could be designed to be maximally accessible to persons with widely varying needs and/or disabilities. The researchers of CAST, which was then a small, non-profit agency providing direct services to children with disabilities and the professionals who worked with them, recognized that the basic premise of universal design had relevance far beyond just physical environments. In response to the recognized variation in learning needs of the wide range of children they were working with, CAST considered how UD could be applied in educational environments. Reviews of neuroscientific research led CAST to the development of a set of core principles for guiding the design of curriculum and learning environments to address the full range of differing needs existing in classrooms. The three core principles of UDL: providing multiple means of engagement, multiple means of representation, and multiple means of action and expression (Rose et al., 2002), now lead CAST's work as an international educational research organization.

Since the time that UDL was first developed, much has happened to support its integration into the educational system. CAST developed comprehensive guidelines and checkpoints to guide educators in how the UDL principles relate to the functions of the classroom and what actions teachers can take to follow the principles in designing lessons, educational units, and curricula. The guidelines explain how to provide multiple means of engagement, representation, and action and expression in one's teaching, and they offer practical strategies for doing so. The graphic representation of the UDL guidelines provides the organizational structure of the three core UDL principles, the nine UDL guidelines, and multiple checkpoints for each of the guidelines (see Figure 1.3). By applying the

FIGURE 1.3 UDL Guidelines Version 2.2

framework of UDL in instructional design, educators can successfully implement many of the aforementioned laws, theories, and frameworks to achieve educational experiences that are truly inclusive, accessible, and responsive to the needs of ALL students.

Recently, UDL has realized broad acceptance within an educational community that continues to search for appropriate and productive ways to implement inclusive education broadly. This is evidenced by the mention of UDL in several US laws, including the National Technology Act, the Higher Education Authority Act, and the most recent comprehensive US educational legislation, the Every Student Succeeds Act (ESSA). One of the best current resources for understanding UDL is the CAST publication, *Universal Design for Learning: Theory and Practice* (Meyer, Rose, & Gordon, 2014). The book captures all of the key areas relating to UDL and presents them in CAST's most recent iteration of UDL and learner variability. Access to this book and the wealth of resources on UDL from CAST are available at www.cast.org.

Conclusions and Recommendations

Reflecting on the purpose of this chapter, UDL needs to be understood in the broad context of diversification in educational design, planning, curriculum, instruction, and policies. To effectively develop and support inclusive practices within our education systems, it is critically important that such an understanding emerges from an informed, solid foundation in educational theory and policy. If we do not recognize and understand what has come before and what is already known, we cannot effectively develop our strategy for systemic change. It is the author's belief that having a better understanding of the key laws, theories, and frameworks of inclusive instructional design will help readers to more easily situate information contained in the later chapters of this text, allowing each reader to better understand the relevance of each chapter to inclusive education, broadly, and to their own instructional practice, specifically. The instructional design framework of UDL is seen as an overarching concept that embraces all other inclusive educational strategies and approaches. UDL, through the simplicity of its three core principles, can provide guidance for designing and developing instruction for any educational situation and for all varieties of learners. It enhances and enriches other inclusive educational theories; however, it is practical at its heart. The UDL framework, guidelines, checkpoints, and resources are meant to be used by educators through applications in practice to create safe, accessible, and engaging learning spaces for ALL students, regardless of need. UDL is being recognized around the world as a means to achieve true inclusion. The foundation set by the laws, theories, and frameworks of education will most certainly strengthen UDL's role in world education.

References

Alverez, B. (2016, June 30). Promising changes for special education under ESSA. *neaToday*. Retrieved from http://neatoday.org/2016/06/30/special-education-essa/

Bergmann, J., & Simms, A. (2012). *Flip your classroom: Reach every student in every class every day*. Alexandria, VA: ISTE.

Bloom, B. (1968). Learning for mastery. *UCLA Evaluation Comment, 1*(2), 1–12. Retrieved from https://programs.honolulu.hawaii.edu/intranet/sites/programs.honolulu.hawaii.edu.intranet/files/upstf-student-success-bloom-1968.pdf

Bloom, B. (Ed.), Engelhart, M., Furst, E., Hill, W., & Krathwohl, D. (1956). *Taxonomy of educational objectives, handbook I: The cognitive domain*. New York: David McKay Co. Inc.

Boss, S., & Larmer, J. (2018). *Project based teaching: How to create rigorous and engaging learning experiences*. Alexandria, VA: Association for Supervision and Curriculum Development.

CAST. (2018a). CAST timeline. Retrieved August 3, 2018, from www.cast.org/about/timeline.html#.W2ScmChKg2w

CAST. (2018b). *CAST: About universal design for learning*. Retrieved from www.cast.org/our-work/about-udl.html#.W2Sk1yhKg2w

Center for Universal Design. (2008). *Universal design principles*. Retrieved from https://projects.ncsu.edu/ncsu/design/cud/about_ud/udprinciples.htm

Cooke, A. (1997). Learning to spell difficult words: Why look, cover, write and check is not enough. *Dyslexia: An International Journal of Research and Practice, 3*(4), 240–243. British Dyslexia Association.

Disability Rights Education & Defense Fund. (2018). *Section 504 of the rehabilitations act of 1973*. Retrieved at https://dredf.org/legal-advocacy/laws/section-504-of-the-rehabilitation-act-of-1973/

Driscoll, M. (2013). *Psychology of learning for instruction* (3rd ed.). Hoboken, NJ: Pearson.

Ellis, E., Gable, R. A., Gregg, M., & Rock, M. L. (2008). Reach: A framework for differentiating classroom instruction. *Preventing School Failure, 52*(2), 31–47.

Fernald, G. (1943). *Remedial techniques in basic school subjects*. New York: McGraw-Hill.

Fernald, G., & Keller, H. (1921). The effect of kinaesthetic factors in the development of word recognition in the case of non-readers. *The Journal of Educational Research, 4*(5), 355–377. doi:10.1080/00220671.1921.10879216

Gagne, R. (1965). *The conditions of learning*. New York: Holt, Rinehart & Winston Publishing.

Gagne, R. (1985). *The conditions of learning and theory of instruction*. New York: CBS College Publishing.

Gardner, H. (1983). *Frames of mind: The theory of multiple intelligences*. New York: Basic Books.

Gardner, H. (1999). *Intelligence reframed: Multiple intelligences for the 21st century*. New York: Basic Books.

Individuals with Disabilities Education Act. (2018). *About IDEA*. Retrieved from https://sites.ed.gov/idea/about-idea/

Koehler, M. (2010). *The history of TPACK: 1999 to present (2010)*. Retrieved from http://matt-koehler.com/hybridphd/hybridphd_summer_2010/wp-content/uploads/2010/06/history_of_tpack.pdf

Meyer, A., Rose, D., & Gordon, D. (2014). *Universal design for learning: Theory and practice*. Wakefield, MA: CAST Professional Publishing.

Mishra, P., & Koehler, M. J. (2006). Technological pedagogical content knowledge: A framework for integrating technology in teachers' knowledge. *Teachers College Record, 108*(6), 1017–1054.

Nunley, K. (1998). *Transform your classroom with layered curriculum.* Retrieved from http://help4teachers.com/layeredcurriculumindex.htm

OHCHR. (2018). *World declaration on education for all of 1990.* Retrieved from www.ohchr.org/EN/Issues/Education/Training/Compilation/Pages/9.WorldDeclarationonEducationforAll(1990).aspx

Puentedura, R. (2006). *Transformation, technology, and education.* Retrieved from http://hippasus.com/resources/tte/

Puentedura, R. (2009). *As we may teach: Educational technology, from theory into practice* [Blog post]. Retrieved from www.hippasus.com/rrpweblog/archives/000025.html

Rose, D., Meyer, A., Strangman, N., & Rappolt, G. (2002). *Teaching every student in the digital age: Universal design for learning.* Baltimore: Association for Supervision & Curriculum Development.

RTI Action Network. (2018). *Tiered instruction/intervention.* Retrieved from www.rtinetwork.org/essential/tieredinstruction

Seaman, M. (2011). Bloom's taxonomy: Its evolution, revision, and use in the field of education. In D. Flinders & P. B. Uhrmacher (Eds.), *Curriculum and teaching dialogue (13) 1 and 2* (pp. 15–28). Charlotte, NC: Information Age Publishing, Inc.

Shulman, L. (1986). Those who understand: Knowledge growth in teaching. *Educational Researcher, 15*(2), 4–14.

Story, M., Mueller, J., & Mace, R. (1998). *The universal design file: Designing for people of all ages and abilities* (rev. ed.). Raleigh, NC: NC State University.

Tomlinson, C. A. (1999). *The differentiated classroom: Responding to the needs of all learners.* Hoboken, NJ: Pearson Education.

UNESCO. (1994, June 7–10). *The Salamanca statement and framework for action on special education needs.* Proceedings of World Conference on Special Education Needs: Access and Quality, Salamanca, Spain. Paris, France: UNESCO.

UNESCO. (2000, April 26–28). *The Dakar framework for action.* Adopted by the World Education Forum, Dakar, Senegal. Retrieved from https://sustainabledevelopment.un.org/content/documents/1681Dakar%20Framework%20for%20Action.pdf

UNESCO. (2009). *Policy guidelines on inclusion in education.* Paris, France: UNESCO.

UNESCO. (2018). *UNESCO in brief.* Retrieved from https://en.unesco.org/about-us/introducing-unesco

US Department of Education. (2010). *Thirty-five years of progress in educating children with disabilities through IDEA.* Office of Special Education and Rehabilitation Services. Archived information. Retrieved from https://www2.ed.gov/about/offices/list/osers/idea35/history/index_pg10.html

US Department of Justice. (2018). *Information and technical assistance on the Americans with disabilities act: Introduction to the ADA.* Retrieved from www.ada.gov/ada_intro.htm

2

CONCEPTUAL FRAMEWORKS FOR DESIGN AND ACCESSIBILITY

The Design of an Online Learning System

Nantanoot Suwannawut

Introduction

The emergence of technologies and telematics services in our era influences almost every sector of society, including education. Online learning media is an area that has been widely adopted in both distance education and on-site traditional classrooms. Since evolving information and technology services are not yet fully accessible and usable by users with disabilities, these students often encounter obstacles in their learning experiences due to barriers to these educational media and technologies. Statistical data indicate that the number of students with disabilities enrolled at the college/university level is on the rise every year (Brett, 2016). Thus, it is important to ensure that educational materials, including those offered through online learning systems, are accessible and usable by this group of students.

There is a need to develop online learning systems that can be used by students with disabilities, particularly those students who have physical challenges. Many methods have been utilized in the development process and in product design, such as incorporating accessibility standards and guidelines or consultation with an expert. Nonetheless, it would be safe to say that users with disabilities still cannot use and interact effectively and easily with many of the available online learning systems (Rangin, Petri, Richwine, & Thompson, 2011). *Online learning system* refers to a course, program, or degree delivered completely online. It utilizes electronic technologies to access educational curriculum outside of a traditional classroom. This may include but is not limited to virtual learning environments, digital repositories, multimedia, web portals, and discussion boards. A suitable theoretical framework is required for better designs of online learning systems that fully support the needs of learners with disabilities. Furthermore, such systems must be readily usable to achieve accessibility.

The ultimate goal of universal design is to make a certain product or service available to a wide range of people, particularly those who have limited functional abilities. In addition, an accurate understanding of users is very important in the design of any accessible online system, particularly in light of increasing demand for information and the diffusion of technologies in daily life. Specific design principles are required to serve within a fundamental framework for accessible design. Inclusive design, on the other hand, emphasizes an understanding of the diversity and uniqueness of each individual. The process of design and the tools used in design need to be inclusive of all users. *Universal design* and *inclusive design* are frequently mentioned in terms of design frameworks, as they share many common attributes. Both concepts originated in a similar rationale, starting with a responsibility toward the experience of the user and aiming toward social inclusion. In fact, these two concepts are not the same; understanding the underlying meanings and differences is important since actions and movements reflecting these terms can have influences on legislation, policy, practice, and, perhaps most importantly, the design process.

Analytic Contemplation of Universal Design and Inclusive Design

Universal design is defined as "design of products and environments to be usable by all people, to the greatest extent possible, without the need for adaptation or specialized design" (Center for Universal Design, 2008). Its underlying idea is to improve the general environment in order to reduce the need for special settings and use of additional devices; it offers a set of seven guiding principles to accommodate people with disabilities, older people, children, and others who are non-average in a way that is not stigmatizing and that benefits all users. Considering such a definition, it is similar to the inclusive design concept in that it is a design approach that ensures that products, services, and environments can be used and accessed by all people to the greatest extent possible, regardless of age or ability (Keates, Clarkson, Harrison, & Robinson, 2000).

The conceptual differences between universal design and inclusive design can be divided into three main categories—target population, process orientation, and strategic approach. First, it is obvious that both concepts are grounded in the idea of social emancipation. They aim to empower people, particularly minority and vulnerable groups, to be able to equally participate in the society. Both design philosophies, therefore, emphasize *users* as the center of the design process. However, their assumptions for approaching target groups are not the same. Universally designed products or environments tend to be usable and accessible by everybody, based on normalization theory (i.e., everyone is equal). On the other hand, inclusive design is a broader paradigm of design that celebrates diversity and is inclusive of all users regardless of age, ability, gender, ethnicity, and economic circumstances. The assumption here is that the society consists of multiple layers, groups, and segments; hence, taking into account the variations among users is significant. Starting with these differing philosophies, both concepts arrive at similar conclusions—namely, that if a product works well for people across the spectrum of functional ability, it works better for everyone (Institute for Human Centered Design, 2016). This premise is somehow justified, although universal design casts it as an abstract ideal. Universal design means design that has to include literally everyone, and encompasses every kind of physical and mental disability. It is generally accepted that the term "universal design" does not imply that everything in this world be fully usable by everybody, or that universal solutions are possible for all situations. This is why it is promoted as a goal to be reached and an attitude to be held rather than a strict and absolute approach.

Furthermore, the applicability issues of affordability, cultural diversity, benchmarking, mainstream customers, and cross-design domains are critical (Steinfeld, 2008). In contrast, inclusive design aims to include as many different people as possible. Its process can start with a targeted group of people and then gradually expand the design concept to include accessibility for people with various challenges based on various conditions. As a result, methods and techniques of inclusive design that embrace diversity should serve the specific needs of individuals while maintaining the integrity of the society as the whole.

In respect to process orientation, universal design focuses on *use*, whereas inclusive design focuses on *design*. Universal design can be considered as a functionalist paradigm, because it caters to utility. Inclusive design, on the other hand, takes a more pragmatic approach. To put it simply, universal design emphasizes usable products, services, and environments, striving to design things/commodities that would fit users. On the contrary, inclusive design emphasizes strategies and design processes that include the participation of users throughout, directly incorporating in the development process features that are usable for the target population (Elokla, Yoshitsugu, & Yasuyuki, n.d.). For example, a universal design approach to web design could involve additions of alternate descriptions or text equivalents to charts and graphics to make visual representations understandable and usable by users who have visual disabilities. On the other hand, an inclusive design perspective would target features (e.g., embedded tagging or special plug-ins) that allow for insertion of text equivalent as part of the design process through suitable technical approaches.

While universal design principles often provide a set of recommendations as prescriptive rules, the solutions that they suggest tend to be so broad that they are hard to implement. Inclusive design provides more concrete solutions, which are often verifiable and straightforward in developing design tools and methods. Universal design and inclusive design also differ in terms of strategy. As the universal design concept was originally developed from the concepts of accessible or barrier-free design, universal design can be considered as a current substitute for accessible design (Duncan, 2007), with its strategic focus primarily on the disabled population. Although universal design encompasses other aspects, such as aesthetics in design, the majority of studies on the topic take the viewpoint of individuals with disabilities as their major consideration (Chan, Lee, & Chan, 2009; Iwarsson & Ståhl, 2003). Consequently, researchers who adopt the perspective of universal design are likely to primarily focus on accessibility (Audirac, 2008). On the other hand, the practice of inclusive design (e.g., design for inclusion) includes potential stakeholders in the design process, providing a more holistic perspective. Therefore, the methods of inclusive design often consider environmental and societal aspects, enhancing opportunities for individual development.

Both universal design and inclusive design strive for similar goals and objectives—equal participation and social justice. However, they have different sets of assumptions, methods, and strategies to achieve those goals. Universal design focuses on prescriptive rules and a performance-based approach, whereas inclusive design emphasizes methods and strategies that promote the participation of users throughout the design. In particular, first-hand involvement and participation of potential users through all the stages of product development are believed to lead to the successful design. Inclusive design, therefore, aims to eliminate disabilities caused by design as well.

Conceptual Framework and Considerations for Design of Accessible Online Learning Systems

The preceding review of universal design and inclusive design demonstrates that these concepts can be appropriately applied to the design of accessible products and systems. Nonetheless, the design of accessible educational media and applications not only focuses on functional limitations of learners, but it also requires consideration of learning components. The following discussion reviews these design frameworks that embrace the teaching and learning elements and are useful for developing learning systems.

Inclusive Teaching and Learning and Universal Design for Learning

Inclusive teaching and learning is the framework that promotes inclusion, reduces stereotype threat, and fosters a growth mindset (Washington University in St. Louis, 2018). It refers to modes of teaching and learning that are designed to consider the diverse needs and preferences of all students to create a learning environment wherein all students feel valued and have equal access to the learning experience. The main strategies of inclusive teaching and learning include: a) diversifying content from multiple perspectives, b) maximizing the varied educational backgrounds and personal experiences of students, c) increasing awareness of problematic assumptions, and d) creating a respectful and productive learning environment (Australian Disability Clearinghouse on Education and Training, n.d.). In other words, apart from individual preferences of learners, their sociocultural backgrounds should also be taken into account when designing accessible learning environments. For example, the learning methods of deaf people in Thailand and in the US are quite different; Thai sign language is developed through posture and gestures in body language and actions in general. whereas the American Sign Language also considers an alphabetical spelling or "fingerspelling" and "manual spelling." Fingerspelling is the process of spelling out words by using hand shapes that correspond to the letters of the word while manual spelling is a set of hand shapes used to spell words (American Sign Language, n.d.). The American Fingerspelled Alphabet consists of 22 handshapes that represent the 26 letters of the American alphabet. Since Thai written language contains many letters (44 basic consonants, 32 vowels, and 5 tone marks), expressing an abstract term through Thai sign language, which often involves alphabetical spelling, is rather impossible or difficult compared to American Sign Language. Consequently, the rate of literacy of American deaf students is presumably higher than that of Thai deaf students, thereby impacting in the preparation of learning media (Woodward, 1996). To put it differently, Thai deaf students may not be able to understand the written instruction clearly since they do not know how to spell the words nor grasp the meaning of the sentence. Therefore, sign language must be employed when designing the learning media for this group of learners.

Another example is the use of shared cultural experiences among learners. Students with intellectual or multiple disabilities often have problems with speech, articulation, and comprehension of complex language generalizations and abstractions (Gargiulo & Bouck, 2017). As a result, the use of multimedia with animated content and shared stories (e.g., cartoons, lifestyle, etc.) is recommended, as these can be more interesting and increase engagement (Hitchcock & Stahl, 2003).

A majority of these strategies are aligned with Universal Design for Learning (UDL) principles. UDL is a framework that aims to accommodate everyone by focusing on learning; it creates environments that enable all learners to gain knowledge, skills, and enthusiasm for learning (Center of Applied Special Technology [CAST], 2018). The central premise of this theoretical framework is that each student can benefit from a flexible curriculum. A major approach of UDL is to design to achieve learning goals by creating flexible instructions, materials, and assessments that accommodate needs of learners, often with the use of a variety of technologies. UDL is composed of three main principles—providing multiple, flexible methods of presentation, varied methods of expression, and options for engagement (CAST, 2018). Each principle aligns to one of the three learner networks (i.e., recognition, strategic, and affective) and prescribes a specific type of curriculum flexibility to address potential individual differences. As such, this network-based framework offers a thoughtful and grounded explanation of human learning. The learner network components not only have great influence in regards to cognition, but they are also involved in specific functions, including language, thinking, problem solving, and memory. These functions are the basic elements that contribute to the learning process.

In the case of students with disabilities, each type of impairment can involve a different focus in regards to each network. For example, the recognition networks can be considered in respect to the learning of students with visual impairments. It is difficult, if not impossible, for this group of learners to perceive visual stimuli, and it may be necessary for people with blindness or low vision to use other senses to compensate for impairments to their sight. Viewing this from a combined neuroscience theory and learning object perspective, the focus on recognition networks translates to the provision of multiple and flexible means of representation. This suggests that learners with visual impairments could benefit from various methods to acquire information. For instance, digital media can supplement the use of print format materials. Due to the rich features of digital media, students would be able to not only access content materials, but the flexible ways of presenting information can also help them focus and practice on specific target skills and strategies (Sapp, 2009).

Additionally, flexible methods of representation are important to academic assessment as they provide students more freedom to demonstrate and express their learning ability, instead of confining them to a single method that might be restricting their actual performance. For example, students with visual or hearing impairments may be asked to submit their work in the form of an electronic text, video, or audio script. "Access to information/activities" and "access to learning" are not the same, although both of them are involved in a learning process (Hitchcock, Meyer, Rose, & Jackson, 2002). Access to information or learning content/materials is an approach that guides students to the knowledge.

Providing access to educational materials, however, does not guarantee that learning will occur; students usually need to be able to read and utilize the learning content as well. Therefore, stimulating and facilitating strategies must be in place to encourage learning and to enhance learning materials to be usable or meaningful to students. Hitchcock and his colleagues (2003) suggested interesting methods of instructions and scaffolds to be integrated into a UDL curriculum, such as offering concept maps highlighting main points and supporting details, showing relationships between events or parts of a complex concept, and stepping learners through an inquiry process. These strategies can be utilized in digital text and online learning systems.

Since the beginning of the 21st century, digital text has become a popular media due to its flexibility and accessibility. One useful feature of digital text is the embedded hyperlink. Hypertext not only highlights important facts to be noticed by students, but it can also help to expand and connect ideas further. Hyperlinks, though, should have meaningful explanations in order to be fully accessible by all learners. Similarly, graphical and complex learning materials may pose problems to students with visual impairments. When converting visual presentations into text format, the resulting descriptions are often quite detailed and complex. Moreover, certain types of instructional activities, such as filling in the blank or matching answers from a series of questions, can present unique challenges to this group of students. Since the visually impaired students cannot perform the skim/scan reading, locating a certain point could take time and require too much effort. Due to the affordances of current technologies, accessibility of these activities can be addressed through adjustable font size, hyperlinked definitions of unknown words, navigating landmarks, screen-reader compatibility, and synchronized text-to-audio capacity; however, they are not efficiently usable by students with visual impairment. Therefore, educators should ensure that students are not only able to access the materials but that they also understand the subject content and they could also help to proofread the materials for clarity.

Furthermore, a variety of instructional approaches should be provided for acting on information and supporting learners' development of metacognition and self-regulation. Strategies can help learners generate patterns, plan actions, and systematically act on information (Hitchcock & Stahl, 2003). Samples of these techniques are insertion of automated prompts, hints, feedbacks, and expert modeling. Instructors can make text-based materials easier to decode by using color contrasts and clear verbal descriptions for figures and other graphics (King-Sears, 2009). These instructional techniques not only help through scaffolding the learning process, but they can also increase student motivation and indirectly encourage them to apply greater effort to the task.

Conclusion

Designing an online learning system is not a matter of only the use of technology; it also involves serious consideration of pedagogical approaches. The learning materials have to be made accessible for all students. The frameworks of inclusive design and universal design provide principles and guidelines to create an accessible platform/environment for the inclusion of the greatest possible number of people, including persons with disabilities. With respect to pedagogy, the strategies of inclusive teaching and learning, as well as the Universal Design for Learning framework, provide feasible learning solutions for diverse learners. A variety of instructional methods can enable students to access learning by addressing personal attributes, capabilities, and goals. Leveraging the advantages of the digital content and online platform, many techniques can be applied to enhance learning and make learning more accessible and inclusive to diverse learners. Furthermore, an accessible online learning system requires collaboration of many stakeholders, such as teachers and programmers, in order to make learning an effective experience for a large number of students.

References

American Sign Language. (n.d.). *Fingerspelling & numbers: Introduction*. Retrieved from www.lifeprint.com/asl101/fingerspelling/fingerspelling.htm

Audirac, I. (2008). Accessing transit as universal design. *Journal of Planning Literature, 23*(1), 4–16.

Australian Disability Clearinghouse on Education and Training. (n.d.). *Information on inclusive teaching*. Retrieved from www.adcet.edu.au/inclusive-teaching/

Brett, M. (2016). Disability and Australian higher education: Policy drivers for increasing participation. In A. Harvey, C. Burnheim, & M. Brett (Eds.), *Student equity in Australian higher education twenty-five years of a fair chance for all* (pp. 87–108). [SpringerLink version].

Center of Applied Special Technology [CAST]. (2018). *Universal design for learning*. Retrieved from www.cast.org/

Center for Universal Design, NCSU. (2008). *Homepage*. Retrieved from https://projects.ncsu.edu/design/cud/about_ud/about_ud.htm

Chan, E., Lee, G., & Chan, A. (2009). Universal design for people with disabilities: A study of access provisions in public housing estates. *Property Management, 27*(2), 138–146.

Duncan, R. (2007). *Universal design—clarification and development*. A report for the ministry of the environment, government of Norway. Retrieved from www.universell-utforming.miljo.no/file_upload/udclarification.p

Elokla, N., Yoshitsugu, M., & Yasuyuki, H. (n.d.). *Understanding of universal design concept among overseas and Japanese institutions and manufacturers*. Retrieved from www.semanticscholar.org/paper/Understanding-of-the-Concept-of-Universal-Design-Elokla/5de30a677b51fe02724cd0a350a2eaa59d2aab34

Gargiulo, R. M., & Bouck, E. C. (Eds.). (2017). *Instructional strategies for students with mild, moderate, and severe intellectual disability*. Los Angeles, CA: Sage Publications.

Hitchcock, C., Meyer, A., Rose, D., & Jackson, R. (2002). Providing new access to the general curriculum. *Teaching Exceptional Children, 35*(2), 8–17.

Hitchcock, C., & Stahl, S. (2003). Assistive technology, universal design, universal design for learning: Improved learning opportunities. *Journal of Special Education Technology, 18*(4), 45–52.

Institute for Human Centered Design. (2016). *History of universal design*. Retrieved from www.adaptiveenvironments.org/index.php?option=Content&Itemid=26

Iwarsson, S., & Ståhl, A. (2003). Accessibility, usability and universal design—positioning and definition of concepts describing person-environment relationships. *Disability and Rehabilitation, 25*(2), 57–66.

Keates, S., Clarkson, P. J., Harrison, L. A., & Robinson, P. (2000). *Towards a practical inclusive design approach*. Paper presented at the Proceedings on the 2000 Conference on Universal Usability, 45–52.

King-Sears, M. (2009). Universal design for learning: Technology and pedagogy. *Learning Disability Quarterly, 32*(4), 199–201. Free Online Library database.

Rangin, H., Petri, K., Richwine, B., & Thompson, M. (2011, March 16–19). *A comparison of learning management system accessibility*. Proceedings of the 26th Annual International Technology & Persons with Disabilities Conference, San Diego. Retrieved from http://presentations.cita.illinois.edu/2011-03-csun-lms/

Sapp, W. (2009). Universal design: Online educational media for students with disabilities. *Journal of Visual Impairment & Blindness, 103*(8), 495–500.

Steinfeld, E. (2008). Universal design/design for all: Practice and method. In A. S. Helal & M. B. Abdulrazak (Eds.), *Engineering handbook of smart technology for aging, disability, and independence*. Online book. John Wiley & Sons, Inc.

Washington University in St. Louis. (2018). *Strategies for inclusive teaching*. Retrieved from https://teachingcenter.wustl.edu/resources/inclusive-teaching-learning/strategies-for-inclusive-teaching/

Woodward, J. (1996). Modern standard Thai sign language, influence from ASL, and its relationship to original Thai sign varieties. *Sign Language Studies, 92*, 227–252. Gallaudet University Press.

3

SNAPSHOT—INTERSECTIONS OF RACE, DISABILITY, CLASS, AND GENDER IN SPECIAL/INCLUSIVE EDUCATION

The Case of Sweden

Girma Berhanu

The message of inclusive education as outlined in the Salamanca statement (June, 1994) has begun to permeate the Swedish language, at least in official documents. The social model of disability and the relational nature of disablement have been officially accepted, which implies that schooling as such can be *more or less disabling or enabling*. There is, however, evidence that schools are becoming more segregated in relation to immigration background, educational background, gender, and grades and that learners from a migrant background are heavily over-represented in special education, particularly in those categories (such as *concentration and behavioral problems* or *unspecified poor talent*) for which there are no clear diagnostic criteria (Berhanu, 2008, 2011; Berhanu & Dyson, 2012; Reichenberg & Berhanu, 2017, 2018). Learners from many (though not all) minority ethnic groups are more likely to be identified as in need of special education than are their majority peers (Gabel, Curcic, Powell, Khader, & Albee, 2009; Luciak, 2008). In a European context, minority ethnicity is often (though not always) associated with migrant status and non-native-speaker linguistic status. However, it is difficult to disaggregate the relative impacts of these factors on disproportionality in special educational placements. Ethnicity is not the only factor in disproportionality. Socio-economic status and gender (specifically, being poor and being male) also play a part as they may interact with minority ethnicity or operate separately from it (Berhanu & Dyson, 2012). Sweden offers a particularly interesting case in this regard.

Some studies indicate that there is disproportional representation in special education in Sweden (e.g., Berhanu, 2008, 2010; Reichenberg & Berhanu, 2018; Rosenqvist et al., 2009). Members of minority ethnic groups (particularly where these groups have migrant status), males, and children from poorer homes are at greater risk than their peers of being placed in special education. The study of the interactions between these factors is not well developed in Sweden, but there is some evidence that ethnicity/race and gender remain factors, even when controls are entered for social class. The implication is that disproportionality reflects the construction of difference in education systems. This refers to the very workings of schools, which partly contributes to the practice of constructing differences or "otherness" based on stereotypes, sets of representational practices, biases, and exaggerated belief associated with categories. This tradition negatively affects equity and equality within educational systems.

The tradition also reflects real differences in educational achievement among the groups, which in turn are a product of wider social inequalities. This has clear implications for the development of inclusive education systems, particularly in urban contexts where inequalities are most marked (Reichenberg & Berhanu, 2018). In particular, it suggests that the development of more equitable procedures in relation to special education must be accompanied by efforts to develop more equitable societies overall. Berhanu and Dyson (2012) argue that the understanding of these issues in Sweden/Europe could be improved by better data and a coherent research effort. Although there are *some* studies investigating intersections of race, disability, class, and gender in inclusive education (e.g., Berhanu & Dyson, 2012; EADSNE, 2009), the evidence tends to be patchy across the Nordic countries as a whole, and comprehensive surveys tend to be lacking even in large cities where the problem is most visible. This is likely due in part to the lack of any centralized database, to the variable quality of statistical information, or to the significant variations in categorizations, as well as eligibility criteria.

Sweden, similar to other Nordic countries, offers a particularly interesting case for a number of reasons. Nordic countries tend to be affluent with well-resourced regular and special education systems. Sweden, in particular, has a long-standing commitment to principles of social justice; and therefore, its affluence tends to be shared fairly equally across the population. This is reflected in the education systems that perform at relatively high levels overall and the relatively small gaps between higher and lower achievers, according to recent PISA results (OECD, 2016). Considerable value has historically been attached to the ideal of the *school for all*, with the result that the special education system has developed along inclusive lines, offering support to a wide range of learners without necessarily segregating them into special settings. Despite this, disproportionality by gender, socio-economic status, and ethnicity is a significant problem that persists in the special education system (Anastasiou, Gardner, & Michail, 2011; Berhanu, 2011; Werning, Löser, & Urban, 2008).

Some studies in Sweden indicate that the number of pupils with special needs has increased mainly in large cities, and different forms of *segregated education* (e.g., preparatory programs for language learners, new arrivals) have expanded (Rosenqvist et al., 2009). Dubious assessment methods and unreflective application of individual evaluation and educational plans have led to many students being viewed as derailed from the "norm" (Skolinspektionen, 2011). It is obvious that the education system has come under serious pressure during the past two decades due to massive migration (Reichenberg & Berhanu, 2017). This exogenous shock has changed the ethnic landscape and composition dramatically and has ushered the country into an era of multiculturalism and globalization. On the negative side, this rapid demographic change has also brought ethnic segregation and inequalities, particularly in large cities, on top of already existing inequalities. That has presented major challenges to current Swedish policymakers in terms of social integration generally and educational inclusion specifically and corresponding measures need to be put into place.

The problem surrounding the overrepresentation of ethnic minorities in special educational arrangements in Sweden is as complex as in the rest of Europe, and some of the evidence presented here points to problems stemming from the home environment, including poverty; sociocultural-related problems, family factors, and language problems; lack of parental participation in decision making and power distances between parents and school authorities; institutional intransigence and prejudices; unreliable assessment procedures and criteria for referral and placement; lack of culturally sensitive diagnostic tools; and large resource inequalities that run along lines of race and class (Berhanu, 2008 and references therein; Reichenberg & Berhanu, 2018). Similarly, Dyson and Gallannaugh (2008) argued, based on recent research on proportionality in England, that

> although the identification of children as having special educational needs may result most immediately from the construction of difference at the school and teacher levels, that construction is itself a response to educational and social inequalities. It follows that a proper understanding of disproportionality, capable of generating effective means of combating it, requires an analysis not only of processes of construction but also of the underlying processes and structures through which social and educational inequality are produced.
>
> (p. 43)

The current Swedish political and educational discourses reflect contradictions and dilemmas among varied dimensions of the educational arena. Swedish social welfare/educational policy has traditionally been underpinned by a strong philosophy of universalism, which includes equal entitlements of citizenship, comprehensiveness, solidarity in approach to social inclusion, and equality of resources. Within the past decades, however, Sweden has undergone a dramatic transformation. The changes are framed within neo-liberal philosophies, such as devolution, market solutions, competition, "effectivity," and standardization. This has been coupled with a proliferation of individual/parent choices for independent schools, which altogether can potentially work *against* the valuing of diversity, equity, and inclusion. Resulting resource differences have widened among schools, municipalities, and pupils.

Swedish efforts in the past to promote equity through a variety of educational policies have been fascinating. Those early educational policies, including the macro-political agenda, focused on the social welfare model and have helped to diminish the effects of differential social, cultural, and economic background on outcomes. This has since come under threat. There is still some hope, however, of mitigating the situation through varied social and educational measures combined with an effective monitoring system and a stronger partnership and transparent working relationship between the central and local government systems. Research and follow-up are crucial in this process (Berhanu, 2009, 2011).

The justification for inclusive education is based in part on the ideals of social justice and the intertwining of social justice goals and inclusive education. However, social justice views in inclusion discourses vary. Rather, "Social justice views can be classified as individualistic or communitarian; both perspectives permeate the discourses on inclusion" (Artiles, Harris-Murri, & Rostenberg, 2006, p. 262). As Artiles and colleagues argue, we must move from a traditional social justice discourse in inclusive education (individualistic/communitarian) to a transformative model of social justice. The values involved relate to a vision of a whole society, of which education is a part. Issues of social justice, equity, and choice are central to the demands for inclusive education. This vision concerns the well-being of all pupils and making schools welcoming institutions through, for instance, measures examining ideological and historical assumptions about difference, critiquing marginalization, debunking merit-based cultures, deliberating/negotiating program goals, tools, and practices, and so on (Artiles et al., 2006). A fundamental change is needed in our educational system. This is as true for Sweden as it is true for many other countries grappling with implementing inclusive education and equitable educational affordances.

References

Anastasiou, D., Gardner, III, R., & Michail, D. (2011). Ethnicity and exceptionality. In J. M. Kauffman & D. P. Hallahan (Eds.), *Handbook of special education* (pp. 745–758). London: Routledge.

Artiles, A. J., Harris-Murri, N., & Rostenberg, D. (2006). Inclusion as social justice: Critical notes on discourses, assumptions and the road ahead. *Theory into Practice, 45*, 260–268.

Berhanu, G. (2008). Ethnic minority pupils in Swedish schools: Some trends in overrepresentation of minority pupils in special educational programs. *International Journal of Special Education, 23*(3), 17–29.

Berhanu, G. (2009, February 1–5). *Challenges and responses to inclusive education in Sweden: Mapping issues of equity, participation and democratic values.* Presented at Research Forum: A Comparative Analysis of Equity in Inclusive Education. Centre for Advanced Study in the Behavioural Sciences (CASBS), Stanford University, Palo Alto, CA.

Berhanu, G. (2010). Even in Sweden excluding the included: Some reflections on the consequences of new policies on educational processes and outcomes, and equity in education. *International Journal of Special Education, 25*(3), 148–159.

Berhanu, G. (2011). Inclusive education in Sweden: Responses, challenges and prospects. *International Journal of Special Education*, 26(2), 128–148.
Berhanu, G., & Dyson, A. (2012). Special education in Europe: Overrepresentation of minority students. In J. Banks (Ed.), *Encyclopedia of diversity in education* (pp. 2070–2073). Thousand Oaks, CA: Sage Publications.
Dyson, A., & Gallannaugh, F. (2008). Disproportionality in special needs education in England. *The Journal of Special Education*, 42(1), 36–46.
EADSNE (European Agency for Development in Special Needs Education). (2009). *Multicultural diversity and special needs education*. Retrieved from http://www.european-agency.org/agency-projects/ multicultural-diversity-and-special-needs-education
Gabel, S. L., Curcic, S., Powell, J., Khader, K., & Albee, L. (2009). Migration and ethnic group disproportionality in special education: An exploratory study. *Disability & Society*, 24(5), 625–639.
Luciak, M. (2008). *Why so many migrant students in schools for children with special needs?* Paper presented at the ninth Network of Experts in Social Sciences of Education (NESSE) seminar on Education and Migration: Lessons from Research for Policy and Practice, Brussels, Belgium. Retrieved from www.nesse.fr/nesse/activites/seminaires/activities/seminars/article_on_seminar_9.doc
OECD. (2016). *Programme for international student assessment (PISA)*. Results from PISA 2015. Retrieved from www.oecd.org/pisa/PISA-2015-Sweden.pdf
Reichenberg, M., & Berhanu, G. (2017). Immigrants' job expectations: A study of what predicts immigrants' job expectations after completing language training programmes. *International Journal of Special Education*, 32(2), 355–386.
Reichenberg, M., & Berhanu, B. (2018). Är pojkar med en annan språklig och kulturell bakgrund än den svenska överrepresenterade i grundsärskolan och specialpedagogiska åtgärder? (Are boys with Foreign cultural and linguistic background represented in special educational placements and Individual Educational Measures/plans?). In K. von Brömssen, S. Risenfors, & L. Sjöberg (Eds.), *Samhälle, genus och pedagogik-utbildningsvetenskapliga perspektiv (Society gender and pedagogical/educational scientific perspective)*. Borås: Stema Specialtryck AB.
Rosenqvist, J., Bengtsson-Tingvar, A., Christiansson-Banck, U., Gislén, E., Jensen, L., Palla, L., . . . Östlund, D. (2009). *Specialpedagogik i mångfaldens Sverige: Särskoleelever med utländsk bakgrund i storstäder. Delstudie 2 [Special education in multicultural Sweden: Immigrant students in education for intellectually disabled in large cities]*. Specialpedagogiska rapporter och notiser, Nr 4. Högskolan Kristianstad (HKr).
Skolinspektionen. (2011). *Mottagandet i särskolan under lupp. Granskning av handläggning, utredning och information i 58 kommuner* (Placement in special educational placements under loupe (under the microscpoic): An investigation of the process and placement procedures in 58 municipalities). Diarienummer 40–2011:348. Stockholm: Skolinspektionen.
Werning, R., Löser, J. M., & Urban, M. (2008). Cultural and social diversity: An analysis of minority groups in German schools. *The Journal of Special Education*, 42(1), 47–54.

4
SNAPSHOT—PROACTIVE DESIGN TO ENSURE ACCESSIBILITY

Lesley Casarez, David Hooks, Gina Shipley, and Dallas Swafford

The Angelo State University (US) Department of Curriculum and Instruction offers five graduate programs, along with five certification plans. With a global reach to students living around the world, program faculty offer instruction from the home campus located in the heart of west central Texas. All courses and programs are delivered asynchronously, with subject matter experts teaching courses through a student-centered online environment. Instructional design methods incorporate advanced pedagogical practices utilizing Universal Design for Learning (UDL) techniques and exemplary course design. Rigorous course content is strengthened through continuous interaction and collaboration among and between faculty and students. Numerous opportunities for learner support are presented through state-of-the-art technology. Every course utilizes open educational resources (OER), presenting students with access to the most current scholarly sources. Course and program content flows through a filter of UDL techniques, such as presenting information and content to learners in different ways (i.e. use of multiple media to convey information about a specific topic) to ensure accessibility for all learners.

Generally, educators impart powerful lessons not only when highlighting classroom successes and "teacher wins," but also when they share with each other the lessons learned from missteps, from students, and through acknowledging the need for growth. Educators are continually seeking to improve upon their abilities to adapt to the burgeoning trend of online education. An ever-increasing number of schools are offering online programs, and in 2015, approximately 30% of all post-secondary students enrolled in at least one online course offering (Allen & Seaman, 2017).

Although online instruction extends student access to digital instructional content, *expanded access* does not necessarily guarantee *equal access* for all students.

When content features a one-size-fits-all curricula, educators run the risk of excluding learners (i.e. those who are gifted and talented, learning English as a second language, or who have disabilities, etc.) from fully reaping the potential benefits of online instruction. "UDL . . . from the outset offered options for diverse learner needs. This approach caught on as others also recognized the need to make education more responsive to learner differences, and wanted to ensure that the benefits of education were more equitably and effectively distributed" (Meyer, Rose, & Gordon, 2014, p. 3).

The following anecdote describes how one institution aligned their online course offerings with UDL Guideline 1.1, to provide options for perception (CAST, 2008), and illustrates the importance of taking into consideration the needs of all students. A student enrolled in the graduate program self-identifies as a student with a hearing impairment halfway through the semester. One course in which she is enrolled has content heavy in videos. Watching the videos is a requirement of the course and is needed to complete the assignment due at the end of each week. At this point, the student shares with her professor that she has been sitting with friends and family members that will view the video with her in order to tell her the words each person in the video is saying.

Upon receiving this information, the faculty member immediately contacts Student Disability Services and work begins to transcribe all required videos in the course in order to meet minimal accessibility requirements, not to mention specifications from Section 508 of the Rehabilitation Act, and help the student meet course requirements in a timely manner. Soon after, work began to add closed-captioning to all videos included in all courses for the program. Working with the student's academic advisor and the director for the program, Student Disability Services quickly ensured that the remainder of the courses in the program are completely accessible, including closed captioning for all instructional videos.

Through resolution of the situation, faculty quickly realize the benefit of having online course content accessible at the point of creation instead of as a response to student accommodation requests. The course designers in this program utilized the UDL framework by incorporating various options for students to respond to assignments. Now, all courses offered have improved accessibility, not only for students with hearing impairments, but also those who have other disabilities. The course content and delivery is designed as a seamless environment in which all students are included in content that is accessible to all, reducing the need for later accommodations and add-ons (Cory, 2013).

References

Allen, E., & Seaman, J. (2017). Distance education enrollment report 2017. *Digital Learning Compass*. Retrieved from https://onlinelearningsurvey.com/reports/digtiallearning compassenrollment2017.pdf

CAST. (2008). *Universal design for learning guidelines version 1.0.* Wakefield, MA: CAST Professional Publishing. Retrieved from www.udlcenter.org/aboutudl/udlguidelines/udlguidelines_graphicorganizer

Cory, R. C. (2013). Universal design of online classes. In K. D. Kirstein, C. E. Schieber, K. A. Flores, & S. G. Olswang (Eds.), *Innovations in teaching adults: Proven practices in higher education* (pp. 97–102). North Charleston, SC: CreateSpace Independent Publishing Platform.

Meyer, A., Rose, D. H., & Gordon, D. (2014). *Universal design for learning: Theory and practice.* Wakefield, MA: CAST Professional Publishing.

SECTION 2
Policies and Structures for Reducing Learning Barriers

5

THE PROSPECTS OF UNIVERSAL DESIGN FOR LEARNING IN SOUTH AFRICA TO FACILITATE THE INCLUSION OF ALL LEARNERS

Marcia Lyner-Cleophas

Background

It is 23 years post the first South African Constitution (Republic of South Africa, 1996) and 25 years after the first democratically elected government of 1994. Democracy emerged after hundreds of years of oppression, marked by colonization and apartheid. Segregation on many levels became endemic in South African society. South Africa (SA) was ripe to create a socially just society. Policy changes naturally had to be put in place to reflect the new democracy.

The educational sector reflected one of the major changes needed toward establishing social justice. This has been both a process and a goal. A socially just society is one in which people can participate respectfully and securely while feeling physically and psychologically safe (Bell, 2016). Education is a way to address the inequalities as a process. The diversity of South African people needed to be embraced and celebrated. In a democratic society, it is vital that all members can develop (Dalton, 2017). Institutional environments also require transformation (Howell, 2015).

This chapter will highlight how curricula can address learner variability in the context of inclusive education. This is done by tracing inclusive education in SA and then proposing a discourse on learning barriers that embraces diversity in a transforming society. UDL is proposed as a way to design curricula to address learner diversity more broadly, rather than focusing on learners with disabilities only.

In the social model, disability is viewed as a component of the environment, with its inaccessible spaces and the various ways in which people with disabilities are excluded from participating in society (Oliver, 1990, 2009; UPIAS, 1976). When people are viewed according to a specific framework of abilities, this is *ableist, exclusionary* and *discriminatory* (Ostiguy, Peters, & Shlasko, 2016). UDL embraces variability in learning for all, hereby being an ideal way to address inclusion and diversity in educational settings from a social model perspective.

People participating in the South African education system have for hundreds of years been subjected to either class differentiation, racial segregation, gender bias, rural-urban divides or traditional notions of schooling and disability, which have contributed to the exclusion of some people from formal education (Mekoa, 2011; Naicker, 2005). These stratifications have created a defocusing from individual differences. In the process, many students dropped out of formal education. Although a multitude of reasons exist for dropping out, life events (like pregnancy), struggles at school, continuance with vocational training and minimal valuing of school are cited by Weybright, Caldwell, Xie, Wegner, and Smith (2017). Statistics reported in South Africa indicate that 52% of students make it from grade 1 to grade 12 in the age appropriate year (Department of Basic Education, 2015). The same department notes that 60% of grade 1 students are likely to eventually drop out of school. Such statistics are worrisome and raise the question, "How is the school system responding to the diverse learning needs of students?"

With the introduction of inclusive education in the South African education system in 2001 by means of White Paper 6 on inclusive education and training (Department of Education, 2001), South Africans began to think differently about education and learning for all people in one education system. This also marked the era of re-thinking the structure of separate special schools for learners with disabilities and considering the inclusion of learners into mainstream schools. This policy was informed by two commissions—the National Commission on Special Needs in Education and Training (NCSNET) and the National Committee on Education Support Services (NCESS) (both in 1996) that reflected on the state of special needs education in SA.

The implementation of inclusive education has been fraught with challenges, given massive educational backlogs and systemic fragmentation. Such challenges have similarly been echoed by Engelbrecht, Nel, Smit, and Van Deventer (2016); Maguvhe (2015); and Murungi (2015). The policy spurred thinking about learners with disabilities differently, such as their having diverse ways of learning and processing information and alternatives to education that went beyond being relegated to a special school only.

Rationale

Given the range of disparities and inequalities in the education system in the past, this presented a challenge for the future of inclusive education. The challenge was not insurmountable, though, as Walton (2011) notes. She argues that such a vision can become a reality, despite complexity fueled by inequalities. Dreyer (2017) cites teacher training (pre- and post-service) as critical human resource factors, together with financial and collaborative efforts required to enhance inclusive education.

With inclusion started at the policy level in the primary school system with White Paper 6, the Post-School Education and Training (PSET) sector also started to engage with transformation and the fact that students coming through a system of inclusive education would eventually continue their studies in the PSET sector. On reflecting about this, notions of universal access (UA), universal design (UD) in physical spaces and Universal Design for Learning (UDL) had limited presence in scholarly circles in SA. Some authors such as Schreiber (2014) mention UDL as important in student affairs and how they engage with students. Dalton, Mckenzie and Kahonde (2012); Lyner-Cleophas (2016) and Lyner-Cleophas and Mavundla (2017) highlight preliminary engagement with the concepts of UDL in particular with some implementation work done at universities in SA. Some educators and policy makers continue to grapple with what *inclusive education* means for schools, teachers and students and how to navigate the paradigm shifts, resource constraints and changing practices in the PSET sector, despite training. Addressing these complexities is a necessary step toward building a society that is truly inclusive of individual differences and similarities.

Peer-reviewed articles on UDL analyzed by Al-Azawei, Serenelli, and Lundqvist (2016) indicated that much research on this issue has been conducted in the USA. They also show that in order to address learning diversity (sensory differences and communication impairments, to name a view) and given the culture of human rights in which we are emerged in the twenty-first century, we need to explore various ways of teaching and responding to diversity. Across the studies, UDL was cited as an effective way of implementing a flexible learning environment with the focus on accessible content. Application of UDL in the articles was described in both blended learning and traditional learning formats that addressed learning diversity. Dalton (2017) questions what the typical student is in the twenty-first century. She also questions what the norms and standards are, if we accept learner diversity. Acknowledging this diversity lends itself to exploring UDL techniques to address the diversity.

Though individual differences and notions of universality seem to be contrasting and contradictory concepts, they can coexist beautifully in the UDL paradigm. If instructional materials are designed from the start with the variability of people in mind, then individual differences are planned for and supported without having to make changes and adaptations afterwards. Students' differing backgrounds, abilities, learning styles and disabilities are taken into account (CAST, 2019; Evmenova, 2018; Rose & Meyer, 2002). In addition, consideration is given to the diverse ways that learners process information, acquire knowledge, engage in learning activities, demonstrate understandings and use products and services. The digital era in which we live lends itself to this kind of engagement more broadly, even in resource poorer or inequitable contexts such as in SA. Integrating the consideration of students' strengths could create more inclusive representation of information, encourage more engagement and create better action and expression of knowledge in technology resource poorer areas.

In 1996, the SA Constitution outlawed discrimination based on disability, language, race and gender, and it broadly echoed what emerged from the Salamanca Statement and Framework for Action on Special Needs Education. This was that all people can learn and have the right to education (UNESCO, 1994). Shortly thereafter, the UN Convention on the Rights of People with Disabilities [UNCRPD] (UN, 2006) was ratified by SA in 2007. It outlined ways in which better access and inclusion should take place in society, with specific reference to people with disabilities. Furthermore, it shed light on UD, which is described as ways of designing products, environments, programs and services so that they are usable to most people without the need for adaptation and specialized design. In the UNCRPD, Article 9 on Accessibility notes access to information and communications technologies and systems to eliminate obstacles and barriers to accessibility. Additionally, Article 24 addresses inclusive education at all educational levels.

Within the SA education and training inclusive education context, the need to respond to learner diversity given inequalities was a key directive in the NCSNET (1997) report and the DoE (2001) policy. Access to curricula, human rights and social justice agendas, and inclusion of SA Constitution principles (1996), underpinned the way forward in the inclusive education and training system, and enhanced participation and social integration were necessary components of the strategy. As the inclusive education and training system definition acknowledges that all children and youth can learn and need support, learning methodologies need to meet learner needs while respecting their differences. There is, therefore, the connection to the social model, wherein methods, curricula, environments, attitudes, approaches to teaching and education management training are considered.

In SA school settings at present, discourses include the importance of curriculum differentiation as a way to respond to learner diversity, as reflected in the Policy on Screening, Identification, Assessment and Support [SIAS] (Department of Basic Education, 2014). This document sets out to ensure support for all learners. Structures to ensure that SIAS is carried out exist at the level of the district-based support teams (DBST), school-based support teams (SBST) and Support Needs Assessment (SNA) structures.

Unsafe structural environments, inappropriate and inadequate provision of support services, lack of parental engagement, lack of human resource development and the unavailability of accessible learning and teaching support materials and assistive technologies challenge this movement toward more inclusive education in SA. Support is about more than just disability; it recognizes that barriers can exist across many areas. In order to move beyond this, questions must be answered, such as, "How can the curriculum be responsive to learner and student diversity?" and "How can student diversity be incorporated into how curricula are delivered, engaged with and assessed?"

This transition shifts the focus away from diagnoses and remediation of deficits using specialist staff to a more holistic approach that envisions inclusive instructional design not just for students with learning barriers but for all students. Curriculum differentiation is noted in education policy, and UDL offers an opportunity for curriculum differentiation. Further, with students' increasing reluctance to disclose specific learning needs (DHET, 2018), planning for student diversity intentionally from the curricular viewpoint is prudent.

Stretching UD to the UDL Context

The 2018 Strategic Disability Framework on the Post-School Education and Training System (DHET, 2018) follows on from the human rights and inclusion principles noted in UNCRPD and relates these principles to the higher education context. An international trend noted in the DHET policy is UD in faculty instruction and curricula and how it can benefit all students. With the increase in teaching and learning centers, disability units and student support services in the PSET sector generally, there is room to consider UDL as the instructional approach noted in the DHET policy, hereby building ways to address learner diversity and foster the integration of human rights and accessibility within the curriculum.

Exploring the idea of UD in the DHET policy (noted earlier), UDL then could be the instructional approach noted as UD refers mainly to physical spaces and products whereas UDL is vested in curricular spaces. UD is rooted in architecture and was coined by Ronald Mace and pioneered by Marc Harrison (Burgstahler, 2015). Its basic premise is to think of design in a way that suits most people, and not design for the average, because thinking in an average way will exclude many people, given our diversity. Seven principles and considerations encompass this concept as adapted by the Centre for Universal Design (1997) when designing services and products: equitable use, flexibility in use, simple and intuitive use, perceptible information, tolerance for error, low physical effort and size and space for approach and use. These mainly relate to physical access to ensure the design is inclusive of all people.

Within a curriculum context, how people process information becomes critical. Neuroscience is a vast field that delves into brain functioning and processing (and not delved into in this chapter). According to Rose, Harbour, Johnston, Daley and Abarbanell (2006), neuroscience assists us in understanding how we learn, how our memory functions and how we process language and information. Three key neural functions are present in the brain, which are pattern recognition, pattern planning and generation, as well as pattern determination of what is important. Given these neural functions, it can be expected that people will engage in diverse ways around these.

Three central guiding principles foster inclusivity and broader access to the curriculum for a diversity of learners through the use of UDL (Al-Azawei et al., 2016; Burgstahler, 2015; Meyer, Rose, & Gordon, 2013). Firstly, the curriculum should be responsive to *multiple means of engagement*, where the aim is to create purposeful and motivated learners. Ways to engage students include pairing them for quick discussions and brainstorming sessions, arranging study buddies, organizing group work with a scribe and using a flipchart to write down responses. Students could range from typical to atypical backgrounds and have a range of ways in which they are motivated to learn (Rose et al., 2006).

Secondly, *multiple means of representation* should be applied in communication of concepts, with the main goal to develop resourceful and knowledgeable learners. Students understand and perceive information in varied ways. No single way exists to represent information (Rose et al., 2006). Varied representation could be through text, captioned videos, diagrams, songs and movement. High- and low-tech measures are possible to use, depending on the resources in the environment. Low-tech techniques could include role-play, psychodrama, worksheets or magazines that can easily be gathered to engage and capture students' attention. High-tech environments could use YouTube videos and talks, webinars and other online and digitized sources.

Thirdly, *multiple means of action and expression* should be supported through providing varied options for learners to demonstrate learning. The aim is the development of strategic, goal-directed learners who can express knowledge in multiple ways (Rose et al., 2006). Group discussions and written exercises that provide opportunities for individual action and expression could be used. Diagrams, flowcharts, drawings, skits and oral presentations are examples of the myriad of ways that students can express their learning.

Considering UDL as a Means Toward Including Learner Diversity

The DHET (2018) policy refers to teaching and learning and acknowledges the value of UD and its application to curriculum design in that it is not only about physical accessibility or accessible font sizes but also about inclusive instruction, engagement and assessment practices. In the context of teaching and learning, the policy describes UD as

> ... an educational approach for instructing all students through developing flexible classroom materials, using various technology tools, and varying the delivery of information or instruction. Infusing universal design techniques as part of information dissemination for diverse learners, including students with disabilities, proved to be an effective strategy for faculty professional development.

(DHET, 2018, p. 22)

This policy then calls attention to the

> ... significant resource implication to provide appropriate staff for a disability support office and the skills and competencies required by such staff members. By implication they would need to play a much bigger advocacy role and give guidance on principles and practical application of universal design methodologies to empower faculty and staff.
>
> *(DHET, 2018, p. 22)*

As part of the disability awareness mandate of staff working in disability support services, UD as it applies to the curriculum and co-curriculum could be developed by way of UDL. Staff in the PSET sector who work with varied learners would do well to consider incorporating UD and UDL principles in the design of curricula.

At the University of Cape Town, for instance, training for teachers and therapists introduced UDL (Dalton et al., 2012). This training was done to get a snapshot view of how professionals perceived UDL and how they could use it in their classrooms to respond to learner diversity. The response to UDL was positive.

A seminal seminar at Stellenbosch University in 2017, where universal access, UDL and UD as means to promote diversity were unpacked (Lyner-Cleophas & Mavundla, 2017), was the first of its kind to start to understand these concepts. Universal access, UD and UDL were introduced in a two-day seminar format to a group of mainly support services staff, including administration, facilities management, faculty (included blended learning staff) and disability unit staff.

UDL was introduced at the Scholarship of Teaching and Learning Conference at Stellenbosch University in Somerset West, South Africa in October, 2018, in a workshop format that addressed how technology can be used to support diverse learners in online courses. The workshop had a particular focus on the accessibility of materials for students with diverse learning needs in the context of technology integration. Challenges with the current learning management system and its accessibility arose during this event and were identified as matters that would need further investigation.

A final example discussed here is Gronneberg and Johnston (2015), who piloted UDL in a history module to see how students can be engaged better. This was also done in response to an increased amount of students seeking test and exam accommodations, as well as high student drop-out. The principles of UDL noted in the previous section were applied in the course design. This allowed for the variability in student engagement with the learning materials, i.e. they could do this using captioned videos or text-to-speech literature. Assessments could be done in their own time using online means, blogging, class presentations or class discussions. Students gave positive feedback about being included, as they did not feel singled out or have to apply for special concessions. They could work successfully according to their learning preferences, given the UDL-designed module.

In summary, UDL-focused professional development presents opportunities to equip educators and instructional designers to be able to reach and benefit many students through mindful, inclusive innovations that are responsive to their diverse students. As indicated by Educause (2015), the principles of UDL take a "holistic approach to learning in which curriculum, procurement, the LMS, and university policy work together to support the needs of all learners." These indicate initial attempts to explore UDL in curriculum design.

Recommendations

Details about UDL implementation shared in this chapter are intended to illuminate how South African educators can think differently about engagement with learning materials and representation and expression of learning, given learner diversity. More professional training with academia and support services are needed to see greater incorporation of UDL as a way of increasing access to the curriculum and co-curriculum to a wide range of SA students. By incorporating a UDL framework in curriculum design, SA educators may be able to move beyond the barriers to more inclusive instruction.

In keeping with the social model of disability, addressing the accessibility and design of curriculum should be core to addressing learner diversity. Envisioning this, fewer students would need to seek out classroom, test and exam accommodations. Students can be provided opportunities to demonstrate their knowledge in various ways and not have to get special permissions to do this. For example, requesting to use a computer during tests and exams or to use a scribe may be eliminated when varied means are already present to use. In a study conducted by Smith (2012), positive interest and engagement were fostered when UDL approaches were incorporated into curricula. Providing multiple ways for students to demonstrate their knowledge can amplify their strengths and reduce limitations of their weaknesses. Al-Azawei et al. (2016), in analyzing peer-reviewed journal articles between 2012 and 2015, found that UDL is not widespread in use internationally, but more so in the USA. Positive elements that emerged from using UDL-inspired course design include positive perceptions by learners, more enjoyable online learning and flexible course design that was stress-reducing. Disability services interventions were also less when UDL was considered in curriculum design.

Conclusion

Policy and political efforts in SA are slowly incorporating UD and UDL in an effort to ensure that no learner is left behind. This echoes the fact that all learners can learn. As educators begin to move beyond barriers to learning, there are opportunities to explore how universal access can be achieved in curricula through UDL, and not just in the spatial environment. This will reduce the need for accommodations by focusing on universal practices, which resonate with the idea of the universality of humanity while also respecting individuals for their differences. This discourse on learning barriers augurs well for embracing student diversity in the post-school sector in particular and contributes to the transformation of South African society and the pursuit of social justice.

References

Al-Azawei, A., Serenelli, F., & Lundqvist, K. (2016). Universal design for learning (UDL): A content analysis of peer-reviewed journal papers from 2012 to 2015. *Journal of the Scholarship of Teaching and Learning, 16*(3), 39–56. http://doi.org/10.14434/josotl.v16i3.19295

Bell, L. (2016). Theoretical foundations for social justice education. In M. Adams, L. Bell, D. J. Goodman, & K. Joshi (Eds.), *Teaching for diversity and social justice* (pp. 4–26). New York: Routledge.

Burgstahler, S. E. (2015). *Universal design in higher education: From principles to practice.* Cambridge, MA: Harvard Education Press.

CAST. (2019). *About universal design for learning.* Retrieved from http://www.cast.org/our-work/about-udl.html#.XQ4C4-gzY2w

Center for Universal Design. (1997). *The principles of universal design, version 2.0.* Retrieved from https://projects.ncsu.edu/design/cud/about_ud/udprinciplestext.htm

Dalton, E. M. (2017). Beyond universal design for learning: Guiding principles to reduce barriers to digital & media literacy competence. *Journal of Media Literacy Education, 9*(2), 17–29. https://doi.org/10.23860/JMLE-2019-09-02-02

Dalton, E. M., McKenzie, J. A., & Kahonde, C. (2012). The implementation of inclusive education in South Africa: Reflections arising from a workshop for teachers and therapists to introduce universal design for learning. *African Journal of Disability, 1*(1), 24–30.

Department of Basic Education (DBE). (2014). *Policy on screening, identification, assessment and support (SIAS).* Republic of South Africa. Retrieved from https://www.naptosa.org/za/what-s-new/1168-policy-on-screening-identification-assessment-and-support-sias-2014

Department of Basic Education (DBE). (2015). *Education statistics in South Africa 2013.* Republic of South Africa. Retrieved from www.education.gov.za/Portals/0/Documents/Publications/Education%20Statistic%202013.pdf?ver=2015-03-30-144732-767

Department of Education (DoE). (2001). *Education white paper 6: Special needs education: Building an inclusive education and training system.* Pretoria, South Africa: Government Printer.

Department of Higher Education and Training (DHET). (2018). *Strategic disability policy framework in the post-school education and training system.* Retrieved from www.dhet.gov.za/SiteAssets/Gazettes/Approved%20Strategic%20Disability%20Policy%20Framework

Dreyer, L. (2017). Constraints to quality education and support for all: A Western Cape case. *South African Journal of Education, 37*(1), 1–11. doi:10.15700/saje.v37n1a1226

Educause. (2015). *Universal design for learning.* Retrieved from www.educause.edu/eli

Engelbrecht, P., Nel, M., Smit, S., & Van Deventer, M. (2016). The idealism of education policies and the realities in schools: The implementation of inclusive education in South Africa. *International Journal of Inclusive Education, 20*(5), 520–535. https://dx.doi.org/10.1080/13603116.2015.1095250

Evmenova, A. (2018). Preparing teachers to use universal design for learning to support diverse learners. *Journal of Online Learning Research, 4*(2), 147–171.

Gronneberg, J., & Johnston, S. (20 15). *Things you should know about universal design for learning [Brief]*. Washington, DC: Educause Learning Initiative.

Howell, C. (2015). *Guidelines for the creation of equitable opportunities for people with disabilities in South African higher education*. Cape Higher Education Consortium (CHEC). Republic of South Africa. Retrieved from www.ru.ac.za/media/rhodesuniversity/content/equityinstitutionalculture/documents/CHECDisabilityguidelinesdocumentfinaldraftOct2015(2).docx

Lyner-Cleophas, M. M. (2016). *Staff and disabled students' experiences of disability support, inclusion and exclusion at Stellenbosch University* (Doctoral dissertation). Retrieved from http://scholar.sun.ac.za/handle/10019.1/11/browse?type=author&value=Lyner-Cleophas%2C+Marcia+Mirl

Lyner-Cleophas, M. M., & Mavundla, S. (2017, June, Spring). Universal access for diversity: Staff magazine. *Life@StellenboschUni*, 3.

Maguvhe, M. (2015). Inclusive education: A transformation and human rights agenda under spotlight in South Africa. *African Journal of Disability*, 4(1). http://dx.doi.org/10.4102/ajod.v4i1.183

Mekoa, I. (2011). Discourses and politics of racism in higher education in South Africa. *Africa Insight*, 40(4).

Meyer, A., Rose, D., & Gordon, D. (2013). *Universal design for learning: Theory and practice*. Wakefield, MA: Centre for Applied Science Technology, Inc.

Murungi, L. N. (2015). Inclusive basic education in South Africa: Issues in its conceptualisation and implementation. *PER /PELJ: Potchefstroomse Elektroniese Regsblad/Potchefstroom Electronic Law Journal*, 18(1). http://dx.doi.org/10.4314/pelj.v18i1.07

Naicker, S. M. (2005). Inclusive education in South Africa. In D. Mitchell (Ed.), *Contextualizing inclusive education: Evalulating old and new international perspectives* (pp. 230–251). London: Routledge..

NCSNET. (1997). *Quality education for all: Overcoming barriers to learning and development*. Report of the NCSNET Department of Education. Needs in Education and Training (NCSNET) and National Committee on Education Support Services (NCESS). Pretoria: Government Printers.

Oliver, M. (1990). *The politics of disablement*. Basingstoke: Macmillan.

Oliver, M. (2009). *Understanding disability*. Basingstoke: Macmillan.

Ostiguy, B., Peters, M., & Shlasko. (2016). Ableism. In M. Adams, L. Bell, D. J. Goodman, & K. Joshi (Eds.), *Teaching for diversity and social justice* (pp. 299–337). New York: Routledge.

Republic of South Africa. (1996). *Constitution of the republic of South Africa*. Act No. 2 of 1996. Pretoria, South Africa: Government Printer.

Rose, D., Harbour, W., Johnston, S. C., Daley, S., & Abarbanell, L. (2006). Universal design for learning in postsecondary education: Reflections on principles and their application. *Journal of Postsecondary Education and Disability*, 19(2), 17.

Rose, D., & Meyer, A. (2002). *Teaching every student in the digital age: Universal design for learning*. Retrieved from www.cast.org/teachingeverystudent/ideas/tes/chapter4_1.cfm

Schreiber, B. (2014). The role of student affairs in promoting social justice in South Africa. *Journal of College & Character*, 15(4), 211–218.

Smith, F. (2012). Analyzing a college course that adheres to the universal design for learning (UDL) framework. *Journal of the Scholarship of Teaching and Learning*, 12(3), 31–61.

UN. (2006). *United Nations convention on the rights of people with disabilities*. Retrieved from www.un.org/disabilities/documents/convention/convoptprot-e.pdf

UNESCO. (1994). *The Salamanca statement and framework for action on special needs education*. Retrieved from www.unesco.org/education/pdf/SALAMA_E.PDF

UPIAS. (1976). *Fundamental principles of disability*. Retrieved from https://disability-studies.leeds.ac.uk/wp-content/uploads/sites/40/library/UPIAS-fundamental-principles.pdf

Walton, E. (2011). Getting inclusion right in South Africa. *Intervention in School and Clinic, 46*(4), 240–245.

Weybright, E., Caldwell, L., Xie, H., Wegner, L., & Smith, E. (2017). Predicting secondary school dropout among South African adolescents: A survival analysis approach. *South African Journal of Education, 37*(2), 1–11. http://dx.doi.org/10.15700saje.v37n2a1353

6

THE GLOBAL UDL VIRTUAL CLASSROOM

A Model for International Collaboration and Learning

Frances Smith and Serra De Arment

Background

In Jamaica, the poverty headcount in 2012 was 19.9% of the total population, compared to 13.5% in the US. Often children under the age of 5 are at great risk due to lower socioeconomic opportunities, limited parental supports, and the effects of poverty (Gertler et al., 2014). Jamaicans live in rural settings and families tend to build their homes one room at time to adjust to anticipated high living costs (The World Bank, 2019). Schools are often equipped with limited technology tools, lighting, ventilation, and overall resources. Compared to the reported US student-teacher ratio of 16.1:1 in 2014, Jamaican educators deal with the realities of 50:1 (National Center for Education Statistics, 2018). Economic opportunities in this country have continued a downward spiral since 2008 with high unemployment and debt rates (Johnston, 2015). Social challenges and high crime and violence levels prevail and have an impact upon the education and employment opportunities of Jamaican youth (The World Bank, 2018).

A commitment to developing educational reform in Jamaica has been underway since 2004 with an emphasis on highlighting learner-centered education, rich learning technologies, and effective professional development programs (Education for All, 2015). The *Vision 2030 Jamaica National Development Plan* highlights a primary goal to "empower everyone to achieve their fullest potential" (Planning Institute of Jamaica, 2010, p. xxiv). Yet, many barriers continue to exist across needs for training for educators and parents, enhancements to infrastructure and equipment, and greater understanding for supporting students with more significant learning needs (Planning Institutes of Jamaica, 2010). Efforts to improve educational opportunities in Jamaica have been growing, yet equitable access remains an issue. While identified as the first country in the Caribbean to acquire computers and Internet access, Gaible (2008) reports that the country of Jamaica's effective implementation and integration of Information and Communications Technology (ICT) into educational practice lags behind. Computers are often non-functional, teachers lack the skills to use these technologies, access by students is questionable, and training for teachers and staff is limited (Ministry of Education and Youth, 2011).

In 2007, discussions at the first National Universal Design for Learning (UDL) Summit outlined needs, opportunities, and recommendations for moving the field forward into the 21st century. In particular, recommendations targeted preparing and sustaining K-12 and postsecondary educators for effectively implementing UDL by "developing learning communities of teachers and postsecondary faculty to share best practices, support and sustain one another, and build support for systemic change around UDL" and "partner[ing] with large corporations and international organizations to scale up distribution of UDL-based media worldwide and give UDL a global reach" (CAST, 2007). This global reach has increased over the past decade and continues to grow with the expanding impact of open educational resources.

The Growth of Online Learning

Online learning has grown as well over the past decade, and forecasts predict this is likely to continue. According to the *NMC 2018 Horizon Report*, the proliferation of open educational resources (OER) is a key mid-term trend for driving educational technology adoption in higher education for the next three to five years (New Media Consortium, 2018). Sharing free and open educational resources has been a common practice of researchers at CAST and continues to involve many of these important partners (CAST, 2018c). OER have great potential to level the educational playing field and provide equitable opportunities for all learners (Young, Daly, & Stone, 2017). In partnership with Jamaican educators, the authors developed the Global UDL Virtual Classroom, a digital classroom designed to be free and accessible for all participants.

Rationale

Globally, educators are confronted with the challenge to prepare students with 21st century skills, to understand student variability, and to provide high quality learning environments (National Research Council [NRC], 2012).

UDL is a transformative framework for developing responsive and adaptive educators who can design and deliver instruction that meets the expected variability of learners in any classroom (Meyer et al., 2014; Reed & Smith, 2013). Through a UDL lens, educators can develop rich learning environments to reach and teach all learners (CAST, 2018a; Meyer et al., 2014; Rose & Gravel, 2010). Teacher training that is informed through the UDL framework encourages the development of skills and understanding that recognize cultural diversity and the importance of learner variability in all individuals. Yet globally, educators may have limited to no access to professional development or training in UDL.

Former Jamaican Minister of Education, The Honorable Reverend Thwaite, emphasized the importance of "setting academic goals, developing strategies to meet those goals, and evaluating and reflecting on performance" (Thwaite, 2014, p. 61). Such approaches are central to an educational plan in which the curriculum is shaped through a UDL lens that focuses on designing clear goals, flexible methods and strategies, and multiple points of assessment that help monitor students' ongoing growth and progress. UDL details three principles and nine guidelines that support learning-centered opportunities by providing multiple means for (1) students to engage with learning, (2) representation of information, and (3) students to act on this information and express their learning (CAST, 2018b). "The practice of the past and sometimes the present has only worked for marginally half of our students ... transformative tasks move away from traditional practices of didactic delivery, rigid curriculum and memorization" (R. Thwaite, October 9, 2014). UDL provides a framework for such transformation.

Design of the Virtual Classroom

Morris and Hiebert (2011) identified using the web to create opportunities for educators to build knowledge about instructional methods by sharing teaching experiences across different contexts and building shared understanding about how to improve instruction over time. They argue that shared construction of knowledge can improve educational equity across settings and that the process is enabled by educators' shared problem-solving, testing of incremental changes to instruction, and use of multiple perspectives for innovation. Online social learning communities can provide important digital spaces that build participatory learning experiences for exchanges of information (Jenkins, Clinton, Purushotma, Robison, & Weigel, 2006). *The Global UDL Virtual Classroom* was designed to build a rich and sustainable online learning community for exploring UDL and its applications. Using open platforms, this virtual classroom aimed to make learning visible, constructive, and applicable through online dialogue, interactive demonstrations, resource curation, and reflection about classroom applications.

Chita-Tegmark, Gravel, Serpa, Domings, and Rose (2012, p. 17) suggest that the UDL framework can be "extended to capture the way in which learning is influenced by cultural variability." The virtual classroom project began with a needs assessment. Through meetings and group discussions with the Jamaican Minister of Education and his cabinet, college deans, faculty, teachers, clinical staff, and community members, US faculty listened to better understand the Jamaican culture and context. Maintaining sensitivity to cultural approaches was paramount for the US faculty as they designed and piloted the virtual classroom. From their first meeting, the Minister of Education and his cabinet endorsed the UDL framework as "the hope for our country" (R. Thwaite, personal communication, February, 24, 2014), as they recognized the opportunities this approach could offer to reach and teach every learner.

Based on these discussions, US faculty and doctoral students designed online modules for educators' exploration of key UDL concepts, identified classroom connections, shared reflections, and piloted applications. In addition, the needs assessment and collaborative design process between Jamaican educators, US faculty, and doctoral students guided the ongoing development of the virtual classroom. Considering the *How People Learn* (NRC, 2000) framework, doctoral students brainstormed initial questions (Table 6.1) around core themes to capture potential knowledge-, learner-, community-, and assessment-focused interests to guide virtual classroom development.

US faculty and doctoral students used these questions to guide discussion with Jamaican educators and to capture their interests for virtual classroom resources and content.

Considering Jamaican culture and context was important given Jamaica's limited access to technology resources, especially within the more rural areas. The design team found that computers were dated desktop models that were housed within a separate classroom and Wi-Fi digital access was often non-existent. These details about the Jamaican context were important for informing the *how* of the international collaboration. Furthermore, though UDL is not synonymous with *high-tech*, limited access to technology in Jamaica also shaped the way participants in the Global UDL Virtual Classroom considered and applied the UDL principles.

The virtual classroom structure was built using the US institution's adopted use of Wordpress© (www.wordpress.com), which allowed the development of

TABLE 6.1 Initial Questions Guiding the Needs Assessment

Questions Generated Through the Core Themes for Designing Successful Learning Environments (NRC, 2000)

Learner-centered
- How are these educators being selected? What are their motivations and interests?
- What types of technology skills do they have? What is their understanding of online learning? Do they understand the importance of accessibility?

Knowledge-centered
- Is there anyone at the US institution who knows about Jamaican culture or education that we can consider?
- What resources do we have?
- What does the average Jamaican know about education?
- Do they use technology in their curriculum?

Assessment-centered
- How do we know what we are building? What are Jamaican educators receptive (or not) to?
- What's practical for their situation?

Community-centered
- How culturally aware are we?
- What do we know about the Jamaican education system? Is this a public or private system? Is it mainstreamed or segregated?

a freely available and open web-based system. This technologically lean design offered benefits of simplicity and accessibility. Costs for ongoing maintenance and hosting were minimal, and the technology was easily adaptable to include needed plugins or web extensions. Online web design principles that supported current learning theory, responsive design, and cross platform compatibility were central for this project.

The team selected the Wordpress theme *Twenty Eleven*, which was accessible and responsive, easily viewed on any screen size, and instantly adjusted to a portable device (see Figure 6.1). This theme also provided a simple and intuitive layout and options to easily adjust for user perception choices, such as selecting a light or dark display. To further support design accessibility, faculty added the Wordpress wp-accessibility plugin to provide users with the ability to easily change the screen contrast from black or white, increase font size, skip navigation links, add long explanatory descriptions to images, and post more descriptive titles.

The virtual classroom design was built around needs identified by the collaborative team. Jamaican stakeholders described the need for UDL supports to help students with and without disabilities who exhibited attention and behavior challenges. US faculty noted the need for resources and supports to be easily accessible on computers with low bandwidth and printable for distribution. US doctoral students considered these requests and developed a cache of resources, including access to many of the free tools on the CAST website (www.cast.org). A list of frequently asked questions (FAQ) offered tips on how to consider using these resources in the classroom.

The US team developed a simple and intuitive navigational design, which included basic menu options to orient users around context, starting points, module content, participants, and resources (Reed, Smith, King, Wojcik, & Temple,

FIGURE 6.1 Initial Design of the Global UDL Virtual Classroom

TABLE 6.2 The Five UDL Instructional Modules

UDL Module	Instructional Focus
Module 1: Getting Started	An introduction to the online community and an overview to the UDL framework, including the three principles and nine guidelines and examples of the three principles applied in context.
Module 2: Focus on Engagement	An exploration of UDL principle: Provide multiple means of engagement, examples illustrated across the engagement guidelines, and applications to context.
Module 3: Focus on Representation	An exploration of UDL principle: Provide multiple means of representation, examples illustrated across the representation guidelines, and applications to context.
Module 4: Focus on Action and Expression	An exploration of UDL principle: Provide multiple means of action and expression, examples illustrated across the action and expression guidelines, and applications to context.
Module 5: Putting it All Together	A review of the three UDL principles, illustration through the CAST Book Builder, and reflection on application to setting.

2014). Table 6.2 highlights the five modules developed on UDL content and components. Each of the five modules had a similar form and function with an introduction, clear goals, guiding questions, first steps, content, and an example application to context. Multiple examples were provided to illustrate content, such as images, hyperlinks, audio files, and transcripts. Throughout, participants were encouraged to share their perspectives on what they took away from the UDL content, how they applied these takeaways to their setting, and why they found this content meaningful.

Impact of the Global UDL Virtual Classroom

Retrospectively, US faculty and doctoral students sought understanding of the impact of this model of open, international collaboration in three areas—(1) participants' engagement in UDL content; (2) participants' perspectives on the accessibility and usability of the virtual classroom model; and (3) perceived challenges and suggestions for improvement (Reed, Arnold, Best, De Arment, & Onorato, 2014). The pilot group for the classroom project included membership from the US university, the Jamaican university, and two interdisciplinary care centers from an urban and a rural location in Jamaica and included 34 participants across Jamaican sites. Each team included two lead facilitators (a total of six) who agreed to explore the modules and resources with their local teams of educators, lead the teams through the module activities (if needed), record their ideas and questions, and share comments. The remaining 28 participants represented local membership of faculty, teachers, counselors, and practitioners. Participants were encouraged to explore the modules and resources, complete activities, record their ideas and comments through online prompts and reply spaces, and share questions. This model reinforced a process for co-constructing and designing UDL knowledge and understanding across cultures.

Facilitator-participants previewed UDL content presented in each of five modules through a video-conference with US faculty in advance of sharing each module with educator-participants. A printed agenda and PowerPoint slide presentation were sent a day ahead of the conference. After each call, a recording of the video-conference and supplemental resources were posted in a private location for later review by Jamaican facilitators and participants. These multiple approaches were developed to support learning and model UDL principles. Within the primary structure of the five UDL modules, all participants (facilitators and educators) responded to specific prompts related to each module's overall instructional focus (see Table 6.3). These prompts were used for ongoing formative assessment and revealed participants' continuing enthusiasm for engaging in the Global UDL Virtual Classroom.

For instance, Module 1 prompts aimed to foster online community not only between US academics and Jamaican educators but also among participants across each of the three Jamaican settings they represented. Participants shared about themselves, described use of technology for communication, professional learning, instruction, and planning, and expressed particular interests in learning about UDL for engaging and teaching diverse learners, identifying curriculum resources and tools, and collaborating with other professionals. This information set the stage for the virtual classroom activities and engagement that would follow through the remaining modules and prompts. It encouraged participants to apply their developing UDL understanding within their own classrooms and contexts and reflect upon its teaching and learning benefits.

Participants could also optionally offer open-ended comments on each module page and use the Wordpress commenting feature to pose questions to one another and US colleagues on the virtual classroom's FAQ page. As visually represented through a word cloud in Figure 6.2, participants' comments emphasized reflection on *students* and *learning* within these unstructured reflections.

Finally, educator-participants engaged with UDL content within their respective groups through their face-to-face interactions with one another and their on-site Jamaican facilitators. To support participation, facilitators prepared handouts, fostered discussion, and used computer access and projection to demonstrate how to access materials available on the virtual classroom website. Knowing that educator-participants were full-time teachers engaging in a learning experience outside of their direct job responsibilities, facilitators noted the need for capitalizing on UDL principles in their roles for supporting teacher learners: "It was imperative that we utilized the principle of multiple representation in our interface with participants. This helped us to maximize the benefits of the session as we all had the opportunity to share in various ways." Some facilitators created bulleted

TABLE 6.3 Virtual Classroom Module Prompts

UDL Module 1: Getting Started
1. What is your role?
2. Which group are you representing? Select: Mico C.A.R.E. Centre, The Mico University College, or St. Ann Community Educators
3. Please share a short bio about yourself, what you do in your work, your interests, etc.
4. How do you use technology to learn or communicate with others?
5. What is most important to you to explore about UDL?

UDL Module 2: Focus on Engagement
1. As you've thought about UDL, how could this be important in your setting?
2. What did we learn about engagement during the first module? What questions do we have about engagement?
3. How does this apply to your students?
4. What engagement strategies would you like to try in your classroom over the next few weeks?

UDL Module 3: Focus on Representation
1. What did you try in your classroom? How did that engage your students? Are there other engagement strategies that you would like to explore further?
2. How does this apply to your students?
3. How would multiple forms of representation benefit your classroom?

UDL Module 4: Focus on Action and Expression
1. What did you try? How did you represent information to your students? Were there other representation strategies that you would like to explore further?
2. How does this apply to your students/learners?
3. How would offering students multiple means for action and expression benefit your learners?

UDL Module 5: Putting it All Together
1. What did you try in your classroom? How did you vary opportunities for students' action and expression? Are there other strategies you would like to explore?
2. In the Book Builder book you began to create, how were you able to design your book to include multiple means of representation?
3. How did you design your book to provide various ways for students to act and express their knowledge?
4. How did you use Book Builder with multiple means to engage student interest and learning?

---

digests of module information that sparked the interest of busy participants who were then more inclined to review module content and identify questions outside of virtual classroom meetings. Facilitators responded to educator-participants' needs and interests and guided their exploration of additional UDL resources outside of the virtual classroom as well. One participant commented, "The facilitators got the participants so engaged. I anticipate our next session as I know that it will be as enthusiastic." The work of on-site facilitators appeared key for tailoring how

FIGURE 6.2 A Visual Representation of Global UDL Virtual Classroom Participants' Comments

participants engaged with UDL content and for supporting the success of the online international collaboration as a whole.

Through these avenues for engaging with UDL content in an online learning community, participants felt empowered to learn, contribute, and act. Rather than being prescriptive, the Global UDL Virtual Classroom promoted participants' integration of new information within their own cultural contexts, thus enhancing the relevance of UDL content for Jamaican educators.

> My exposure to UDL has shown that engagement, representation and action and expression (strategy) are interwoven. All of the above are evident in my daily classroom activities. I am now catering to students' learning styles in a more effective and efficient way. I have brought back what I have learned to the members in my faculty at Steer Town Academy. At Mico Care, I have explored, I have learned, and I have shared my teaching experiences. I look forward to meeting with my group every other week. I know that I will learn new ways to cater to the learning styles of my students.
>
> *(Educator-participant)*

Facilitators appreciated the video-conference meetings with US faculty and access to materials ahead of module implementation. These approaches allowed Jamaican facilitators to ask questions, address issues, and familiarize themselves with the information and identify the modalities that would be most effective in engaging the participants. Facilitators also found these meetings to be encouraging and helpful to them to feel supported and connected to the project. Constructive feedback revealed a need for more time for facilitators to preview module content and more time spent by US faculty to demonstrate the use of resources. During implementation of the virtual classroom, facilitators felt the module content was well packaged with multiple means of representing information and encouraging participant action and expression. At the same time, the modules were readily available which allowed participants to access the information at their own convenience. Facilitators perceived video clips, hyperlinks, prompts, and the ability to view one another's comments online as effective for helping participants learn the material presented.

Generally, participants agreed that the resources, design, and navigation of the virtual site were effective in promoting accessibility and that the content supported collaboration and reflection while modeling the UDL principles in action. A noted strength of the model was the collaborative nature of the learning community. Participants also found the links and materials beneficial and acknowledged the affordances of the virtual format such as convenience, enhanced interaction and engagement, and flexibility.

Facilitator-participants identified challenges in technology access, including connectivity issues due to unreliable Internet availability and password issues that affected access to materials. Scheduling across international partners and the breadth of Jamaican participants also posed challenges along with the time commitment required by participants during the summer months. Educator-participants indicated a need for more time, examples, and support for enhancing lesson planning, using tools such as the UDL Book Builder, and tailoring resources for specific student populations (e.g., preschoolers, specific disability categories, high school contexts, boys, English language learners). For some, access to the virtual classroom was limited to the collaborative sessions facilitated by their colleagues. If these participants missed a session, then they were unable to work on the module from another location.

Participants' ideas for improving the Global UDL Virtual Classroom included technical supports, such as a password helpdesk, and structural suggestions, such as including online tutorials for engaging in activities and using resources as well as separating the introduction of UDL principles and the exploration of related resources. Participants also expressed a need for more time engaging in the virtual classroom, particularly through more group sessions to allow participants to fully grasp concepts, as well as ongoing support with using UDL so that the principles could be applied in their classrooms that academic year. Again, participants expressed the desire for more feedback from their US counterparts, possibly through video-conferencing, including immediate feedback, responses to questions as they emerge, and a process for submitting their UDL-based lesson plans for vetting.

Conclusion and Recommendations

The Global UDL Virtual Classroom project demonstrated the utility and effectiveness of the UDL framework in supporting Jamaican educators' responsiveness to learner variability, adaptive teaching, and commitment to Jamaican students' success. Though many educators had little access to digital resources and technology-enhanced tools, they appreciated the bigger impact of considering UDL in their settings (Smith, Reed, & Arnold, 2015). They appreciated values offered by the UDL framework for supporting the variability in learners, particularly in the areas of support for struggling learners, teaching of diverse learners, technology integration, and resources for teaching teachers.

Access to free and open digital instructional tools was appreciated by teachers who were both with and without access to computer-enhanced classrooms. At each of the interdisciplinary care centers, the enhanced computer lab became a space where participants could continue to learn together, expand their hands-on expertise in using free UDL digital tools, and build ongoing teacher learning communities.

Jamaican educators teaching in low socioeconomic, no-tech settings eagerly embraced the opportunities to learn about this transformational framework. They folded this into their practice, noted changes in how students reacted to new teaching approaches, and prioritized a goal to broaden their involvement in online UDL communities. Rural educators worked overtime to refashion a small teaching space into one that offered computers and Internet connections that could bring new information, expand understandings, and widen opportunities for students. Though technology challenges existed, responses from both emerging US doctoral faculty and Jamaican educators echoed the value this online classroom offered as a free and open platform for learning and collaborating about UDL. To encourage ongoing research and expanded global access to professional development around UDL, resources and details for developing a similar online classroom are available at the Open Educational Resource Commons (www.oercommons.org/authoring/23414-the-global-universal-design-for-learning-udl-class).

References

CAST. (2007). *Summary of 2007 national summit on universal design for learning working groups*. Wakefield, MA: CAST Professional Publishing.

CAST. (2018a). *UDL and the learning brain*. Wakefield, MA: CAST Professional Publishing. Retrieved from www.cast.org/our-work/publications/2018/udl-learning-brain-neuroscience.html

CAST. (2018b). *The UDL guidelines*. Wakefield, MA: CAST Professional Publishing. Retrieved from http://udlguidelines.cast.org/

CAST. (2018c). *Providing UDL resources for colleges and universities*. Retrieved from www.cast.org/our-work/capacity-building/projects/open-education-resources-higher-education.html#.W5Ald9hKgsk

Chita-Tegmark, J., Gravel, J. W., Serpa, M. D. B., Domings, Y., & Rose, D. H. (2012). Using the universal design for learning framework to support culturally diverse learners. *Journal of Education, 192*(1), 17–22.

De Arment, S., Reed, E., & Wetzel, A. (2013). Promoting adaptive expertise: A conceptual framework for special educator preparation. *Teacher Education and Special Education, 36*(3), 217–230. doi:10.1177/0888406413489578

Education for All (EFA). (2015, May). *2015 national review report: Jamaica*. Retrieved from http://unesdoc.unesco.org/images/0023/002300/230020E.pdf

Gaible, E. (2008). *Survey of ICT and education in the Caribbean: A summary report, Basedon 16 country surveys*. Washington, DC: InfoDev, World Bank. Retrieved from www.infodev.org/en/Publication.441.html

Gertler, P., Heckman, J., Pinto, R., Zanolini, A., Vermeerch, C., Walker, S., . . . Grantham-McGregor, S. (2014). Labor market returns to an early childhood stimulation intervention in Jamaica. *Science, 344*(6187), 998–1001. http://doi.org/10.1126/science.1251178

Jenkins, H., Clinton, K., Purushotma, R., Robison, A., & Weigel, M. (2006). *Confronting he challenges of participatory culture: Media education for the 21st century*. Retrieved from www.macfound.org/media/article_pdfs/JENKINS_WHITE_PAPER.PDF

Johnston, J. (2015). *Partners in austerity: Jamaica, the United States and the international monetary fund*. Center for Economic and Policy Research. Retrieved from http://cepr.net/documents/Jamaica_04-2015.pdf

Meyer, A., Rose, D. H., & Gordon, D. (2014). *Universal design for learning: Theory and practice*. Retrieved from http://udltheorypractice.cast.org/login

Ministry of Education and Youth. (2011). *ICT in Jamaica's education system*. Initiative and Challenges, World Bank Regional Event. Retrieved from http://siteresources.worldbank.org/EDUCATION/Resources/Jamaica_ICTintheJamaicanEducationSystemrevised.pdf

Morris, A. K., & Hiebert, J. (2011). Creating shared instructional products: An alternative approach to improving teaching. *Educational Researcher, 40*(1), 5–14.

National Center for Education Statistics. (2018). *Characteristics of public school teachers*. The Condition of Education. Retrieved from https://nces.ed.gov/programs/coe/indicator_clr.asp

National Research Council (2000). *How people learn: Brain, mind, experience, and school* (Expanded ed.). Washington, DC: National Academies Press.

National Research Council. (2012). *Education for life and work: Developing transferable knowledge for life and work*. Retrieved from www.nap.edu/openbook.php?record_id=13398

New Media Consortium. (2018). *NMC horizon report preview: 2018 higher education edition*. Retrieved from https://library.educause.edu/~/media/files/library/2018/4/previewhr2018.pdf

Planning Institutes of Jamaica (2010). *Executive summary*. Vision 2030. Jamaica: National Development Plan. Retrieved from www.vision2030.gov.jm/Portals/0/NDP/Executive%20Summary.pdf/

Reed, M. E., Arnold, A., Best, K., De Arment, S., & Onorato, P. (2014, July). *Teacher educators examine UDL/AE applications in international learning community*. Presentation at Braga 2014 International Conference on Special Education—Embracing Inclusive Approaches. University of Mino, Braga, Portugal.

Reed, M. E., & Smith, F. G. (2013, June). *Selected roundtable discussion: Two lenses for disrupting professional education: Adaptive expertise and universal design for learning*. Tobago, West Indies: International Roundtable, Division on International Special Education Services.

Reed, E., Smith, F. G., King, A., Wojcik, A., & Temple, P. (2014, May). *Building a universal design for learning (UDL) virtual classroom*. 2014 VCU Online Learning Summit. Richmond, VA: Virginia Commonwealth University.

Rose, D. H., & Gravel, J. (2010). Universal design for learning. In E. Baker, P. Peterson, & B. McGraw (Eds.), *International encyclopedia of education* (3rd ed.). Oxford: Elsevier.

Smith, F. G., Reed, M. E., & Arnold, A. (2015). *Building solid bases: Designing culturally responsive UDL professional development with Jamaican educators*. 2015 Conference Proceedings, 2015 UDL-IRN National Summit, Gulfport, MS.

Thwaite, R. (2014). *Sectoral presentation 2014–15: Student achievement*. Retrieved from www.moe.gov.jm/sites/default/files/HMEsectoralD21-May7-2.pdf

The World Bank. (2018). *Overview*. The World Bank in Jamaica. Retrieved from www.worldbank.org/en/country/jamaica/overview

The World Bank. (2019). *Data*. Jamaica. Retrieved from http://data.worldbank.org/country/jamaica

Young, L. C., Daly, U. T., & Stone, J. (2017). OER: The future of education is open. *Educause Review, 52*(5), 1–2.

7

DECAFFEINATED UDL

Chile in Quest of Inclusive Education

Boris Alvarez, Paola Andrea Vergara, and Irma Iglesias

UDL: The Authentic Coffee

Due to its fragrance, color, and intensity, coffee is an undeniable part of human culture. In Chile, for example, coffee helps many to begin the day, to partake in conversations, to get through the workday, and to round out a delightful dinner (Karaouglu, 2004). Inspired by great coffee, a whole story is written that begins in country fields and ends in the cups of consumers. Coffee growers work tirelessly in fields, preparing the soil, planting seeds, and collecting carefully just those beans that are mature enough. To meet this goal, it is necessary to look forward between six to eight years to obtain an optimal production of the coffee tree.

As coffee growers strive to obtain the best coffee beans from the fields, educators must make the most of their own and their students' capabilities in order to obtain the best production in learning. UDL invites educators to transform old practices, to erase beliefs linked to undervalued learning capacities, to operationalize curriculum, and to change content representation formats that are single, standardized, and fixed. Technological and neuroscientific advances are exciting education professionals' interests to learn about brain functions as well as understand the impacts of experience and emotions in learning. This neuroscientific evidence is the basis of the UDL framework that promotes access, inclusion, participation, and progress in education for all (Riviou, Kouroupetroglou, & Oikonomidis, 2015).

Although one's national context and current normative practices may lead views toward inclusive education, support is needed to develop practices based on UDL that reduce learning gaps. This chapter aims to approach this issue, taking into consideration the drivers that have affected Chilean policy and the challenges met in the implementation of the UDL framework in Chile. It describes steps taken toward the development of an educational system that is inclusive and equitable.

Hundreds of stories are written about good coffee coming to tables everywhere. So too, hundreds of stories are written in the implementation of Universal Design for Learning in Chile.

Chile: Policies and Structure

The legal framework of Chile is based on Decreto N° 100 of the Political Constitution of the Republic (Ministerio Secretaría General de la Presidencia, 2005), which states general guarantees regarding Rights and Duties. The first article decrees equality of dignity and rights. In the nineteenth article, guarantees such as the right to life and the right to receive an education are listed. This main legal framework declares that the equality of each person must be protected and corroborates with the Convention on the Rights of Persons with Disabilities (2006) and the Law N° 20,422 (2010). Together, these laws establish the legal foundation regarding the rights of people with disabilities (Servicio Nacional de la Discapacidad [SENADIS], 2015).

In 2004, the first survey about disability in Chile was performed. Up to that year, there were no statistics available that could drive public policies about different scenarios, barriers, and the magnitude of disability in the country (El Fondo Nacional de la Discapacidad [FONADIS], 2004). The second survey about disability was performed in 2015. It was conceptually framed on a biophysical-social model that considered the social and environmental dimensions of disability and was based on the criteria of the International Classification of Functioning, Disability and Health (ICF). Furthermore, the second survey was performed after Chile ratified the Convention on the Rights of Persons with Disabilities (CRPD) in 2008. It has since led to a more complete reality of disability in the country. CRPD is a mandate that promotes, protects, and guarantees the full enjoyment of the human rights of people with disabilities in Chile (SENADIS, 2016).

In 2010, Law 20,422 was enacted, making way for equality of opportunities and social inclusion of people with disabilities. This led to the creation of the National Service of Disability, a government institution in charge of promoting the rights of people with disabilities through social inclusion and the elimination of any form of discrimination based on disability (SENADIS, 2010). The Non-Discrimination Law 20609 followed in 2012, mandating that state agencies (including the Ministry of Education) "guarantee to every person that they will not receive arbitrary discrimination, as well as they will have guaranteed the enjoyment and exercise of their rights recognized for the Political Constitution of the Republic, the laws and international agreements ratified by Chile and that be valid, particularly when they be based on reasons such as race or ethnicity . . . and disease or disability" (Ministerio Secretaría General de Gobierno, 2012, p. 1). Most recently, the Higher Education Law 21091 was passed in 2018, assuring non-discrimination and full social inclusion of people with disabilities through reasonable adjustments (Ministerio de Educación, 2018).

The history depicted in Figure 7.1 can be perceived as an evolution regarding the development of disability-related policies in Chile from an integrative model

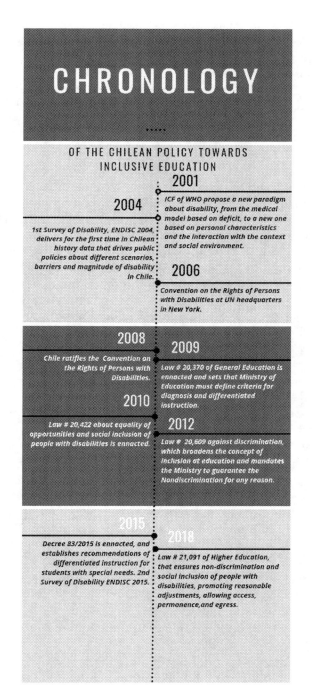

FIGURE 7.1 Chronology of the Chilean Policy Toward an Inclusive Education

toward a model based on human rights and inclusion. It should be mentioned that these changes not only have occurred in the legal framework but also in society. Though some Chileans persist in seeking to conserve traditional exclusionary systems, many others seem eager to create new spaces for inclusion, viewing mistakes from previous generations as opportunities for the future. Further, individuals with disabilities, their families, and advocates are actively involved in the creation, implementation, follow-up, and assessment of the public policies that concern them (SENADIS, 2016).

Perhaps most relevant to inclusive instructional design is Decree 83/2015, which approved criteria and orientations of curriculum adjustments for students with special educational needs from pre-school, elementary, and middle school levels. This has contributed to a major shift in Chilean education, due to explicit referencing of UDL to address diverse learners in this decree—"Universal Design for Learning is a strategy that responds to diversity, whose goal is to maximize learning opportunities of all students, considering the broad spectrum of abilities, learning styles and preferences" (Ministerio de Educación Gobierno de Chile, 2015, p. 6).

Although most of the written statements of the decree are based on a classic UDL definition of providing multiple means of expression, representation, and action and expression, it also included elements from Special Education, creating a mixture called "Diversification of Teaching." For example, it describes the use of curricular adaptations:

> When strategies for responding to diversity based on Universal Design for Learning do not meet the learning needs of some students, it is necessary to carry out an individual diagnostic evaluation to identify whether they present special educational needs and whether they require curricular adaptations.
>
> *(Ministerio de Educación Gobierno de Chile, 2015, p. 7)*

This decree marked a pivotal point in Chilean legislation in which students with disabilities now have access to regular education, rather than being segregated to special education schools or to integration programs (integration programs allow access of students into regular classrooms but they are incorporated through accommodations and adjustments, based on diagnosis and a medical model).

Further, applications of UDL are supporting new skills and choices and the creation of learning communities that value differences and curricular innovations. Implementation of an authentic UDL model, though, has been challenging, as the local version has a series of accommodations that have led to misconceptions. The experiences with the start-up of this policy relayed through this chapter can be a reference to other countries to detect barriers and propose solutions that allow, through the UDL framework, progress toward an inclusive education. The following paragraphs will dig deeper into these challenges and will share proposals for overthrowing barriers.

Decaffeinated UDL

Just like carefully selected, high quality coffee beans, UDL is a valuable approach that can have varied "roasts" and styles. UDL recognizes the unique essence within each student. UDL's potential, as the one of *authentic coffee*, is the ideal or ultimate goal. *Diversified teaching* may be viewed as the decaffeinated version of UDL (see Figure 7.2). Because caffeine naturally occurs in coffee beans, procedures used to decaffeinate (such as soaking them in methylene chloride) will affect taste and aroma (Muy Interesante, 2019). So, too, decaffeinated UDL has remains from the process that affect the final result of its implementation, in the following ways:

1. Decaffeinated UDL sees UDL as *a strategy* and not as *a framework* that considers learner variability, approaches to overcoming barriers, and iteration.
2. Decaffeinated UDL *tags* learners. Diversified teaching invites educators to use UDL; however, when the learning needs of some students are not addressed by UDL, diagnostic evaluations and curricular adaptation measures follow.
3. Decaffeinated UDL considers study plans for the illusive *average learner*, without considering needs of students from the margins.
4. Decaffeinated UDL *does not anticipate* context and curriculum barriers.

FIGURE 7.2 UDL: Authentic Bean and Decaffeinated Bean

Implementation of Authentic UDL

Chile's pioneering of UDL as the implementation framework for inclusive education has involved some trial-and-error in the process. Similar to an expert barista, who knows the appropriate grind method, temperature, and time of brewing to enhance the properties and attributes of coffee, Chile is working to achieve the expertise to implement UDL fully and authentically. As such, two challenges that have decaffeinated UDL need to be addressed: 1) shifting the conceptual view of UDL as a strategy to UDL as a framework and 2) transitioning from labeling and focusing on deficits of learners to an inclusive instructional design approach.

Challenge 1: Conceptual Shift

UDL is a framework that is centered around the learner and curriculum and is defined by the way it supports and accommodates his/her variability (Meyer, Rose, & Gordon, 2014). Oxford Living Dictionaries define *framework* as "a basic structure underlying a system, a concept or a text" (Oxford University Press, 2019). Accordingly, UDL forms the basic structure of an educational system that is both inclusive and of high quality, redefining and changing the focus from *abilities and disabilities of certain learners* to identifying that the *curriculum and context* are *disabled*.

Chile needs to work toward the conceptual shift to view UDL as a framework, rather than just a strategy, and as such to recognize that UDL does not dictate a single design or plan. The use of a wider perspective, as opposed to a single design, is based on the significant diversity present in classrooms. Differences are intrinsic to human beings, and these differences are evident in learning approaches and preferences. Chile's decaffeinated version of UDL considers individual differences but does not systematize teaching as a function of variability. UDL involves instructional planning that proactively addresses this learner variability, considering voices of students in the design and delivery of learning experiences that facilitate options and choices for different levels of challenge (Novak, 2017).

The decaffeinated version of UDL does not eliminate barriers but coexists with them and sets specific workarounds for those students who are not able to overcome them. This can increase educator workload, because alternates have to be created for each student who faces an obstacle. In contrast, authentic UDL invites reflection and anticipation regarding what can impede learning or what could cause learning failure in the future. This becomes the starting point of teaching, because it enables detection and elimination of potential learning barriers. Realizing what must be changed is fundamental to achieving access for each person and reaching expert learning (Guzmán, 2018). Moreover, overcoming barriers is not a static process but one that invites iteration.

Change is underway in Chile, as a new conception of disability (SENADIS, 2015) has stimulated the understanding that barriers are not in the person but in the context, such as facilities, culture, policies, curriculum, and ways to interact (Booth & Ainscow, 2002). Barriers may also be present in the design of a lesson. Through the UDL lens, barriers can be identified, anticipated, and minimized through inclusive instructional design.

As a fully caffeinated UDL expert "barista," an educator continues to build his/her skills and practices. Feedback received will be relevant to determine which elements worked and potential areas to improve. This process is performed daily, iterating to achieve mastery. UDL implementation, therefore, can be viewed as a process of iteration, not a set of rigid steps to follow. It centers on continuous improvement that supports learning and professional growth (National Center on Universal Design for Learning, 2012).

Challenge 2: Deficits of Learners vs. Deficits in Curricular Design

In Chile, the use of labels is strongly ingrained for *tagging* groups of students. Understanding that deficit by itself does not determine the disability of a student but also involves the context and associated barriers; a truly inclusive approach must assure that these qualifications be removed. Authentic UDL posits that everybody has different requirements, motivations, and ways to access and engage with information. While it promotes multiple pathways to learning, it does so from the curricular outset, instead of through individual accommodations. Rather than focusing on deficits and labels, UDL attributes barriers to the curricular design, instead of the learners. Learners who do not fit the mold of an *average* learner are provided opportunities to show their high capacities when the learning context plans for that (Meyer et al., 2014; Núñez, Careaga, Fornoni, Ruiz, & Valverde, 2003). UDL gives us a clear framework to address this. Though people learn in different ways, each one has the right to learn and the potential to achieve it.

Conclusion

Learners have wide variability in learning. They can present different needs or benefit from different supports to achieve a task. Authentic UDL thus does not respond to *ability* or *disability*; rather, authentic UDL responds to *variability*. Decaffeinated UDL, like decaffeinated coffee, becomes more evident when one sees and experiences authentic UDL practices. However, someone only familiar with the decaffeinated version of UDL may not know what is missing. Educational change agents are working toward more authentic and effective implementation of UDL, addressing key challenges of reframing instructional design to be inclusive and supportive of all students.

Chile faces several challenges. One of them is creating *UDL Learning Communities* wherein teachers can share success stories and support those who are interested in inclusive education. There is increasing interest in going deeper into using this framework, as evidenced by the publication of technical guides, establishment of consultancy projects, and opportunities for continuing education to institutions and professionals. These are crucial to equipping Chilean teachers with needed tools and strategies to implement UDL in their schools. Regarding this purpose, the creation of strategic alliances with expert institutions would be welcomed, and research about UDL implementation in Chile is needed to contribute to deeper understanding of its important value toward developing a more inclusive society.

References

Booth, T., & Ainscow, M. (2002). *Index for inclusion: Developing learning and participation in schools*. Bristol: CSIE.

El Fondo Nacional de la Discapacidad (FONADIS). (2004). *Primer Estudio Nacional de la Discapacidad en Chile (ENDISC)*. Retrieved from www.senadis.gob.cl/descarga/i/3011

Guzmán, A. (2018). *Concepto de Variabilidad y su Contribución en el Aprendizaje*. Chile: Curso de Introducción al DUA, Unidad 2. SENCE.

Karaouglu, Y. (2004). *Culto al Café*. Barcelona: Oceano Ambar.

Meyer, A., Rose, D. H., & Gordon, D. (2014). *Universal design for learning: Theory and practice*. Wakefield, MA: CAST Professional Publishing.

Ministerio de Educación. (2018). *Sobre Educación Superior* (Ley 21091). Retrieved from www.leychile.cl/Navegar?idNorma=1118991&idParte=

Ministerio de Educación Gobierno de Chile. (2015). *Diversificación de la Enseñanza* (Decreto 83/2015). Retrieved from http://especial.mineduc.cl/wp-content/uploads/sites/31/2016/08/Decreto-83-2015.pdf

Ministerio Secretaría General de Gobierno. (2012). *Establece Medidas Contra la Discriminación* (Ley 20609). Retrieved from www.leychile.cl/Navegar?idNorma=1042092

Ministerio Secretaría General de la Presidencia. (2005). *Fija el texto refundido, coordinado y sistematizado de la Constitución Política de la República de Chile* (Decreto 100). Retrieved from www.leychile.cl/Navegar?idNorma=242302

Muy Interesante. (2019). *¿Cómo se hace el café descafeinado?* Retrieved from www.muyinteresante.es/curiosidades/preguntas-respuestas/como-se-hace-el-cafe-descafeinado-381473863668

National Center on Universal Design for Learning. (2012). *Learner variability and UDL (Online seminar presentation)*. UDL Series, No. 1. Retrieved from http://udlseries.udlcenter.org/presentations/learner_variability.html

Novak, K. (2017). *Let them thrive: A playbook for helping your child succeed in school and in life*. Wakefield, MA: CAST Professional Publishing.

Núñez, J., Careaga, S., Fornoni, J., Ruíz, L., & Valverde, P. (2003). La evolución de la plasticidad fenotípica. *Revista Especializada En Ciencias Químico—Biológicas, 6*(1), 16–24.

Oxford University Press. (2019). *Framework*. Retrieved from https://en.oxforddictionaries.com/definition/framework

Riviou, K., Kouroupetroglou, G., & Oikonomidis, N. (2015). A network of peers and practices for addressing learner variability: UDLnet. *Studies in Health, Technology and Informatics, 217*, 32–39.

Servicio Nacional de la Discapacidad (SENADIS). (2010). *Quienes Somos. Introducción*. Retrieved from www.senadis.gob.cl/pag/2/1144/introduccion

Servicio Nacional de la Discapacidad (SENADIS). (2015). *Discapacidad y Salud Mental: Una Visión desde SENADIS*. Retrieved from www.senadis.gob.cl/descarga/i/3179/documento

Servicio Nacional de la Discapacidad (SENADIS). (2016). *Estudio Nacional de la Discapacidad en Chile*. Retrieved from http://observatorio.ministeriodesarrollosocial.gob.cl/endisc/docs/Libro_Resultados_II_Estudio_Nacional_de_la_Discapacidad.pdf

8
UNIVERSAL DESIGN FOR LEARNING IN CHINA

Haoyue Zhang and George Zhao

Introduction

Universal Design for Learning (UDL) is a framework aiming to optimize learning outcomes by considering systematic learner variation when designing a course. Learner variation is addressed through the framework by having instructors provide multiple means of engagement to learners, multiple means of representing the course content, and multiple means of expression to determine learner understanding. By adopting the UDL framework, learners of different backgrounds and abilities are able to access and understand the curriculum in their own ways.

The Center for Applied Special Technology ([CAST], 2018) proposes using multiple means to make teaching and learning activities satisfy the learning needs of students of different backgrounds, learning abilities, and cognitive styles. When designing their instruction, CAST recommends considering a wide range of learner abilities such as learner perception, listening comprehension, reading comprehension, writing performance, organization, and learning retention. With these abilities in mind, instructors can use this information when deciding learning objectives, selecting instructional materials, organizing learning activities, executing instruction, and designing learner assessments for their course.

UDL offers benefits in three aspects (Chen & Pei, 2016). First, it is helpful in cultivating the expert learner, who is resourceful and knowledgeable, strategic and goal-directed, and purposeful and motivated. Second, it suits a core goal of school education in the 21st century, which is learning to know. Third, it responds to the query on the effectiveness of educational technologies, such as whether technology promotes effective learning. By dismantling the environmental barriers that could impede the learning of students, UDL transfers the source of the barriers from the learners to the curricular design.

Inclusive learning was proposed in China in the 1980s (Li, 2015). As a result, schools were no longer able to refuse students with intellectual disabilities from receiving a general education. This was done in an effort to minimize the differences between students in a special education system and those in a general education system (Deng & Zhu, 2007; Shen, 2004). Later on, educators (Gao & Gao, 2009) introduced and proposed the application of UDL in general curriculum instruction. Though it is beneficial to adopt UDL to facilitate teaching and learning, there are many challenges. As a primarily English framework, it would be difficult to implement the UDL framework into a country that speaks primarily another language besides English. This is made especially difficult without the support of local organizations. The mission of this chapter is to describe the situation in China with the UDL framework and inclusive learning, describe the educational transformation of China, and identify the challenges and solutions for future researchers and educators to apply UDL in China.

Current Status in China

Government Policy

The inclusion of students with special needs in general schools was first stated in the government issued document "The Notification of Additional Teaching Guidelines for Full-Time Schools or Classes for the Mentally Disabled" in 1988 (National Education Committee, 1988). In this document, the government described the integration as *Learning in Regular Classes*. It proposed that students with mild learning disabilities are allowed to enroll in general classes. Students suffering from more severe mental ailments would remain in special classes or special schools (Deng & Jin, 2013). However, students with special needs fortunate enough to be allowed admittance into general courses often did not receive attention from their teachers (Deng & Jin, 2013). The students with special needs were supposed to take responsibility to catch up with class schedules and perform like other students (Deng & Jin, 2013). No changes were made to curricula or course content. The only *inclusion* that the students with special needs experienced was physical.

To change the situation, *Equal Regular Education* was proposed, which provided equal rights, environments, positions, and education for students with special needs. Under this proposition, students would have equal rights to enroll in regular classes regardless of the severities of their disabilities. This inclusion would be more than physical. In addition, students with special needs would experience mental and social inclusion as well as special curriculum considerations. Equal Regular Education is grounded in the premise that the boundary between general education students and students with special needs should not exist. All students should have access to high quality education that suits their individual characteristics.

In January 2014, the State Council issued the *Special Education Promotion Plan (2014–2016)*. Written by the Ministry of Education and other government departments, the objective of this document was to provide better educational opportunities to students with special needs. It proposed the overall developmental goal of "promoting inclusive education in an all-round way so that every child with special needs can receive appropriate education" (Ministry of Education of the People's Republic of China, 2014). Additionally, the latest *People with Disabilities Educational Ordinance Act of 2017* stated that "Governments at all levels should gradually improve the ability of ordinary kindergartens and schools to receive students with disabilities, promote inclusive education, and ensure that disabled people enter ordinary kindergartens and schools to receive education" (Li, 2017). The promulgation and implementation of these policies fully demonstrate that the Chinese Ministry of Education has recognized the concept of *inclusive education* and has begun to put it into practice.

Developmental Result

When the UDL framework was first proposed, it was primarily theoretical in nature, based upon neurological processing research (Rose & Meyer, 2002). As support for the framework has grown, CAST has developed UDL tools based on their research projects. Tools such as the UDL guidelines, the UDL Studio, and the UDL Toolkit have been instrumental in UDL's growth. Additional tools such as the Carnegie Strategy Tutor and Read with Me eBooks have also been recommended in China (Chen & Pei, 2016; Jia & Xin, 2017; Yan & Deng, 2014). Furthermore, tools from other websites have also been mentioned by Chinese researchers, including Math ML (www.w3org/Math/) and Mathematics Glossary (www.ronblond.com/MathGlossary) (Chen & Pei, 2016).

However, all of the tools referenced are English-only applications and created with Western culture in mind. The upstarting UDL Chinese instructor would hardly be able to understand and utilize these tools to their full potential without translation. Additionally, students may not receive the maximum benefit to their learning outcomes from these tools without appropriate connections to the students' background culture. Currently, there is no Chinese UDL website to attract, gather, and connect educators, researchers, instructional designers, and educational administrators. Finally, without a local leadership to rally behind, it will be extremely difficult to spread the UDL framework throughout China.

An investigation into the published literature on the terms *inclusive learning* and *UDL* illustrates the difference in the concept's presence in China and in the West. Using the Education Resource Information Center (ERIC) database to search for publications on *inclusive learning*, 645 academic journal articles from between 1979 to 2018 were found. Searching instead for *Universal Design for Learning* rendered 270 academic journal articles from 1991 to 2018 with greater quantities of publications releasing in more recent years, prior to 1991 no articles on UDL exist within ERIC.

When searching *inclusive learning* in the China National Knowledge Infrastructure (CNKI) database, the most utilized Chinese academic database, only 38 articles (including unpublished dissertations) were found, starting from the first in 2004 to the most recent in 2018. A paltry number, especially when compared to the American database. Of the CNKI articles, 10 of these were published in the *Chinese Journal of Special Education* and *Modern Special Education*, which implies that there is a lack of attention toward the idea of inclusion in general education. Prior to 2012, there was merely one publication every year on average. Since 2012, there have been an average of four publications every year. Unfortunately, the number of publications does not show a tendency of increasing. Only nine articles were found when searching for *Universal Design for Learning* between 2009 to 2018 within the CNKI database, and none prior to 2009. This lack of relevant literature in Chinese databases will likely slow the *implementation* of the recently approved ordinance for inclusive learning as educators seek ways to better support the needs of diverse learners in China.

The dramatic contrast in publication volume between the Western and Chinese databases is understandable, given the genesis of inclusive learning and UDL in China being decades after its conceptualization in the United States. Currently, though, neither inclusive learning nor UDL are hot topics in Chinese educational research. The development of UDL in China is still in the beginning stage at best, as few are paying attention to it and even fewer have actually adopted it.

Evaluation

Regarding the effect of the UDL approach, CAST conducted a series of studies based on UDL principles and found that UDL has a positive impact on stimulating learning motivation and increasing the learning outcomes for learners with learning barriers (Coyne, Pisha, Dalton, Zeph, & Smith, 2012; Kortering, McClannon, & Braziel, 2008; Smith, 2007). Haley-Mize and Reeves (2013) described how UDL helps instructors consider how to actively prepare the curriculum for learners with different cognitive preferences from the start, rather than modifying the curriculum when learners encounter learning problems. Hitchcock, Meyer, Rose, and Jackson(2002) believe that UDL is an effective way to achieve inclusive learning by satisfying the diverse needs of students with all backgrounds. More research evidence supporting UDL guidelines can be found on the CAST website (http://udlguidelines.cast.org/more/research-evidence).

The execution of the UDL framework is further enhanced by educational technology, but unfortunately socio-economic limitations pose challenges in some parts of China (Yan, Guan, & Deng, 2015). For example, the rural areas of China are impoverished and even basic technology such as computers is scarce. For these rural students, the benefits of a technological UDL approach would be hindered. Furthermore, many teachers still have a superficial understanding about UDL. They know that UDL can mean providing multiple ways to present information. However, they don't know how it works, which has inhibited the integration of UDL into curriculum design (Jia & Xin, 2017).

Transformation of Education in China

Teaching Philosophy

The UDL approach acknowledges and recognizes learner diversity. The foundation is based on the tenet that cognitive ability and neurological networks need to be considered to facilitate the optimal learning outcomes of learners with various needs through a combination of educational strategies and technologies (Cao, 2015). UDL's features of openness, flexibility, and foresight have the potential to enlighten teaching and learning practice in China. The traditional teaching philosophy in China focuses on instructional materials and not the learners (Cao, 2015). Teachers typically design the curriculum around the content, instead of the learners' abilities. As a result, it is hard to motivate students and satisfy their needs, especially for students with special needs.

However, due to translation issues, distance, and cultural differences, UDL has not been adopted rapidly in China. Additionally, the UDL framework that does exist in China has varied dramatically from its original form. Chinese people have a different understanding of how UDL functions from the aspects of their audience, instruction, and context. The teachers tend to understand UDL through the lens of the traditional teaching framework and view UDL as targeting students with special needs exclusively (Jia & Xin, 2017). Some teachers misunderstand UDL as an assistive tool for students with disabilities, which significantly weakens the effect of UDL overall (Jia & Xin, 2017). It does appear, though, that a majority of teachers in China comprehend what UDL means; however, some teachers design the curriculum based on the needs of the majority of students and provide a watered down version to the students with special needs, which eventually hurts overall learning potential. Ideally, the UDL approach will likely need to change teachers' teaching philosophy in order to provide better development opportunities for students.

Teacher Professional Development

The use of educational technology tools can be greatly beneficial in the application of the UDL approach. Educational technology can be used to expand the multiple means aspects of UDL. However, the reality is that in rural areas and in Midwest area, there is little to no access to modern technology at schools (Chu, 2015). Additionally, teachers in elementary and secondary schools are usually undergraduates majoring in education. An *Introduction to Educational Technology* course may be the only educational technology that they have been exposed to. Their ability to use or integrate digital media into a curriculum is limited. Special education teachers may have the mindset that technology tools are assistive tools that are used only when students encounter certain problems, which conflicts with UDL principles that are concerned with the needs of all students (Jia & Xin, 2017). Relevant professional development opportunities are needed, so that teachers are able to understand the concepts and principles of UDL, gain the skill sets to adopt educational technology tools, and practice applying UDL into the curriculum. Also, the school administrators need further training on how to enhance students' learning experience through their policy designs.

Situated Guidelines and Tools

In China, researchers, educators, and policymakers are working to cultivate expert learners through curriculum reform (Chen & Pei, 2016). The way CAST promotes UDL application provides a practical way to change the traditional teaching method and cultivate expert learners, which would be worthwhile for China to adopt. Situated guidelines and tools are needed to spread the UDL approach in China and eventually change the traditional teaching methods that are currently being used. Teachers will then be able to use their past experiences in connection with the UDL principles to help them understand the framework and how to apply it in their classrooms. A quick way to connect UDL with the Chinese teachers' past experiences is comparing UDL with differentiated instruction, which has been known by Chinese teachers since the 1990s (Yan et al., 2015). Both differentiated instruction and UDL acknowledge learner differences in terms of backgrounds, learning abilities, and cognitive styles. However, in differentiated instruction, teachers instead design different learning materials and learning activities according to student abilities. In UDL classes, teachers design multiple ways to present information and assess learning outcomes, which leaves the choice of learning method up to the student. Situated UDL guidelines reinforced with tools that appeal to the preferences of Chinese teachers and students are more likely to be adopted.

Educational Technology Challenges in China

Technology tools play a strong supplementary role in applying UDL. Even though Chinese teachers may have limited understanding of UDL, they may be applying it through the use of projectors, interactive whiteboards, multimedia, and other common classroom devices. Unfortunately, many specific tools designed in support of the UDL approach are not currently available in Chinese. Furthermore, many of the common tools available to Western teachers cannot be accessed while in China. Perhaps the most critical example is the popular video sharing website YouTube, which is blocked by the Chinese government. While China has similar complementary services, the Chinese versions are not as feature-rich as the original. For example, *Youku* is a popular Chinese video sharing website that is near-identical to YouTube but lacks key features such as auto-captioning, which makes fulfilling the multisensory instruction promoted by the UDL framework more difficult. Operating systems on school computers and software versions are another potential obstacle worth considering. In China, the schools and universities purchase life-long licenses of computer software and typically only update their programs when needs force them to do so. It would not be strange to see a computer running Windows XP or Microsoft 2000 in many schools. Teachers may need to consider the strong possibility of software incompatibility issues when using UDL tools in China.

Conclusion

Through the UDL approach, instructors and students are able to reduce the loss of learning opportunities due to environmental limitations by providing multiple selections to the students. The Chinese government offers a welcome environment for the development of UDL in China by promoting inclusive education. The UDL framework has a lot of potential to benefit education in China, such as increasing learners' motivation and learning outcomes. However, the developmental status of UDL in China is far behind that of America, in terms of practical guidelines and tools and research progress. Chinese teachers need more support on changing their traditional teaching philosophy and mastering digital skill sets to embed a UDL approach in their curriculum. Situated UDL tools are under development in terms of language accessibility.

References

Cao, R. (2015). The principle of universal design for learning and teaching applications. *Psychology: Techniques and Applications, 17*(1), 41–44.

CAST Timeline. (2018, August 29). Retrieved from www.cast.org/about/timeline.html#.XHropej0k2w

Chen, S., & Pei, X. (2016). Preparing expert learner in digital age- universal design for learning. *e-Education Research, 277*(5), 58–65.

Chu, Z. (2015). Talking about the 'management' and 'use' of rural educational technology equipment. *Experiment and Equipment for Primary School, 25*, 44–46.

Coyne, P., Pisha, B., Dalton, B., Zeph, L., & Smith, N. (2012). Literacy by design: A universal design for learning approach for students with significant intellectual disabilities. *Remedial and Special Education, 33*(3), 162–172.

Deng, M., & Jing, S. (2013). From learning in regular classrooms to equal regular education: Reflections on the localization of inclusive education in China. *Chinese Journal of Special Education, 158*(8), 4–9.

Deng, M., & Zhu, Z. (2007). "Learning in regular class" and inclusive education: A comparison between Chinese and western model for special education. *Journal of Huazhong Normal University, 46*, 125–129.

Gao, W., & Gao, Y. (2009). Universal design for learning: Realizing inclusive teaching and learning. *Studies in Foreign Education*, *227*(36), 11–15.

Haley-Mize, S., & Reeves, S. (2013). Universal design for learning and emergent-literacy development: Instructional practices for young learners. *Delta Kappa Gamma Bulletin*, *79*(2), 70.

Hitchcock, C., Meyer, A., Rose, D., & Jackson, R. (2002). Providing new access to the general curriculum: Universal design for learning. *Teaching Exceptional Children*, *35*(2), 8–17.

Jia, C., & Xin, W. (2017). Universal design for learning: Development, commentary and enlightenment. *Modern Special Education (Higher Education)*, (4), 21–25.

Kortering, L., McClannon, T., & Braziel, P. (2008). Universal design for learning: A look at what algebra and biology students with and without high incidence conditions are saying. *Remedial and Special Education*, *29*(6), 352–363.

Li, K. (2017). *People with disabilities educational ordinance act*. Retrieved from www.hbdpf.org.cn/xwzx/qgdt/162986.htm

Li, L. (2015). The three-decade-long developments of China's policy of inclusive education: The process, dilemma and strategies. *Chinese Journal of Special Education*, *184*(10), 16–20.

Ministry of Education of the People's Republic of China. (2014). *Special education promotion plan (2014–2016)*. Retrieved from http://old.moe.gov.cn/publicfiles/business/html files/moe/moe_1778/201401/162822.html

National Education Committee. (1988). The notification of additional teaching guidelines for full-time schools or classes for the mentally disabled. *People's Education*, (6).

Rose, D., & Meyer, A. (2002). *Teaching every student in the digital age: Universal Design for Learning*. Alexandria, VA: Association for Supervision and Curriculum Development.

Shen, R. (2004). Ecological construction of inclusive learning environment. *Chinese Journal of Special Education*, *43*, 1–4.

Smith, F. (2007). *Perceptions of universal design for learning (UDL) in college classrooms* (ProQuest Dissertations and Theses Global). (3296852).

Yan, T., & Deng, M. (2014). Reflection on universal design for learning in inclusive classroom. *Chinese Journal of Special Education*, *163*, 17–22.

Yan, T., Guan, W., & Deng, M. (2015). A comparative analysis of differentiated instruction and universal design for learning in inclusive classrooms. *Chinese Journal of Special Education*, *176*(2), 3–9.

9

SNAPSHOT—REDUCING LEARNING BARRIERS THROUGH THE USE OF THE FACE PROGRAM

Radhike Khanna and Elizabeth M. Dalton

The Indian Context

In the words of Mahatma Gandhi, "True education must correspond to the surrounding circumstances or it is not a healthy growth" and "by education I mean an all-round drawing out of the best in the child and man—body, mind and spirit" (Sridharan, 2018). Gandhi's words seem to hold true for today's mainstream educational system in India, as well as in the rest of the world. Students' performance is often reduced to marks or percentages and education is primarily tailored to the requirements of the job market. "Most students are unable to transfer and effectively apply the gained knowledge outside the classroom" (Khanna & Buechler, 2015, p. 10). Subjects are often taught completely isolated from each other and disconnected from practice. "Additionally, education today focuses mainly on imparting *academic* knowledge with an emphasis on natural sciences or empiricist approaches to the social sciences, while the humanities and disciplines such as cultural studies, developmental psychology, art and spirituality are neglected" (ibid., p. 10). True education should be a liberating and transformative experience for the students, as Gandhi indicated, allowing each individual to fully explore himself or herself, gain multiple perspectives and consequently, develop holistically into an integral human being. The desperate need for more holistic integrated forms of education has been emphasized by both Indian sages and international scholars (The Economic Times, 2018).

A pioneering example of a holistic approach to education is that of VR Purnatva and its methodology, that of the "FACE program that leads to the transformation of many *specially-abled* students, allowing them to develop their full potential and become valuable and earning members of the society" (ibid., p. 10). This successful educational approach brings about a change in the lives of many special students and has become a catalyst for societal evolution in India. "The four dimensions of the FACE program are profoundly connected to the

FIGURE 9.1 Examples of FACE Program Applications

respective societal dimensions, mirroring the need for more holistic perspectives" (ibid., p. 11). The FACE program was formulated for students on the autism spectrum, however, it has been successfully applied, over time, to encompass all developmental handicaps (see Figure 9.1).

Rationale

Modern science and knowledge creation, as commonly existing in today's educational environment, encourage human independence and specialization, which can often lead, unfortunately, to the development of separation in schools for those with disabilities, and potentially to greater disintegration in broader society. While western therapeutic approaches for individuals with developmental disabilities (i.e. autism) are primarily pragmatic and behaviorally based, recent support for alternative approaches to therapy and education has begun to emerge (Brondino et al., 2015; Lind & Archibald, 2013). A tool like the FACE program guides teachers to work toward holistic transformation. It highlights the ability of oneself or an institution to bring forth latent talents and gifts of an individual, and then nurture them in a safe space. The FACE program is based on the belief that science and art must be equally used to develop skills in specially-abled students, and uses multiple means of both engaging students and encouraging varied means of expression of both gained understandings and skills, which follows the principles of Universal Design for Learning (UDL) (CAST, 2019). The students, once accepted in school and community, become catalysts for societal change, directly influencing everyone around them. It leads to a complete balance in the integration of the student with the environment of normalcy.

FACE Program Model

In response to the need for alternative support for students with autism and other challenging behaviors and potential gifts, the FACE model was developed (see Figure 9.2) and is described next.

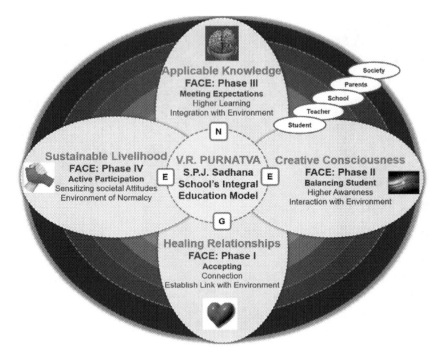

FIGURE 9.2 FACE Program Model (Khanna, 2009)

Phase 1 — Healing Relationships. *Process: Facing AUTISM Through COMMUNICATION with the ENVIRONMENT (FACE)*

The first phase of this program was aimed at creating thinking individuals with the capacity to extend their thinking to everyday situations. By establishing relationships, the educator is accepting students as a whole with challenging behaviors and helping students to communicate with the environment. Behaviors are changed by physical modification of the site and class to make the learning scenario conducive. This helps to create thinking individuals.

Phase 2 — Creative Consciousness. *Process: Kriya, Empowerment, Yoga and OM Meditation (KEY OM)*

Over the years, the FACE program has repeatedly surmounted barriers and evolved through dynamic progression to create a therapeutic environment enabling each participant to attain their full potential. Development of the right brain (creativity) to facilitate whole brain activity is emphasized by use of alternate therapies, creating better balance between right and left-brain areas. This strengthens the moral and mental fiber of the person.

Phase 3 — Applicable Knowledge. *Process: Linking and Initiating a Network of Communication Through Synergy (LINCS)*

Association between mentor and student is built on the understanding that if the student is treated as a respected member of society, he/she has the potential to rise to the required expectation. Synchronization of the work of the staff mentor and trainee creates a systematic flow of synergy between mentors and trainees and is extended to the students. The student gradually builds up a primary LINC with his/her mentor that forges connections with other teachers, peers and society.

Phase 4 — Sustainable Livelihood. *Process: Sensitizing Attitudes for Normalizing Tendencies and Offsetting Latent Adult Non-acceptance of Autism (SANTOOLAN)*

The final stage of FACE is *Santoolan*, where the student is placed in an environment of normalcy and integrated at the work place. The imbalance, created due to psychological blocks of parents who may not have completely accepted the child as a whole being, undergoes a focus shift, from the child to parental and societal influences, moving toward a shared holistic view of the normalcy of the student.

Conclusion

This program's functional evolution has built personal relationships between clients, parents, staff, volunteers, schools, etc., through education, training, alternate activities such as yoga and meditation, creative product production and direct community-based experience. This approach supports creation of awareness of the value and worth of all individuals, and is in keeping with UDL principles to celebrate human diversity and help society better understand and accept special individuals.

References

Brondino, N., Fusar-Poli, L., Roccetti, M., Provenzani, U., Barale, F., & Politi, P. (2015). Complementary and alternative therapies for autism spectrum disorder. *Evidence-Based Complementary and Alternative Medicine, 2015*. Retrieved from www.ncbi.nlm.nih.gov/pmc/articles/PMC4439475/

CAST. (2019). *UDL guidelines*. Retrieved from http://udlguidelines.cast.org/

The Economic Times. (2018, March 18). *Indian education sector needs holistic relook: Experts*. Retrieved from https://economictimes.indiatimes.com/industry/services/education/indian-education-sector-needs-holistic-relook-experts/articleshow/63352334.cms

Khanna, R. (2009). *Face program to Santoolan*. Mumbai: David Printing Press.
Khanna, R., & Buechler, S. (2015). *V R Purnatva*. Mumbai: Silverpoint Press Pvt Ltd.
Lind, A., & Archibald, N. (2013). *Structuring new service delivery models for individuals with intellectual and developmental disabilities* [Revised]. Trenton: Center for Healthcare Strategies, Inc.
Sridharan, M. (2018). *13 quotes by Mahatma Gandhi on education*. Retrieved from www.careerindia.com/features/13-quotes-on-education-by-the-mahatma-gandhi-jayanthi-018049.html

10

SNAPSHOT—A DISTRICT'S JOURNEY TO MEASURE UNIVERSAL DESIGN FOR LEARNING (UDL)

Katie Novak and Laura Chesson

Groton-Dunstable is a PreK-12 regional school district with an enrollment of approximately 2,500 students, 35 miles northwest of Boston, Massachusetts, USA. The towns of Groton and Dunstable are unique in their own ways, with Groton being the home of a quaint downtown area that boasts history and fine dining, while Dunstable holds onto much of its rural charm, with several working dairy farms in the community.

Annually, the district completes an institutional self-evaluation, which includes an equity audit to ensure that all students, regardless of variability, have equal opportunities to achieve at high levels. This process highlights achievement gaps and inequities for students with disabilities, English language learners, and economically disadvantaged students. The district vision seeks to eliminate these inequities through implementation of Universal Design for Learning (UDL), yet it is difficult to quantify the depth of implementation of UDL (Davies, Schelly, & Spooner, 2013). Community members and school committee members often inquire how the district knows UDL is, in fact, being implemented, and this nagging question led the district to create procedures to measure implementation of UDL so it could correlate the results to student growth, especially with groups who typically fail to make academic gains.

To begin to establish a baseline understanding of UDL implementation, the Assistant Superintendent, the Director of Technology, and the Director of Pupil Personnel Services walked through 300 classrooms in one year, observing instruction and looking for examples of UDL. The three principles of UDL, providing multiple means of engagement, multiple means of representation, and multiple means of action and expression, were noted during the walkthroughs. As an example, administrators observed teachers providing students with options and choices to increase engagement 24% of the time they were in classrooms. Once the administrative team established an understanding of basic implementation, the district examined the depth of implementation using the UDL Progression Rubric (Novak & Rodriguez, 2018), a tool designed to identify when practices are emerging, proficient, and approaching expert practice.

Although administrators saw educators offer choices in what students learn (e.g., "choose a country to study" rather than "study France"), how students learn (e.g., use books, videos, and/or teacher instruction to build understanding), and how they express what they know (e.g., "you can create a multimedia presentation or an audio recording or write a paragraph"), 24% of the time, the vast majority of these practices were *emerging* on the UDL Progression Rubric. Therefore, the district realized they were still in the initial implementation phase. Sharing these outcomes with teachers and providing them with the opportunity to review the UDL Progression Rubric and set goals for their own improvement created a culture with a shared understanding of the framework and its impact on the design of teaching and learning experiences for all students.

Annually, during the institutional self-evaluation, the administration plans to use the results from continued informal walkthroughs using the UDL Progression Rubric, as well as teacher evaluation write-ups, to identify classrooms that are *emerging, proficient*, and *approaching expert practice* consistently. These results will then be correlated with multiple data points to measure the correlation between UDL practices and student growth on standardized measures. There is incredible promise in this practice for all districts looking to partner with educators to both understand and provide diagnostic and formative measures of UDL implementation to increase transparency and accountability among stakeholders.

References

Davies, P. L., Schelly, C. L., & Spooner, C. L. (2013). Measuring the effectiveness of universal design for learning intervention in postsecondary education. *Journal of Postsecondary Education and Disability, 26*(3), 195–220.

Novak, K., & Rodriguez, K. (2018). *UDL progression rubric*. Retrieved from http://castpublishing.org/novak-rodriguez-udl-progression-rubric/

SECTION 3

Inclusive Classroom Design and Instructional Strategies

11

ACCESS TO THE CURRICULUM FOR STUDENTS WITH DISABILITIES

Moving Closer to the Promise of UDL in Inclusive US Classrooms

Rita Brusca-Vega and Anastasia Trekles

A Model for Making Decisions About Instructional Supports and Adaptations

Based on the work of experts in assistive technology (AT) and Universal Design for Learning (UDL), this chapter proposes a simple model that can be used to ensure that needed supports and adaptations can be properly accommodated and integrated into learning environments and that this integration plan can be evaluated and improved systematically (Bryant & Bryant, 2003; Cook & Polgar, 2013; de Jonge, Scherer, & Rodger, 2007; Gamble, Dowler, & Orslene, 2006; Kouroupetroglou, Pino, & Paraskevi, 2017; Meyer, Rose, & Gordon, 2014; Rose & Meyer, 2002; Trekles, 2009). The *Making Decisions to Support All Students* model introduced in this chapter includes six primary components: evaluating the *tasks and demands*, evaluating the *environment*, investigating *potential obstacles* for the student, investigating *adaptations for improved performance*, obtaining *training and instructional support*, and evaluating ongoing *effectiveness* (see Figure 11.1).

Each step in this model depends on the one before for success and requires that general education teachers, special educators, and support staff work together (see Table 11.1). Depending on the situation and the individual student, families may also play a key role by supporting the maintenance and generalization of new knowledge and skills. Further, like the UDL framework, which asks teachers to provide multiple means of engagement, representation, and action and expression in the teaching and learning process (Meyer et al., 2014), this model provides for a student-centered, flexible environment focused on providing personalized pathways toward reaching classroom goals (Freiberg & Lamb, 2009). Next, each of the model components are described in further detail.

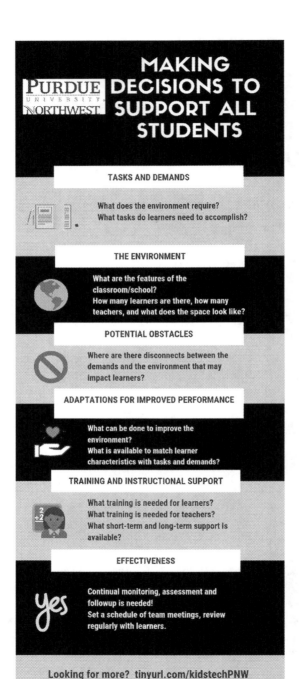

FIGURE 11.1 Decision-Making Model

TABLE 11.1 Implementation Steps for the Making Decisions to Support All Students Model

Step 1. What are the physical, social, and cognitive demands of the learning task?
- **Physical demands**: small & large motor movements? sensory expectations?
- **Social demands**: minimal or high engagement with teacher & peers?
- **Cognitive demands**: sustained attention? sequential memory? speed? comprehension of oral & written vocabulary & form? comprehension of oral & written content? transfer of input into output such as teacher lecture into written notes?

Step 2. What are the features of the environment and expectations for behavior?
- **Setting characteristics**: personal space allotment? noise? interruptions? number of students in room? distance to teacher & visual displays?
- **Behavior expectations**: need for silence? raising hand? timeliness in responding to teacher request?

Step 3. What are potential barriers for students with different characteristics and needs?
- **Oral communication barriers**: difficulty comprehending (vocabulary, form)? difficulty expressing (physical issues? limited output, inappropriate output)? In the case of new language learners, lack of proficiency?
- **Written communication barriers**: difficulty reading (physical issues? visual/auditory processing issues?) difficulty writing (physical issues? word/sentence formation issues?)
- **Sensory, physical, health barriers**: hearing or vision impairments? motor impairments? attention deficit hyperactivity? effects of medication? fatigue?
- **Content barriers:** lack of academic or experiential context? level of presentation exceeds level of understanding? concepts exceed level of understanding? inadequate modes of input?
- **Intrapersonal barriers**: behavioral & personality traits—shyness, aggressiveness, dependency?
- **Interpersonal barriers**: cultural or language differences?

Step 4. What instructional and other adaptations are needed for students?
- **IEP requirements**: accommodations—changes to how lesson material or test is presented? modifications—changes to curricular content? assistive technology—supportive tech devices?
- **Input adaptations**: print-to-speech software? braille, enlarged print? paired visual & auditory input? simplifying vocabulary? simplifying directions? picture boards? assigning peer helper?
- **Engagement adaptations**: placement in class? small group work? learning stations? one-on-one time with teacher? quiet space? allowing for movement?
- **Output adaptations**: speech-to-print software? response options—talk, show, do? if-then options (show mastery on selected items, reduce number of items)? Low or high tech communication device?

(Continued)

TABLE 11.1 (Continued)

Step 5. What training and supports are needed for educators?
- **Professional development**: technical training on equipment or software use? outside consultant? time for collaboration with colleagues?
- **Instructional support**: co-teacher? peer helpers? peer tutors? follow-up in resource room? parent homework help?
- **Curricular support**: who will adapt materials? who will find alternative materials? what materials need to be purchased?

Step 6. What refinements are needed to improve student outcomes?
- **Sources of data**: test scores on unit? performance on projects? behavioral observations? student input? parent satisfaction?
- **Planning for improvement**: how often will reviews occur? who will implement changes? what are follow-up procedures?

Tasks and Demands

Analyzing the demands of the environment is the first step in the process. What are the setting-specific demands regarding tasks that must be performed, and what prerequisite abilities would a student need in this environment? For example, the average fourth grader at a US elementary school is typically expected to read and write in English, perform basic arithmetic, hold and use writing utensils, converse with the teacher and with peers, sit at a desk and attend to the teacher's instructions, and interact with a computer using a standard keyboard and mouse interface. Thus, this child is expected to have a certain level of manual dexterity, an age-appropriate command of the English language, problem-solving skills, and conversation skills.

The Environment

Examining the features and expectations within the setting is the second and complementary step in the process. What basic physical features are present and what behaviors are expected of students using this space? For example, a typical fourth-grade American classroom might be made up of 25 to 30 children, sitting at individual student desks arranged in close rows. Students may have technology at their desks, but they may also have workstations at the back of the room or in another room entirely. Considering what furniture layouts and features of the room would best suit all students in this scenario is highly useful, such as ensuring that students have adequate room to move around for grouping. This may mean investing in flexible furniture such as adjustable, mobile desks.

Potential Obstacles

Considering how the performance of students with special needs may be affected by environmental features and demands is the third step in the process. What obstacles might students encounter to be successful in the environment? For example, students with mobility impairments may be hindered by desks that are not height-adjustable or are grouped too close together. Working with writing utensils and the computer may not be feasible without the use of AT. Students with learning disabilities may struggle with silent reading and concept development without options for learning the material orally. Students with intellectual disabilities may be unable to grasp concepts if the pace of instruction is too fast or they have minimal instructional support.

Adaptations for Improved Performance

Selecting adaptations to make the learning environment more accessible to students is the fourth step in the process. Teachers should first ask themselves what changes to the learning tasks, demands, and space can be made for improved academic and social functioning to best meet the characteristics of the group. Then, teachers should consider what additional adaptations are needed to meet specific characteristics of individual students. In a class of struggling readers, for example, a teacher might change her typical whole-group instruction to include expanded opportunities for independent reading where students listen to a story and follow along in print at their own pace, personally controlling the device used. If a student with a short attention span and acting out behaviors was part of the class, the teacher might consider additional changes for that student, such as having shorter stories to read and writing an individual learning contract where a mutually agreed upon number of stories would need to be completed for class credit.

When considering the *Making Decisions to Support All Students* model within the framework of UDL, note that adaptations for improved performance can and should provide for multiple means of engagement, representation of concepts, and expression of learning, resulting in multiple benefits to all students within the classroom (Meyer et al., 2014). Linking to the examples in the earlier paragraph on potential obstacles, classroom layouts can be reconfigured to allow for easier wheelchair accessibility, and at least one height-adjustable desk or table can be made available. The teacher can have simple alternative input devices, such as trackballs and keyboards with large keys or touch-sensitivity, on hand for students with mobility impairments to use during computer time, and all computers can have onscreen keyboard access. Print materials can be read aloud in class or made orally available using text-to-speech applications such as *Dragon NaturallySpeaking*, or built-in tools available in the Mac OS, Windows, or Chrome OS. Specified students may be assigned a peer buddy who repeats teacher directions and provides support.

Training and Instructional Support

Determining what professional development and instructional supports are necessary to implement the adaptations with fidelity is the fifth and perhaps most critical step in the process. Will teachers and students need training on AT devices and instructional support in the form of co-teachers or paraprofessionals? What materials and devices may need to be purchased and/or adapted? With regard to AT, both the student (the AT user) and the people who work with him or her daily should be trained on the operation of the AT, especially when it comes to complex devices and software. Even regularly available devices such as iPads have assistive features built into their operating systems that teachers may or may not be aware of, thus providing further opportunities for training (Cook & Polgar, 2013; Ok, Kim, Kang, & Bryant, 2016). No student with a disability should be forced to wait for a counselor or aide to come to the "rescue" with a malfunctioning piece of equipment because other support personnel are unable to assist. In the US, the vast majority of states have state- or grant-funded special education centers that provide training and support locally and on-site for AT usage in the schools and throughout the community, such as Wisconsin (see http://wati.org) and Indiana (see www.patinsproject.com). If local special education personnel cannot provide training themselves and no service is otherwise available, most AT manufacturers can be contacted to provide on-site workshops and support.

For supports and adaptations involving technology, a rubric has been developed using this model for evaluating assistive and instructional technologies, primarily those apps and web-based programs and subscription services that are commonly used by teachers in the classroom (Frazier, Trekles, & Vega, 2018). The rubric allows educators to examine apps, devices, and other software based on the major framework components and includes attention to areas such as the technology's interface, presentation of information, engagement methods, input and output types, embedded biases, content accuracy, and available support. It is intended to be a tool that prompts educators in their evaluation processes to look beyond content and into all aspects of how the technology works and adheres to the tenets of UDL (Meyer et al., 2014; Ok et al., 2016).

Effectiveness

Finally, once adaptations have been put into place, monitoring student progress and the fidelity of the adaptations is essential to maintaining student success and fulfilling the legal requirements of the individualized education program (IEP), a document which defines the special education services provided to students in the United States. The needs of students with disabilities change over time, so how do support personnel help ensure that their adaptations change with them? And, how do they ensure that agreed upon adaptations are actually implemented in the course of a busy classroom day? Regular team meetings, the collection and analysis of qualitative and quantitative data ranging from scores on unit tests to regular communication with parents, and a commitment to shared responsibility for student performance by general and special educators and support staff are recommended.

For further understanding of how this framework looks in practice, examine the classroom vignette in Box 11.1.

BOX 11.1   VIGNETTE: MR. CLINE'S HIGH SCHOOL WORLD CULTURES CLASS

Mr. Cline is an enthusiastic young teacher with two years of experience in the classroom. As he begins his third year, he is informed by the principal that he will have 25 students for World Cultures, including four students with mild disabilities. He has not dealt with such a range of diverse learning needs previously and uses the first days before the term starts to meet with the special education teacher. Ms. Arturo is impressed that he sought her out for advice and provides good information about the students, each with different learning issues. Steven is very bright and learns well by listening but has a severe reading disability that makes deciphering text laborious. Max has attention deficit-hyperactivity disorder (ADHD) that medication partially controls. He does well in classes when he knows what is going to happen each day and can review the content ahead of time. Sheila can usually keep up with class assignments but she has problems interpreting social cues and can become loud and inappropriate with the teacher and other students.

Mr. Cline shares with Ms. Arturo that he has taught his World Cultures class in the past using fairly traditional approaches, including having students read textbook selections and answer questions in writing. He thinks his lectures are very good because of the pictures and video clips he uses, but students do have to take notes on their own. He also likes his classroom layout because he has plenty of space and moveable tables for small group discussion. In addition, he explains that he has never implemented a structured behavior management system, because the students have usually responded well to gentle reminders and occasional loss of points.

Ms. Arturo shares a copy of the students' IEPs with Mr. Cline along with a copy of the *Making Decisions to Support All Students* model with implementation steps for decision-making about adaptations to instruction. They decide that most of the adaptations he will need to make for the students with disabilities he can use for the entire class: (a) recording his live slide presentations for students and posting them on the class website, (b) using reading selections that are available online and allowing all students the choice of reading silently or using the text-to-speech software on their computers to listen to the material with headphones, (c) creating a *what's next* space on the class website to provide students and parents with a heads-up about upcoming daily assignments, and (d) having classroom rules about civility and other expected behaviors and corresponding daily points that count toward the class grade. Mr. Cline understands that he will also need to be flexible regarding individual students. For example, since Steven has a print barrier due to his learning disability, his IEP states that he be given alternate ways to express his knowledge, including recording his oral answers to questions or using speech-to-text software to produce a paper. Sheila may need to have a specialized behavior plan, such as a behavioral contract, in addition to the rules in class to support her behavioral needs. This will be decided based on her classroom performance. Ms. Arturo and Mr. Cline decide to meet weekly for at least the first month of school to review student progress and make needed adjustments. These meetings will become less frequent if students are consistently successful.

Discussion and Conclusion

What do you think of Mr. Cline and Ms. Arturo's decisions? If you were Mr. Cline, would you do anything differently or make any other changes based on your new understanding of the students with disabilities arriving in your classroom? If you were Ms. Arturo, would you consider any other suggestions in terms of ensuring your students have the best support possible? How does this model match up with practices you have witnessed in your own work setting?

It may be clear based on the vignette that Mr. Cline and Ms. Arturo are not only following the *Making Decisions to Support All Students* model as described in this chapter, but that they are also following UDL principles. By examining what happens in the class and creating an environment where students can express and receive their learning in multiple ways, through multiple channels, Mr. Cline has ensured that all students have equal chances at success. Ultimately, this is the goal of both AT and UDL. When educators work together to create flexible, accommodating classrooms, they provide opportunities for all students to work at their full potentials. What Mr. Cline and other general educators will hopefully experience in this process is that planning initially for inclusive instruction, in partnership with special educators, is mutually beneficial for all students in a class as well as the teachers. Even minor instructional or curricular adaptations can substantially increase access and engagement and decrease the need for time-intensive adjustments for individual or small groups of students with disabilities or other special needs.

Further, the vignette shows the importance of instructional support and continual evaluation. Teachers cannot work in silos; they must be able to communicate and help one another in order to do the best for their students. Routine and consistent plans for assessing where students are on all levels— not just academically — allows teachers to respond quickly and provide timely critical adjustments. This may indeed mean that additional time is spent outside of the school day to meet and make decisions; but when general and special educators work together in this way, they not only better meet the needs of their students with disabilities, but also help bridge gaps for all learners.

Of course, it is important to remember that the most critical partner in such an education team is the student. Combined with the UDL framework (Meyer et al., 2014), the model helps teachers to offer students a variety of ways to achieve the same learning goals as all students, those with and without disabilities, learn differently. In evaluating the tasks and demands of the environment, it is important to consider what students must be able to do in order to be successful, as well as the many different means available to reach those goals. In evaluating obstacles and finding adaptations that meet their needs, considering each student's unique and individual requirements is necessary. In evaluating the need for training and designing assessment plans, teachers must continually reflect on what is happening, what they would like to happen, and how they can best serve students. This framework may not always be simple to follow, as there are many things to consider along the journey, but the benefits are numerous in ensuring that students are not only served well, but that they are also respected and treated fairly throughout their learning.

References

Bryant, D. P., & Bryant, B. (2003). *Assistive technology for people with disabilities.* Boston: Allyn and Bacon.

Cook, A. M., & Polgar, J. M. (2013). *Cook & Hussey's assistive technologies: Principles and practice* (4th ed.). St. Louis, MO: Mosby.

De Jonge, D., Scherer, M. J., & Rodger, R. (2007). *Assistive technology in the workplace.* St. Louis, MO: Mosby.

Frazier, D., Trekles, A., & Vega, R. (2018). *Evaluation rubric for apps.* Retrieved from https://tinyurl.com/yaqs2fpy

Freiberg, H. J., & Lamb, S. M. (2009). Dimensions of person-centered classroom management. *Theory into Practice, 48*(2), 99–105. doi:10.1080/00405840902776228

Gamble, M. J., Dowler, D. L., & Orslene, L. E. (2006). Assistive technology: Choosing the right tool for the right job. *Journal of Vocational Rehabilitation, 24*(2), 73–80.

Institute of Education Sciences. (2018). *Children and youth with disabilities.* National Center for Educational Statistics website. Retrieved from https://nces.ed.gov/programs/coe/indicator_cgg.asp

Kouroupetroglou, G., Pino, A., & Paraskevi, R. (2017). A methodological approach for designing and developing web-based inventories of mobile assistive technology applications. *Multimedia Tools and Applications, 76*(1), 5347–5366. doi:10.1007/s11042-016-3822-3

Meyer, A., Rose, D., & Gordon, D. (2014). *Universal design for learning: Theory and practice.* Wakefield, MA: CAST Professional Publishing.

Ok, M. W., Kim, M. K., Kang, E. Y., & Bryant, B. R. (2016). How to find good apps: An evaluation rubric for instructional apps for teaching students with learning disabilities. *Intervention in School and Clinic, 51*(4), 244–252. doi:10.1177/1053451215589179

Rose, D. H., & Meyer, A. (2002). *Teaching every student in the digital age: Universal design for learning.* Alexandria, VA: Association for Supervision and Curriculum Development.

Trekles, A. (2009). *Putting people first: Human issues in instructional technology.* Valparaiso, IN: Zelda 23 Publishing.

12

BALANCING REQUIREMENTS, OPTIONS AND CHOICE IN UDL

Smorgasbord or Nutritious Diet?

Britt Tatman Ferguson

Introduction

UDL, a promising practice for all learners, is receiving attention in education. It provides a framework which supports learning by removing barriers and increasing access. Stevens (2004) discusses the phenomenon of how education innovations have come and gone since the 1990s. Will UDL be the next to go? Insufficiency of teacher training in learning, learning theory and motivation has been identified as one factor that may impact UDL's sustainability.

Educators with insufficient understanding of how students learn and how instruction and motivation impact learning are more likely to take "... a 'bag of tricks' approach to teaching than a rational, theory driven approach to making instructional decisions" (Stevens, 2004, p. 391). Decisions to operationalize UDL as easy assignments from "the bag of tricks" or allowing students to decide what they want to do may not be theory based and could negatively impact UDL's success. This chapter considers the importance of making theory driven instructional decisions to effectively employ UDL with fidelity, thus ensuring its benefits and sustainability.

Understanding UDL

Although the impact has not yet been demonstrated, UDL is considered an effective methodology for all students (Capp, 2017). Research supporting UDL falls into four categories: foundational research, UDL principles, promising practices and implementation (National Center for Universal Design for Learning, 2011).

UDL recognizes the unique learning needs of individual students in diverse classrooms around the world. Its goal is to address individual needs through intentional, flexible planning (CAST, 2018), eliminating barriers and maximizing access. Based on neuroscience, UDL has three primary principles, the provision of multiple means of engagement, multiple means of representation and multiple means of action and expression, so each learner can access and master their curriculum (National Center for Universal Design for Learning, 2014). How do UDL principles fit into the process of learning?

A Learning Process

Teaching and learning can be thought of as an information processing approach through which knowledge and skills are transmitted to a learner (Driscoll, 2005). The process can be diagrammed as shown in Figure 12.1.

Although simple in design, the diagram is not intended to suggest that the *learning process* is simple or simplistic. There are complexities in each of the areas.

- During **input**, information must be encoded and transferred in such a way that it can be received by the learner.
- **Processing** results from the learner decoding the input, making sense of the information, making conceptual connections and adjusting previous understandings accordingly. Effective processing results in stored information that can be retrieved for future use.
- **Output** requires retrieving and expressing the stored information to demonstrate learning or to apply it in similar or new situations.

Underlying Principles

The three principles of UDL can enhance the learning process. Providing **multiple means of representation** necessitates presenting information through multiple media with varied supports (National Center on Universal Design for Learning, n.d., 3:15). Information inputted and perceived through the five senses is transmitted to the brain. Some individuals access information better via one sense than another. By anticipating learning needs, the teacher can present information through multiple representations increasing the likelihood everyone will receive it and achieve the learning objective. A lecture accompanied by manipulatives and signed by an interpreter benefits deaf students and hearing students alike.

Providing **multiple means of engagement** heightens involvement and attention by securing and keeping student interest (National Center on Universal Design for Learning, n.d., 4:17). To engage his class on the Bill of Rights, a

FIGURE 12.1 Information Processing Model of Learning

high school teacher, Clell, asked students what they do on Friday evenings. They responded that they meet and hang out at a fast food restaurant. "What if you were told you could not hang out anymore?" Clell asked. Indignant, students replied it was their right to get together . . . and a lively discussion of the origin of that right, the Bill of Rights, ensued, meeting the learning objective. The more engaged the student, the more likely information will be connected and stored in the brain in a way that can be retrieved and utilized.

Providing **multiple means of action and expression** encourages learners to interact with, apply and express new learnings and demonstrate mastery. Teachers can provide options for involving students with the material and showing what they know, providing models, feedback and supports (National Center on Universal Design for Learning, n.d., 3:27). *Key is that each option for demonstrating mastery is evaluated against the same rubric for a given learning objective.* A math student can complete a written set of problems alone, at home and submit it for evaluation or complete the problems by explaining the process to a partner while the teacher observes and evaluates mastery. In each example, the learner acts on the material and expresses understanding, albeit through different means (output), while the teacher assesses against the same criteria. Multiple opportunities to engage with and express learning can provide triangulation for assessment.

Multiple means of representation and **multiple means of engagement** facilitate the inputting of new information while **multiple means of action** facilitate processing. Through **multiple means of expression** students engage with the material but also demonstrate mastery of learning objectives.

The Importance of UDL

UDL provides a comprehensive organization for instructional experiences that flexes according to the learning needs of each student to remove barriers and increase access. Teachers who comprehend the learning process and roles of instruction and motivation will succeed with UDL because they will understand how to operationalize each underlying principle to support the learning process. Teachers with insufficient understanding may waver and resort to practices not shown to be effective or which are implemented without fidelity, e.g. the "bag of tricks."

For example, providing choice is an effective practice in UDL but can become one of the tricks in the bag when used without deliberation and planning. Choice is a tool. A tool is only as good as the person using it. Teachers may misuse the tool of choice.

Students perceive activities as more important when given a choice (Marzano, 2018). Choice of content or the means for learning the content can facilitate motivation and engagement and lead to students identifying learning as within their control, as their own (National Center for Universal Design for Learning, 2011). If "choice" is seen as an easy remedy, not employed appropriately, not based on theory, it will not address underlying issues or learning goals and may ultimately fail as an intervention.

Careful consideration of the teacher's and student's roles in the process of choice is needed. The teacher creates options designed to ensure achievement of each learning objective. Students must be taught and learn to make informed decisions so they can later identify options supporting their own learning needs.

Choice: Smorgasbord or Nutritious Diet?

UDL has been compared to differentiated instruction (DI) through the analogy of a dinner party (Novak, 2017). The host individually plans and prepares separate dishes, precisely accommodating each guest's dietary preferences and needs, a time consuming, labor intensive approach that does not guarantee that each guest will like his dish or not prefer the dish of another guest!

Alternatively, the host could put out many dishes and have guests select the foods "... best for them, what they believe will work with their individual diet" (Novak, 2017, para. 5), requiring less labor and freeing the host to relax and interact more. This buffet, analogous to UDL, has great appeal requiring *less labor*, less guessing about which foods *will please* the guests. Rather, it provides freedom for guests to choose and the host to interact more but does not ensure each guest selects foods best for them.

Would this "buffet" approach work in the classroom? Telling students to choose what they need or what will please them from an activity smorgasbord may not result in a "nutritious diet" of learning. With the buffet approach, responsibility for choosing appropriate learning activities is placed in the hands of the student. However, it is the teacher's responsibility to provide the students with what they need, not necessarily *many* choices but appropriate choices leading to achievement of learning objectives.

Careful attention to *how* student choice is operationalized within UDL is needed to ensure success. Having students make choices about their own learning is empowering, facilitating ownership and independence *when they know how to choose*. Complete freedom over what they will do and when they will do it puts too much responsibility in the hands of young learners. Rather, the thoughtful teacher creates options with each of the three principles to support achievement of the learning objective while addressing ability, language, prior learning, culture, styles, interests, strengths, individualized education plans and standards.

The learning objective *defines* the intended learning. Learning options must be designed which lead to the intended learning and which enable the teacher to evaluate whether the objective has been met. A self-choice smorgasbord may not result in the students' nutritional requirements being met.

What if we narrowed the "buffet" with many dishes to a "build-your-own-taco"? The objective is to build a taco taking into consideration vegetarian and gluten free needs. Each guest prepares a taco choosing from limited ingredients:

corn or flour shell, ground beef or black beans, lettuce and tomatoes, cheese or sour cream, salsa optional.

Applying the taco analogy to the classroom, the teacher can determine the learning objective: For example, *to demonstrate knowledge of the seven continents, students will name and identify the location of each continent telling which continent(s) it touches, alone or with a partner during geography, correctly for seven/seven continents, by the end of the week.*

The teacher determines the media used to present information to garner attention and buy in (engagement) and to structure involvement with the new information (action and expression). The teacher determines how to assess the objective, necessitating some form of expression by the learner *that demonstrates the objective.* The class includes several students learning English and a student with a processing disorder.

The teacher plans to introduce and show "The Seven Continents Song," a short Internet video utilizing color, images, words and song to teach the information. She presents the seven continents on a large map, telling the students a little about the geography of each continent, encouraging questions and presenting realia and pictures of each terrain, labeled in English and other language(s) spoken by the students. She places English speakers and English learners in cooperative learning pairs with a blank map of the world and directs them to paint each continent a different color (requiring careful examination of the shape and location of each continent) and labeling each (practicing the name). Students cut the map into seven pieces, so each continent is on one piece, creating a puzzle, and take turns putting the pieces together, naming each continent as they put it in place. Students choose the colors for the continents, where they write the names, and who cuts first. All three principles of UDL are present.

While students may have multiple means of expression to demonstrate their mastery, it is *essential that any means of expression be sufficient to determine if the learning objective has been achieved*. It is not responsible to tell students to decide how they want to demonstrate their learnings. Suzie may like Antarctica and draw a penguin. While relevant and engaging, Suzie's picture does not demonstrate the criteria of the learning objective, and it cannot be determined if Suzie mastered the learning objective.

More appropriate would be to have students pick a means of expression that best suits their strengths and preferences:

- Draw a map of the world, label each continent noting which continent(s) each touches.
- Write a paragraph naming each continent, telling where it would be found on a map and which continent(s) it touches.
- Prepare a two-minute video, with oral narration naming and labeling each of the seven continents on a blank map of the world, noting which continent(s) each touches.

Essential *is grading each option with the same rubric* assessing the criteria from the objective. Regardless of which option students choose, they will be demonstrating equivalent mastery of the learning as operationalized in the learning objective.

Determining which choices will support the student's learning need(s) and facilitate mastery of the objective can be confusing for novice users of UDL. It may be confusing if UDL is perceived and misunderstood as a means to make assignments "easier" or to let students do what they like, forgetting or perhaps never understanding that UDL is about removing barriers, increasing access and producing better learners.

Barriers are obstacles, difficulties. If the difficulty presents an *impossibility*, such as requiring a deaf student to listen to a lecture without an interpreter, then it would be absurd to make this a requirement. But if a difficulty presents a *challenge* which can be overcome by the student, with support, then it is reasonable to expect the student to take the challenge and grow by the experience. When the student has overcome a challenge, it is no longer a barrier and access has been increased. Success empowers the individual as a learner. If the teacher or student views a challenge as an impossibility when it is not, then the barrier remains in place, the challenge will be avoided and access will be denied.

For example, Suzie's teacher prepares a learning objective to address a common core standard: "Recount and describe key ideas or details from a text read aloud or information presented orally or through other media." The objective reads, "To demonstrate ability to recount ideas orally, students will orally tell which book they chose and why they chose it, standing before the class during reading, correctly as measured by comparing information stated with book chosen, by the end of the period."

Suzie can talk in front of the class, but she does not like to do it. The teacher has options. She may:

1. Let Suzie choose not to share;
2. Let Suzie draw a picture representing her choice;
3. Demand that Suzie get up and share no matter what;
4. Scaffold support by sitting in front of the class next to Suzie and asking Suzie which book she chose and why she chose it.

The selected option will need to reduce barriers, increase access to the curriculum and support Suzie in achieving the learning objective. Option one provides no means of action, leaves the barrier in place, denies access to the curriculum and does not allow Suzie to achieve the objective. Option two provides an alternative means of action, but does not allow Suzie to achieve the objective, hence the barrier remains in place, access is limited. Option three does not address the barrier and does not facilitate access. While it could allow Suzie to meet the objective, it does not support Suzie's learning needs. Option four provides support for the required action by the teacher's presence and behavior, removing the barrier, facilitating access. With this support, Suzie will be able to achieve the learning objective.

Option four as a mean of expression desensitizes the situation and supports Suzie in completing the assignment, which is empowering for Suzie. This is UDL in action.

Mistakes of Novices

Novice users make mistakes when they do not understand motivation and instruction or how students learn. Most teachers recognize that using force violates the principles of UDL and other successful approaches to learning. One error is to believe a child should be allowed to avoid something he does not want to do. However, providing less stressful ways of engaging in the challenging endeavor, like the teacher sitting with Suzie, reduces the self-imposed barrier and facilitates access. Misunderstanding the point of the objective is another mistake. If the point of Suzie's objective is to identify the book she chose and the reason she chose it, she could write a report or create a poster. However, the point is to "recount orally," and the details about her book are simply the content of the recounting. Simply completing an activity or learning sequence does not verify mastery of the objective. Some type of expression that reflects *the criteria of the learning* objective is necessary. Novices may see no harm in allowing all students the support provided to Suzie, but UDL provides support when the learner cannot perform independently and has not moved beyond the barrier. Support is not appropriate for those who passed the zone of proximal development (Vygotsky, 1978). Veteran users will know that the only reasonable option is to provide support and scaffolding, to overcome the barrier and achieve the learning objective, appropriate to the learning needs of the student.

Conclusion

UDL provides a framework for reducing barriers and increasing access for learners. Three principles guide designing flexible instruction to accommodate learner needs. Successful teachers apply the principles with deliberation and intention. UDL is NOT license to allow students to do what they want, when they want, how they want. It is not intended *not* to challenge learners, nor does it provide an excuse for giving less rigorous assignments. UDL is a structure to provide students what they need to succeed when faced with challenges. Learners still complete work toward learning objectives and are evaluated against the same criteria regardless of the means they employ. Successful teachers understand the learning theory behind UDL and how it impacts motivation and learning. Successful teachers ensure that UDL is not one more come-and-go phenomenon, but a sustained instructional approach that ensures a nutritious educational diet.

References

Capp, M. J. (2017). The effectiveness of universal design for learning: A meta-analysis of literature between 2013 and 2016. *International Journal of Inclusive Education, 21*(8), 1–17.

CAST. (2018). *About universal design for learning*. Retrieved from www.cast.org/our-work/about-udl.html#.W5HkZ-hKjIU

Driscoll, M. (2005). *Psychology of learning for instruction* (3rd ed.). Hoboken, NJ: Pearson.

Marzano, R. J. (2018). *Tips from Dr. Marzano*. Retrieved from www.marzanoresearch.com/resources/tips/hec_tips_archive#tip24

National Center for Universal Design for Learning. (2011). *Types of evidence supporting UDL*. Retrieved from www.udlcenter.org/research/researchevidence/checkpoint7_1

National Center for Universal Design for Learning. (2014). *The three principles of UDL*. Retrieved from www.udlcenter.org/aboutudl/whatisudl/3principles

National Center on Universal Design for Learning. (n.d.). *UDL at a glance*. Retrieved from www.udlcenter.org/resource_library/videos/udlcenter/udl#video0/

Novak, K. (2017). *The dinner party analogy*. Retrieved from http://katienovakudl.com/udl-vs-di-dinner-party-analogy/

Stevens, R. J. (2004). Why do educational innovations come and go? What do we know? What can we do? *Teaching and Teacher Education, 20*, 389–396.

Vygotsky, L. (1978). Interaction between learning and development. In *Mind in society: The development of higher psychological processes*. Cambridge, MA: Harvard University Press.

13

UDL PRACTICES IN INDIA

Paving a Path From Equality to Equity in Learning

Aashna Khurana

Differing Learner Needs in India

Variation, not homogeneity, in learning is a norm. Every child in the classroom learns differently, which leads to the conclusion that learning is highly person-specific and unique in nature. This realization further gave birth to Universal Design for Learning (UDL), which aims to include all the learners, ensure equitable access, and enhance their learning outcomes. The term *UDL* originates from universal design (UD), which focuses on proactively designing products, buildings, and environments which can be accessed by most of the users, without any need for adaptations or changes (UNCRPD, 2006). The UDL framework extends the idea of universal design from primarily physical environments and applies it to the process of learning. It removes or reduces the barriers from the beginning that might hinder the learning of children (Bhattacharya, 2017). This proactive approach of designing lessons and activities helps in addressing learner variability and diversity.

Diversity is the essence of India. India presents endless varieties of cultures, values, religions, languages, and people. Further, this diversity is also evident in schools where children from affluent families, economically weaker sections, first generation learners, vernacular medium, and with and without disabilities learn the same content under a common roof. Inclusion in the school environment is the result of various acts and policies formulated by the government, such as *Integrated Education for Disabled Children (1976–77)*, *Sarva Shiksha Abhiyan 2001*, *Right to Education Act (RTE) 2009*, and *Rights of Persons with Disabilities Act 2016* (Ministry of Human Resource Development—Government of India, Sarva Shiksha Abhiyan, 2010; Ministry of Law and Justice—Government of India, 2009, 2016; Ministry of Welfare—Government of India, 1974). However, enrollment is not the sole aim here; the aim is to have all these learners learn to the maximum of their abilities.

Similar to education systems in other countries, the Indian school system is structured by age and grade. The curricular expectations increase as learners clear one level and move toward the next higher level. In India, 96.9% of rural children aged 6 to 14 are enrolled in schools, yet only 50% of the learners in grade 5 can read grade 2 level texts and solve subtraction problems (ASER, 2017). When this trend is shown graphically, it is reflected in a flat learning trajectory illustrating that most Indian children complete schooling without acquiring foundational skills. Lack of use of level appropriate materials and an unclear understanding of teaching methodology are possible contributors to this problem.

With this in mind, it is important to realize that learners make sense of information in different ways, work at different paces, and have varied ways of approaching and completing the tasks. Meyer, Rose and Gordon (as cited in Rao & Meo, 2016) reiterate that personal qualities and abilities of an individual are dynamic and ever-evolving, as these intersect between the individual and his or her environment. Since one size does not fit all, designing curricula to ensure equitable learning is an ultimate goal and requires deliberate and rigorous planning. Rabindranath Tagore, a famous Indian philosopher said, "The problem is not how to wipe out the differences but how to unite with the differences intact" (Tagore, 1994, p. 712). Therefore, the need to intentionally provide equitable learning opportunities to all the learners along with inclusion emerges.

UDL focuses on systematically designing varied learning activities and materials. This is a flexible approach that refutes the traditional one-size-fits-all approach and aims to customize and adjust content, material, method, and assessment according to individual needs (Meo, 2008). To make the teaching-learning process interactive, constructivist, and meaningful, it is important to adapt content, learning materials, and most importantly the learning environment. Hence, this chapter further analyzes three nationwide practices, from the dimensions of instructional framework, learning environment, and materials. These practices include the instructional framework developed by Pratham Education Foundation, Building as Learning Aid (BaLA), and the Barkhaa—A Reading Series for All. The aforementioned practices have changed the way of transacting curriculum and delivering instruction. Furthermore, these practices have been incorporated in the context of UDL implementation in the learning environment with the intention to develop accessible materials to make classrooms more inclusive and provide appropriate and meaningful experiences to all the learners under one roof.

Rationale

Pratham's instructional framework, BaLA, and the Barkhaa series are innovative practices that address the question—*how do children learn?*—through the creation of age-appropriate, child-centered experiences that further bridge the gap between what is being *taught* and what is being *learned*. In India, Pratham Education Foundation designed learning level appropriate content to address the needs of children at the margins, to promote their successful inclusion. The content keeps in mind the level, interest, and need of learners to enhance a particular competency and ensure better generalization of concepts. It focuses on enhancing foundational skills by approaches like Combined Activities for Maximized Learning (CAMaL), which address multiple pathways to learn and provide multiple means to express the learned content.

Secondly, BaLA is an innovative initiative by Vinyas supported by UNICEF that focuses on full utilization of the learning environment by adapting it and also ensuring maximum possible correspondence with the curriculum. BaLA eliminates physical and instructional barriers from the learning environment and focuses on how best to use school infrastructure like classrooms, walls, corridors, windows, and outdoor spaces as learning resources (Vinyas, 2012) to transform the physical and instructional environment and make the experience enriching for learners.

The third pertinent aspect that influences learning is equitable access to learning materials, particularly the textbooks. Recently, the Department of Education of Groups of Special Needs (DEGSN), National Council for Educational Research and Training (NCERT) adapted the original Barkhaa series into Barkhaa: A Reading Series for 'All' to include all the learners. The adaptations follow principles of UDL and aim to provide information in Braille, tactile, sign language, and digital versions to ensure equitable access to all readers (NCERT, 2016).

The abovementioned unique initiatives provide multi-sensory experiences to children, thus catering to multiple pathways to learn and respecting diverse learning paths and choices. These inclusive instructional designs provide autonomy to learners, support self-regulated learning, and help in reducing barriers by creating accessible instructional resources and environments. They help to ensure equity in learning according to need, interest, and level by offering appropriate learning materials and experiences for the varied learners in the classroom.

Nationwide Inclusive Initiatives

Pratham's Instructional Framework

Despite achieving nearly a 97% enrollment rate, the education system of India, especially in rural areas, experiences significant shortcomings (Wadhwa, 2019). To combat this situation, Pratham developed its own teaching-learning approach, which focuses on building a strong foundation of fundamental skills. The teaching methodology used is commonly referred to as *CAMaL* and is also referred to as *Teaching at the Right Level (TaRL)*. It involves adaptations at every level rather than providing additional input without changing pedagogy.

Pratham's instructional practice is comprised of a set of seven basic elements, starting with assessment to understand the current functioning level of the children (Pratham, 2017).

1. The current level (out of four levels) of the learners is ascertained by *assessments* using ASER tool.
2. Then, *goals* are set to identify the destination, that is, where learners are expected to reach.
3. After that, *children are grouped according to their current learning* level rather than by grade. The educators understand the value of beginning with present student interest and level as a point of departure, giving direction to move forward.
4. Later, *various activities are combined* for maximizing the learning and catering to diverse interests and learning styles.
5. The fifth element, *scalability*, involves judicious and efficient use of manpower, materials, and other resources.
6. Further, *appropriate materials* are needed to facilitate learning and support the teaching. Each child is given material of their own which is based on contexts and situations familiar to the children.
7. Finally, *measurements are used to monitor the progress*, reviewing movement toward the target and making changes, if necessary.

Pratham's education program fulfills one of the key functions of an educational program, which is to broaden and deepen the student's interest so that he/she continues education lifelong. It helps to provide opportunities for the students to enter actively into, and to deal wholeheartedly with, whatever interests them at their learning levels, which makes them deeply engrossed and skillful to carry on a spectrum of activities effectively (Tyler, 1949).

Building as Learning Aid

As per the NCERT (2014) research, children *construct their own knowledge* from their experiences and don't just imbibe what is handed over to them, as they have different learning styles. The research also highlights that children *learn all the time* even beyond the four walls of the classroom. Further, children *don't just learn from the teacher* but also from interacting with other children; therefore, opportunities for interaction and cooperative play should be promoted while teaching. Another important dimension discussed is that *learning occurs in a spiral;* therefore, the learning opportunities should be given multiple times, in a new format, so that it lasts long.

Children tend to learn in a holistic way and not in a segmented fashion (Hargreaves & Shirley, 2012; Miller, 1999). Learning, therefore, becomes more meaningful if it's integrated. BaLA comprehensively and meticulously takes into account the aforementioned aspects of a child's learning and creatively designs school infrastructure in a way that promotes equity by giving every child the opportunity and ability to use every feature of the school environment easily and freely, without any inhibitions (Kaushika, 2008; Vajpeyi, 2010). It looks at a student's relation with school, explores physical spaces in the educational environment, which is one of the most neglected components, and pays due attention to bridging the interface between building design and teaching-learning program design. The framework makes the school infrastructure, which previously was conceived merely as a brick and mortar structure, a new space that houses enriching activities, experiences, and opportunities to learn. BaLA develops school spaces—the classrooms, the floors, walls, doors, windows, pillars, outdoor spaces, and the natural environment—as learning spaces. The three-dimensional space offers a unique setting for a child to learn by involving a range of learning situations and materials and using multiple senses to give abstract concepts real form. It aims to create an enriching school environment to support subconscious learning at every step and maximizes the educational value of the built structure (see Figure 13.1 for examples). Additional information can be found at www.jinglebellschool.org/facilities-iti/bala-jbs

Many of the activities are designed to captivate the essence of the constructivist pedagogy approach under the National Curriculum Framework 2005, enabling children to build their own knowledge through assimilation from the environment. BaLA emphasizes the need to establish inclusive settings and child-friendly learning environments in schools. This encourages children to use school spaces to learn through an activity-based process of discovery and exploration mandated under the RTE Act, 2009. This further strengthens children's

FIGURE 13.1   Examples of BaLA Educational Spaces

language, communication, and numeracy skills, reinforces their observation skills by involving multiple senses in the learning process, and facilitates understanding of abstract notions through concrete examples available from the school environment. It establishes a healthy, welcoming, child-centered setting throughout a child's school progression (Grover & Kaur, 2017; Indian Express, 2012; Sharma, Adsure, & Varjani, 2012; Vajpeyi, 2010).

Barkhaa Series—A Reading Series for All

Another initiative in India taken up by the Department of Education of Groups of Special Needs (DEGSN) at NCERT is a project titled *Adapting the Barkhaa Series for Visually Challenged Children and other CWSN according to UDL* (NCERT, 2016). The project aimed to address the unique learning needs of children in the early years, which are considered to be foundational to the literacy development in the later period. Barkhaa is a supplementary graded reading series and a pedagogical tool that helps early graders (Grades I and II) to read with meaning. The stories in the books revolve around every day experiences of children and are available in four levels. Level 1 is comprised of one illustration with one sentence on each page, level 2 has one illustration and two sentences, level 3 has an illustration with three sentences, and level four has an illustration and four sentences.

Abiding by the ethos of inclusion, the book is adapted in ways that support the inclusion of children with disabilities, who have been widely ignored or excluded in the reading process. The series incorporates numerous innovations by providing the same information in various formats, such as in Braille, tactile, sign language, and digital mode so that all the learners regardless of their differences have full access to the content of the series, ensuring optimum participation. The books are available in print and digital versions. The text version has text in print as well as Braille written together, which makes it more accessible to all learners. Further, to reinforce the tactile experience, the pictures are embossed with certain textures that are constant throughout the book. Pages have black arrows to indicate that children have to move to the next page. In addition to this, there are green and red dots indicating the beginning and the end of sentences. This makes it easier for children to navigate through the book. To support the vocabulary, every page has windows, which have key words and their meanings underneath.

Additionally, the book is adapted into digital formats with an introductory note given before every story to arouse the interest and set the backdrop of the story. The introductory note is also available in sign language, which takes into account learners with hearing impairments who use this mode of communication. The key visuals are in high resolution to ensure that learners focus on the events of the story. Additionally, the text and background in each story are provided in a combination of three colors, white, black, and yellow, which the learners can select according to their visual preference and need. Similar to the print version, the digital version also has windows for keywords, and red and green dots to mark the beginning and end of the sentences. These adaptations give learners the alternatives to access the content in their desired ways and ensure maximization of learning.

Conclusion

The core objectives of the three nationwide practices described in this chapter are to respect diverse choices, facilitate access for each child to learning materials, and acquaint teachers with systematic ways of delivering instruction that include flexible pathways and supports to help students progress toward mastery of content. Incorporation of these practices broadens access for varied learners and establishes supports that include and acknowledge a range of learner needs. Therefore, these practices are flexible in nature and leave room for learner-specific adaptations.

Additionally, the focus of all these inclusive practices is to provide customized alternatives and opportunities to make teaching-learning captivating and joyful for the learners. These practices also support accessibility and equity; and most importantly, they empower teachers to be more effective in promoting inclusion. The combination of dimensions used to construct inclusive learning designs and strategies provides insight into the inclusive practices followed in India that are equipping students to self-regulate their learning, providing them with equal opportunities to learn, ensuring the movement of India toward inclusion and equity for all learners.

References

ASER. (2017). *Annual status of education report (Rural) 2016*. New Delhi: ASER Centre.

Bhattacharya, T. (2017). Adoption of universal design for learning for meaningful inclusion. In S. Prasad, D. Sonpal, & S. Vaishnav (Eds.), *Empowering children with disabilities* (pp. 404–424). New Delhi: Prabhat Prakashan. Retrieved from http://people.du.ac.in/~tanmoy/papers/UDL_for%20distribute.pdf

Grover, J., & Kaur, K. (2017). *Study of impact of building as learning aid (BaLA): Project interventions on students' learning outcomes*. Retrieved from http://ssachd.nic.in/sites/default/files/BaLA%20Project%20report.pdf

Hargreaves, A., & Shirley, D. (2012). *The global fourth way: The quest for educational excellence*. London: Sage Publications, Integrated Education for Disabled Children Scheme 1974 (IEDC) (In.).

Indian Express. (2012, September 19). *North corporation to use building as learning aids in its schools*. Retrieved from https://indianexpress.com/article/cities/delhi/north-corporation-to-use-building-as-learning-aids-in-its-schools/

Kaushika, P. (2008, January 14). Building as a learning aid education. *The Times of India*. Retrieved from https://timesofindia.indiatimes.com/home/education/news/Building-as-a-learning-aid/articleshow/2697206.cms

Meo, G. (2008). Curriculum planning for all learners: Applying universal design for learning (UDL) to a high school reading comprehension program. *Preventing School Failure*, *52*(2), 21–30. http://dx.doi.org/10.3200/PSFL.52.2.21-30

Miller, J. P. (1999). Making connections through holistic learning. *Educational Leadership*, *56*(4), 46–48.

Ministry of Human Resource Development—Government of India. Sarva Shiksha Abhiyan. (2010). Retrieved from http://planningcommission.nic.in/reports/peoreport/peoevalu/peo_ssa2106.pdf

Ministry of Law and Justice—Government of India. (2009). *The right of children to free and compulsory education*. Retrieved from https://mhrd.gov.in/sites/upload_files/mhrd/files/upload_document/rte

Ministry of Law and Justice—Government of India. (2016). *The rights of persons with disabilities act*. Retrieved from www.disabilityaffairs.gov.in/upload/uploadfiles/files/RPWD%20ACT%202016.pdf

Ministry of Welfare—Government of India. (1974). *Integrated education for disabled children*. Retrieved from www.edudel.nic.in/circulars_file/IEDC(FINAL_COPY).htm

NCERT. (2014). *Learning indicators and learning outcomes at the elementary stage*. Retrieved from www.dsek.nic.in/Misc/learningoutcome.pdf

NCERT. (2016). *Barkhaa—A reading series for all*. Retrieved from www.ncert.nic.in/departments/nie/degsn/pdf_files/DEGSNbarkha1_3_16.pdf

Pratham. (2017). *Improving reading and arithmetic learning at scale in India: Pratham's approach to teaching and learning*. Retrieved from www.pratham.org/templates/pratham/images/1_Pratham-s-Teaching-Learning-Approach.pdf

Rao, K., & Meo, G. (2016). Using universal design for learning to design standards-based lessons. *Sage Open*, *6*(4), 1–12. https://doi.org/10.1177/2158244016680688

Sharma, R., Adsure, R., & Varjani, S. (2012). *Study on impact of BaLA (Building as Learning Aid) in state of Gujarat*. Gandhinagar: Gujarat National Law University.

Tagore, R. (1994). *The English writings of Rabindranath Tagore: A miscellany*. New Delhi: Sahitya Akademi.

Tyler, R. (1949). *Basic principles of curriculum and instruction*. Chicago: The University of Chicago Press.

UNCRPD. (2006). *Convention on the rights of persons with disabilities and optional protocol*. New York: UN. Retrieved from www.un.org/disabilities/documents/convention/convoptprot-e.pdf

Vajpeyi, K. (2010). BaLA- its roots and the spread. *Teacher Plus*. Retrieved from www.teacherplus.org/bala-%E2%80%93-its-roots-and-the-spread/

Vinyas. (2012). *Effectively using BaLA (Building as Learning Aid) in elementary schools-a teacher's manual*. New Delhi: Vinyas, Centre for Architectural Research & Design. Retrieved from www.edudel.nic.in/upload_2013_14/145_52_dt_03102013/SecA.pdf

Wadhwa, W. (2019, March 4). Simple policies, major learning gains. *The Tribune*. Retrieved from www.tribuneindia.com/news/in-focus/simple-policies-major-learning-gains/738000.html

14

UDL-INSPIRED PEDAGOGICAL PRACTICES AND A CASE STUDY IN REGULAR JAPANESE CLASSES

Kiyoji Koreeda

UDL in Japan

In Japan, approximately 6.5% of the students enrolled in regular classes exhibit symptoms of learning disabilities (LD), attention deficit hyperactivity disorder (ADHD), or high-functioning autism (HFA). These students present special educational needs in learning and behavior (Ministry of Education, Culture, Sports, Science and Technology [MEXT], 2012). The maximum regular class size in primary and secondary schools is 40 students. An average class would enroll two to three students with special educational needs.

To promote *reasonable accommodations* that cater to the educational needs of the individual student, it is important for faculty members to understand the characteristics of students with various needs (Ministry of Foreign Affairs of Japan [MOFA], 2014). As such, the Universal Design for Learning (UDL) framework (Meyer, Rose, & Gordon, 2014), proposed by researchers at the Center for Applied Special Technology (CAST) in the United States, has been increasingly adopted by Japanese ordinary schools. The UDL guidelines are organized according to three main principles—providing options for representation, action and expression, and engagement (CAST, 2011). UDL emphasizes the viewpoint of how students can become expert learners through variation and control of input for, connection with, and demonstration of learning. Critical to the implementation of UDL is the advanced preparation and design of the curriculum based on the guidelines (Hall, Meyer, & Rose, 2012).

Developing accessible classes based on the UDL guidelines facilitates students' understanding and promotes inclusive education in regular classes. In Japan, the number of students using a *special support service inventory* (a system that offers guidance according to individual needs) has increased sharply over the last decade, from 43,078 in 2007 to 96,996 in 2017 (MEXT, 2017). It is critical for classroom teachers and individual guidance teachers to share detailed background information about their students and to work closely together in offering optimal support for target students in regular classes. Promoting these efforts is also likely to enhance understanding of the lesson, build self-esteem, and increase confidence of all students in the class. For example, in a class where there are multiple students who require additional time to read examination sentences, the teacher may read the examination sentences for these students, but through this reading the understanding of the whole class may be promoted. Using tools like digital textbooks, electronic blackboards, and personal computers can support students with special needs. The UDL framework advocates for environments wherein all students can learn in diverse ways. The framework anticipates various needs of students and prompts teachers to rethink their present instructional practices.

The concept of UDL provides common learning ease not only for students with special needs but also for all students belonging to the class. In regard to students with special educational needs, teachers can provide more effective assistance by planning for students' varied characteristics and needs using different instructional methods. Students who experience different conditions (LD, ADHD, HFA, etc.) are expected to respond in similar ways to other students. However, in some cases, different instructional approaches may be necessary depending on individual characteristics and needs. For example, some students with Autism Spectrum Disorder (ASD) have indicated preferences for visual over verbal information (Kamio & Toich, 2000).

Prior Research

Educational support practices like the UDL framework have remained an established topic in the areas of regular education and special needs education in Western countries; however, it was only recently introduced to Japan. Therefore, in Japan, it has not been possible to systematically advance UDL throughout schools as a whole (Kawamata, 2014). The ratification of the Convention on the Rights of Persons with Disabilities (MOFA, 2014) brought forward recommendations regarding the systematic implementation of environmental supports in a classroom setting. Guidance was based on individual students' characteristics and needs. Initially, UDL workshops for teachers were generally organized by private research groups. In recent years, however, an increasing number of UDL workshops have been organized by the Regional Board of Education and prefectural education centers (Kanagawa Prefectural Education Center, 2018).

Evidence against making unnecessary changes to the classroom environment (e.g., arrangement of seats and lockers) has also been presented (Ueno & Nakajima, 2012). Similarly, research on classroom interventions for students with

ADHD suggests that a reduction in classroom posters and incorporation of specific seating arrangements (e.g., seating that subjects students to less disruption from the surroundings) can support students with ADHD (Dupaul & Weyandt, 2006). In Japan, it is common to respond individually to the characteristics and needs of students. The use of design flexibility to address varied needs of an entire class, as with the UD framework, is not yet accepted. Therefore, it is important to accumulate the case results of individual guidance situations (e.g., what kinds of supports and considerations are given to each student with special educational needs). The adjustments made on behalf of an individual student's needs may be beneficial for all students throughout the class.

In addition to researching other emerging educational practices, the number of researchers working on UDL at Japanese universities and educational institutions is rising. There have been recent studies on applications of UDL to support inclusion at Japanese primary schools and university students with ASD (Harada & Edahiro, 2017; Sato & Noutomi, 2018). However, despite UDL's increasing popularity among educators in Japan, empirical studies on the pedagogical value and effectiveness of UDL in the Japanese context are still lacking. Thus, evidence from case studies conducted in various contexts is of value for the applicability of UDL principles in Japan and other cultural settings. This chapter describes one such case study within the Japanese context and explores connections to the UDL framework.

UDL Implementation and Case Study in Japanese Regular Classes

UDL-Inspired Pedagogical Efforts in a Japanese Regular Class

The described case takes place in a writing class at a regular primary school. The Japanese language is comprised of three types of characters: (1) Hiragana; (2) Katakana; and (3) Kanji. Students with LD in Japan tend to experience greater difficulties in learning handwriting (especially Kanji) compared to reading (Koike, Kumoi, & Kuboshima, 2002). A number of UDL-inspired strategies were applied in this case study to address this situation. For instance, the Hiragana and Katakana letters (a total of 100) and the list of Kanji were posted on the classroom wall for daily review to promote understanding. This relates to UDL checkpoints of varying the display of information (checkpoint 1.1) and offering alternatives for auditory information (checkpoint 1.2) among the three principles of the UDL guidelines.

Other observations within this classroom offer examples of UDL implementation related to clarifying vocabulary and symbols (checkpoint 2.1) and clarifying syntax or structure (checkpoint 2.2). There is a poster of the classroom rules which are written using positive phrases (e.g., "Students who can do . . . are excellent.") rather than negative ones (e.g., "Students who do . . . are bad."). This is designed to encourage self-motivated adjustments by the students. Auxiliary teaching materials with visuals are available to aid students' learning by providing multiple means of content representation. For instance, specific visual presentations (see Figure 14.1) are provided to support students' understanding of demonstrative (e.g., "this," "that") usage.

Optimizing individual choice and autonomy (checkpoint 7.1), which relates to the UDL guideline of providing options for recruiting interest, was also applied in this case. Multiple printed teaching materials (e.g., copies of lessons on learning simpler Kanji or Kanji with a higher degree of difficulty or sheets showing examples) are prepared to provide options for various student levels of understanding. This flexibility in materials for the same subject allows students at different levels to choose the materials at their appropriate degree of difficulty. In addition to the environmental supports, the teacher's attitude and way of thinking also played a vital part in lesson planning and classroom management. It is critical that teachers feel motivated to familiarize themselves with the UDL approach in developing effective teaching methods that address learner characteristics and needs, thereby developing greater understanding and confidence in the UDL methodology.

FIGURE 14.1 Visual Presentations Illustrating Demonstrative Usage

Teaching Practices Focusing on Student Strengths

The pedagogical efforts just described were impactful to one student in particular. Student A, a male third grader with ASD, has an amiable personality and abundant knowledge in subjects in which he shows interest, such as insects. In the writing class, however, he was found to show difficulty in writing Japanese characters. He eventually became uneasy in dealing with increasingly difficult tasks. After consulting with his classroom teacher and parents, the author conducted weekly one-hour individual guidance sessions using a special support service inventory and decided to provide individual support according to the student's needs.

Characteristics of Student A

Student A is generally animated and likes to talk. However, he shows reluctance when it comes to writing. For instance, he was found to have difficulty in recalling what he had just heard. He would spend a long time writing one word. Although he showed no difficulty in writing Kanji with the expected proficiency and accuracy, he found Hiragana difficult to perform. To explore the reasons and to use it as a reference for individual guidance, the author and guidance teacher conducted the Kaufman Assessment Battery for Children (K-ABC) with the student (Kaufman & Kaufman, 1983). Based on the results and the observations of Student A's behaviors in receiving guidance, the following conclusions were drawn regarding his characteristics:

1. He has the ability to capture shapes.
2. He has the ability to remember what he sees.
3. He finds it difficult to remember what he hears.
4. He is better at processing information as an overall set (simultaneous processing) than processing information in sequence (sequential processing).

Though he could accurately distinguish the shapes of letters, he was poor at memorizing auditory information and found it difficult to transcribe a sound into letters, particularly for Hiragana. He was more successful with transcribing Kanji, because it encodes meaning in the shape of the character. Therefore, the researchers took Student A's cognitive features into consideration. They adopted a method that focuses on visual stimuli and is grounded in the UDL principle of providing multiple means of representation.

Painting and Cartography in Teaching Writing and Social Skills

Student A expressed interest in drawing pictures. When he failed to retell a story properly, he would draw a picture and explain it. It was necessary to mitigate the difficulties in *connecting sounds and shapes* and to find a meaningful way to explain the letters using visual aids. In connection to UDL, the researchers identified optimizing individual choice and autonomy (checkpoint 7.1) as insightful to the incorporation of *Karta* (a traditional Japanese card game) made up of Hiragana. In this game, the student:

1. Chooses the letter he wants to make from a list of difficult-to-remember words (e.g., "C," "F," etc.).
2. Thinks about words associated with the selected letters ("A"→"Apple," "C"→"Cake," etc.).
3. Draws a picture of that word (playing cards) (see Figure 14.2).
4. Thinks and writes a short sentence including that word (reading cards) (see Figure 14.3).
5. Listens to the teacher read the sentence, remembering the picture he drew, and practices answering quickly.

This game enabled Student A to enjoy the freedom to decide what to learn in each class. He decided to draw inspirations from his daily life and his favorite insects. Furthermore, by working one-on-one with the teacher who utilized the special support services inventory, it was also possible to improve the student's social and communication skills including greeting, eye contact, and speech appropriateness to respond appropriately to classmates.

FIGURE 14.2 Student A Working on a Picture Tag

UDL-Inspired Pedagogical Practices **117**

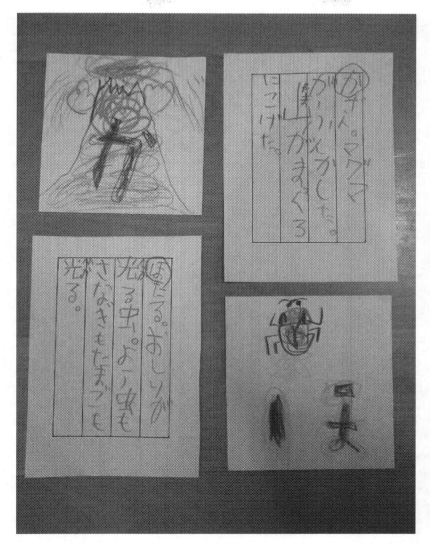

FIGURE 14.3 Sample of Character Tags and Painted Cards Created by Student A

Outcomes

In this case study, the researchers were trying to find ways to make use of visual memory and coordination to supplement the student's audial memory. While receiving individual guidance, Student A no longer required time to recall Hiragana. He did not express reluctance (e.g., "I do not want to write"), and his emotional resistance to writing gradually diminished. In general, his uneasiness in writing was alleviated. During his Japanese language lessons offered in a regular classroom, he was able to write calmly without becoming emotionally unstable.

It is noteworthy that the difficulties and weaknesses of students with special educational needs are diverse. Different difficulties are experienced by individual students in dealing with the same challenging task of handwriting. With individual guidance using Student A's positive cognitive characteristics, the difficulty of writing was reduced. The student was able to participate with confidence in regular classes. This case clearly demonstrates the importance of using his strengths.

Through this case study, the author felt it important to understand the student's good cognitive characteristics. For example, the author thinks that it is possible to develop a learning method that conforms to UDL's ideas by dividing the class into groups with the same characteristics and presenting different tasks for each strategy, such as simultaneous processing, sequential processing, etc. However, it should be noted that the characteristics of ASD students are diverse and the needs of individual learners will be different. The author believes that it is desirable to use the support of the entire class following the UDL guidelines, as well as support that takes into consideration the characteristics of individual students, such as the challenges associated with ASD faced by Student A. It is necessary to carefully consider the needs of each student and enrich individual support while guiding the whole class.

Conclusions and Recommendations

Special needs education is growing in Japan through increased use of the special support service inventory and other inclusive efforts (MEXT, 2017). As described through this case study, instructional guidance grounded in the UDL framework can consider individual learner characteristics, such as their cognitive strengths, along with the improvement of the classroom environment overall. These efforts are likely to enhance student self-esteem and confidence. Future efforts are needed to advance inclusion of concrete and systematic UDL-based practices in regular classrooms in Japan. Research on UDL applications in the Japanese culture and educational system, including further case analyses, is needed.

Acknowledgement

The author thanks the stakeholders who contributed to the preparation of this publication. The case study reported here was conducted with the consent of Student A, his parents, the classroom teacher, the individual guidance teacher, and the school principal. The author would also like to thank Editage (www.editage.jp) and eContent Pro (www.econtentpro.com) for English language review.

References

CAST. (2011). *Universal design for learning guidelines version 2.0*. Wakefield, MA: CAST Professional Publishing.

Dupaul, J., & Weyandt, L. (2006). School-based intervention for children with attention deficit hyperactivity disorder: Effects on academic, social, and behavioral functioning. *International Journal of Disability, Development and Education, 53*(2), 161–176.

Hall, T., Meyer, A., & Rose, D. (2012). *Universal design for learning in the classroom: Practical applications (What works for special-needs learners).* New York: Guilford Press.

Harada, S., & Edahiro, K. (2017). A discussion of universal design for learning for active learning in the university. Reprinted from *Bulletin of Center for Teacher Education and Development, Okayama University, 7,* 137–146.

Kamio, Y., & Toich, M. (2000). Dual access to semantics in autism: Is pictorial access superior to verbal access? *Journal of Child Psychology and Psychiatry, 41*(7), 859–867.

Kanagawa Prefectural Education Center. (2018). *Fundamental training for 2018* [in Japanese]. Retrieved from www.edu-ctr.pref.kanagawa.jp/h30kihon/30index.html

Kaufman, A., & Kaufman, N. (1983). *Kaufman assessment battery for children.* Circle Pines, MN: American Guidance Service.

Kawamata, T. (2014). Practice of universal design at Japan and other countries. In M. Tsuge (Ed.), *Instruction and classroom making utilizing the viewpoint of universal design* (pp. 12–24). Tokyo: Kaneko-Shobou.

Koike, T., Kumoi, M., & Kuboshima, T. (2002). *Hiragana/Kanji support for persons with LD.* Kyoto: Airi-Shuppan.

Meyer, A., Rose, D., & Gordon, D. (2014). *Universal Design for Learning: Theory and practice.* Wakefield, MA: CAST Professional Publishing.

Ministry of Education, Culture, Sports, Science, and Technology (MEXT). (2012). *Survey results on students who need special educational support with potential developmental disabilities enrolled in regular classes* [in Japanese]. Retrieved from www.mext.go.jp/a_menu/shotou/tokubetu/material/1328729.htm

Ministry of Education, Culture, Sports, Science, and Technology (MEXT). (2017). *Special needs education survey data (2017 edition)* [in Japanese]. Retrieved from www.mext.go.jp/a_menu/shotou/tokubetu/material/1406456.htm

Ministry of Foreign Affairs of Japan (MOFA). (2014). *Convention on the rights of persons with disabilities* [in Japanese]. Retrieved from www.mofa.go.jp/mofaj/fp/hr_ha/page22_000900.html

Sato, H., & Noutomi, K. (2018). Learning support to train children independently on Foreign language activities. *Bulletin of University of Teacher Education Fukuoka, 67,* 221–229.

Ueno, K., & Nakajima, T. (2012). Fieldwork study on acoustical environment of learning and living spaces for children with disability. *Journal of Environmental Engineering, 77*(682), 933–940.

15

LOW-TECH SOLUTIONS FOR UTILIZING THE UDL FRAMEWORK IN THE INCLUSIVE MATHEMATICS CLASSROOM

Marla J. Lohmann, Ruby L. Owiny, and Kathleen A. Boothe

Through Sustainable Development Goal 4, UNESCO has identified the need for "inclusive and equitable quality education for learners worldwide" (UNESCO, 2014); the UDL framework is one way to meet this goal. However, this goal can be hard to achieve for many teachers, especially in developing countries, where resources for education are few. The challenges in many developing countries are similar.

The first author spent time working in Zambia, where teachers have large class sizes of as many as 70 students in one room. Meeting the needs of all learners by responding to individual needs that have arisen is often impossible. The teachers there wanted to make changes to meet the needs of specific learners, but felt pulled in many directions and simply could not find time in the day to differentiate based on individual students. For these teachers, using the UDL framework to proactively design instruction that was accessible to all learners was a better option.

The second author worked in Guatemala with teachers in both Guatemala City and rural areas. Resources are scarce and training is minimal. In addition, challenges occur with indigenous students speaking their native language when their teachers may not. Challenges for bilingual learning coupled with a lack of special education support creates a situation in which using the UDL framework to create an inclusive classroom with minimized barriers is crucial. The second author also spent time working with teachers in rural mountainous areas of Bolivia. The challenges encountered in Guatemala were very similar there. Large class sizes and minimal materials required teachers to be creative in designing instruction to meet needs. The UDL framework provided a means by which to allow teachers to be more effective and students to reach higher levels of achievement.

In addition to time considerations and large class sizes, teachers in developing countries, such as Zambia, Guatemala, and Bolivia, often have limited teaching materials and a lack of funds to purchase computer-based technologies to support learning. While the second author was in Uganda and Tanzania, she encountered a classroom with one computer that did not have internet access. While the classroom had technology, it was limited in its scope. With this in mind, it is critical to support teachers in finding ways to implement the UDL framework with the use of low-tech supports, such as illustrated in the vignette in Box 15.1.

BOX 15.1   VIGNETTE: MISS PHIRI IN ZAMBIA'S EASTERN PROVINCE

Miss Phiri is a new teacher in a small village in Zambia's Eastern province. She is looking for ways to ensure that she is meeting the learning needs of the 50 students in her classroom. She knows that each student comes to school with unique learning needs and challenges; she wants to design instruction to proactively meet students' needs. Miss Phiri wants to make learning engaging and challenging, but she has no budget for purchasing materials and is unsure of how she might differentiate instruction for a large class. One day, she hears about Universal Design for Learning and begins exploring how it might meet her needs.

For many teachers, including those in developing countries, the use of UDL may seem daunting due to limited resources and the large class sizes that exist in many schools. Teachers should be aware that, while UDL can be enhanced through the use of technology, it does not require technology (Rose, Gravel, & Domings, 2010). As noted earlier, teachers can meet the needs of all learners with a limited budget and amidst other challenges, such as very large class sizes. This chapter provides teachers with practical, evidence-based strategies for utilizing the UDL framework to teach mathematics to diverse learners in primary and secondary classrooms without the use of computer-based or digital technology.

A variety of mathematics strategies have proven to be effective for increasing access to learning for all students. These strategies can include educational games (Buchheister, Jackson, & Taylor, 2017), math manipulatives (Carbonneau, Marley, & Selig, 2013), peer tutoring (Hogan & Prater, 1993), visual models (Woodward & Brown, 2006), word problems (Moran, Swanson, Gerber, & Fung, 2014), active responding (Owiny, Spriggs, Sartini, & Mills, 2018), project-based learning (PBL; Bottge, Rueda, Grant, Stephens, & LaRoque, 2010), and explicit instruction (Archer & Hughes, 2011). These strategies were specifically selected due to their ease in implementation when resources are few. This chapter will discuss each of these strategies and provide practical examples of their use in the classroom.

Mathematical Challenges and UDL

Mathematics concepts permeate multiple school subjects and daily life (Shamsuddin, Mahlan, Ul-Saufie, Hussin, & Alias, 2011). However, mathematics can be perceived as difficult by many students (Dauda, Jambo, & Umar, 2016) due to its conceptual and procedural concepts. Making these abstract concepts more concrete while assisting students to see the practical application of mathematics captures the essence of UDL: developing lifelong, independent learners. In addition, the application of UDL principles in mathematics instruction has the potential to increase active engagement of students in their own learning to help them develop a greater interest in mathematics and assist them in better understanding and using the abstract concepts often presented in mathematics.

Mathematics Strategies in the UDL Framework

The UDL framework includes three principles with specific guidelines and checkpoints for each principle. These checkpoints provide teachers with descriptions and examples to enhance understanding and implementation. This framework is outlined in the Universal Design for Learning Guidelines 2.2 (CAST, 2018). In order to effectively meet the needs of learners, teachers should strive to regularly incorporate concepts from each guideline in their classroom instruction. For mathematics, the UDL guidelines can be met through a variety of strategies. Table 15.1 outlines these strategies, as well as the principle and guidelines with which they are associated. It is important to remember that, even though only a few strategies are listed for each checkpoint, several of these strategies are more versatile and meet the expectations of multiple guidelines.

TABLE 15.1 Examples of Evidence-Based Mathematical Strategies within the UDL Framework

	Multiple Means of Engagement	*Multiple Means of Representation*	*Multiple Means of Action & Expression*
Access	Options for recruiting interest 1. Visual models 2. Project-based learning	Options for perception 1. Manipulatives 2. Visual models	Options for Physical Action 1. Games 2. Active responding
Build	Options for sustaining effort and persistence 1. Peer tutoring 2. Active responding	Options for language and symbols 1. Manipulatives 2. Visual models	Options for expression and communication 1. Word problems 2. Visual models
Internalize	Options for self-regulation 1. Project-based learning 2. Explicit instruction	Options for comprehension 1. Word problems 2. Visual models	Options for executive functions 1. Project-based learning 2. Manipulatives

Educational Games

For students at all grade levels, mathematics instruction includes both mastering the math facts and enhancing problem-solving skills. One way to practice these skills is through the use of games. When children play games, they are required to defend their mathematical reasoning to others and engage in mathematics discourse (Buchheister et al., 2017). Educational games align with the UDL framework in one way by providing options for physical action. When choosing games to include in lessons, teachers must ensure that those games include solid math concepts, are engaging and challenging, and can be played independently with little teacher interaction (Buchheister et al., 2017). The authors have identified several no-tech mathematics games that can be incorporated in the inclusive classroom. These include: card flip (see Figure 15.1), trashcan basketball, dice duel, UNO, and math flash cards relay.

Manipulatives

In many classrooms, physical objects are used to support student learning and the use of these *manipulatives* has an impact on students' long-term retention (Carbonneau et al., 2013). Manipulatives can be used to teach basic math facts, fractions, area and perimeter, algebra, and geometry concepts (Carbonneau et al., 2013) and align with the UDL framework by providing options for perception, options for language and symbols, and options for executive functions.

Everyday materials can be used to build hands-on instructional tools, such as an abacus (see Figure 15.2). The use of an abacus can increase long-term spatial working memory (Barner et al., 2016). While commercial products are popular items, they are not the only hands-on tools that teachers can provide for student use; research supports the idea that the *use* of manipulatives is what matters, not the specific item used (Bouck & Park, 2018). Ideas for no-tech, easy-to-access manipulatives include rocks, sticks, seashells, leaves, flowers, and beans.

Peer Tutoring

Peer tutoring has proven effective for all ages, grades, and subject areas (Hott & Walker, 2012) and provides options for sustaining effort and persistence. The use

---

Math Skills: Additional, Subtraction, Multiplication, Division
Grades: K–8
How to Play:
1. Deck of cards is turned upside down.
2. Student turns over two cards.
3. Student completes chosen math operation using the two numbers.
Additional Notes: Can be played individually or in pairs. Can use deck of cards, UNO cards, or teacher-made number cards.

FIGURE 15.1 The Card Flip, Illustrating How to Play a Math Game Using Cards

124 Marla J. Lohmann et al.

Materials Needed:
- One stiff piece of paper or cardboard (one side of a cereal box would be perfect)
- One spool of string or yarn
- 100 small circular items with a hole in the center (e.g., beads, buttons, acorns, or seashells with a hole drilled in the middle)
- Tape or glue

Instructions:
1. Draw 10 equal horizontal lines on the paper.
2. Cut 10 pieces of string the same sizes as the lines you drew in Step 1.
3. Using the tape of glue, attach each piece of string to the paper on the left side of each line.
4. Put 10 circular items on each piece of string.
5. Attach the other end of the piece of string to the right side of the line using the tape or glue.

FIGURE 15.2 How to Build a Homemade Abacus to Use in the Classroom

of peer tutoring benefits students from individualistic cultures, such as most in Europe and North America, while also serving the collectivism reflected in many African, Asian, Latin American, and Middle Eastern cultures (Hogan & Prater, 1993). Benefits include an increase in student engagement and on-task behavior, promoting academic and social development, and an increase in self-confidence and self-efficacy (Hott & Walker, 2012). Peer tutoring provides a way for students to learn from one another, which is a way to vary representation. Hott and Walker identify five ways to incorporate peer tutoring into the classroom. These include class-wide peer tutoring, reciprocal peer tutoring, same-age peer tutoring, peer-assisted learning strategies (PALS), and cross-age peer tutoring.

Visual Models

Increasing visual instructional materials can support the learning of students at all grade levels by aligning with the UDL conceptual guidelines of options for recruiting interest, options for perception, option for language and symbols, options for expression and communication, and options for comprehension. Using visual models helps students make abstract mathematics concepts more concrete, which enhances understanding of both basic math facts and more complex problem solving skills (Gonsalves & Krawec, 2014). Examples of visual models include number lines for learning basic math facts (Gonsalves & Krawec, 2014), visual chunking for geometry concepts (Zhang, Ding, Stegall, & Mo, 2012), and diagrams for problem solving (Pantziara, Gagatsis, & Elia, 2009), along with posters listing and demonstrating multiple steps required to solve complex problems. Figure 15.3 provides an example of visual chunking for solving a geometry problem.

Steps to Visual Chunking:
1. Look at the geometry problem.
2. Break it into smaller pieces.
3. Put the smaller pieces together to solve the problem.

Example of Visual Chunking:
In the figure below, AB and CD are parallel, and lengths are given in units. What is the area, in square units, of trapezoid ABCD?

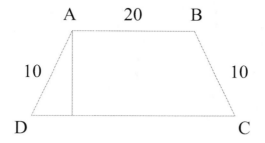

A. 100
B. 208
C. 200
D. 104
E. 250

To Solve This Problem, Students Should:
1. Look at the problem.
2. Note that there are two distinct shapes—the right triangle on the left and the quadrilateral on the right.
3. Identify two separate math problems to solve—the area of the triangle and the area of the quadrilateral.
4. Solve for the area of the triangle.
5. Solve for the area of the quadrilateral.
6. Add the two answers together.
7. Discover that the correct answer to the problem is B.

FIGURE 15.3 Steps on How to Visually Chunk a Geometry Problem and How to Solve the Problem

Word Problems

There is a strong interdisciplinary connection between reading and math skills. When students are presented with word problems, it is beneficial to paraphrase the problem by eliminating unnecessary words and putting the problem into mathematical equations; doing so will increase student comprehension (Moran et al., 2014). The use of word problems aligns with the UDL framework by providing options for expression and communication and options for comprehension. Figure 15.4 provides an example of a paraphrased word problem.

Active Responding

By allowing students to respond using active response methods, students become more engaged in their coursework. The use of active responding aligns with the UDL framework by providing options for physical action and options for sustaining effort and persistence. One way active responding can be used is when a teacher asks a question or creates a poll and has students answer using various methods. Evidence-based practices such as choral responding (Kretlow, Cooke, & Wood, 2012) and response cards (Owiny et al., 2018), along with writing, talking, drawing, holding up fingers, creating a model, or using manipulatives to demonstrate learning, are methods to vary response types, providing multiple opportunities for representation and action/expression. Educators can also vary active responses when creating assignments for their students. Examples of varying responses for assignments include creating a diorama; writing a song, play, or story; acting out a scene; and creating a dance.

Project-Based Learning

For many students, skills can be enhanced by applying them to complete projects of interest to the student. The use of project-based learning (PBL) fits into the UDL framework by providing options for recruiting interest, options for self-regulation, and options for executive functions. Potential PBL activities include building, crafting, cooking, and designing. Because mathematics skills are necessary to complete many daily tasks, popular hobbies may lend themselves well to

---

Original Problem:
Today is payday for Mary, Juan, and Rahim. After receiving their pay, the three friends go to the local store and make purchases. Mary buys 4 books, 4 CDs, and 2 video games; she pays $560. Juan purchases 9 books, 9 CDs, and 6 video games and pays $1290. What will Rahim pay for 1 book, 1 CD, and 1 video game?

Paraphrased Problem:
1. People are buying books, CDs, and video games.
2. $4b + 4c + 2v = 560$
3. $9b + 9c + 6v = 1290$
4. $1b + 1c + 1v = ????$

Answer:
  $150

FIGURE 15.4 How to Create a Paraphrased Problem From a Given Word Problem

TABLE 15.2 Project-Based Learning Ideas

Grade Level & Math Skill	Project	References
High School Problem Solving, Algebra, Geometry	Teams built a machine that involved energy; each team chose what type of machine; project lasted 25 weeks.	Kokko et al., 2015
Middle School Money, Algebra, Geometry	Students designed an amphitheater for their community; students were in charge of using math and science skills for the design and creating the budget; the student project was used to build the amphitheater.	Newman, Dantzler, & Coleman, 2015
Lower Primary School Money	Students grew vegetables in a garden and then sold those vegetables at the market.	Selmer, Rye, Malone, Fernandez, & Trebino, 2014
Any age Money, Time Management, Algebra, Geometry	Students planned and implemented the plans to improve a public space in their school or community. Projects could be small (e.g., redesigning the classroom) or large (e.g., re-designing the city park).	Duke, Halvorson, & Strachan, 2016

PBL in math. When students have the opportunity to use math skills to complete projects of interest, their motivation and enjoyment increases (Kokko, Eronen, & Sormunen, 2015). Table 15.2 provides examples of PBL ideas for enhancing student mathematics skills.

Explicit Instruction

Explicit instruction is another way for teachers to reach *all* students. When teachers utilize scaffolded instruction, they are incorporating all principles of UDL. The use of explicit instruction principles supports a model of "I do it" (teacher model), "We do it" (guided practice), and "You do it" (independent practice) (Archer & Hughes, 2011). Through the use of explicit instruction, students slowly develop independence with the skill through the "I do it" and "We do it" stages. Specifically, explicit instruction supports expression and communication, but also addresses language and symbols and sustaining effort and persistence.

Applications in Practice

When planning for the implementation of the UDL framework in the mathematics classroom, it is critical to design and implement lesson plans that reflect the UDL principles. The authors have provided a sample lesson plan in Table 15.3,

TABLE 15.3 Sample UDL Mathematics Lesson Plan

Lesson Topic: Order of Operations

Introduction	Review lesson from yesterday, while reminding students about the order they should use (refer to poster/note on blackboard). Ask questions while students answer on a slate, small whiteboard, a piece of cardboard, or a piece of paper. Have students write four letters of the alphabet in each corner (i.e., A, B, C, D). Ask students multiple-choice questions with up to four answer options. Students hold up their paper and use their thumb and index finger to "mark" the correct answer. For example, "With a problem such as this (written on board): 4 + 8 X 9 – 2, which operation do you solve for first: A) addition, B) multiplication, or C) subtraction?" UDL Checkpoints addressed: Options for physical action, Options for sustaining effort and persistence, Options for comprehension
I do it	Practice a few problems, starting simple and increasing in difficulty. Use small pebbles or cut-up paper for students to group simpler problems to visualize the process. Talk through the steps as they are completed. UDL Checkpoints addressed: Options for perception, Options for physical action, Options for language and symbols, Options for executive functions
We do it	Give students direction to write their own problem independently or with a peer. Each student must have two problems. Ask for volunteers to write their problem on the board. Students work through problems together with teacher guiding. UDL Checkpoints addressed: Options for sustaining effort and persistence, Options for comprehension
You do it	Students trade the problems they wrote in guided practice (except the ones already modeled) for peers to solve. Once completed, peers check work for accuracy and partners work together to fix errors with teacher monitoring. UDL Checkpoints addressed: Options for sustaining effort and persistence, Options for comprehension
Conclusion	Review relevant vocabulary with a game, such as Bingo. Demonstrate a problem using students as the "numbers" to move around as they are grouped according to the order of operations. UDL Checkpoints addressed: Options for sustaining effort and persistence, Options for physical action

utilizing scaffolded instruction and exemplifying the use of the UDL principles in practice.

Conclusions and Recommendations

As teachers of diverse students, the authors know that it is critical to use best practices in instruction, including UDL. Utilizing UDL in one's classroom will reduce barriers to learning, encourage students to enjoy learning, and ultimately develop lifelong, independent learners. In the opening vignette, Miss Phiri can

TABLE 15.4 UDL Web-Based Resources

Website	Information Available
The UDL Project https://www.theudlproject.com/math-k-5.html	Lesson plans for K-5 mathematics.
UDL Guidelines in Practice Video http://www.udlcenter.org/resource_library/videos/udlcenter/guidelines#video2	Video of 1st grade sample math lesson.
High Measurement Unit https://wiki.ncscpartners.org/index.php/High_School_Mathematics_UDL_Instructional_Unit	Unit lesson plans for secondary mathematics unit.
Universal Access Chapter of the Mathematics Framework for California Public Schools https://www.cde.ca.gov/ci/ma/cf/documents/mathfwuniversalaccess.pdf	Suggestions and specific activities for ensuring that all students can access the mathematics curriculum in grades K-12.
2018 UDL-IRN International Summit Handout https://schd.ws/hosted_files/2018udlirninternationalsummit/6d/UDL%20resources%20handout.pdf	Links to videos with specific recommendations for using the UDL framework in mathematics lessons.
UDL Aligned Strategies https://goalbookapp.com/toolkit/strategies	Strategies, organized by principle and guideline, with hyperlinks to descriptions. Subscription required.

begin meeting the learning needs of her classroom by using the framework and utilizing materials that are readily available to her.

The authors recommend starting small. It is not advisable to attempt to try all the strategies at once; one strategy can be selected and applied first, and, then slowly others can be added in. The authors recommend that Miss Phiri begin incorporating the UDL framework into her mathematics classroom by having students collect objects from the schoolyard to use as manipulatives. Engaging the students in preparing the learning materials is likely to increase engagement and motivation for learning.

In addition to the ideas provided in this chapter, the authors recommend a variety of web-based resources for locating ideas to implement the UDL framework in the mathematics classroom. These resources can be found in Table 15.4.

References

Archer, A. L., & Hughes, C. A. (2011). *Explicit instruction: Effective and efficient teaching.* New York, NY: The Guilford Press.

Barner, D., Alvarez, G., Sullivan, J., Brooks, N., Srinivasan, M., & Frank, M. C. (2016). Learning mathematics in a visuospatial format: A randomized, controlled trial of mental abacus instruction. *Child Development, 87*(4), 1146–1158.

Bottge, B., Rueda, E., Grant, T., Stephens, A., & LaRoque, P. (2010). Anchoring problem-solving and computation instruction in context-rich learning environments. *Exceptional Children, 76*(4), 417–437.

Bouck, E. C., & Park, J. (2018). A systematic review of the literature on mathematics manipulatives to support students with disabilities. *Education and Treatment of Children, 41*(1), 65–106.

Buchheister, K., Jackson, C., & Taylor, C. E. (2017). Maths games: A universal design approach to mathematical reasoning. *Australian Primary Mathematics Classroom, 22*(4), 7–12.

Carbonneau, K. J., Marley, S. C., & Selig, J. P. (2013). A meta-analysis of the efficacy of teaching mathematics with concrete manipulatives. *Journal of Educational Psychology, 105*(2), 380–400.

CAST. (2018). *Universal design for learning guidelines version 2.2*. Retrieved from http://udlguidelines.cast.org

Dauda, B., Jambo, H. E., & Umar, M. E. (2016). Students' perception of factors influencing teaching and learning of mathematics in senior secondary schools in Maiduguri Metropolis, Borno State, Nigeria. *Journal of Education and Practice, 7*(20), 114–122.

Duke, N. K., Halvorson, A., & Strachan, S. L. (2016). Project-based learning not just for STEM anymore: The research is clear that social studies and literacy are fertile ground for robust project-based learning units. *Phi Delta Kappan, 98*(1), 14–19.

Gonsalves, N., & Krawec, J. (2014). Using number lines to solve math word problems: A strategy for students with learning disabilities. *Learning Disabilities Research & Practice, 29*(4), 160–170.

Hogan, S., & Prater, M. A. (1993). The effects of peer tutoring and self-management training on on-task, academic, and disruptive behaviors. *Behavior Disorders, 18*(2), 118–128.

Hott, B., & Walker, J. (2012). *Peer tutoring*. Retrieved from https://council-for-learning-disabilities.org/peer-tutoring-flexible-peer-mediated-strategy-that-involves-students-serving-as-academic-tutors

Kokko, S., Eronen, L., & Sormunen, K. (2015). Crafting maths: Exploring mathematics learning through crafts. *Design and Technology Education: An International Journal, 20*(2), 22–31.

Kretlow, A. G., Cooke, N. L., & Wood, C. L. (2012). Using in-service and coaching to increase teachers' accurate use of research-based strategies. *Remedial and Special Education, 33*(6), 348–361.

Moran, A. S., Swanson, H. L., Gerber, M. M., & Fung, W. (2014). The effects of paraphrasing interventions on problem-solving accuracy for children at risk for math disabilities. *Learning Disabilities Research & Practice, 29*(3), 97–105.

Newman, J. L., Dantzler, J., & Coleman, A. N. (2015). Service in action: How middle school students are changing the world through STEM service-learning projects. *Theory into Practice, 54*(1), 47–54.

Owiny, R. L., Spriggs, A. D., Sartini, E. C., & Mills, J. R. (2018). Evaluating response cards as evidence-based. *Preventing School Failure, 62*(2), 59–72.

Pantziara, M., Gagatsis, A., & Elia, I. (2009). Using diagrams as tools for the solution of non-routine mathematical problems. *Educational Studies in Mathematics, 72*(1), 39–60.

Rose, D. H., Gravel, J. W., & Domings, Y. M. (2010). *UDL unplugged: The role of technology in UDL*. Retrieved from www.cast.org/our-work/publications/2012/udl-unplugged-role-technology.html#.W5FKoc5KjIU

Selmer, S. J., Rye, J. A., Malone, E., Fernandez, D., & Trebino, K. (2014). What should we grow in our school garden to sell at the farmer's market? Initiating statistical literacy through science and mathematics integration. *Science Activities, 51*(1), 17–32.

Shamsuddin, M., Mahlan, S. B., Ul-Saufie, A. Z., Hussin, F., & Alias, F. A. (2011). *An identification of factors influencing student's attitude and perceptions towards mathematics using factor analysis*. Paper presented at AIP National Symposium on Mathematical Sciences. https://doi.org/10.1063/1.5041706

United Nations Educational, Scientific, & Cultural Organization. (2014). *Education for sustainable development goals*. Retrieved from http://unesdoc.unesco.org/images/0024/002474/247444e.pdf

Woodward, J., & Brown, C. (2006). Meeting the curricular needs of academically low-achieving students in middle grade mathematics. *Journal of Special Education, 40*(3), 151–159.

Zhang, D., Ding, Y., Stegall, J., & Mo, L. (2012). The effect of visual-chunking-representation accommodation on geometry testing for students with math disabilities. *Learning Disabilities Research & Practice, 27*(4), 167–177.

16

SNAPSHOT—SCIENCE FOR ALL THROUGH UDL

Using UDL as a Framework for Science Education for the English Learner

Heather Pacheco-Guffrey and Jeanne Carey Ingle

Background

America's population of English learners (EL) is rising (U.S. Department of Education, National Center for Education Statistics, 2018). To ensure that we are producing people who are college and career ready and prepared to fill roles in leadership and innovation, efforts to close persistent achievement gaps between ELs and native English speakers should be prioritized (U.S. Department of Education, National Center for Education Statistics, 2018).

In 2016, the authors were approached by a local urban school with ~50% EL population to help their EL 5th graders reading at K-1 levels. School science texts matched students' K-1 reading proficiencies but also targeted K-1 level concepts. Their peers reading at grade-level had science texts on related topics but the texts were appropriately abstract and complex, reflective of 5th grade standards. ELs, bored and angry trying to learn from the *babyish* K-1 texts, refused to use them. As observed in this case, limiting ELs to below-grade texts can be demotivating and can lead to learning deficits over multiple years, hampering ELs' progress in science and subsequently limiting access to future opportunities in STEM.

Technology and UDL for English Learners (EL)

Next Generation Science standards (NGSS) are best supported by instructional strategies such as inquiry, discovery, collaboration in integrated environments and hands-on experiences (NGSS, 2016). Teachers must learn how to enact these strategies while also ensuring equitable access to learning for all their students.

The authors leveraged the schools' digital infrastructure to connect teachers with technology-rich strategies because technology is supportive of EL education (Echevarria, Vogt, & Short, 2016; Mikyung et al., 2016) and provides high levels of engagement for ELs (Bunch, Walqui & Pearson, 2014; Sinatra, Mukhopadhyay, Allbright, Marsh, & Polikoff, 2017). The Universal Design for Learning (UDL) framework (Meyer, Rose, & Gordon, 2014) is employed here as a powerful ally for educators creating inclusive learning experiences. In the authors' work with elementary educators, two technology-based UDL approaches are employed.

Authentic Science and Engineering Practices With Apps

Practice-oriented learning environments inclusive of ELs provide the hands-on and communication-rich experiences that can support student development of *language for use*, fostering language learning for all students alongside content learning (Quinn, Lee, & Valdés, 2012). Simulation apps, such as Marco Polo *Arctic*, enable learners to collect and analyze data to build scientific arguments. Using First8Studios' *Wonderfarm* and *Plant Journal*, students can plan and carry out investigations and also make connections between the virtual and physical worlds with real-world data collection for in-app analyses and interpretation. These experiences engage all learners in authentic practices and support grade-level learning.

Flexible Science Text Resources that Build Literacy

The *Crack the Books Series* apps present developmentally and grade-appropriate science content with embedded literacy supports such as leveled readings, clickable in-text links to videos, images and glossary. The *Namoo Wonders of Plant Life* app from Crayon Box aligns with NGSS and includes in-app literacy supports that complement the well-designed and leveled interactive simulations designed to target the wide range of K-6 learning needs.

Conclusions

These UDL-connected approaches enable teachers to employ flexible and engaging resources to target student learning and motivation through hands-on experiences with developmentally and cognitively appropriate strategies and technologies. Using high-quality technologies to support UDL-based teaching and learning creates accessible and equitable learning experiences that are inclusive of English learners.

References

Bunch, G., Walqui, A., & Pearson, P. D. (2016). K-12 standards-based educational reform: Implications for English language learner populations (September 2014). *TESOL Quarterly*, *48*(3), 533–559.

Echevarria, J., Vogt, M. E., & Short, D. J. (2016). *Making content comprehensible for English language learners: The SIOP Model* (5th ed.). Boston, MA: Allyn & Bacon, Pearson.

Meyer, A., Rose, D. H., & Gordon, D. (2014). *Universal design for learning: Theory and practice.* Wakefield, MA: CAST Professional Publishing.

Mikyung, K. W., Guzman-Orth, D., Lopez, A., Castellano, K., Himelfarb, I., & Tsutagawa, F. S. (2016). Integrating scaffolding strategies into technology-enhanced assessments of English learners: Task types and measurement models. *Educational Assessment, 21*(3), 1257–1275.

NGSS. (2016). *Next generation science standards: For states, by states: Next generation science standards fact sheet.* Washington, DC: The National Academies Press.

Quinn, H., Lee, O., & Valdés, G. (2012). *Language demands and opportunities in relation to next generation science standards for English language learners: What teachers need to know.* Stanford, CA: Stanford University, Understanding Language Initiative at Stanford University.

Sinatra, G., Mukhopadhyay, A., Allbright, T., Marsh, J., & Polikoff, M. (2017). Speedometry: A vehicle for promoting interest and engagement through integrated stem instruction. *Journal of Educational Research, 110*(3), 308–316.

U.S. Department of Education, National Center for Education Statistics. (2018). *The condition of education 2018* (2018–144). English Language Learners in Public Schools. Retrieved from https://nces.ed.gov/fastfacts/display.asp?id=96

17

SNAPSHOT—RECONSTRUCTING ASYNCHRONOUS ONLINE LEARNING WITH UDL

Kathryn Nieves

About the Course

In a middle school intervention course in New Jersey, the author implements the UDL process in order to help build the confidence and skills of the special education students in her class. The course, *Multisensory Reading*, is for students who struggle in reading, writing, phonology, and spelling.

The curriculum for the course requires one-on-one work between the teacher and the student. Due to its intensity and the size of the class, there are portions of time where students will need to work on skills independently. An online course had to be built in order to support these students as they work on language arts skills on their own. The online portion of the course used the UDL framework (CAST, 2018) in order to build an experience wherein the students received the remediation for the skills they needed and continued to practice strategies to use in their language arts classes.

Each of the students was observed on an individual basis, examining the details of their individualized education program (IEP), their self-determined strengths and weaknesses, and their classroom and pre-assessment performances. The barriers these students had against the grade-level curriculum were also considered, including the need for small group focus, a slower pace of the content, and multisensory-based instruction. From there, a series of end goals were set for the group. The end-of-course expectations for these students were to reach grade-level standards in reading, writing, and grammar.

UDL Applications

Multiple Means of Representation in Online Learning

Once the final expectations for all students were determined, they were used to shape the online learning modules for the course. Students worked asynchronously through these modules when they were not completing intensive instruction with the teacher.

Students were:

- Self-pacing through the curriculum, reviewing and redoing activities to assist learning
- Using multiple means of representation to access the data, including video resources that were professionally produced and teacher-made, presentations, digital anchor charts, various notes strategies, and slideshows
- Drawing on their background knowledge during introduction sections for each module
- Empowered to make their own choices for notes and documenting new information, including sketchnotes, standard bullet points, or speak-to-text dictation on the computer

Multiple Means of Engagement, Action, and Expression in Online Learning

The remainder of the modules contained application activities and assessment choices that appealed to the UDL guidelines of multiple means of engagement and action and expression. Using the interests of the students, the modules hosted different options to practice the newly learned material, including:

- Hands-on activities with class resources, such as task cards and physical manipulatives
- Collaborative experiences for students working within the same module to practice and discuss the skill
- Choice assessments to demonstrate new knowledge gained
- Connections to other content areas or real-life situations to make the concept relevant

Recommendations for Replication

Educators looking to build an online course should use the UDL framework in order to appeal to the unique needs of the class while still building toward grade-level standards. Making note of any IEP goals and determining obstacles in the way of learning the content are the most important factors in planning each learning module. The embedded online activities can allow instructors to observe and formatively assess student progress toward the learning goals (Bauder, Simmons, & Gronseth, 2019). If possible, content area connections to students' lives and the real world should be considered to help students understand each concept.

References

Bauder, D. K., Simmons, T. J., & Gronseth, S. (2019). Technology ideas for monitoring student progress: Through a UDL lens. *Closing the Gap (December 2018–January 2019)*, 3–10.

Center for Applied Special Technology (CAST). (2018). *About universal design for learning*. Retrieved from www.cast.org/our-work/about-udl.html

SECTION 4
Technology Innovations for Inclusive Learning

18
SAMR STRATEGIES FOR THE INTEGRATION OF TECHNOLOGY THROUGH UDL

Debra K. Bauder, Katherine M. Cooper and Thomas J. Simmons

Introduction

To meet the diverse needs of learners in our increasingly heterogeneous society, it is paramount to consider unique ways to provide access to the curriculum for all students (Head & Fain, 2018). The idea of the Universal Design for Learning (UDL) framework (Rose & Meyer, 2002) was developed to offer guidance and resources to meet all students' learning goals. This is often realized by implementing a flexibility and scaffolding framework. The UDL framework centers on developing an instructional environment for the learner to gain knowledge at their own pace using preferred activities and products to demonstrate comprehension of concepts, issues and learning. UDL can be thought of as a framework that provides choice and options for learners to engage, represent and express themselves. These can include the use of technology, physical activities, written products, electronic productions, visual representations and various other stratagems (Edyburn, 2010; Meyer, Rose, & Gordon, 2014). Thus, UDL challenges us to rethink our instructional pedagogy in such a way that we can widen and expand what students can learn or do to demonstrate understanding. With this as a context, this chapter will focus on the relationship of technology within the UDL framework and look at processes to consider in its implementation and integration into instructional efforts to meet the needs of students.

Substitution, Augmentation, Modification and Redefinition (SAMR)

As technology continues to be a growing force in education, teachers must learn to integrate it into the classroom in more expansive ways (Baran, Correia, &

Thompson, 2013; Ruday, 2011). To assist in technology integration and to hold teachers to a standard, school districts have turned to technology models. There are several suggested methods and strategies for incorporating the latest technological tools and addressing changing pedagogies (Blackwell, Lauricella, Wartella, Robb, & Schomburg, 2013; Machado & Laverick, 2015). One such structure is the substitution, augmentation, modification and redefinition (SAMR) model, which was developed by Puentedura (see Puentedura, 2006). Within the model, the components allow teachers to approach technology as a separate task from lesson planning by offering scaffolding (Hilton, 2015). The idea of integrating technology into the classroom through such an organized manner of SAMR instinctively provides access to the curriculum in a variety of ways. Additionally, through using this model, it also offers an approach to providing accessible content to all students in the classroom.

According to Hilton (2015), the SAMR approach to technology integration started to gain popularity in 2012 and continued to grow after an endorsement from the Apple Computer Corporation that same year (Couch & Towne, 2018). While the SAMR graphic appears to be a progression of levels in technology integration, it should be looked at as a way to enhance lessons to create a richer learning experience through technology. When creating or redesigning a lesson, one could work through each level to create experiences for students that could not exist without technology (Kirkland, 2014). Furthermore, the SAMR model includes increasing levels of technology integration and provides a schematic to support educators (see Figure 18.1). These levels can also be considered as aspects of scaffolding within the UDL framework.

It is imperative that the learner outcome, as well as the process, be thoroughly vetted, and digital tools intentionally selected for specific pedagogical goals when considering technology integration (Baran et al., 2013; Ruday, 2011). Specifically, each component of the SAMR structure provides a level of complexity from simple/uncomplicated to more complex and requiring greater depth of understanding to answer or explain an assessment-related item or classroom activity. For example, at the *substitution* level, teachers are encouraged to replace traditional education materials with technology alternatives (Gorman, 2017; Gromik, 2012). At this level, an eBook or a tablet, rather than a print version of a book, could be used. There is no functional change to the task in this scenario, but it is worthwhile to note that the task may intrinsically become more accessible using technology. In the *augmentation* level, the use of technology to provide a functional change to the task *is* the goal, such as using an audiobook in our previous example, allowing students access to the reading materials in a different medium (Gorman, 2017). When moving into the *modification* level, a teacher begins to transform the lesson using technology so that it fuels a redesign of instruction (Gorman, 2017; Wang, Yu, & Wu, 2013). As an example, a teacher uses multimedia options, such as video, audio or interactive graphic organizers, to enhance a digital text. In the utmost level of *redefinition*, novel tasks are reimagined through technology. Researchers

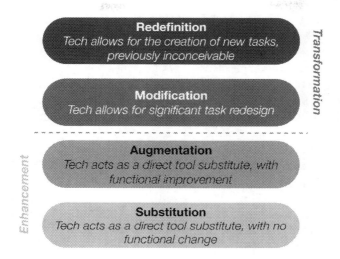

FIGURE 18.1   Puentedura's (2006) Substitution, Augmentation, Modification and Redefinition (SAMR) Model

Source: from www.hippasus.com/rrpweblog/

have demonstrated this by having a student show knowledge by creating a video or a game to demonstrate comprehension of the assigned reading (Gorman, 2017; Hamilton, Rosenberg, & Akcaoglu, 2016; Liu & Tsai, 2013). Using technology to move curriculum and tasks through the SAMR model will give teachers an opportunity to create a more dynamic and engaging environment for all students (Hartman & Weismer, 2016; Hooker, 2014).

UDL and SAMR Pedagogy

Recent research has shown that increasing access alone does not automatically equate to greater or higher quality of technology usage (Ertmer, 1999; Ertmer & Ottenbreit-Leftwich, 2010). Barriers to technology integration have included, but are not limited to, valuing technology in the classroom (Inan & Lowther, 2010), knowledge of technology and its use (Angeli & Valanides, 2013) and teacher attitudes toward technology (Cubukcuoglu, 2013; Mills, & Tincher, 2003). However, the growing availability of new technology has created a shift in classroom pedagogy and challenged traditional understandings of teaching content knowledge (Donnelly & Kyei-Blankson, 2015; Hooker, 2014). While both UDL and SAMR can be implemented independently of each other, applying them in combination can be a powerful way of enhancing student engagement and academic achievement. In order for teachers to embed UDL/SAMR scaffolds, they need to know the technology, its uses and functionality (Pamuk, Ergun, Cakir, Yilmaz, & Ayas,

2015). Figure 18.2 provides an illustration of the UDL framework (*representation, engagement* and *expression*) and the infusion of the SAMR structure.

The UDL/SAMR integration utilizes the three UDL principles and SAMR at various depths and complexity in light of a student's effort and engagement in completing a task. In the UDL/SAMR technology integration model, multiple means of representation and substitution are easily coupled. The idea of incorporating multiple means of representation/substitution (R/S) provides both teachers and students with an uncomplicated and straightforward way to integrate technology into lessons and tasks.

At the *augmentation* level, the technology acts as a new tool that provides beneficial improvement (Puentedura, 2013). As noted in the UDL/SAMR integration graphic, *augmentation* aligns well with all three UDL principles at equal intensity. For example, when incorporating *augmentation*, the use of multiple ways of engagement, representation and action are all equally addressed in the manner that a lesson, activity or lecture is conceptualized and taught. An example of this could be the manner in which a teacher provides instruction through the use of an interactive whiteboard. First of all, an interactive whiteboard is a tool that can substitute for pencil and paper tasks (representation). Secondly, the use of interactive whiteboards can increase teacher-student engagement (engagement). This type of technology also allows students to demonstrate their understanding (expression), such as labeling parts of a picture or matching words with their respective meanings.

At the *modification* level, a teacher redesigns the instruction using technology. This level also aligns well with all three UDL principles at equal intensity, as illustrated in the UDL/SAMR technology integration model. The task for students could be to create a document using Google Docs that discusses global warming (representation/expression). Using the dictation feature in Google Docs (engagement/expression), students verbally express their ideas on the elements of the topic. Once completed, the document is then shared either on Google Docs or using an online program such as Peerceptiv (a program that allows peer feedback) (expression/engagement). By sharing the document, students can receive feedback on their assignment from their peers. This activity supports writing skill development.

FIGURE 18.2 Conceptualization of UDL/SAMR Integration

Lastly, at the *redefinition* level of the SAMR model, the UDL principle of multiple means of expression represents the greatest potential of this type of technological integration, while engagement and representation are evenly divided. At this level, the technology would equate as a transformative tool for educators; in other words, a higher degree of student expression that demonstrates their understanding in a more complex way. One of the transformative technology tools is best described through the use of augmented and virtual reality. This type of technology provides avenues that allow students to engage in a social, collaborative and active learning environment (Dunleavy, Dede, & Mitchell, 2009; Sotiriou & Bogner, 2008). Augmented reality (AR) is commonly accepted as real-time technology of a physical environment that has been augmented by adding virtual information to it (Carmigniani et al., 2011), and virtual reality (VR) is an interactive computer-generated experience taking place within a simulated environment (Babich, 2018). Research shows that both VR and AR simulations increase student motivation and improve collaboration and knowledge construction (Babich, 2018; Cheng & Tsai, 2013). There are many AR/VR type of apps for teachers to choose from, including Quiver (AR coloring book), Layr (scanning and viewing print in an interactive way) or Metaverse (interactive content creation).

Applications for Use

Creating a lesson that includes the principles of SAMR and UDL can make for rich lessons that include multi-tiered supports available to all students. The example in Box 18.1 could be used during a class field trip or as a homework assignment that students complete independently.

BOX 18.1 APPLICATION EXAMPLE

Mrs. Bronger wants her students to learn about Lewis and Clark's Corps of Discovery Expedition. The local history museum has an interactive exhibit that allows students to learn about their journey through hands-on artifacts and replicas of what they experience. Mrs. Bronger is taking her students to the museum on a field trip, enhancing the experience by embedding the principles of UDL and SAMR into the trip. The lesson was introduced in the classroom. Students drew a map on their tablet of what they thought the United States looked like in 1804, just before Lewis and Clark left on their expedition. Then, they used their tablets to research what the map actually looked like making adjustments. Students also used pictures they found on the Internet to represent people, animals, plants, etc. that were native to the area in 1805. When the students finished their maps from 1805, they

> compared them to current maps available on the Internet. The groups presented the information they had collected in a variety of ways to demonstrate what they had learned. Students were encouraged to be creative, and Mrs. Bronger suggested using performing arts, technology, models or any other method of the groups' choosing.
>
> Student groups used their tablets to explore the Lewis and Clark Experience exhibit. When they located tagged artifacts, they were required to perform a task, answer questions or create entries that could be viewed by other students. Mrs. Bronger used interactive areas in the exhibit to guide the activities. Using the built-in camera on their tablets, students used "dress up" clothes to reenact part of Lewis and Clark's journey. Inside of the replica tipi, students practice storytelling, recording the audio on their tablet.
>
> When the students returned to class, they collected the videos, the audio and the pictures they took on the tablet to create a presentation to share with the rest of the class. Mrs. Bronger gave the link to the AR scavenger hunt that she created in the museum to parents so they could take their children back to the museum to extend the activity for extra credit.

A variety of educational technology tools can be used to support the UDL-SAMR Integration Model. Table 18.1 offers suggested strategies and supportive technologies associated with each UDL principle and SAMR scaffold. Many of the supportive technologies included in this table can be used in multiple areas.

Conclusion

UDL provides a broad palette by which educators can develop and articulate educational curricula. As Rose and Meyer (2002, p. 5) stated in their original text on the subject, UDL provides us with

> a Copernican shift toward a new position. . . . In the rapidly expanding capabilities of digital content, tools, and networks, we see the possibility of conceiving, designing, and delivering a curriculum that will accommodate widely varying learner needs. Essentially, this will transfer the burden of adjustment from students to the materials and methods they encounter in the classroom.

With this as a backdrop, added structures and practices need to be provided to further articulate how UDL can be implemented. This chapter provided a conceptual method for integrating SAMR and UDL to align technology use with pedagogy. The provided examples illustrated how SAMR connects to UDL

TABLE 18.1 Potential Technologies Supporting UDL/SAMR Integration

UDL Principle	SAMR Scaffold	Strategies	Supportive Technologies
Multiple means of representation	Substitution	• Use text-to-speech program, large print books or eBooks to modify texts and audiobooks. • Provide access to audiobooks with paired texts. • Use podcasts (audio files, MP3 files).	• Learning Ally • Bookshare • Google Docs • Google Slides • Podcasts: Content Acquisition Podcast (CAP)
	Augmentation	• Use digital text/textbooks featuring defining words, personalizing format to be more user-friendly. • Highlight & copy/paste key points of text. • Provide simplified narration-based animation program. • Create a complete animated, narrated video.	• Google Docs with Read Write Add-ons • Adobe Spark Video app • Amazon Kindle • iBooks
	Modification	• Have students review online materials such as videos at home so class time can be used for hands-on activities. • Use an iPad as a recordable whiteboard. • Create dynamic interactive lessons, activities, assessments and tutorials.	• Educreations • Explain Everything • Thinglink • Nearpod
	Redefinition	• Collaboration among peers. • Share ideas and discuss key concepts of lessons. • Collate ideas and collaborate online. • Create a customized comic. • Create a custom drawing and then animate it.	• Google Suite • Google Classroom • Padlet • Comic Life • Animation Desk
Multiple means of engagement	Substitution	• The technology used must assist in student engagement. • Students take a quiz using a Google Form instead of using pencil and paper. • Use alerts and reminders to complete tasks.	• Tablets & apps • Apple Watch • Chromebook • Google Forms

(Continued)

TABLE 18.1 (Continued)

UDL Principle	SAMR Scaffold	Strategies	Supportive Technologies
	Augmentation	• Have students explore other languages using a text and audio translation tool. • For math, have students measure an environment using augmented reality apps. • Collaboration.	• Google Translate • Aruler • AR Dragon
	Modification	• Create a video on classroom topic. • Pair recorded audio with a photo. • Use QR codes to enhance a scavenger hunt digitally.	• PowerPoint • Prezi • iMovie • Camtasia • Speech Journal • QR Code Creator
	Redefinition	• A story could be changed into a picture book, a slideshow or even a movie. • Experience otherwise inaccessible environments using VR and AR apps. • Create geotagged works of art drawn or painted on walls.	• Book Creator • Flipboard • VoiceThread • VR apps, such as Google Expeditions • AR apps, such as Metaverse and WallaMe • Just A Line • Google Lens
Multiple means of expression	Substitution	• Have students record themselves as they read. • Apply spelling, grammar, punctuation, conventions, rules in writing.	• Google Docs • Notetaker • Grammarly • Read & Write • Fluency Tutor • Snapverter

Augmentation	- Have students answer questions as part of the video. - Complete math assignments. - Increase vocabulary skills with an online graphical dictionary. - Record narration to a book to tell a story. - Use digital calculators or spreadsheets to solve a problem.	- Edpuzzle - EquatIO - Virtual Manipulatives (online program) - Visuwords - Bunsella Bedtimes Story - Tellagami
Modification	- Caption video to improve listening skills/spelling skills. - Create digital stories. - Compile research using a bookmarking tool.	- YouTube captioning manager - Little Bird Tales - Diigo - Animoto - Make Beliefs Comix - Story Creator - PuppetPals
Redefinition	- Create an augmented reality story. - Create a virtual reality for students to explore different realities and alternative learning experiences. - Create scenario in response to classroom topics. - Build a virtual tour. - Create timelines. - Create a photosphere.	- Google Earth TourBuilder - MyHistro - SmartDraw - TimeToast - Google Streets

scaffolding at multiple levels. The SAMR structure offered a great deal of direction and substance to expanding one's framework for implementing technology in the classroom in order to help students learn and achieve goals in an individualized systematic method. Although educators can aim for ultimately using technology so that it redefines what's possible in their classrooms, there will be "times when even the most proficient educators with technology conduct a task at the substitution level" (Gorman, 2017, Conclusions, para. 1). That is why the use of UDL principles and SAMR scaffolds embraces the concept of fitting the task and learning target with the type of technology. Much more thought and attention is required to be placed on the structures we use to facilitate student performance and involvement in learning. With the technology integration of UDL and SAMR, the challenge for teachers is to rethink pedagogy in such a way that teachers can expand the opportunities for students to learn and to demonstrate their understanding.

References

Angeli, C., & Valanides, N. (2013). Technology mapping: An approach for developing technological pedagogical content knowledge (TPCK). *Journal of Educational Computing Research, 48*, 199–221. doi:10.2190/ec.48.2.e

Babich, N. (2018). *How virtual reality will change how we learn and how we teach* [Blog post]. Retrieved from https://theblog.adobe.com/virtual-reality-will-change-learn-teach/

Baran, E., Correia, A., & Thompson, A. (2013). Tracing successful online teaching in higher education: Voices of exemplary online teachers. *Teachers College Record, 115*(3), 1–41.

Blackwell, C., Lauricella, A., Wartella, E., Robb, M., & Schomburg, R. (2013). Adoption and use of technology in early education: The interplay of extrinsic barriers and teacher attitudes. *Computers & Education, 69*, 310–319. doi:10.1016/j.compedu.2013.07.024

Carmigniani, J., Furht, B., Anisetti, M., Ceravolo, P., Damiani, P., & Ivkovic, M. (2011). Augmented reality technologies, systems and applications. *Multimedia Tools and Applications, 51*(1), 341–377.

Cheng, K. H., & Tsai, C. C. (2013). Affordances of augmented reality in science learning: Suggestions for future research. *Journal of Science Education and Technology, 22*(4), 449–462.

Couch, J. D., & Towne, J. (2018). *Rewiring education: How technology can unlock every student's potential*. Dallas, TX: BenBella Books, Inc.

Cubukcuoglu, B. (2013). Factors enabling the use of technology in subject teaching. *International Journal of Education and Development Using Information and Communication Technology, 9*(3), 50–60.

Donnelly, H., & Kyei-Blankson, L. (2015). Administrator insights, evaluation, and support of new teacher use of educational technology. *Journal of Education and Training, 2*(1), 110–133.

Dunleavy, M., Dede, C., & Mitchell, R. (2009). Affordances and limitations of immersive participatory augmented reality simulations for teaching and learning. *Journal of Science Education and Technology, 18*(1), 7–22.

Edyburn, D. L. (2010). Would you recognize universal design for learning if you saw it? Ten propositions for new directions for the second decade of UDL. *Learning Disability Quarterly, 33*(1), 33–34.

Ertmer, P. A. (1999). Addressing first- and second-order barriers to change: Strategies for technology integration. *Educational Technology Research and Development, 47*(4), 47–61.

Ertmer, P. A., & Ottenbreit-Leftwich, A. T. (2010). Teacher technology change: How knowledge, confidence, beliefs, and culture intersect. *Journal of Research on Technology in Education, 42*(3), 255–284.

Gorman, M. (2017). Part 5 ... beyond the shine: Supporting technology with the SAMR model plus ten great resource sites [Blog post]. Retrieved from https://21centuryedtech.wordpress.com/2015/06/10/part-1beyond-the-shine-supporting-technology-with-the-samr-model-plus-ten-great-resource-sites/

Gromik, N. (2012). Cell phone video recording feature as a language learning tool: A case study. *Computers & Education, 58*(1), 223–230. doi:10.1016/j.compedu.2011.06.013

Hamilton, E. R., Rosenberg, J. M., & Akcaoglu, M. (2016). The substitution augmentation modification redefinition (SAMR) model: A critical review and suggestions for its use. *TechTrends: Linking Research and Practice to Improve Learning, 60*(5), 433–441.

Hartmann, E., & Weismer, P. (2016). Technology implementation and curriculum engagement for children and youth who are deafblind. *American Annals of the Deaf, 161*(4), 462–473.

Head, C. N., & Fain, A. C. (2018). Curriculum design: Principles, methods, & strategies. In N. D. Young, E. Jean, & T. A. Citro (Eds.), *Stars in the schoolhouse: Teaching practices and approaches that make a difference* (pp. 1–14). Wilmington, Delaware: Vernon Press.

Hilton, J. T. (2015). A case study of the application of SAMR and TPACK for reflection on technology integration into two social studies classrooms. *The Social Studies, 107*(2), 68–73. http://dx.doi.org/10.1080/00377996.2015.1124376

Hooker, C. (2014). *SAMR swimming lessons* [Blog post]. Retrieved from https://hookedoninnovation.com/2014/08/01/samr-swimming-lessons/

Inan, F. A., & Lowther, D. L. (2010). Factors affecting technology integration in K-12 classrooms: A path model. *Educational Technology Research and Development, 58*(2), 137–154.

Kirkland, A. B. (2014). Models for technology integration in the learning commons. *School Libraries in Canada, 32*(1), 14–18.

Liu, P-H. E., & Tsai, M-K. (2013). Using augmented-reality-based mobile learning material in EFL English composition: An exploratory case study. *British Journal of Educational Technology, 44*(1), E1–E4. doi:10.1111/j.1467–8535.2012.01302.x

Machado, C., & Laverick, D. (2015). Technology integration in K-12 classrooms: The impact of graduate coursework on teachers' knowledge and practice. *Journal of Technology and Teacher Education, 23*(1), 79–106.

Meyer, A., Rose, D. H., & Gordon, D. (2014). *Universal design for learning: Theory and practice*. Wakefield, MA: CAST Professional Publishing.

Mills, S. C., & Tincher, R. C. (2003). Be the technology. *Journal of Research on Technology in Education, 35*(3), 382–401. doi:10.1080/15391523.2003.10782392

Pamuk, S., Ergun, M., Cakir, R., Yilmaz, H. B., & Ayas, C. (2015). Exploring relationships among TPACK components and development of the TPACK instrument. *Education and Information Technologies, 20*(2), 241–263. doi:10.1007/s10639-013-9278-4

Puentedura, R. R. (2006). *Transformation, technology, and education* [Blog post]. Retrieved from http://hippasus.com/resources/tte/

Puentedura, R. R. (2013). *SAMR: Moving from enhancement to transformation* [Web log post]. Retrieved from www.hippasus.com/rrpweblog/archives/000095.html

Rose, D., & Meyer, A. (2002). *Teaching every student in the digital age*. Alexandria, VA: Association for Supervision and Curriculum Development.

Ruday, S. (2011). Expanding the possibilities of discussion: A critical approach to the use of online discussion boards in the English classroom. *Contemporary Issues in Technology and Teacher Education, 11*(4), 350–361.

Sotiriou, S., & Bogner, F. X. (2008). Visualizing the invisible: Augmented reality as an innovative science education scheme. *Advanced Science Letters, 1*(1), 114–122.

Wang, J., Yu, W., & Wu, E. (2013). Empowering mobile assisted social e-learning: Students' expectations and perceptions. *World Journal of Education, 3*(2), 59–70. doi:10.5430/wje.v3n2p59

19

ENGAGEMENT, REPRESENTATION, AND EXPRESSION IN ONLINE MIND MAPPING ACTIVITIES

Rosa Cendros Araujo and George Gadanidis

Today's classrooms and learning materials are filled with images. After many years of research about pedagogy, learning psychology, and neuroscience, it would be unthinkable to teach complex concepts without the facilitative aid of a diagram, an illustration, or a photo. In this context, mapping—as in mind mapping and concept mapping—is understood as an alternative form of thinking (Hyerle, 2009).

Mind maps are defined as "visual and graphic holistic thinking tool[s] that can be applied to all cognitive functions, especially memory, creativity, learning, and all forms of thinking" (Buzan & Buzan, 2010, p. 31). The main characteristic of a mind map is that it has a central image or word, and ideas branching out of it. This is referred to as a radiating structure and has been related to a more creative and aesthetic approach to thinking. According to Brown and Czerniewicz (2014, p. 93), "As a genre, mindmaps enable certain semiotic possibilities that conversation and writing do not." These possibilities include more options in arranging items, sizing, highlighting, linking, or separating ideas (Gao, Zhang, & Franklin, 2013). Using these elements, instead of relying on pure language to describe a concept and its relationships, increases the conceptual complexity that can be handled in a discussion (Suthers & Hundhausen, 2003). Mind maps also encourage brainstorming, which adds different discourse characteristics to discussions and allows a quick view of the main concept (Ng & Hanewald, 2010).

Beyond these advantages, technology has increased the possibilities of mind mapping. For example, Ng and Hanewald (2010) compared manually created concept maps to electronic versions and noted that digital mind maps allow the flexibility of hypertext, which enables infinite changes and the insertion of media (images, videos, hyperlinks, and others). In the 21st century, visual representations for education have had an upturn with the rise of Universal Design for Learning (UDL) and its correspondence with many curricular trends, such as *multiliteracies*, a pedagogical approach that emphasizes multimodal forms of linguistic expression and representation (Kalantzis & Cope, 2015). According to Eisner (2002, p. 148), curriculum needs to consider that "humans employ different knowledge systems to acquire, store, and retrieve understanding, and they use different performance systems to express what they know about the world."

In terms of UDL, mind maps have the potential to include multiple means of representation and expression by providing ways to improve remembering, understanding, and knowledge organization through different modes that combine text, images, colour, and layout. This chapter will present a descriptive case study of the Mathematics Education program at Western University, wherein online mind mapping has been included as a strategy for collaborative work for over three years. For this purpose, three different tools—Popplet, Mindmeister, and Mindomo—were used in the courses. This chapter describes the development of the mind mapping activities, along with general reflections in terms of engagement, representation, and expression.

Rationale

Some studies have documented how visual representations have helped students with diverse learning needs and preferences to understand concepts. For example, Balım (2013) showed that concept maps done in teams led to more active and participatory learning during lessons because they increased comprehension and recall. Similarly, Himangshu-Pennybacker (2016) found that collaborative concept maps had a positive impact on knowledge visualization and concept linkage. This is supported by other studies that show how concept maps can highlight students' contradictions (Johnson, 2016) and that mind maps can be useful to help students identify misconceptions and knowledge gaps (Wilson, Copeland Solas, & Guthrie-Dixon, 2016).

Also, some studies have documented student engagement and participation during collaborative building of visual representations. A key finding is that visual representations, whether concept maps or mind maps, can increase motivation and interest toward learning (Ahmed & Abdelraheem, 2016; Balım, 2013; Lin, Chang, Hou, & Wu, 2016). Specifically, Wilson et al. (2016) found that building mind maps affords a creative and fertile learning environment that can be motivating to students and supportive of varied learning needs.

Presenting information in multiple formats and providing options for students to participate and express their understandings are key aspects of inclusive learning. Mind maps can provide a new range of multimodal possibilities, such as layout, colour, image, and video, that can enrich student interaction through multimodal collaboration, discussion, and assessment. In this chapter, the UDL guidelines (CAST, 2018) will be used as a framework to describe and analyze results. The following sections will detail the development of the mind mapping activities used in the math education program at Western University, along with general reflections in terms of engagement, representation, and expression.

Application in Practice

Online mind mapping activities were incorporated using online activities as a support for face-to-face learning in three blended courses in the math education program at Western University. Three different mind mapping tools—Popplet, Mindmeister, and Mindomo—and different scaffolding techniques in terms of prompts and number of participants per group were explored. Each course will be treated as a case and is described later (see summary in Table 19.1). It is relevant to note that the focus of this chapter is the mind mapping implementation through the lens of UDL. For a more thorough description of the case studies along with experiential and learning outcomes comparing the three different tools and two different kinds of prompts, the reader may refer to Cendros and Gadanidis (2017).

Case 1

The first case was a computational thinking in mathematics education course in the Winter of 2016. It had a duration of nine weeks, two hours per week, where the five odd-numbered sessions were face-to-face and the four even-numbered sessions were online. Participants were 143 teacher candidates (TCs) who agreed to participate in the research, out of a total of 157, distributed among five sections. Each online week included the collaborative knowledge construction and reflection in small groups (four to seven participants) of mind maps through Popplet (http://popplet.com/), which replaced the more traditional, text-based discussion forum. Popplet was chosen initially due to its simplicity. The instructor and researchers believed that fewer features would facilitate an easier introduction to the activity.

There was a total of 31 small groups across the five sections. The mind mapping activity was implemented during every online week (weeks 2, 4, 6, and 8). Prior to each online week, TCs received a link with access to their group's mind map, which was initially blank. For weeks 6 and 8, each group used only one canvas; so for week 8, students continued ideas and topics within the mind map that they had begun in week 6. The prompts used by the instructor to guide TCs to develop the mind maps included an explanation on how Popplet can help students make connections between the online and in-class activities, a list of suggested topics to address in the mind map, and a video on how to use the tool. Figure 19.1 shows a mind map created by a group of students in Case 1.

TABLE 19.1 The Three Cases and Their Characteristics

	Term-Year	Course	Tool Used	Prompt	Participants
Case 1	Winter-2016	CT+ Math Education	Popplet	Topics List	143 (Set A)
Case 2	Fall-2016	CT+ Math Education	Mindmeister	Topics List	194 (Set B)
Case 3	Winter-2017	Math Methods	Mindomo	Questions	194 (Set B)

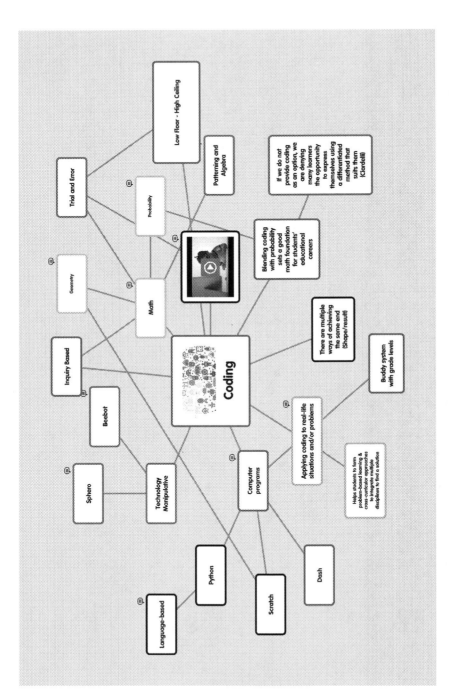

FIGURE 19.1 Sample Mind Map Created by Participants in Case 1

Source: http://bit.ly/case1map

Case 2

The second case was a new cohort of the computational thinking in mathematics education course, in the following Fall 2016. Characteristics of this case were the same as in Case 1 in terms of duration, mode of delivery, and contents. However, in this case, the number of participants was larger than in the first case, with 194 TCs (out of the 240 enrolled) agreeing to participate in the research. In regard to mind map construction, this case included the collaborative knowledge construction and reflection in larger groups (eight participants, as compared to four–seven in Case 1) using a different online tool, Mindmeister (www.mindmeister.com). The instructor and researchers decided to use Mindmeister after facing technical problems in the previous experience with Popplet. In this case, only weeks 2 and 4 required mind map construction. As a result, a total of 60 mind maps were created (30 from week 2 and 30 from week 4).

As in Case 1, TCs received a link with access to their group's mind map and a prompt to guide construction that included a list of suggested topics to address. In addition, an instructor-led live presentation was added in each section to provide opportunities for students to ask questions about how to use the tool. Additionally, tutorial videos about the use of Mindmeister were made available for students in their online course site. Figure 19.2 shows a mind map created by a group of students in Case 2.

Case 3

In the Winter of 2017, instructors decided to include the mind map activity in the math methods course for TCs. Since students in this program register for the entire year in sets of courses for the subject of their choice, participants of the mathematics education stream were simultaneously enrolled for the CT in mathematics education and the math methods courses. So, participants from Cases 2 and 3 belong to the same cohort (194 participants that gave permission, out of 240 enrolled). The math methods course had a total duration of 17 weeks, using mainly a face-to-face delivery mode coupled with an online learning component that included discussion groups and mind map development. The mind map activity was used during weeks 9 to 11.

Collaborative knowledge construction and reflection was done in groups of six to eight participants using a third online tool, Mindomo (www.mindomo.com/). In this case, the tool was chosen by the instructors because it is provided to teachers for free by Ontario's Ministry of Education. A total of 96 mind maps were obtained from this case (32 for each week). Figure 19.3 shows a mind map created by a group of students in Case 3.

Since this group of participants had prior familiarity with collaborative mind maps, instructors only provided a video about the tool and prompted TCs to create their own mind maps and invite the instructors to view them (rather than the

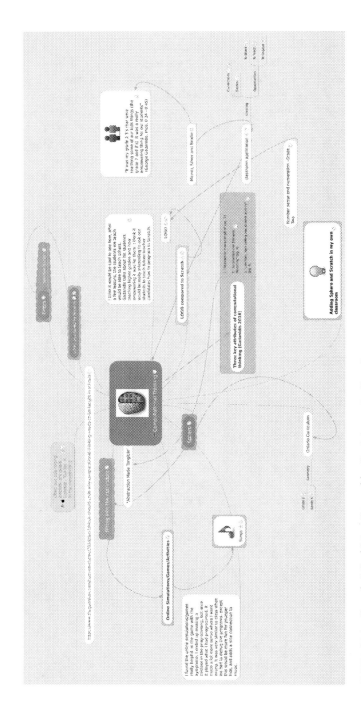

FIGURE 19.2 Sample Mind Map Created by Participants in Case 2

Source: http://bit.ly/case2map

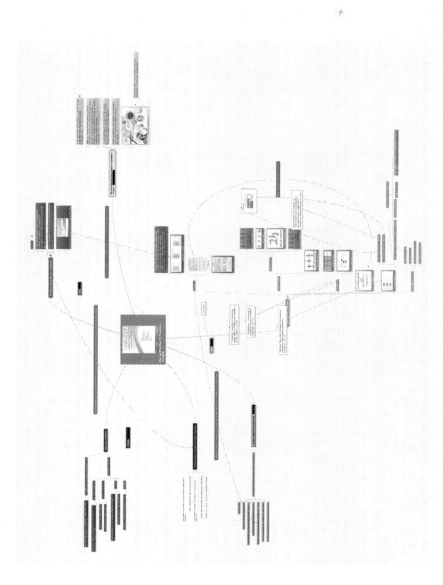

FIGURE 19.3 Sample Mind Map Created by the Participants in Case 3

Source: http://bit.ly/case3map

instructors creating blank canvases and sending the links to the TCs). In this case, instructors decided to use questions as prompts to guide the activity.

Reflections about UDL and the Online Mind Mapping Application

Engagement

The principle of multiple means of engagement was considered at the planning stage of these courses. Mind mapping was incorporated to foster variety in the online discussions by providing access to a new tool as an alternative to threaded forums. During the mind map activities, instructors observed evidence of negotiation and organization as group members worked together to complete the tasks. For example, some groups decided on the colour that each member would use for individual contributions. They then agreed that when connecting concepts, they would use a connector with the other person's colour in order to better visualize relationships between ideas.

Furthermore, the use of Mindomo in Case 3 responded to a need to increase relevance, value, and authenticity. The instructors purposefully selected this tool because it is approved by the Ontario Software Acquisition Program Advisory Committee (OSAPAC), which advises the Ministry of Education on the acquisition of provincial licenses for publicly-funded schools in Ontario. So, using Mindomo in the course provided TCs with an opportunity to become familiar with a visual tool they could later use in their own classrooms.

Representation

Even though the mind mapping activities were not intended to be presentations, they did seem to have impacts on student perceptions of the topics during the discussions. In end-of-course questionnaires, many students commented about organizational features of the mind maps. For example, one student wrote that mind maps "made information easy to be sorted and viewed." Another student described how the mind maps made it possible to see everyone's participation at a glance, which enabled students to decide easily where they wanted to include their contributions.

It is important to note, though, that this visual way of representing the discussion was found to be overwhelming for some students. Some expressed that seeing all contributions at a glance, with all the different colours and images, made it harder for them to understand what was going on in the discussion. This study did not assess if these students had particular difficulties in other academic activities or their daily lives, but perhaps the visual aspect of the mind mapping experience was an inadequate match for their learning style or individual learning needs. However, the tools do offer ways of customizing the information displays, allowing participants to select between outline and diagram views, and future implementations could inform students of this tool feature.

Action and Expression

Promoting multiple forms of action and expression was key in the mind mapping activity, as students were able to organize, display, and elaborate using images, words, and connecting lines to show their understandings. Variability in action and expression was evident in the mind maps, with some students using images, very little text (only concept headers), and lots of connectors to express their knowledge and others using long text notes attached to concepts to explain their thoughts. This kind of flexibility allowed participants to choose a mode of action/expression that suited their needs.

Conclusions and Recommendations

There are many online tools that can provide multiple ways for viewing, organizing, and engaging with course content. In order to meet students' diverse learning needs, it is beneficial for course developers and instructors to consider UDL guidelines when designing online learning experiences, whether it is as support of face-to-face courses or fully web-based ones. Online mind mapping implementations, such as the one described in this chapter, have the potential to cover some important UDL curricular guidelines (CAST, 2018), including:

- Vary demands and resources to optimize challenge (checkpoint 8.2).
- Foster collaboration and community (checkpoint 8.3).
- Optimize relevance, value, and authenticity (checkpoint 7.2).
- Offer ways of customizing the display of information (checkpoint 1.1).
- Illustrate through multiple media (checkpoint 2.5).
- Provide options for expression and communication (guideline 5).

Based on observations from the mind mapping cases described in this chapter, the involved researchers and instructors have been able to continue to improve these activities to implement with new student cohorts. In sum, lessons learned along the way have generated several guidelines:

- Allow participants to choose how to contribute to the mind map, whether it be through long text notes or concept imagery and connections. The prompts used should encourage and support multiple approaches.
- Inform students about display options for the visual information on mind maps. Demonstrate how to change the visualization of the mind map from a diagram to an outline.

- In the activity prompt, emphasize the importance of collaboration. Encourage participants to negotiate how they will distribute the concepts, colours, and layout and collectively decide on how they will respond to others' contributions, such as through connectors, notes, and additions of concepts to the same branch.

Finally, opportunities for further research emerge in the ways that online collaborative mind mapping can benefit people with disabilities who require support for reading, spelling, and/or handwriting. Beyond the power of visualization, perhaps mind mapping activities would provide supportive and mistake-tolerant access for these individuals.

References

Ahmed, A., & Abdelraheem, A. (2016). Investigating the effectiveness of digital—based concept mapping on teaching educational technology for undergraduate students. *Journal of Educational & Psychological Studies/Magallat Al-Dirasat Al-Tarbawiyyat Wa-Al-Bafsiyyat, 10*(4), 737–747.

Balım, A. G. (2013). Use of technology-assisted techniques of mind mapping and concept mapping in science education: A constructivist study. *Irish Educational Studies, 32*(4), 437–456. https://doi.org/10.1080/03323315.2013.862907

Brown, C., & Czerniewicz, L. (2014). Students' mindmaps of the role of technology in academic and social communication networks. In A. Archer & D. Newfield (Eds.), *Multimodal approaches to research and pedagogy* (pp. 91–107). New York: Routledge.

Buzan, T., & Buzan, B. (2010). *The mind map book: Unlock your creativity, boost your memory, change your life*. Hampshire, UK: Pearson, BBC Active.

CAST. (2018). *Universal design for learning guidelines version 2.2*. Retrieved from http://udlguidelines.cast.org

Cendros Araujo, R., & Gadanidis, G. (2017). Experiences of online collaborative mind mapping. In L. Gómez Chova, A. López Martínez, & I. Candel Torres (Eds.), *ICERI2017 Proceedings* (pp. 3690–3697). Seville, Spain: IATED.

Eisner, E. W. (2002). *The educational imagination: On the design and evaluation of school programs*. Upper Saddle River, NJ: Prentice Hall.

Gao, F., Zhang, T., & Franklin, T. (2013). Designing asynchronous online discussion environments: Recent progress and possible future directions. *British Journal of Educational Technology, 44*(3), 469–483. https://doi.org/10.1111/j.1467-8535.2012.01330.x

Himangshu-Pennybacker, S. (2016). Transforming science pedagogy: Using concept mapping to design an interdisciplinary approach to teaching middle school science. In A. Cañas, P. Reiska, & J. Novak (Eds.), *Innovating with concept mapping: CMC 2016. Communications in computer and information science* (pp. 265–274). Cham: Springer. https://doi.org/10.1007/978-3-319-45501-3_21

Hyerle, D. (2009). *Visual tools for transforming information into knowledge*. London: Corwin.

Johnson, L. L. (2016). Writing 2.0: How English teachers conceptualize writing with digital technologies. *English Education; Urbana, 49*(1), 28–62. Retrieved from https://search.proquest.com/docview/1831204826/fulltextPDF/2105384C0B214E37PQ/1?accountid=15115

Kalantzis, M., & Cope, B. (2015). Learning and new media. In *The Sage handbook of learning* (pp. 373–387). London: Sage Publications. https://doi.org/10.4135/9781473915213.n35

Lin, Y-T., Chang, C-H., Hou, H-T., & Wu, K-C. (2016). Exploring the effects of employing Google Docs in collaborative concept mapping on achievement, concept representation, and attitudes. *Interactive Learning Environments, 24*(7), 1552–1573. https://doi.org/10.1080/10494820.2015.1041398

Ng, W., & Hanewald, R. (2010). Concept maps as a tool for promoting online collaborative learning in virtual teams with pre-service teachers. In P. Lupion Torres & R. Marriot (Eds.), *Handbook of research on collaborative learning using concept mapping* (pp. 81–99). IGI Global. https://doi.org/10.4018/978-1-59904-992-2.ch005

Suthers, D. D., & Hundhausen, C. D. (2003). An experimental study of the effects of representational guidance on collaborative learning processes. *The Journal of the Learning of Sciences, 12*(2), 183–218.

Wilson, K., Copeland Solas, E., & Guthrie-Dixon, N. (2016). A preliminary study on the use of mind mapping as a visual-learning strategy, in general education science classes for Arabic speakers in the United Arab Emirates. *Journal of the Scholarship of Teaching and Learning, 16*(1), 31–52. https://doi.org/10.14434/josotl.v16i1.19181

20
HANDCRAFTED CUSTOMIZED CONTENT AND SCHOOL ACTIVITIES WITH NEWLY DEVELOPED TECHNOLOGIES

Shigeru Ikuta and Yumi Hisatsune

Introduction

More than 12 years ago, the first author started helping students with various difficulties by using Scan Talk code, developed by Olympus Co., Japan (Olympus, 1999). With it, voices/sounds were encoded, and links to the files were printed directly onto paper as two-dimensional dot codes. To reproduce the voices and/or other sounds, the students had to trace the fairly long dot codes with great care using a Scan Talk Reader or a Sound Reader device. This first system was a very powerful tool for students with difficulties, both because the specially designed software could be used to create original, handcrafted teaching materials focused on individual needs and desires, and because of its ease of use and low cost (Ikuta, Endo, Nemoto, Kaiami, & Ezoe, 2013; Ikuta et al., 2015). However, some students at special needs schools with mental and severe hand and finger challenges were unable to trace the long, straight Scan Talk codes correctly and were therefore unable to join in with class activities. Therefore, an alternative system was sought that would enable students to easily touch the dot codes with a sound pen to reproduce the voices/sounds clearly. Such a system could enable a greater number of students with disabilities to learn to use the dot code content. With the first author, Gridmark (2009) developed *Grid Onput* multimedia-enabled dot codes and began distributing related software, *Sound Linker* and *File Linker*, that made it possible for users to create their own handcrafted content. Presently, an iOS app version of the software will be released soon; the readers may now ask the first author to use it.

The first author created original sheets (called "Magical Sheets") with "Post-it"-like removable sticker icons overlaid with dot codes (Figure 20.1). The sheet has paper controller icons that allow users to change the mode from reading

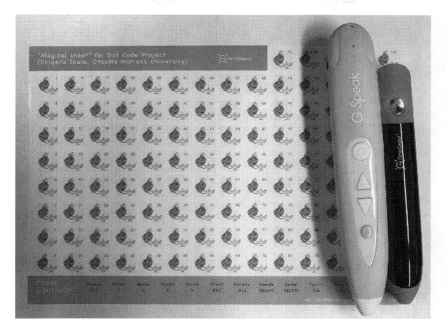

FIGURE 20.1 Magical Sheet with "Post-it"-Like Sticker Icons with Dot Codes, Together with Sound (G-Speak) and Scanner (G-Pen Blue) Pens

to recording, thus enabling students and teachers to record voices/sounds using the internal microphone of a sound pen and link the recordings to sticker icons directly. Using the provided tools, teachers are able to create their own original booklets. To do this, the "Post-it"-like sticker icons are first removed from the magical sheets and affixed to real items. Voices/sounds and multimedia are then linked to the icons. By touching an icon using a G-Speak sound pen, students are able to hear the voices/sounds very clearly (Ikuta et al., 2017; Ikuta, 2018). Further, using the G-Speak as a scanner pen, multimedia can be viewed on a computer screen or with the newer G-Pen Blue (with Bluetooth functionality) on iOS devices (Ikuta et al., 2019). The specially designed sheets with dot codes and associated software and hand-tools (sound and scanner pens) have been provided for free to schoolteachers in the United States, China, Korea, Oman, Saudi Arabia, United Arab Emirates, and Myanmar in addition to more than 180 schoolteachers in Japan.

Main Focus of the Chapter

Teachers of students with significant learning challenges are often faced with a quandary of whether the teaching materials and tools that had been effective for the previous year's students will be appropriate for new students. This is because the needs, desires, personalities, and other characteristics of each student tend to be unique to that student. Thus, differentiated content and special access tools need to be prepared individually for each student. This perspective is very much related to Universal Design for Learning (UDL), which is a framework for designing instruction to address the wide range of learner variation in today's inclusive classrooms (CAST, 2019). To create *original* teaching materials for each student, having access to easy-to-handle and free software is indispensable for schoolteachers; having access to less costly tools for enabling the use of such original content is also quite important (Dell, Newton, & Petroff, 2016).

The first author started organizing a research project with schoolteachers at both special-needs and general-education schools more than 12 years ago. The schoolteachers have since been creating original teaching materials with multimedia-enabled dot codes and using them in their teaching. The dot code technology addresses the need for specialized assistive technologies in a manner that enables schoolteachers to create the supports for specific learner needs.

Multimedia-Enabled Dot Codes

Grid Onput multimedia-enabled dot codes are comprised of sets of novel two-dimensional codes with extremely small dots (Gridmark, 2009). The dot codes can invisibly overlay any graphically-printed letter, photo, and illustration with little to no impact on the image design, meaning that the visual can be changed into an information-trigger icon. A maximum of four voices, sounds, movies, Web pages, and other media can easily be linked to each dot code icon. Simply touching the dot codes (printed on ordinary paper) with a sound pen (e.g., G-Speak) and/or a scanner pen with Bluetooth functionality (e.g., G-Pen Blue) enables students to access the digital information directly. In contrast, printing a document that includes the "invisible" Grid Onput dot codes involves industry-standard Cyan-Magenta-Yellow-Black (CMYK) processes that use a specially designed software program (*GM Authoring Tool*) and a costly printer. More specifically, carbon ink that absorbs infrared rays is used only for dot code printing, while non-carbon ink is used to print graphics.

School Activities With Multimedia-Enabled Dot Codes

Software for Creating Original Teaching Materials

Three software programs—*GM Authoring Tool*, *Sound Linker*, and *File Linker*—are available for Windows PC:

- The *GM Authoring Tool* puts the multimedia-enabled dot codes on one's designed document at any place, in any size, and in any number as the user might like. This specially designed, costly software has not yet been released into the market, but the readers may ask the first author to try it.

- The *Sound Linker* program creates content for a G-Speak sound pen and enables the user to link a maximum of four audio files to each dot-code icon with a simple drag-and-drop procedure. The content created is copied to the MicroSD Card in a sound pen—making it ready for use.
- The *File Linker* program creates a standalone application that can replay a maximum of four multimedia files linked to each icon on a screen of one's Windows PC to which the same G-Speak sound pen is connected. The created application (a standard executable file) is launched by double clicking on the file.
- A new program—*GCV*—will soon be available for Apple devices. *GCV* will enable users to easily create content with multimedia (such as movies, photos, audio files, and Web pages) and replay it on iOS devices (such as the iPad and the iPhone) using the G-Pen Blue with Bluetooth functionality.

School Activities With Original Handcrafted Teaching Materials

The second author is a teacher at Nakatsu Special Needs School and has created handcrafted, original content and conducted several school activities for a second grader (Student A) at her special needs school. Student A uses a wheelchair due to total disorders of the upper and lower limbs (paralysis of the extremities) caused by acute encephalitis sequelae (a condition that is the consequence of a previous acute inflammation of the brain). She has an epileptic seizure almost every day. In addition, the student always has stridor (a harsh vibrating noise when breathing) and cannot speak. She is apt to feel sick due to difficulties with body temperature regulation and receives nutrition by means of a nasogastric tube. She has nystagmus (rapid involuntary movements of the eyes) but can gaze and visually pursue. She enjoys good relationships with people, and she smiles brightly and laughs aloud when she feels happy. A goal for the student was that she could talk with teachers and other students in the class and enjoy such talking. The sound pen was identified as a possible communication tool for the student.

Let's Preside Over a Morning Meeting

Adaptations were made to meet the unique needs of this student. She had great difficulty with touching the "Post-it"-like sticker icons using the sound pen. Only when she was nervous could she grasp the sound pen. So, a handcrafted aid made of cardboard was created to support her touching of the icons with a sound pen. The teacher recorded the student's voice and linked the recordings to the sticker icons with the dot-codes pasted on the handcrafted cards. The cards were then used to enable the student to preside over a morning meeting in the class. One element of the morning meeting involved checking other students' physical conditions. The sticker icons were affixed near each student's photo, where the spoken names of each student and "How are you feeling today?" were linked.

On the day of her duty, Student A presided at a morning meeting in the class. Until then, the teacher had presided over it, instead of the student, by standing next to her. All the classmates were so surprised to hear their own names being spoken by the sound pen. In response to seeing how amazed her friends were, Student A smiled (Figure 20.2).

The student was able to preside over the morning meeting by touching icons with dot codes, which allowed her to ask questions to classmates by means of voice. She was observed smiling while watching the classmates reacting to her calling their names (such as their standing up and moving forward), following the replaying of the linked voices with the sound pen. Student A also expressed satisfaction that all her classmates paid attention to her activities. Other students expressed interest in presiding over the morning meeting together with her and to interact with her. To address her difficulty in grasping the sound pen, she could be supported with the aid of a cardboard with a gradient.

Investigation of Favorite Doughnuts

In a *social skill learning* activity in the school, all the classmates went to buy doughnuts, learning how to do shopping. However, Student A could not eat doughnuts since she took nutrition through a nasogastric tube. So, while other students

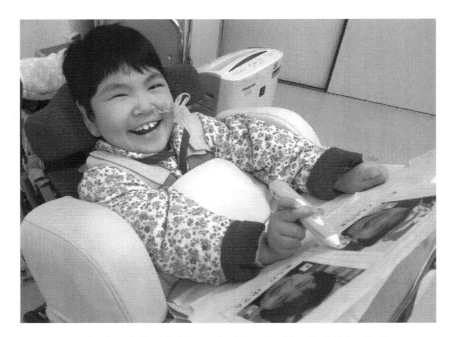

FIGURE 20.2 Student A Presided Over the Morning Meeting With a Smile

tried to buy doughnuts, she asked them about their favorite doughnuts. With the help of a sound pen, she asked each classmate to affix a seal on a space of a whiteboard corresponding to the doughnut she/he selected (see Figure 20.3). By touching an icon with dot codes with a sound pen, she also asked each student in other classes to affix the sticker icon corresponding to her/his favorite doughnut. In an *exchange learning* with a same regional general-education school, she also asked each second grader about her/his favorite doughnut by means of the same method noted earlier (Figure 20.4).

This activity was particularly lively. With the help of a sound pen, she asked classmates, "Which doughnut do you want to eat?" The second-grade classmates responded with, "I have eaten this [one]," "I like [this] chewy doughnut," and "It's sweet and yummy." Their responses to her leading question went on to produce wonderful conversations. Student A expressed enjoyment with these conversations, and they afforded her invaluable experiences with many students of a general-education school. Through the technology, Student A could communicate with many friends and experience the enjoyment of looking at how she/he selected a favorite doughnut. Student A smiled upon learning that many friends could not easily decide their favorite doughnuts and over how her classmates were gathering around her and talking to her.

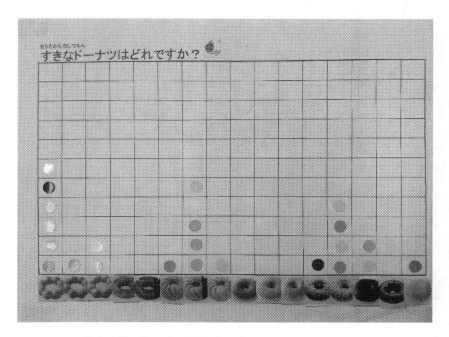

FIGURE 20.3 Seals Affixed on the Whiteboard

FIGURE 20.4 Exchange-Learning Activity Performed with a General-Education School in the Same Region

Conclusions

Original teaching materials created with multimedia-enabled dot codes are quite useful and effective for a student with acute encephalitis sequelae in promoting communications with others. It is crucial that schoolteachers develop their own *original* content accessible for all students in their classes, as each student has different thoughts, feelings, and learning histories. Students with nonverbal communication, in particular, have difficulty in expressing what they want to say. In such cases, tools such as the sound pen—which can reproduce the recorded voices of teachers, classmates, and parents—are often very effective. Student A, presented in this paper, was able to well understand that tools such as the sound pen could assist her in making her needs and desires known to others. The present school activities have described the importance and role that handcrafted materials could play in achieving greater access to instruction and learning for students who have special needs or disabilities, and to fully grasp how such materials can be used by educators to develop diversified and accessible learning environments for all students.

The UDL framework, which provides educators with parameters for differentiation and diversification of materials, and assistive technologies can reduce many barriers to both content and learning, such as providing more accessible and varied means of communication. The technology presented in this chapter supported school activities for students with severe disabilities through means of augmentative and alternative communication (AAC); the multimedia-enabled dot codes and software can aid schoolteachers in designing instruction that addresses the wide range of learner variation in today's inclusive classrooms. This integration of handcrafted or customized materials provides options for learners, as advocated in the UDL framework (Dalton, 2019).

For the development of focused school activities, collaboration with software and hardware is an important issue. The help of university students is also a strong motivation for the development of individual content. Collaboration with teachers from various special needs and general education schools may provide useful insights for the learning classification of each disability, which would assist both in the development of more focused software and hardware and in the sharing of activities for students with a variety of disabilities. International collaboration with teachers and researchers could also lead to new developments in materials designed for use by students with disabilities around the world.

The study was approved by the Ethics Committee of Otsuma Women's University. Before the study, the schoolteacher received permission from her principal to conduct the current school-based activities. The study's purpose and methods were explained orally, and informed consent was obtained from the student and her parent.

Acknowledgements

Shigeru Ikuta offers thanks for the support of "JSPS KAKENHI Grant Number: JP16K04844" and of the "Otsuma Grants-in-Aid for Individual Exploratory Research (Research Number: S2912)." The authors would like to thank eContentPro International (www.econtentpro.com) for the English language review.

References

Center for Applied Special Technology (CAST). (2019). *Until learning has no limits*. Retrieved from www.cast.org

Dalton, M. E. (2019). Diversity, disability, and addressing the varied needs of learners. In S. Ikuta (Ed.), *Handmade teaching materials for students with disabilities* (pp. 1–19). Hershey, PA: IGI Global. doi:10.4018/978-1-5225-6240-5.ch001

Dell, A. G., Newton, D. A., & Petroff, J. G. (2016). *Assistive technology in the classroom: Enhancing the school experiences of students with disabilities* (3rd ed.). Upper Saddle River, NJ: Pearson Education.

Gridmark. (2009). *Grid onput*. Retrieved from http://gridmark.co.jp/en/

Ikuta, S. (2018). Multimedia-enabled dot codes as communication technologies. In M. Khosrow-Pour (Ed.), *Encyclopedia of information science and technology* (4th ed., pp. 6464–6475). Hershey, PA: IGI Global. doi:10.4018/978-1-5225-2255-3.ch561

Ikuta, S., Endo, E., Nemoto, F., Kaiami, S., & Ezoe, T. (2013). School activities using handmade teaching materials with dot-codes. In D. G. Barres, Z. C. Carrion, & R. L-C. Delgado (Eds.), *Technologies for inclusive education: Beyond traditional integration approaches* (pp. 220–243). Hershey, PA: IGI Global. doi:10.4018/978-1-4666-2530-3.ch011

Ikuta, S., Morton, D., Kasai, M., Nemoto, F., Ohtaka, M., & Horiuchi, M. (2015). School activities with new dot code handling multimedia. In L. Lennex & K. Nettleton (Eds.), *Cases on instructional technology in gifted and talented education* (pp. 314–340). Hershey, PA: IGI Global. doi:10.4018/978-1-4666-6489-0.ch015

Ikuta, S., Urushihata, C., Ishitobi, R., Yamaguchi, K., Nemoto, F., & Nakui, H. (2017). Handmade content and school activities for autistic children with expressive language disabilities. In Y. Kats (Ed.), *Supporting the education of children with autism spectrum disorders* (pp. 85–115). Hershey, PA: IGI Global. doi:10.4018/978-1-5225-0816-8.ch006

Ikuta, S., Yamashita, S., Higo, H., Tomiyama, J., Saotome, N., Sudo, S., . . . Watanuki, M. (2019). Original teaching materials and school activities with multimedia-enabled dot codes. In S. Ikuta (Ed.), *Handmade teaching materials for students with disabilities* (pp. 50–75). Hershey, PA: IGI Global. doi:10.4018/978-1-5225-6240-5.ch003

Olympus. (1999). *Scan talk reader R 300 and personal computer software "sound print workshop"—new feeling multimedia that can easily print "voice" on paper* [Japanese]. Retrieved from www.olympus.co.jp/jp/news/1999b/nr990823r300j.jsp

21
CONNECTING THE WORLD IN A DISCONNECTED CLASSROOM

Vivian B. Intatano

Background

Filipino teachers are always ready for change, ones that will benefit the welfare of the Filipino learners. One of these changes is the effect of technology. *Technology* is a widely used word in conversation worldwide, as its impact is far-reaching across lines of age and gender. With increasing spread of technology tools and online resources, the use of information and communication technology (ICT) in the classroom is very important in providing opportunities for students in this information age. ICT has also become an important part of most modern-day functions of organizations and businesses (Zhang & Aikman, 2007). Computers began to appear in schools in the early 1980s, and ICT will likely be an important part of education for the next generation as well (Bransford, Brown, & Cocking, 2000).

Rodrigo (2001) stated that just like other developing nations, the Philippines resorted to ICT to improve the teaching and learning process. Likewise, Lachica (2015) stated that developing countries like the Philippines invest in ICT in education to decrease social inequalities among schools and their respective graduates. Education sectors are aware of how these technologies affect the lives of every student. The Department of Education (DepEd) is the agency of the Philippine government that is responsible for ensuring equal access to basic education in the Philippines and improving quality of service. In 2004, DepEd issued the *Guidelines on the Use of Computer Laboratories in Teaching and Learning* (DO 23, s. 2004), which states that a shift from teaching *about* technology to teaching *with* technology should be implemented. In 2009, DepEd launched the *Internet Connectivity Project and Directing All Public High Schools to Subscribe to Internet Connectivity Services* (DO 50, s. 2009). Thus, it is clear that the DepEd supports ICT integration in classroom instruction to enhance teaching and learning in all subject areas.

DepEd has demonstrated its commitment to ICT integration through funding, capacity building, facilities, and collaboration with non-governmental organization (NGO) support. It has incorporated a computer literacy program and development of 21st century skills as part of the K-12 curriculum. Although schools can choose to allocate funds from their budget to technology integration in general classrooms, there are still public schools that only teach about the technology tools in segregated ICT classes. For instance, the author has observed public schools that contain computer laboratories used to teach the technology, such as how to use MS Office, the Internet, and other applications, but provide no specific technology that teachers in other subject areas can use as part of their lessons.

It is understandable, then, why many teachers view ICT as a driver of change, a conduit for learning, and an instrument for teaching (Lachica, 2015). The Internet offers opportunities for students to tap into global expertise, which enables them to become part of a broader community and helps them to become more aware of the world around them through different learning environments, simulations, and computer-based activities for science, math, and language skills (Rodrigo, 2001). Indeed, the availability of an Internet connection for teachers and students is important to help them be updated with the issues relevant to the curriculum. For example, the *Text2teach* project of SEAMEO INNOTECH reduced absenteeism in grades 5 and 6 science classes, and students found science learning interesting and fun (Rodriguez, 2008). Teachers in the project were trained to use digital satellite broadcasting and video materials that were transmitted via mobile phone technology.

Technology is also being used to support students with special needs, both in software or hardware forms (Balmeo et al., 2014). For instance, a special education teacher in a public school in Manila has been studying the use of a reading program, *Alpabasa*, with her students who have intellectual disabilities (personal communication, L. Galvez, February 10, 2019). Alpabasa is a reading program that uses manipulatives and videos to provide reading practice and instruction. The teacher has thus far observed how eager her students appear to be to learn how to read using the videos in the Alpabasa program.

To make ICT a transformative tool in the teaching and learning process, there is need for a clear strategic plan, concrete actions, continuous measurement and evaluation, and strong leadership. Caluza et al. (2017) conducted a needs assessment to measure the level of ICT competencies of teachers in order to design an ICT program suitable for their professional development needs. They found teachers have basic knowledge of ICT but not full competence. The teachers needed training to become proficient in the use of technology for teaching and other related tasks. In addition, challenges such as budget constraints, human resources, time, infrastructures, technical issues, and teacher motivation can limit instructional ICT use, as was found in a recent Philippines case study (Kubota, Yamamoto, & Morioka, 2019). Even with limited resources, strong leadership can make a difference in supporting teachers in their use of ICT as part of classroom instruction.

This chapter uses the term *disconnected classroom* to refer to schools without technology available for teachers and students to be used for classroom instruction. There is a need for policy development for equitable distribution of ICT resources in all learning areas (Manaligod, 2012). As mentioned previously, though schools may have some ICT tools, they may only be using them for learning how to use or operate computers and other applications, but not in teaching lessons. Due to the limited resources of the Philippines government, a public-private partnership program needs to be strengthened. Also, resources from nearby universities can help to address some of the challenges, with collaborations between schools and universities fostering workshops, seminars, and other teacher trainings to help address ICT knowledge gaps. In this chapter, the author explores how Philippine teachers cope with challenges in using ICT, particularly when their schools do not have sufficient facilities. For this study, six teachers were interviewed to find out their best practices and approaches to countering these challenges.

Study Highlights

Participant Profiles

A convenience sample of six public secondary (junior high) schoolteachers who utilize technology for classroom instruction were interviewed. Four teachers were interviewed face-to-face, and the other two had online interviews with the author due to their remote locations. The focus of the interviews was on their best practices in using technology in classroom instruction, specifically the frequency of using technology, how they cope with the challenges they meet in using technology, and how they prepare lessons for diverse learners. Four of the participants teach in Manila, two at one school (JC and Dharyl) and two at another school (Catherine and Bernadette). Marivi came from the province of Mindanao, which is in the Southern part of the Philippines, and Rose is from the province of Bicol. Table 21.1 summarizes frequency of the participant instructional technology use.

Key Findings

When asked about who provides the facilities for their technology use, only Marivi reported school-provided facilities, which were funded in part through a partnership of the DepEd and an adopt-a-school NGO. The adopt-a-school program is a DepEd initiative that encourages private companies and organizations to provide schools with the facilities needed in order to implement the curriculum. The schools where the other participants are teaching each have a computer laboratory, but these labs are used for technology classes offered through the Vocational Department. The Vocational Department has computer lab priority, which means

TABLE 21.1 Participant Instructional Technology Use

Participant	Frequency of Instructional Technology Use
Teacher Marivi	Every day
Teacher Dharyl	2–3 times a week
Teacher JC	3 times a week
Teacher Catherine	1–2 times a week
Teacher Rose	Once a week
Teacher Bernadette	Twice a month

that other subject teachers can only use the labs when they are not being used by the vocational teachers. The school in which Catherine and Bernadette teach also has an e-classroom that was initiated by the Science Department and funded by the school, and it can be used by all teachers, if they will be using technology in their lessons. Table 21.2 details the teacher responses in regards to facilities.

In regards to the use of online resources, only Rose said that she does not use them in her classroom teaching due to a lack of Internet connectivity. The others reported using online resources such as games, YouTube videos, Google Classroom, Quipper, Edutopia, Kahoot, and other formative assessment tools, sometimes through their own personal data connections. Catherine and Bernadette are able to use an e-classroom where Internet connection is available, which they find helpful in enabling them to use varied instructional technology tools as they prepare their lessons. They also use crowdsourcing, involving parents to help them in providing data connections that students can use in their classes. Sometimes, they download materials, such as videos and simulations, to be able to use them without an Internet connection.

In regards to using technology to promote inclusive learning, it was evident from the participant responses that they valued careful planning, including considering the wide variety of available tools, matching the varied skills of their students with the tools that they will use, and seeing to it that activities are engaging and interactive to meet the needs of the diverse learners. Furthermore, one of the participants said that her students have a voice in choosing what applications they want to use in learning activities, as long as the tools are relevant and beneficial for the lesson. For example, she asks her students which application to use for games - Kahoot, Poll Everywhere, or both. Oftentimes, the decision she makes depends upon the learning needs of individual students. Another teacher uses a tool known as Strategic Intervention Materials (SIM) to meet the needs of diverse learners. SIM is a teacher-made learning tool composed of different activity cards used to improve the performance levels of students. Overall, the participants seem to believe that a successful integration of technology in classroom instruction needs preparation, skills in using technology, and understanding of the diversity of learners in the classroom. This small sample of teacher respondents offers evidence

TABLE 21.2 School Facilities for Teaching with Technology

Participant	Facilities Described
Teacher Marivi	We have provisions from the Department of Education under the DepEd Computerization Program (DCP) in which they provide my school with the 100 units of computers, four sets of LCDs, speakers, and four white screens. We are also one of the recipients of the Global Filipino School adopt-a-school program under the partnership of Globe Telecom and DepEd. We have eight units of laptops, new models of LCDs (small ones), eight HP printers, and more. We also have personal property in terms of laptops used in the classroom by a number of teachers.
Teacher Dharyl	Sometimes when the ICT room or TechVoc computer lab is available. Most of the time, personal property.
Teacher JC	When I was starting, I usually borrowed the school's LCD projector from time to time from the in-charge custodian. Aside from that, most of my co-teachers in the department bought their own, so it was from them I usually borrowed then. It was only three years ago that I bought my own projector. On a side comment, borrowing facilities like such from the school custodian usually takes time and would require extra effort in convincing the custodian to lend it to you.
Teacher Catherine	The school provides because we have e-classroom where we can bring our students to use computers with Internet connection. But since the e-classroom is just one and if it is used by another teacher, I can't use it often. So, there are times that I use my own equipment and even my own data connection if I need to use online applications.
Teacher Rose	The school does not provide. I use my own personal property.
Teacher Bernadette	The school has e-classroom. But inside my classroom I use my own laptop and projector.

of interest, current practice, and apparent continuing need for improvements in ICT inclusive integration in Philippine schools.

Conclusion

The Government of the Philippines supports and advocates for the effective use of ICT in classroom instruction through policy and programs such as the adopt-a-school program that help provide the facilities needed for ICT integration in classroom instruction. There is evidence that Filipino teachers seem to recognize the value of technology in classroom instruction, though they often face challenges of resource limitations. Lack of facilities does not always deter ICT integration, as some teachers purchase and use their own technology as part of their overall instructional strategy to reach diverse learners. Further, inclusive instruction is also happening in the Philippines using teacher-made strategies such as SIM (Strategic Intervention Materials) that can be used without significant costs for technology resources.

References

Balmeo, M. L., Nimo, E. M. A., Pagal, A. M., Puga, S. C., Quiño, A. D., & Sanwen, J. L. (2014). Integrating technology in teaching students with special learning needs in the SPED schools in Baguio City. *IAFOR Journal of Education, 2*(2), 149–178.

Bransford, J. D., Brown, A. L., & Cocking, R. R. (2000). *How people learn: Brain, mind, experience, and school committee on developments in the science of learning.* Washington, DC: National Academy Press.

Caluza, L. J. B., Verecio, R. L., Funcion, D. G. D., Quisumbing, L. A., Gotardo, M. A., Laurente, M. L. P., . . . Marmita, V. (2017). An assessment of ICT competencies of public school teachers: Basis for community extension program. *IOSR Journal of Humanities and Social Science, 22*(3), 1–13.

Department of Education. (2004). *Guidelines on the use of computer laboratories in teaching and learning (DO 23, s. 2004).* Retrieved from www.deped.gov.ph/2004/03/25/do-23-s-2004-guidelines-on-the-use-of-computer-laboratories-in-teaching-and-learning/

Department of Education. (2009). *Launching the DepEd internet connectivity project and directing all public high schools to subscribe to internet connectivity services (DO 50, s. 2009).* Retrieved from www.deped.gov.ph/2009/05/15/do-50-s-2009-launching-the-deped-internet-connectivity-project-and-directing-all-public-high-schools-to-subscribe-to-internet-connectivity-services/

Kubota, K., Yamamoto, R., & Morioka, H. (2019). *Promoting ICT education in developing countries: Case Study in the Philippine.* Retrieved from www.researchgate.net/publication/228655099_Promoting_ICT_education_in_developing_countries_Case_Study_in_the_Philippine

Lachica, L. P. F. (2015). Classroom communication and ICT integration: Public high school teachers' notions. *International Journal on Integrating Technology in Education, 4*(2), 1–11.

Manaligod, H. J. T. (2012). *Integration of information & communication technology in public secondary schools in metro-Manila, Philippines* (Doctoral dissertation). Retrieved from https://minerva.usc.es/xmlui/bitstream/handle/10347/6112/rep_250.pdf?sequence=1

Rodrigo, M. T. (2001). Information and communication technology use in Philippine public and private schools. *Loyola Schools Review: School of Science and Engineering, 1,* 122–139.

Rodriguez, C. (2008). Building teachers' capacity to make better use of ICT in Philippines schools. In E. Meleisea (Ed.), *ICT in teacher education: Case studies from the Asia-Pacific region* (pp. 74–85). Bangkok: UNESCO. Retrieved from https://unesdoc.unesco.org/ark:/48223/pf0000156757

Zhang, P., & Aikman, S. (2007). Attitudes in ICT acceptance and use. In J. A. Jacko (Ed.), *Proceedings of the 12th international conference on human computer interaction* (pp. 1021–1030). Berlin: Springer-Verlag.

22

SNAPSHOT—WEARABLE ASSISTIVE TECHNOLOGY

An Illuminated Glove Project With Conductive Thread and LilyPad Technology

Cindy L. Anderson and Kevin M. Anderson

Background

One of the authors of this snapshot has a rare disease known as *Ledderhose Disease* (Genetic and Rare Diseases Information Center, 2019). This disease causes fibromas filled with tissue that appear on the bottom of the feet, thus limiting the author's walking. A disability scooter is used to navigate long distances. However, in crowded places, people tend to not see the scooter below eye level. This limits the user's mobility in many environments. The authors developed a solution in the wearable project that will be described next.

Project Design

A blinking glove cover was designed to make the scooter visible in all environments, reflecting universal design principles (National Disability Authority, 2014). To create the glove, the project used conductive thread and a needle, a TinyLily, a Lilypad coin battery holder, Lilypad light-emitting diode (LED) lights, and a circular elastic bandage that acted as a glove cover. The resulting product provided blinking signal functionality that showed the presence of the disability scooter.

To develop the device, the authors sought out a plan for a stitched circuit that would meet their needs and eventually adapted the plan from Sparkfun's LilyTiny Plush Monster with blinking eyes (Sparkfun, 2019), adding an additional LED light. The steps for constructing the circuit are outlined in Table 22.1, with the completed circuit design shown in Figure 22.1.

The authors cut off a glove-length piece of tubular elastic elbow bandage. A needle with conductive thread was used to stitch the coin battery holder onto the bandage. Then, a seam was stitched from the positive connection of the LilyPad

TABLE 22.1 Steps for Constructing an LED Project

1. Select and cut a length of tubular elastic bandage (hand-length).
2. Using conductive thread for all sewing, attach the battery holder.
3. Connect the battery holder to the TinyLily microprocessor (+ side).
4. Connect the battery holder to the TinyLily microprocessor (− side).
5. Connect the + side of the LED lights to the TinyLily (+ side) in series.
6. Connect the − side of the LED lights to the TinyLily (− side) in series.
7. Insert the battery and test the connections using the on/off switch.

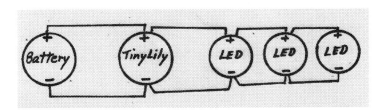

FIGURE 22.1 Diagram of the Completed Circuit

coin cell battery holder to the positive connection of the TinyLily microprocessor which was stitched to the elastic, just below the location of the index finger. This microprocessor controls the blinking speed of the LED lights, with three speeds of twinkling available. A medium blinking speed was chosen.

Conductive stitching was attached to the appropriate terminal of the TinyLily microprocessor, and the thread circuit was continued up the index finger where the positive end of the first LilyPad LED light was attached with stitches. The stitching then continued from this positive end of the first LED and to the positive ends of the second and third LEDs. This stitching continued up the index finger, connecting one circuit element to the next positive one. The thread was snipped at the last of the three LED lights. The circuit then repeated, beginning at the negative end of the last LED light and continuing in the same manner through the negative ends of the three LED lights, connecting to the negative end of the TinyLily microprocessor, and finishing at the negative end of the LilyPad coin cell battery holder. When stitching was complete, a coin cell battery was installed and the battery holder off/on switch was tested to see if the LED lights blinked as programmed.

The resulting glove cover slips over the scooter user's hand or driving glove, so that the driver can raise his or her hand when wanting to enhance visibility. It can also be used to facilitate turns, using bicycle hand signals. In this way, crowds who do not regularly look down to the level of a scooter will see the blinking lights and avoid tripping over the disability scooter and its rider.

This wearable project was tested at the Walt Disney World theme park in Orlando, Florida. During a crowded night at the Magic Kingdom park, the blinking glove cover enabled surrounding crowd members to see the blinking lights in the dark and avoid the scooter and its rider. This enhanced the accessibility of the environment and made the theme park experience more universally designed for the rider.

Conclusion

This project is an example of a simple technology modification that can be made to support the differing needs of learners. It uses materials that are widely available at hobby shops or online retailers, with a total project cost of $25 or less. Further, this type of activity can be incorporated as a service learning experience in teacher preparation courses to show how such simple hands-on projects may be undertaken as teacher-led or student-led activities in adapting teaching materials, toys, and learning devices for specific learning needs. It can be a worthwhile learning opportunity for beginning teachers to see that materials may be easily planned, adapted, and utilized through the perspective of inclusive instructional design.

References

Genetic and Rare Diseases Information Center. (2019). *Ledderhose disease*. Retrieved from https://rarediseases.info.nih.gov/diseases/6873/ledderhose-disease

National Disability Authority. (2014). *Centre for excellence in universal design: What is universal design*. Retrieved from http://universaldesign.ie/What-is-Universal-Design/

Sparkfun. (2019). *LilyTiny plush monster*. Retrieved from https://learn.sparkfun.com/tutorials/lilytiny-plush-monster

23

SNAPSHOT—AQUATIC ADVENTURES

Deep Dive Investigation of UDL Through a Pond Keepers Project

Juliet Boone

Background

Pond Keepers is an educational initiative of a local nature conservation, Mohonk Preserve, that has been adapted for use in a New York high school class of students identified with a range of developmental disabilities. The environmental educator creates classroom mini-habitats that mirror local ponds, using available organisms to create an ecosystem. Pond Keepers have an opportunity, through hands-on activities, to study the diverse ways in which organisms breathe, feed, move, defend themselves and respond to pollution.

Rationale

The program contains a variety of learning activities within a 10 lesson unit. Students independently or with a team select from and complete the learning activities in their preferred order. The unit demonstrates how globally available educational technology applications can be adapted to study flora and fauna that are local to the students in their part of the world. Also, it facilitates online student interaction and supports development of global competencies through engagement around issues, like pollution, that affect local ecosystems as well as have broader applications. Through these processes, the unit supports multiple means of engagement for the students, one of the three core UDL principles (CAST, 2018).

Technology in the unit provides options that help learners develop sustained effort. For some, this is developed through collaboration and community. For others, grit is augmented through frequent, mastery-oriented feedback facilitated via technology. In this program, gamification with Kahoot, Quizlet Live and Brainpop quizzes (played with buzzers) increases the motivation to accept challenges, and thus to learn content. The gamification dimension provides immediate feedback and harnesses student interest (David, 2016).

Highlights

Multiple Means of Engagement

The students tend to cater to the tadpoles and avidly watch as they grow legs and lose tails. Students are provided opportunities to contribute to a tadpole Padlet (a digital bulletin board tool), as well as a paper-based bulletin board. The tadpole activity, "What's the Job of the Tadpole?," focuses on ecological relationships and has a work-based-learning emphasis. Propelled by natural curiosity and emotional connection with tadpoles, students explore and post jobs that in any way connect with amphibians. They investigate and report on topics ranging from New York state environmental laws (such as those that prohibit the removal of amphibians without appropriate licensing), food webs, pollution, wetlands, water technology and life cycles.

Digitized Craft

Students create a pond-craft bulletin board (see Figure 23.1) that combines formative assessment, review and interaction with the larger school community through an interactive online Thinglink (www.thinglink.com/scene/109772520840128 1025). They post QR codes around the school, inviting others to read their summaries and take their Google Forms mini-quizzes and Kahoot challenge quizzes on the creature or life process of their choice. They monitor and analyze participation using the data generated from the quizzes.

Multiple Means of Action and Expression

In order to make the learning activities more authentic, students are invited to use the pond facts to write thank you notes to the Pond Keepers scholarship benefactors and educators. Students value their artifacts because they are included in their electronic portfolios for showcasing their learning and experiences to their families, learning community and prospective employers. Learning activities and artifacts include:

- Stop-motion animations that depict adaptations and ecological relationships and pollution and incorporate homemade kinetic sand (to portray pond ecosystems) and other crafts
- Images captured from document camera and digital microscope, and incorporated into posters created on Smore (web-based newsletter tool)
- Poetry that incorporates observed breathing, feeding and defense strategies
- Demonstrations of ecological relationships through computer programing using Hummingbird, Snap, and Scratch

FIGURE 23.1   Pond-Craft Bulletin Board with QR Code to Interactive Online Thinglink

References

CAST. (2018). *CAST: About universal design for learning*. Retrieved from www.cast.org/our-work/about-udl.html#.W2Sk1yhKg2w

David, L. (2016). *Learning theories: Gamification in education*. Retrieved from www.learning-theories.com/gamification-in-education.html

SECTION 5
Issues in the Design of Accessible Instructional Materials

24

UNIVERSAL ACCESS IN ONLINE DISTANCE EDUCATION

A Case Study From the Philippines

Melinda dela Peña Bandalaria

Introduction

The right to education is recognized by all nations. As such, it has become an expectation for governments to provide education opportunities to all of its citizens not only because it is a social responsibility but also because of other imperatives in which education has direct and indirect impact on the country's overall performance and status. As stated by UNESCO (2019),

> Education itself is an empowering right and one of the most powerful tools by which economically and socially marginalized children and adults can lift themselves out of poverty and participate fully in society. In order to do so there must exist equality of opportunity and universal access.

However, UNESCO also pointed out that "millions of children and adults remain deprived of educational opportunities, many as a result of social, cultural and economic factors" (ibid.). Personal circumstances also often present access barriers to conventional ways of learning, like the physical condition of the individual. The UN Convention on the Rights of Persons with Disabilities specifically mentioned the rights of this group to education, information and communication as being fundamental to enjoying all human rights and freedom (NCDA, 2019). The conceptualization of Universal Design for Learning (UDL) provides strategy to consider in addressing the identified barriers to education as articulated by UNESCO. In general, UDL means "meeting the diverse and variable needs of all students in your classroom" (New Zealand Ministry of Education, 2019). UDL originated as a framework used primarily in face-to-face classrooms (Rose & Meyer, 2002). Given the increasing integration of modern information and communication technologies (ICTs) in education and proliferation of open distance eLearning offerings, models of integrating the UDL principles in this mode of learning have become necessary.

The Philippines Case Study

The Philippines is a developing country where all the barriers to education as articulated by UNESCO are present. In addition to the challenge of addressing these barriers, there is also the additional concern of working toward the achievement of the sustainable development goals (SDGs), which involves every citizen, no matter their context. Sustainable development goal #4 (SDG#4), also referred to as *the Education Agenda 2030*, specifically states *quality education*, but embedded in this goal are targets that imply *inclusivity*, or the making available to all citizens the educational opportunities they need in order to be productive members of society (United Nations, 2019). Specific mention is made regarding the inclusion of the vulnerable sectors, such as women, persons with disabilities, indigenous peoples and children in vulnerable situations. Likewise, specific mention is made regarding access to affordable and quality technical, vocational and tertiary education (including university), as well as to the knowledge and skills needed to promote and contribute to sustainable development.

One indicator of a country's competitiveness status is the *Global Competitiveness Index*, which provides insights for the country's drivers of productivity and prosperity. It consists of 12 pillars—institutions, infrastructure, macroeconomic environment, health and primary education, higher education and training, goods market efficiency, labor market efficiency, financial market development, technological readiness, market size, business sophistication and innovation (World Economic Forum, 2017). Notable is the fact that these pillars are either directly or indirectly related to education; either it is education itself or education is an input for the pillar to perform well.

One Philippine mechanism to facilitate access to education opportunities is the Republic Act 10650, or the *Open Distance Learning Act* (Republic of the Philippines, 2014). Implementing courses and programs in open distance eLearning (ODeL) mode can already be considered as an initiative to promote access to education. As implied, ODeL is a mode of instructional delivery that combines the basic features of distance education. Though ODeL involves the physical separation of learners from the teachers, the university and other elements of the teaching and learning environment, it employs modern and networked technologies (via the Internet) to deliver instructional content and learner support services. This is the mode of instructional delivery employed by the University of the Philippines Open University (UPOU), one of the constituent units of the University of the Philippines, the only national university in the country. Offering programs in ODeL revealed learning barriers that drove development of the *Universal Access to Learning for Development Framework (UAL4D)*, in which UDL is the main component. Moreover, in ODeL, the use of assistive technologies, including hardware, software and peripherals, can be used to enable individuals with visual and hearing impairments, hand function limitations and speech impairments (NIH, 2019) to participate fully in a learning experience.

Access Barriers in a Distance eLearning Context

Various access barriers in Filipino ODeL course offerings were identified, and they became the imperatives for the UAL4D initiative. Each of these barriers are described in further detail next.

Geographical Location of the Learners

The Philippines is a developing country in Southeast Asia with a population of more than 105 million. It is an archipelagic country consisting of 7,107 islands. In her paper "Geographies of Social Exclusion: Education Access in the Philippines," Symaco (2013) cited natural instabilities, conflict areas in some parts of the country and remote geographic features as problems for education access.

Poverty/Financial Constraints

Poverty is a significant barrier to education access (Montgomery College, 2017). Specific to the Philippines, poverty is a primary reason for why students leave school both at the basic education and higher education levels (Pennington, 2017). Years before the implementation of the K-12 Program (Republic Act No. 10533), the education system in the Philippines was already characterized by high drop-out rates from basic to higher education. Of the 100 pupils who enter Grade 1, only 68 will complete 6th grade, only 57 will then go on to high school, and ultimately only 42 will graduate (Gutierrez, 2013). Unfortunately, out of these 42 who finish tertiary education, they also face another problem, that of *job mismatch*. In 2017, the estimated 1.2 million who would finish college were projected to be facing difficulty in landing jobs because of the growing mismatch between their training and the skills required by most employers (Depasupil, 2017).

The impact of poverty to access of basic education has resulted in half of school children dropping out of school (Philippine Institute for Development Studies, 2016), and the situation is not much different in higher education. The 2016 *Global Education Monitoring Report* examined disparities between the richest and poorest students in terms of completion of higher education. It found that in 2013, of those who completed at least four years of higher education, 52% came from the richest households and only 1% from the poorest families.

Physical Disabilities

Based on a household survey in 2010, 1.57% of the Philippines population had a disability (Philippine Statistics Authority, 2013). About half of these were males (50.9%) and the majority were in the working age group of 13–64 years old

(Philippine Statistics Authority, 2013). The approximately 1.6 million Filipinos could contribute to the country's productivity and have greater economic independence if they were provided with relevant training and skills.

Technology and the Digital Divide

Technology is an important resource to facilitate full participation by students to learning activities. This is more critical in the context of technology-driven modes of learning like ODeL. Technology and the digital divide exists in the following forms: lack of physical access to hardware and software, including the Internet; lack of skills needed to use the hardware and software; costs involved in accessing needed hardware and software; and language barriers. In 2017, only 60% of Filipinos had accessed to the Internet (Subido, 2017). The digital divide also results in lack of access to information as well as social exclusion.

Courses and Learning Materials Not Designed for Universal Access

There is a need for greater conscious effort to integrate the principles and features of Universal Design for Learning (UDL) in online programs and courses in order to facilitate full participation of all learners. Course sites and contents need to be accessible to learners with visual and hearing impairments as well as other disabilities. Moreover, costs of learning resources prescribed to achieve learning goals can prohibit some from being successful in the education environment.

Fragmented Approach to Inclusive Education

In some cases, design for inclusivity covers minimal aspects of the learner's activities. For instance, inclusive practices could be more widely implemented in areas of learner support and other administrative processes like enrollment, library, counseling, etc.

The UAL4D Framework: Components and Strategic Implementation Mechanics

To address these barriers, the University of the Philippines Open University developed the *UAL4D Framework*. There are six key components of this framework (see Table 24.1), and each will be described next.

University Website Redesigned to Adopt the Website Content Accessibility Guidelines

The university website (www.upou.edu.ph/), which contains the basic information about programs, courses and how students can avail of these learning

TABLE 24.1 Key Components of the Universal Access to Learning for Development (UAL4D) Framework

1. University website redesigned to adopt the *Web Content Accessibility Guidelines*.
2. Student Portal redesigned.
3. Course materials as Open Educational Resources (OERs).
4. Massive open distance eLearning (MODeL) courses.
5. Access through mobile phones.
6. Links to industry.

opportunities, was redesigned to integrate the different features contained in the *Web Content Accessibility Guidelines (WCAG 2.0) (W3C Web Accessibility Initiative, 2019)*. Web content included text, images and sounds and code or markup that defined structure and presentation. The design team felt that the university website was a key place to start, as it is often the first point of call for those who are interested in university opportunities. This component aimed to address the barrier of information access, and the redesigned website made web content more accessible to all users and responsive to mobile phone access.

Student Portal Redesigned

The Student Portal (http://our.upou.edu.ph/student/) is a web-based application that contains student academic records and connections to the different support services. Like the university website, the Student Portal was redesigned to better follow WCAG 2.0. Mobile responsiveness is another aim of this redesign.

Course Materials as Open Educational Resources (OERs)

Study guides and lessons within the course packages have been expanded to multimedia formats, e.g., video, text and podcast, to cater to different learning preferences and learners' contexts. These materials are mostly Open Educational Resources (OERs) and are licensed under Creative Commons (CC-BY-NC-ND) to facilitate free/open access to learning. The University has a repository for all the materials it has produced—the *UPOU Networks* (http://networks.upou.edu.ph/), which is an open access site. The UPOU Networks facilitate learning engagements that are essential for course and degree completion at no cost. The UPOU Networks also contains open access eJournals and eBooks and can be accessed using a mobile phone. This component of the UAL4D also addresses poverty, physical disabilities and potential conflicts of learning schedule with other personal and professional/work engagements. The ubiquity of the whole mechanism allows anyone to learn anywhere and anytime and using any gadget that is accessible to the learner.

Massive Open Distance eLearning (MODeL) Courses

MODeL courses are designed using the concept and principles of massive open online courses (MOOCs) (Drake, O'Hara, & Seeman, 2015). MODeL courses have the following features:

- designed to accommodate massive enrollment (150 learners and up)
- are open such that there are no qualification requirements for an individual to enroll and be part of the learning program, no course fees and no limit to the number of participants
- offered online or make use of the Internet to make courses ubiquitous and available to the learners wherever they are
- designed with defined learning objectives and assorted lessons to help students achieve the learning objectives through the different types of interaction—learner-teacher; learner-learner; learner-content; and learner-community of practice (Barasa, 2014)
- assessed by certifications used to validate and attest the learning acquired
- provided assorted, asynchronous learning engagements
- diversified course materials to be available in multimedia formats, which lend themselves to different learning contexts and preferences (see Figure 24.1)
- designated course materials as OERs to facilitate access to lessons and other learning engagements)

The University MOOCs are also being aligned with the *Philippines Qualification Framework (PQF)* (RA 10968), which is aimed at institutionalizing the harmonized qualifications that should be achieved at the different levels of education. The MOOCs are also aligned with University objectives, including the following:

1. Response to the *Paris Message*, which projected demand for higher education to reach more than 400 million by 2030 and called for responses from the global education community to provide accessible, affordable and quality higher education through open and non-formal learning activities (UNESCO, 2015).
2. Provide *universal access* to lifelong learning opportunities to school leavers at various levels and borderless Filipino workers who need continuing professional development programs.
3. Enhance quality education in the country and contribute to the attainment of all 17 sustainable development goals, with education as the prime mover of each of the goals.
4. Address the gap that exists between the skills possessed by college graduates and the knowledge and skills required by industries (job mismatch) in order to face concerns of unemployment and underemployment.

FIGURE 24.1 Sample Learning Objectives/Resources in Multimedia Formats

In 2018, the University started offering the following certification programs: ODeL (Open Distance eLearning), Child Rights Protection and Promotion Certification, Technology for Teaching and Learning, eService Management and Business Analytics (Business Management Track and Information Technology Track). Each program consists of a set of three to four MOOCs. Completion of each MOOC entitles the learner to a Certificate of Completion; and after completing the required MOOCs and passing the final comprehensive assessment, the learner is given the associated University Certificate.

Access through Mobile Phones

UAL4D also includes design of websites, learning portals and course materials for access through mobile phones. Using mobile phones is also supported by the government project of providing free wi-fi in public places (Ranada, 2017). In

Access our courses through your phones

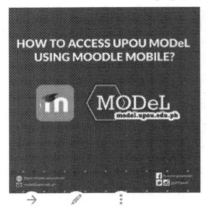

FIGURE 24.2   Instructions on How to Access the Courses Using Mobile Phone

2017, there were 110 mobile cellular subscriptions for every 100 people in the Philippines (World Bank, 2019), so being able to access learning through these devices can expand learning opportunities (see Figure 24.2).

Links to Industry

The university links with industry for a seamless transition from university to employment. One example is the offering of MOOCs on eService Management. The courses and materials were designed in collaboration with experts from the Business Process Outsourcing (BPO) industry, and certifications acquired through MOOCs are recognized by BPO companies for employment and job promotion. In the International Business Process Association of the Philippines' (IBPAP) General Membership Assembly Meeting held June 26, 2018, supports for Persons with Disability (PWDs) will be provided through the Project DI (Diversity and Inclusion). This project is the result of a partnership of the IBPAP, Contact Center Association of the Philippines (CCAP), Unilab Foundation and Edulynx Corporation. Project DI aims to place 18,000 PWDs in the workforce by the year 2022 (Muñiz, 2018). For example, ensuring wheelchair-accessible entrances, exits and bathrooms can reduce barriers for individuals with disabilities to attain gainful employment (PWD Philippines, 2015).

Conclusion

Exclusion to learning opportunities and engagements is not a consequence of physical disabilities alone. There are many barriers to universal access to learning, and these are being addressed in the Philippines through the development and implementation of the UAL4D framework. This holistic and comprehensive approach to universal access to learning can contribute to social transformation and to a country's development.

References

Barasa, S. D. (2014). *Modes of interaction in distance education: A review of the literature.* Retrieved from www.academia.edu/8372938/MODES_OF_INTERACTION_IN_DISTANCE_EDUCATION

Depasupil, W. (2017). 1 Million graduates face job-skill mismatch. *The Manila Times.* Retrieved from www.manilatimes.net/1-million-graduates-face-job-skill-mismatch/317111/

Drake, J. R., O'Hara, M., & Seeman, E. (2015). Five principles for MOOC design: With a case study. *Journal of Information Technology Education: Innovations in Practice, 14,* 125–143. Retrieved from http://jite.org/documents/Vol14/JITEv14IIPp125-143Drake0888.pdf

Gutierrez, N. (2013). College graduate? Teach in a public school. *Rappler.* Retrieved from www.rappler.com/move-ph/20250-college-graduate-teach-in-a-public-school

Montgomery College. (2017). *Poverty biggest barrier to accessing higher education.* Retrieved from http://mcblogs.montgomerycollege.edu/atmc/poverty-is-biggest-barrier-to-access-to-higher-education/

Muñiz, S. (2018). *BPO sector welcomes persons with disability.* Retrieved from https://andersonbpoinc.com/bpo-sector-welcomes-pwds/

NCDA. (2019). *United Nations convention on the rights of persons with disabilities.* National Council of Disability Affairs. Retrieved from www.ncda.gov.ph/international-conventions-and-commitments/united-nations-conventions-on-the-rights-of-persons-with-disabilities/united-nations-conventions-on-the-rights-of-persons-with-disabilities/

New Zealand Ministry of Education. (2019). *Guide to universal design for learning.* Retrieved from www.inclusive.tki.org.nz/guides/universal-design-for-learning/

NIH. (2019). *What are some types of assistive technology and how are they used?* National Institutes of Health, US Dept. of Health and Human Services. Retrieved from www.nichd.nih.gov/health/topics/rehabtech/conditioninfo/device

Pennington, J. (2017). Education, inequality, poverty—a paradox in the Philippines. *ASEAN Today.* Retrieved from www.aseantoday.com/2017/03/education-inequality-poverty-a-paradox-in-the-philippines/

Philippine Institute for Development Studies. (2016). *Policy Notes No. 2016-19.* Retrieved from https://pidswebs.pids.gov.ph/websitecms/CDN/PUBLICATIONS/pidspn1619.pdf

Philippine Statistics Authority. (2013). *Persons with disability in the Philippines (Results from the 2010 Census).* Retrieved from https://psa.gov.ph/content/persons-disability-philippines-results-2010-census

PWD Philippines. (2015). *PWDs in the BPO industry.* Retrieved from http://pwdphil.com/2015/06/01/pwds-in-the-bpo-industry/

Ranada, P. (2017). Duterte signs law providing free Internet in public places. *Rappler.* Retrieved from www.rappler.com/nation/177540-duterte-free-wifi-internet-law

Republic of the Philippines. (2014). *Republic act no. 10650.* Retrieved from https://senate.gov.ph/republic_acts/ra%2010650.pdf

Rose, D. H., & Meyer, A. (2002). *Teaching every student in the digital age: Universal design for learning.* Alexandria, VA: Association for Supervision and Curriculum Development.

Subido, L. K. (2017). *Growing 27% in 2016, PH now has 60 million Internet users.* Retrieved from www.entrepreneur.com.ph/news-and-events/ph-now-has-60-million-internet-users-growing-27-in-2016-a36-20170124

Symaco, L. P. (2013). Geographies of social exclusion: Education access in the Philippines. *Comparative Education*, *49*(3), 361–373.

UNESCO. (2015). *Paris message*. Retrieved from www.icde.org/assets/WHAT_WE_DO/POLICY/parismessage13072015final.pdf

UNESCO. (2019). *Right to education*. Retrieved from https://en.unesco.org/themes/right-to-education

United Nations. (2019). *Sustainable development goals, 4 quality education*. Retrieved from www.un.org/sustainabledevelopment/education/

World Bank. (2019). *International Telecommunications Union, world telecommunications/ICT development report and database, mobile cellular subscriptions, Philippines*. Retrieved from https://data.worldbank.org/indicator/IT.CEL.SETS.P2?locations=PH

World Economic Forum. (2017). *The Global Competitiveness Report 2017-2018*. Retrieved from http://www3.weforum.org/docs/GCR2017-2018/05FullReport/TheGlobalCompetitivenessReport2017–2018.pdf

W3C Web Accessibility Initiative. (2019). *Web content accessibility guidelines (WCAG): Overview*. Retrieved from www.w3.org/wai/standards-guidelines/wcag/

25
APPLYING UDL PRINCIPLES IN AN INCLUSIVE DESIGN PROJECT BASED ON MOOCS REVIEWS

Francisco Iniesto, Covadonga Rodrigo, and Garron Hillaire

Recommender Systems and MOOCs

While massive open online courses (MOOCs) may be attracting a wide range of learners, there is a need to provide access to learners that have varying needs (Iniesto, McAndrew, Minocha, & Coughlan, 2017). As learners may have likes and dislikes regarding course designs, there is a need to organize feedback from such a wide range of participants into a coherent and actionable structure. Selection of courses to enroll in among many electives is one of the most influential decisions learners have to make in their educational life. These courses may result in a different career path or educational benefits. Although this selection may be thought to be trivial, the ambiguity of the factors to be considered leads learners to miss chances or make wrong decisions.

The need to reduce the massive amount of information that a user must process to find something of interest on the Internet has influenced the emergence of recommender systems (Adomavicius & Tuzhilin, 2005). Recommender systems are a step forward in the recovery of traditional information and provision of a set of recommendations of interest to the user that match users' expectations (Abhihek, Kulkarni, Kumar, Archana, & Kumar, 2011). Recommendations have significant dependencies between the user and the activity that are centered on the result. For instance, if someone is interested in moving forward professionally, it is more likely that the person will register in an educational program that fits the objectives of the future professional role he/she wants to play.

Adjusting learning based on learners' particular needs has been a priority for educators for years, and artificial intelligence (AI) allows a level of differentiation between learners in different online environments. AI techniques may be useful for several reasons, including their ability to develop and imitate human reasoning and decision-making processes (learning-teaching model) and to minimize the sources of uncertainty in order to achieve an active learning-teaching context. These abilities ensure both learner and system improvement over the lifelong learning mechanism (Colchester, Hagras, Alghazzawi, & Aldabbag, 2017). The idea of customizing curriculum for every learner's needs is not yet viable today, but it will be for AI-powered machines. It is expected that AI in US education will grow by 47.5% from 2017–2021, according to the *AI Market in the US Education Sector* report (Education Artificial Intelligence Market Report, 2018).

Recommender systems, applied in many domains, have recently been used in the educational context (Lu, Wu, Mao, Wang, & Zhang, 2015) by advising learners to enroll in specific courses depending on learners' performance in previous courses, their grades, and similarity of content. Drachsler, Verbert, Santos, and Manouselis (2015) found that all recommender systems reviewed aimed to support educational stakeholders by personalizing the learning process, and that previous learner feedback was a critical factor in making appropriate recommendations.

MOOCs are courses delivered through specific eLearning platforms available through the Internet. Literature on MOOCs shows cases of adaptive intervention utilizing real-time clickstream data tracking of learners' behaviors and dynamic adaptations of content (Pardos, Tang, Davis, & Le, 2017) and the use of collaborative filtering to extract learner-specific latent interest from historical access behaviors to provide recommendations (Jing & Tang, 2017). The recommendations can be applied to particular parts of the MOOCs, such as forums where discussions can be difficult to track (Mi & Faltings, 2017), or use external sources like opinions in social media (Wang, Maruyama, Yasui, Kawai, & Akiyama, 2017). The curriculum recommendation mechanism has not gone unnoticed by the big MOOC providers, including edX and Coursera, for whom trying to offer courses of interest for their learners is a priority in their sustainable development and business model (Tan & Wu, 2018).

Due to the high amount of MOOC offerings around the world, over 800 universities have launched at least one MOOC; the total number of MOOCs that have been announced stands at 9,400 in 2017 (Shah, 2018), and the need for specific recommender sites is indisputable. YourMOOC4all is a recommender system influenced by other systems that use learners' feedback. It is similar to other MOOC aggregator sites, such as Class Central, MOOC List, and CourseTalk, where learners can add feedback about the MOOCs they are participating in and receive recommendations. YourMOOC4all also supports review of various pedagogical aspects of the MOOCs through ratings, free text comments, and posted opinions about the content of the MOOC, the provider, or the instructor.

MOOCs and Inclusive Design

There is a critical point ignored in prior MOOC recommender systems in regards to the area of inclusive design—the lack of detailed information regarding accessibility to ensure learners with disabilities can access the eLearning platform and the content. In the development of YourMOOC4all, the goals are to provide information to MOOC providers to integrate accessibility features into the courses and platforms and to inform the learners who are in search of relevant and accessible MOOCs. The project is grounded in the premise that learners' experiences on eLearning platforms offer useful information for others to use to fulfill their interests and to inform special needs regarding accessibility. For instance, if a platform is especially accessible for learners with a visual impairment, that information is of great interest to another learner in a similar situation.

UDL in the MOOC Context

Universal Design for Learning (UDL) offers a framework to evaluate MOOCs design and determine improvements at their early stage of development. This framework considers how to design learning environments to develop expert learners, defined in this framework as resourceful, strategic, and motivated (CAST, 2017). UDL is comprised of three design principles, which contain 31 checkpoints. The three design principles are *multiple means of engagement*, *multiple means of representation*, and *multiple means of action and expression*. These outline the overall goal while the checkpoints provide specific design advice that considers accessibility and learning. In the most recent version of the UDL Guidelines (CAST, 2018), the checkpoints have been further organized into *access*, *build*, and *internalize* categories.

To take a closer look at the checkpoints and their relationship with accessibility, the *multiple means of representation* principle is explored in depth. In the context of MOOCs, the checkpoint "to offer alternatives for visual information" (1.3) is categorized as *access*, providing options for perception (CAST, 2018). This focus on access is reflected by accessibility standards, such as the Web Content Accessibility Guidelines ([WCAG 2.1] W3C Web Accessibility Initiative, 2018) in guideline 1.1 which also recommends alternative text for non-text material. Specifically, UDL checkpoint 1.3 includes the suggestion to use alternative text when there is an image as an option for perception. While the alternative text of an image provides access to support learning, it is also crucial to building on that access.

For example, if a MOOC uses images to illustrate two examples of amphibians with depictions of a salamander and a frog, the alternative text is likely to include the words *frog* and *salamander*. A learner may be unfamiliar with the word *salamander*, which would make the term a potential candidate for a glossary item. Checkpoint "clarify vocabulary and symbols" (2.1) is an example of providing options for language and symbols, suggesting the design should clarify vocabulary (CAST, 2018). Checkpoint 2.1 is supported by research that indicates providing glossaries in the text is linked with vocabulary gains for language learners and struggling readers (Proctor, Dalton, & Grisham, 2007).

UDL guidelines suggest that to help *internalize* information about amphibians, checkpoint "highlight patterns, critical features, big ideas, and relationships" (3.2) outlines how the design should potentiate ways to provide options for comprehension (CAST, 2018). For images of the frog and the salamander, one image might highlight the critical feature that a frog has no tail placing it in the order *Anura*, while the salamander image would have a visible tail placing it in the order *Urodela*. The images of the frog and salamander may also illustrate that both Anura and Urodela are orders within the species of amphibians to highlight this relationship. Using the UDL Guidelines, one can look at a MOOC about amphibians and ask:

- Do the images of the frog and salamander have alternative text?
- Is there a glossary of terms?
- Do the images highlight key features and relationships?

The design would then support access to learning materials that provided answers to those questions, building on the access to learn and internalize the key features and relationships. While this example illustrates how the UDL guidelines might inform the creation of images that teach about amphibians, there are parallels to how learners might consider concepts within a MOOC and how one course might relate to other courses.

There is evidence that when interacting with an online course, like a MOOC, concept mapping the course can lead to better learning outcomes (Huang et al., 2012). It illustrates the parallel nature of how concept maps can be used in instructional design and how internalizing this approach when evaluating a MOOC can produce improved learning outcomes. YourMOOC4all is a project that offers these options.

YourMOOC4all: An Inclusive Design Project

YourMOOC4all is designed with the objective of developing expert learners. If learners are developed as experts, they may be considering both the MOOC elements as well as the relationships between MOOCs. To be successful, expert learners need to be able to recognize the tools and resources that help them to learn (strategic), organize tools and resources to facilitate their learning (resourceful), and evaluate the design of MOOCs they take (motivate) (CAST, 2017). The YourMOOC4all project has designed a MOOC aggregator site with the following aims:

1. Provide information to MOOC developers and recommendations to learners seeking accessible MOOCs.
2. Support learner evaluation of inclusive instructional design aspects of MOOCs using the UDL framework and retrieve recommendations, helping learners to locate MOOCs that fit their needs.

At this time, the project is a programmed prototype hosting more than 700 MOOCs for testing (Iniesto & Rodrigo, 2018). The website is multi-language and enables learners to search by free text, enabling them to refine the search by course title, theme, or related course information. It is possible to order the results by title, institution, platform, and average score obtained in previous evaluations. Some of the YourMOOC4all main features can be seen in Figure 25.1 (note the search engine and MOOC available information on the left and the rating system for the means of representation on the right).

The dynamically captured course information includes general information about the MOOC such as name, platform, and provider institution, thematic information, learning objectives, expected prior knowledge, recipients and required level to participate, and accessibility information about the availability of sign language, transcriptions, audio-description, and captions.

YourMOOC4all in Practice

An evaluation matrix was created following the UDL framework, with a total of 31 indicators directly related to the checklists (Table 25.1). These indicators have been developed by the authors based on the UDL guidelines (CAST, 2018) and with the support of a UDL expert. Learners apply this matrix to quantitatively rate any of the optional indicators using a Likert scale. All the indicators offer a small tip to help learners understand each question with an example, as can be observed in Figure 25.1.

In the evaluation process, learners can answer open-ended questions, enriching the qualitative content of the feedback for MOOC providers and offering valuable information to other learners. The YourMOOC4all design captures quantitative information through the ratings and qualitative information from comments to triangulate the data.

The project and associated development research promotes a better understanding of the accessibility barriers MOOCs have and establishes a fluent communication with MOOC providers, providing recommendations to assist them in improving accessibility to reduce the identified barriers in MOOCs. The design of the project records the different runs of a single MOOC. For example, if a *Pedagogical Methodologies* MOOC has three editions, this is reflected and shown in YourMOOC4all, tracking the changes and improvements. Therefore, the communication is bidirectional, allowing evaluation of new MOOC runs wherein MOOC designers and instructors have implemented the suggested recommendations.

Table 25.2 indicates the key areas at guideline level where recommendation and improvement feedback is expected to be delivered to MOOC providers. If followed, these recommendations for integrating UDL into a MOOC could prove to significantly extend access and understanding of course content through diversified design features. This is a temporary table since the input provided by

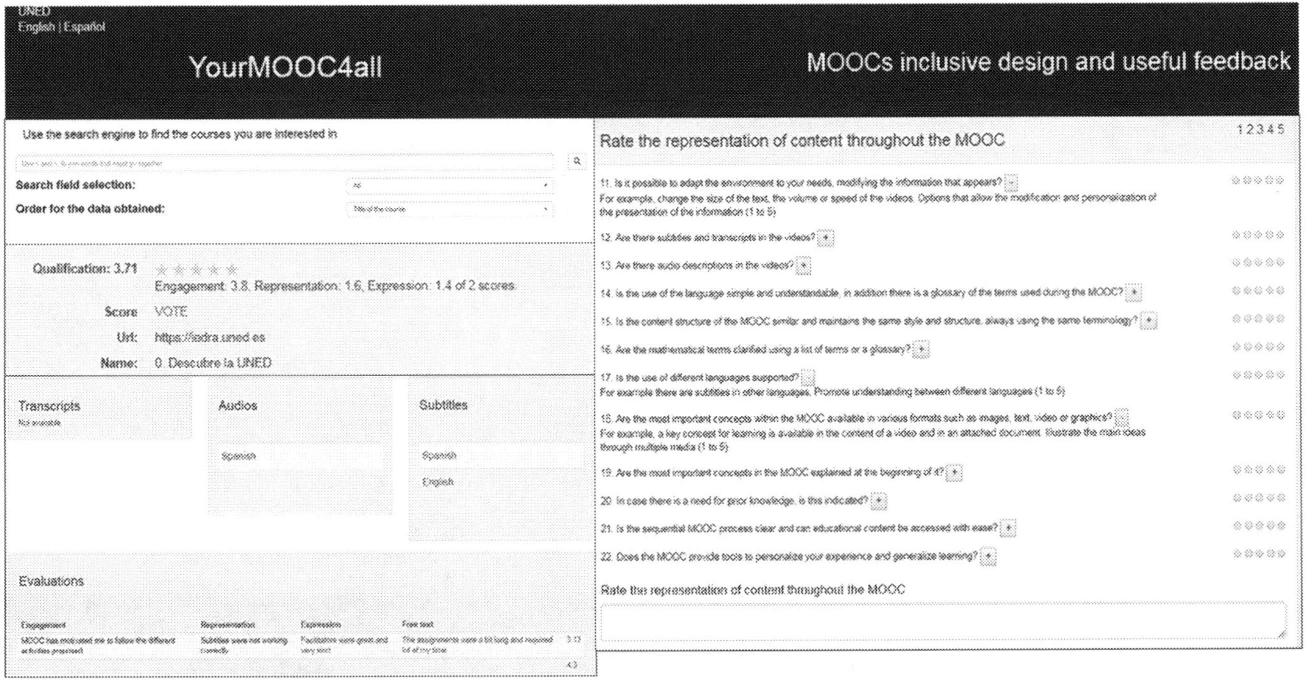

FIGURE 25.1 YourMOOC4all Features

TABLE 25.1 YourMOOC4all Evaluation Matrix Indicators Distributed by UDL Principles and Checklist Items

	Multiple means of engagement	Multiple means of representation	Multiple means of action and expression
Access	Provide options for recruiting interest • Can you participate whenever you want in the discussions or activities and work without time limits? (7.1) • Did the proposed activities match what you wanted to learn, giving you the possibility to explore the content and be creative? (7.2) • Is the information about the activities notified in advance (at the beginning of the MOOC or with email)? Is there access to a calendar with all the information? (7.3)	Provide options for perception • Is it possible to adapt the environment to your needs, modifying the information that appears? (1.1) • Are there captions and transcripts available in the videos? (1.2) • Are there audio descriptions available in the videos? (1.3)	Provide options for physical action • Is there a time limit to perform the tests or activities when you start them? (4.1) • Is it possible to move around the MOOC using only the keyboard or the mouse? (4.2)
Build	Provide options for sustaining effort & persistence • Do you have space to formulate what you are expecting to learn at the beginning of the MOOC? (8.1) • Is the level of difficulty in the activities proposed in the MOOC differentiated? (8.2) • Can you discuss what you want to learn in the MOOC with other partners? (8.3) • Are the responses from the facilitators positive and oriented to help you? (8.4)	Provide options for language & symbols • Is the use of the language simple and understandable; also, is there a glossary of the terms used during the MOOC? (2.1) • Is the structure of the MOOC similar and maintains the same style, using the same terminology? (2.2) • Are the mathematical terms clarified using a list of terms or a glossary? (2.3) • Is the use of different languages supported? (2.4) • Are the most important concepts within the MOOC available in various formats, such as images, text, video, or graphics? (2.5)	Provide options for expression & communication • Are there social networks or external tools available in the MOOC? (5.1) • Are external links and complementary readings offered in the MOOC? (5.2) • Do the MOOC facilitators help in the process of communication and reflection? (5.3)

(*Continued*)

TABLE 25.1 (Continued)

	Multiple means of engagement	Multiple means of representation	Multiple means of action and expression
Internalize	Provide options for self-regulation • Do the tests provide feedback that helps your learning? (9.1) • Is there a space available to talk freely about the difficulties encountered? (9.2) • Is there any help in case you have not been able to participate in the whole MOOC? (9.3)	Provide options for comprehension • Are the most important concepts in the MOOC explained at the beginning of it? (3.1) • If there is a need for prior knowledge, is this indicated? (3.2) • Is the sequential ordering of tasks in the MOOC logical? (3.3) • Does the MOOC provide tools to personalize your experience and generalize learning? (3.4)	Provide options for executive functions • Is it clear at the beginning of each module what is to be learned and the calendar of activities? (6.1) • Are there quizzes during the MOOC to facilitate reflection on what has been learned? (6.2) • Are guides provided to assist in the learning process and the use of the platform? (6.3) • Does the MOOC show the progress you have made? (6.4)

TABLE 25.2 Key Areas for Recommendation and Improvement by Guideline to MOOC Providers

	Multiple means of engagement	Multiple means of representation	Multiple means of action and expression
Access	Provide options for recruiting interest Indicators to engage learners in discussion and activities, to deliver full access to the content, and notify in advance the workload	Provide options for perception Standardization around the adaptability of the educational environment, production of captions, transcripts, and audio descriptions	Provide options for physical action Configurations to avoid time limits when performing tests or activities and access through the keyboard
Build	Provide options for sustaining effort & persistence Suggestions to allow learners to formulate goals, identify activities' difficulty, and allow discussion between peers providing oriented feedback from the facilitator's side	Provide options for language & symbols Guidelines to provide consistent and straightforward language, structure, style, and terminology, allowing support to different languages and formats	Provide options for expression & communication Guidelines to provide use of social networks, external links, and complementary readings, and orientations to facilitators to help in the process of communication and reflection
Internalize	Provide options for self-regulation Indicators to provide non-academic discussion spaces and help when unable to participate in the MOOC	Provide options for comprehension Orientation on explicit prior knowledge, concepts, and sequential ordering of tasks from the beginning of the MOOC	Provide options for executive functions Indications on a calendar of activities of progress made, provision of quizzes to facilitate reflection and guidelines to help the learning process

learners will determine which key areas to improve in the learning design. In that sense, the open-ended questions answered by learners will have an impact on MOOC providers, since they may offer new ideas and perspectives that could be related to the UDL framework, current MOOC development processes, and beyond.

Conclusions and Future Work

YourMOOC4all is designed to develop expert learners through the application of UDL principles to crowd-sourced MOOC design evaluation. It supports learners internalizing UDL guidelines and offers a structure to MOOC providers to compare their design quality processes. Future work includes adding user profiling options to the search (for example, language preferences or existence of captions) and increasing the sample of MOOC providers.

References

Abhihek, K., Kulkarni, S., Kumar,V., Archana, N., & Kumar, P. (2011). A review on personalized information recommendation system using collaborative filtering. *International Journal of Computer Science and Information Technologies (IJCSIT)*, 2(3), 1272–1278.

Adomavicius, G., & Tuzhilin, A. (2005). Toward the next generation of recommender systems: A survey of the state-of-the-art and possible extensions. *IEEE Transactions on Knowledge and Data Engineering*, 17(6), 734–749.

CAST. (2017). *Top 5 UDL tips for fostering expert learners*. Retrieved from http://castprofessionallearning.org/wp-content/uploads/2017/08/cast-5-expert-learners-1.pdf

CAST. (2018). *Universal design for learning guidelines version 2.2*. Wakefield, MA. Retrieved from http://udlguidelines.cast.org

Colchester, K., Hagras, H., Alghazzawi, D., & Aldabbagh, G. (2017). A survey of artificial intelligence techniques employed for adaptive educational systems within e-learning platforms. *Journal of Artificial Intelligence and Soft Computing Research*, 7(1), 47–64.

Drachsler, H., Verbert, K., Santos, O. C., & Manouselis, N. (2015). Panorama of recommender systems to support learning. In F. Ricci, L. Rokach, & B. Shapira (Eds.), *Recommender systems handbook* (pp. 421–451). Boston, MA: Springer.

Education Artificial Intelligence Market Report. (2018). *United States education artificial intelligence market report 2018–2022*. Retrieved from www.prnewswire.com/news-releases/united-states-education-artificial-intelligence-market-report-2018-2022-sector-to-grow-at-a-cagr-of-47-77-300703244.html

Huang, H. S., Chiou, C. C., Chiang, H. K., Lai, S. H., Huang, C.Y., & Chou,Y.Y. (2012). Effects of multidimensional concept maps on fourth graders' learning in web-based computer course. *Computers and Education*, 58(3), 863–873.

Iniesto, F., McAndrew, P., Minocha, S., & Coughlan, T. (2017). *An investigation into the perspectives of providers and learners on MOOC accessibility*. Proceedings of the 5th International Conference on Technological Ecosystems for Enhancing Multiculturality. ACM, 95.

Iniesto, F., & Rodrigo, C. (2018). *YourMOOC4all: A MOOCs inclusive design and useful feedback research project*. Paper presented at Learning with MOOCS 2018: MOOCs for All—A Social and International Approach.

Jing, X., & Tang, J. (2017). *Guess you like: Course recommendation in MOOCs*. Proceedings of the International Conference on Web Intelligence. ACM, 783–789.

Lu, J., Wu, D., Mao, M., Wang, W., & Zhang, G. (2015). Recommender system application developments: A survey. *Decision Support Systems, 74*, 12–32.

Mi, F., & Faltings, B. (2017). *Adaptive sequential recommendation for discussion forums on MOOCs using context trees*. Proceedings International Conference Educational Data Mining, 24–31.

Pardos, Z. A., Tang, S., Davis, D., & Le, C. V. (2017). *Enabling real-time adaptivity in MOOCs with a personalized next-step recommendation framework*. Proceedings of the Fourth ACM Conference on Learning@ Scale. ACM, 23–32.

Proctor, C. P., Dalton, B., & Grisham, D. L. (2007). Scaffolding English language learners and struggling readers in a universal literacy environment with embedded strategy instruction and vocabulary support. *Journal of Literacy Research, 39*(1), 71–93.

Shah, D. (2018). By the numbers: MOOCs in 2017. *Class Central Report*. Retrieved from www.class-central.com/report/mooc-stats-2017/

Tan, M., & Wu, M. (2018). An association rule model of course recommendation in MOOCs: Based on edX platform. *European Scientific Journal, ESJ, 14*(25), 284–292.

W3C Web Accessibility Initiative. (2018). *Web content accessibility guidelines (WCAG) 2.1*. Retrieved from www.w3.org/TR/WCAG21/

Wang, Y., Maruyama, N., Yasui, G., Kawai, Y., & Akiyama, T. (2017). *A Twitter-based recommendation system for MOOCs based on spatiotemporal event detection*. iConference 2017 Proceedings, vol. 2.

26
GENERAL ACCESSIBILITY GUIDELINES FOR ONLINE COURSE CONTENT CREATION

Kathleen Bastedo and Nancy Swenson

Introduction

The design of online content should take into consideration the diverse audience on the other side of the computer screen. Online materials need to be accessible to all students. As a scientifically based set of principles, UDL recognizes that not everyone learns the same way and that the differences need to be considered when designing curriculum.

The World Wide Web Consortium (W3C) develops and updates the Web Content Accessibility Guidelines, or WCAG 2.1, that are recognized and adopted by users throughout the world (W3C, 2018). Having web accessibility standards available that countries around the world follow has been instrumental in guiding the development of accessible online content for people with disabilities. The W3C takes into consideration the fact that people will be accessing the Internet for a multitude of reasons using a variety of devices. One of W3C's goals is to make the web accessible to everyone regardless of hardware, software, native language, or culture (W3C, 2018). The application of Universal Design for Learning principles, along with WCAG 2.1, help guide development of online course materials that are accessible for diverse learners.

Basic Guidelines

Whether online course content is created utilizing tools within an LMS such as a content editor or with programs outside the LMS such as Microsoft Word or Adobe Acrobat, the same general principles for creating an accessible document apply. The WCAG 2.1 standards guide how to develop content that can be accessed by everyone. These tips, which follow the WCAG 2.1 standards and promote the principles of UDL, should be applied in the creation of accessible online course content:

- **Headings**—Use proper heading structure (e.g., H1, H2, H3) when creating documents (e.g., heading information is located in the content editor in LMSs and in the Styles Ribbon in Microsoft products) so the headings of a website or online course content can be quickly scanned by screen readers.
- **Content**—Divide large pieces of course content into smaller, easier to remember chunks (Shank, 2012). Smaller chunks are also easier to view on a mobile device.
- **Tables**—Add row and column headers to tables to allow a screen reader to read aloud the information as it was intended. Adding a caption and/or summary is also recommended as it will provide more context to the table. To learn more about various options for setting up rows and headers (e.g., tables with one header, tables with two headers, table with multi-level headers), see the W3C Table Concepts in the provided resources.
- **Links**—Use descriptive links (e.g., "Funny Dog Pictures") when linking a web address instead of just "click here" so that screen reader users know where the link will be taking them.
- **Color**—Use of color should not be the only distinguishing feature when providing information (e.g., color shading on a course schedule of face-to-face meetings should also be supplemented with corresponding text information).
- **Color contrast**—Use a color contrast checker to make sure the color contrast meets W3C Level AA guidelines. Insufficient color contrast could make it difficult for people who are colorblind or have low vision to view content. WebAIM (2018) has created a free Color Contrast Checker (see Resources) that allows anyone to check text for appropriate color contrast, and it provides the tools to fix the text if the appropriate color contrast ratio is not met.
- **Images**—Add alternative text (e.g., a word or phrase that describes an image) to inserted images so that a screen reader user will know the intention of the image. The W3C includes tutorials on their website regarding various types of images (informative images, decorative images, images of text, image maps).

Creating Online Course Content Using LMS Tools

An LMS helps to organize all the components of an online course, e.g., quizzes, assignments, and discussions, into one place (Ippakayala & El-Ocla, 2017). Each LMS also comes with options to create content within them. This section will focus on using various LMS tools to create accessible online course content of four LMS systems, specifically Blackboard Learn, Instructure Canvas, D2L

Brightspace, and Moodle that are commonly used by educational systems around the world (McKenzie, 2018).

Each LMS is equipped with its own version of a content editor (e.g., Canvas' Rich Content Editor) that supports the creation of course content pages, discussions, announcements, quizzes, and more. Each tool provides users with the ability to format text as headings, add alternative text to images, identify column and row headers, and add captions to tables. Figures 26.1 and 26.2 are images of what formatting options are readily available in the Canvas Content Editor and the Blackboard Course Sites Editor. The formatting options in each are similar to what most people have come to expect with software packages that offer content creation or editing.

When adding an image to a page using a content editor, the designer will be prompted to add alternative text (*alt text*) information. Alt text provides context and meaning of the image and is particularly important for individuals who are unable to see images and may use screen readers for accessibility. Many LMS content editors also offer the option to indicate whether an image is decorative, which would allow a user to skip over this information. It is important to take into consideration the purpose of the image as well as the intended message. For example, the image in Figure 26.3 is a cat wearing an Elizabethan collar following surgery. The alternative text may be different if the image was a personal image vs. an image that is being used for a veterinarian course. In this case, the applicable alternative text is "Cat wearing an Elizabethan collar after surgery." If it were an image used as decoration, the "Decorative Image" box in Canvas can be checked (Figure 26.3) so that the screen reader will ignore the image.

The formatting area of content editors also provides the opportunity to select appropriate headings for structure, organization, and accessibility. Document headings also make a document more accessible as they allow screen reader users to scan a document using only the headings. Figure 26.4 provides an example of how to add headings using Canvas's Rich Content Editor.

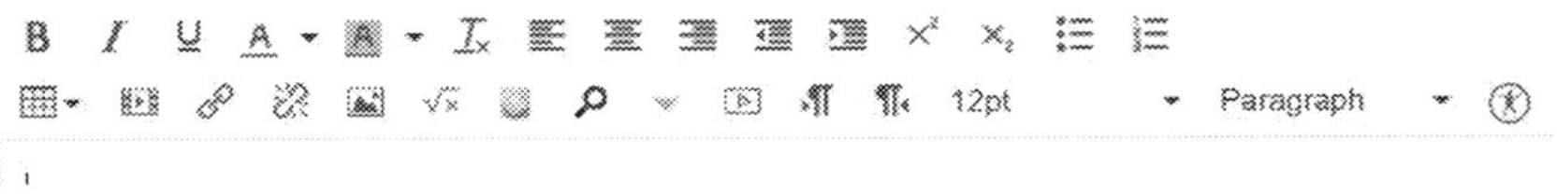

FIGURE 26.1 Instructure Canvas Rich Content Editor

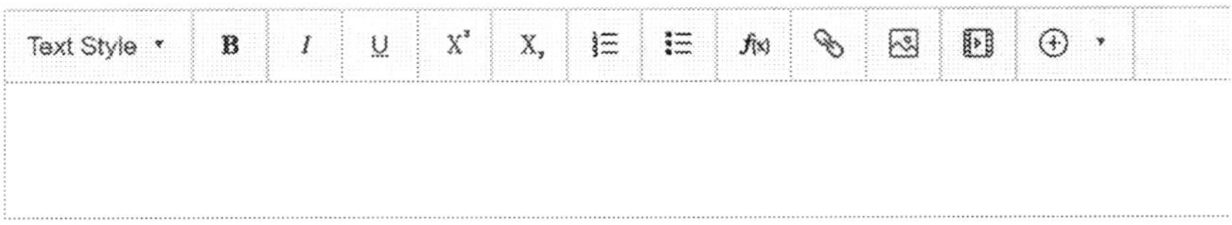

FIGURE 26.2 Blackboard Course Sites Content Editor

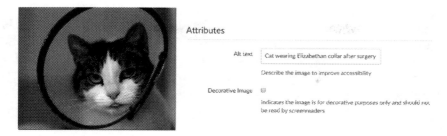

FIGURE 26.3   Cat Wearing an Elizabethan Collar after Surgery

FIGURE 26.4   Heading Options from the Canvas Rich Content Editor

Accessibility Checkers

Accessibility of online materials remains a time and financial challenge; however, the products and strategies described next will help to decrease the burden on course developers. Accessibility checkers can help to identify accessibility issues present in course materials and offer recommendations for addressing problematic areas. Accessibility checkers are products with the ability to determine the accessibility of specific materials, such as websites and online course materials. Some of these checkers are built into an LMS, while other checkers are external to an LMS.

LMSs such as Canvas and Brightspace have built-in accessibility checkers. These can be used to check content pages that are created within the LMS; and they identify general accessibility issues, such as need for table headers, image alt text, and page headings, and provide recommendations for how to fix the issues.

Ally is an external accessibility evaluation product that was recently purchased by Blackboard. It works well with Blackboard LMS products, Canvas, and Moodle. As of this writing, Ally is currently not compatible with Brightspace. For many file types uploaded to a course by the instructor, Ally is able to create several alternate formats of that file, such as a tagged PDF, an audio file, electronic Braille, and an e-pub file. This particular process is automatic, but it can be turned off at any time. These files are made available to all students in the course. As of this writing, this process is not yet available to student-generated content. Ally also can check instructor-created content and provide guidance for how to fix any outstanding accessibility issues; however, none of the suggested fixes are completed automatically. Finally, Ally offers the capability to generate a report on how the institution is doing overall in relation to accessibility.

UDOIT (Universal Design Online content Inspection Tool; pronounced "You Do It") is an open source product created by the University of Central Florida that can be used to scan a course, generate a report, and provide resources and suggestions on how to fix general types of accessibility issues within various areas of a course site, such as native content pages, announcements, assignments, and discussions. UDOIT also checks to see if YouTube videos linked in the course have accurate captions. UDOIT is free for use by any institution that uses Canvas. The source code is available for download from GitHub (https://github.com/ucfopen/UDOIT).

UDOIT Case Study

As instructional designers, the authors recently worked with an instructor that was new to the online learning environment and wanted to redesign several of his courses to be taught online. In one particular course, there were tables, images from copyright-free sites, and links to videos. When advised that he should run the UDOIT tool on his course and address the identified accessibility areas before teaching the course, he was hesitant to do so, as he thought it would be better to address those needs as they arose.

His assigned instructional designer explained that if some students (especially those with disabilities) were not able to access all the course materials at the beginning of the semester, it would create barriers for these students, as they would likely get behind in the course before student accessibility services would be able to address the accessibility areas. The instructor reconsidered and ran the UDOIT accessibility checker. Using the provided suggestions in the resulting accessibility report, he added alternative text to images and appropriate headings to tables. He also took advantage of a captioning pilot for YouTube videos (supported by the distance learning fee at the institution) and submitted his course videos for captioning. These efforts yielded immediate returns, as students with disabilities who enrolled in the course were able to immediately access and engage in the course without barriers or delays relating to accommodations.

Creating Accessible Online Course Content Using Tools Outside the LMS

Consideration also needs to be given to the accessibility of materials created outside an LMS and uploaded to an online course. The types of files that may be uploaded to online courses include Word documents, PDFs, PowerPoint or

Keynote presentations, and multimedia components such as video and audio. There are many tutorials online related to creating accessible online content (see Resources). Most of the LMS product websites also include tutorials and user help knowledge banks. Considerations for improving accessibility of the most common types of online course files will be described next.

Microsoft Word

When creating documents in Microsoft Word, it is important to follow the general accessibility guidelines for online course content creation mentioned earlier in this chapter. For example, readings, such as H1, H2, and H3, should be used to provide structure in a document. The incorporation of headings meets WCAG 2.1 Criterion 2.4.10 and is an application of the UDL principle of Action and Expression, Checkpoint 6.3 — *Facilitate managing information and resources by chunking information aids in comprehension and memory* (CAST, 2019).

The Microsoft Word interface contains a formatting *ribbon* (see Figure 26.5) to select headings.

There is also an embedded accessibility tool in Microsoft Word that can review items such as headings, alternative text, and row and/or column headers in a data table for proper formatting. The Microsoft Word accessibility checker is located under File, then Info, then Check for Issues, then select Check Accessibility (see Figure 26.6 for details).

PDF

There are two types of documents that are typically converted to PDFs and added to online courses. The first type is a document created in a word processing program such as Microsoft Word and then converted to a PDF (for example, a syllabus). The second type is a PDF that was creating by scanning a printed document. If the Optical Character Recognition (OCR) feature was not applied in this case, it may present difficulties in being searchable and screen reader accessible.

The key to making an accessible PDF is to begin with a digital file. Regardless of the original file type, care should be taken to apply the WCAG 2.1 standards. For example, the file should be structured using headings, images should include alternative text, and tables should have proper row and column headings. The more accessible the original document is, the less chance retrofitting will be required to achieve accessibility when the document is converted to a PDF.

FIGURE 26.5 Microsoft Word Formatting Ribbon

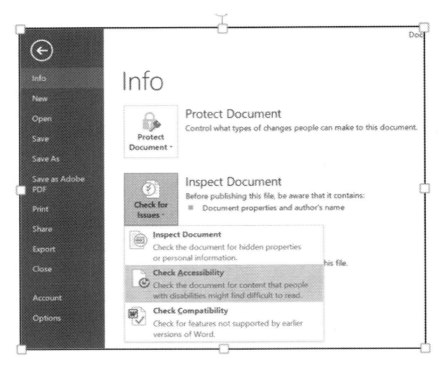

FIGURE 26.6 Microsoft Word Check Accessibility Command

A general tip to check the accessibility of a PDF is to open the PDF and use the *read-aloud* feature to identify areas where adjustments may be needed. For example, incorporating *tags* in a PDF allows a screen reader to access the information in the file in the correct order.

Newer scanners equipped with OCR can convert paper-based documents into readable and searchable text so that it can easily be read by a screen reader. ABBYY FineReader, a product with OCR capabilities, can also be used to create or convert a document or an existing PDF into an accessible PDF that is editable and searchable. ABBYY FineReader can be used to convert PDF documents to various formats or applications, such as word processing or spreadsheet files.

Presentations

The tips included earlier in this chapter for creating accessible content apply to presentation programs as well. Alternative text can be applied to images, headings can be incorporated, and row and column headers can be added in tables. In addition, accessible templates are available for popular presentation software, including Microsoft PowerPoint, Google Slides, and Apple Keynote.

Mobile Learning Recommendations

Mobile device usage (including laptops, tablets, and smartphones) by students to access online course materials has continued to increase over the years (Magda, 2017). Most learning management systems provide apps for both the iOS and the Android operating systems. With students increasingly using mobile devices to access online course materials, the accessibility guidelines described in this chapter are also relevant to the design of course materials for mobile access (Nasta & Adams, 2017). Designers should consider using the native LMS content editor when creating content as it tends to display online content better than non-native types of content editors on mobile devices. Other formats such as Doc/Docx, PDF, PPT can be included as part of online course materials, but the content/text may appear smaller and more difficult to read in these formats on mobile devices. When considering adding various types of multimedia, such as audio or video, it is worthwhile to note that not all mobile devices can easily access all types of these file formats. For student access on mobile devices, files types such as MP4 are generally recommended for video, and MP3 file formats are generally recommended for audio files.

Conclusion

With the increase of online education, it is critical that online course materials be accessible to a diverse student population. Although it is ideal to create online course materials that are accessible from the start, the reality is that many course materials may need remediation. Accessible design can start with strategically selecting key items in a course that can easily be made accessible. Existing documents, presentations, and PDFs can be converted to content pages using an LMS content creation tool, and designers can apply the UDL and W3C accessibility best practices and strategies suggested in this chapter. Creating accessible online course materials helps to form a solid basis for the implementation of UDL, and both work together to meet the needs of all students. As course materials are likely to expand to include emerging technologies such as Augmented/Virtual Reality (Chandrasekera & Yoon, 2018; Chen, Liu, Cheng, & Huang, 2017) and various active learning approaches, it is imperative that the accessibility of these technologies be considered from the start so that all students can benefit.

Resources

TABLE 26.1 Resources for Online Course Accessibility

Resource	Website
Adobe Acrobat Professional: Create and Verify PDF Accessibility	https://helpx.adobe.com/acrobat/using/create-verify-pdf-accessibility.html

(Continued)

TABLE 26.1 (Continued)

Resource	Website
Blackboard Accessibility Documentation	https://www.blackboard.com/accessibility.html
Blackboard Learn Mobile Accessible App	https://help.blackboard.com/Blackboard_App/Accessibility
Canvas Accessibility (Instructure)	https://community.canvaslms.com/docs/DOC-2061-accessibility-within-canvas
Canvas Mobile App	https://community.canvaslms.com/thread/21918-mobile-app-accessibility
Desire2Learn (Brightspace)	https://www.d2l.com/accessibility/
D2L Mobile App	https://www.d2l.com/products/pulse/
Moodle Accessibility	https://docs.moodle.org/dev/Accessibility
	https://docs.moodle.org/35/en/Accessible_course_design
Moodle Mobile App	https://docs.moodle.org/36/en/Moodle_app
Pennsylvania State University Accessibility Resources	https://accessibility.psu.edu/
University of Washington Accessibility Resources	https://www.washington.edu/accessibility/
University of Washington, DO-IT	https://www.washington.edu/doit/20-tips-teaching-accessible-online-course
University of Western Australia Accessibility Resources	https://www.web.uwa.edu.au/accessibility
WebAIM Color Contrast Checker	https://webaim.org/resources/contrastchecker/
WebAIM Microsoft Word Tutorial	https://webaim.org/techniques/word/
W3C Table Concepts	www.w3.org/WAI/tutorials/tables/
W3C Tutorials Overview	www.w3.org/WAI/tutorials/

References

CAST. (2019). *UDL guidelines checkpoint 6.3 facilitate managing information and resources.* Retrieved from http://udlguidelines.cast.org/action-expression/executive-functions/information-resources/information-resources

Chandrasekera, T., & Yoon, S. (2018). Augmented reality, virtual reality and their effect on learning style in the creative design process. *Design and Technology Education: An International Journal, 23*(1), 55–75.

Chen, P., Liu, X., Cheng, W., & Huang, R. (2017). A review of using augmented reality in education from 2011 to 2016. In E. Popescu (Ed.), *Innovations in smart learning: Lecture notes in educational technology.* Singapore: Springer.

Ippakayala, V. K., & El-Ocla, H. (2017). OLMS: Online learning management system for e-learning. *World Journal on Educational Technology: Current Issues, 9*(3), 130–138.

McKenzie, L. (2018). Canvas catches and maybe passes Blackboard. *Inside Higher Ed/Inside Digital Learning.* Retrieved from www.insidehighered.com/digital-learning/article/2018/07/10/canvas-catches-and-maybe-passes-blackboard-top-learning

Nasta, S., & Adam, P. J. (2017). Mobile applications and litigation: Why accessibility is important and what to consider before launching, part 1 of 2: Critical development considerations for mobile application accessibility. *Digital Accessibility Digest*. Retrieved from www.microassist.com/digital-accessibility/mobile-application-accessibility-part-1-of-2/

Shank, P. (2012). More on designing and teaching with returning adults in mind, part 2. *Faculty Focus*. Retrieved from www.facultyfocus.com/articles/online-education/more-on-designing-and-teaching-online-courses-with-adult-students-in-mind/

W3C Web Accessibility Initiative. (2018). *Web content accessibility guidelines (WCAG) overview*. Retrieved from www.w3.org/WAI/standards-guidelines/wcag/

WebAIM. (2018). *Color contrast checker*. Retrieved from https://webaim.org/resources/contrastchecker/

27

SNAPSHOT—CREATING UDL LEARNING AND TEACHING STRATEGIES TO ADDRESS THE UNDERREPRESENTATION OF PRESENT-DAY INDIGENOUS PERSPECTIVES

Kerry Armstrong, Brenda Boreham, and Terri Mack

Background

To ensure that Indigenous Peoples are represented in a contemporary context, educators at Strong Nations Publishing in Nanaimo, British Columbia, Canada responded to UNDRIP articles 14 & 15 by creating respectful, contemporary and culturally authentic resources (United Nations, 2013).

These materials relate to the UDL framework (Meyer, Rose, & Gordon, 2014) as they:

- support learner variation
- provide support for accessibility
- support teachers to navigate curriculum diversity and the contemporary context of indigenous ways of knowing

Rationale

"We Are All Connected," a recently published series of eight books, is one example of a Strong Nations resource that fulfills the three objectives listed (see Table 27.1). Each book is designed to link young readers to place-based science and literacy with authentic cultural content. Vetted Traditional Knowledge, reflecting an oral tradition, is applied to the learning across the curricular areas that are imbedded in each of the books.

The following are some of the UDL teaching and learning strategies implemented in the series:

1. The same structure is used in each of the eight books. This provides multiple/varied entry points to the cultural and science content, as well as practice in

TABLE 27.1 UDL Practices in the "We Are All Connected" Series

UDL Principles	UDL Connections to the "We Are All Connected" Series	Supports for Learners	Supports for Teachers
Multiple means of representation	• same structure in each of the eight books • text feature variation • designed for interactive strategies	• entry points to diverse cultural content • partner and/or small group work • designed with small chunks of information	• predictable routine • provides choice • designed for diverse learners
Multiple means of action and expression	• designed for inquiry • stewardship calls to action • suggestions	• each learner can transform learning • self-regulation	• support learners to take action • embedded teaching strategies
Multiple means of engagement	• designed for assessment for learning strategies	• opportunities for self-assessment • metacognition	• ongoing assessment to inform instruction

making connections, predictions, asking questions, inferring and determining importance.

2. The text features provide small chunks of information that are found in different places on the page and provide various ways to access information.
3. The inquiry and call to action provide agency for students to transform their thinking into action planning to make change in their community.
4. The assessment for learning strategies in the text provide opportunities for learners to start, stop and go back to interact with the text in order to self-assess.
5. Interactive strategies that are imbedded in the text provide opportunities for partner and small group interactions.

Finally, to help teachers remove barriers, there is an Educational Resource Guide (Armstrong & Mack, 2018). Strong Nations provides respectful, authentic cultural content that includes the past, present and future continuum (Younging, 2018) coupled with inquiry, literacy and assessment for learning pedagogy that follows the principles of UDL and inclusive instruction.

References

Armstrong, K., & Mack, T. (2018). Learning intentions guide. *Strong Nations*. Nanaimo, BC. Retrieved from www.strongnations.com/store/item_list.php?it=3&cat=3633

Meyer, A., Rose, D. H., & Gordon, D. (2014). *Universal design for learning: Theory and practice*. Wakefield, MA: CAST Professional Publishing.

United Nations. (2013). *UNDRIP*. Geneva, Switzerland. Retrieved from www.un.org/development/desa/indigenouspeoples/declaration-on-the-rights-of-indigenous-peoples.html

Younging, G. (2018). *Elements of indigenous style: A guide for writing by and about indigenous peoples*. Toronto, ON: Brush Education Inc.

28

SNAPSHOT—USING THE YOUTUBE AUTOMATED CAPTIONING TOOL FOR VIDEO LECTURES

Sandra A. Rogers

This case took place at a small, Catholic, and Jesuit college located in the United States. The Theology graduate program decided to convert their traditional courses to an online format to maximize efficiency and outreach. Previously, they offered an occasional course online, and instructors and students drove to major cities in the tristate area to deliver and attend seminars. This transition necessitated the creation of multimedia lectures. These needed to be accessible, as the US Department of Labor requires federally funded institutions to provide closed captions (CC) for media in distance education (ADA, 2008; Section 504, Rehabilitation Act, 1973).

The college could not afford to outsource captioning; however, instructors were incentivized to build their courses and took on the task. Instructors not only had to learn how to produce and caption media but also share it via an unlisted YouTube channel. The author provided training, guides, and video tutorials for the instructors to achieve these tasks. Additionally, the training material addressed the need to correct the automated caption errors that YouTube often produces. See the YouTube captioning user interface in Figure 28.1. Most of the instructors involved in the project self-reported having limited technology skills; nevertheless, they persisted and over time became adept online instructors.

This learning experience optimization lends itself to UDL. For example, Jesuit institutions advocate for teaching to the whole person (Kolvenbach, 1987). Therefore, providing CC media was welcomed even though no student enrolled at that time required it. Besides meeting the needs of learners with hearing impairments, these instructors provided multiple means of representation, as espoused in UDL. For example, captioning ". . . aids the reading and literacy skills development of many others" (DCMP, 2018). Linder (2016) found 71% of collegians nationwide without hearing impairments used CC as a learning aid for comprehension,

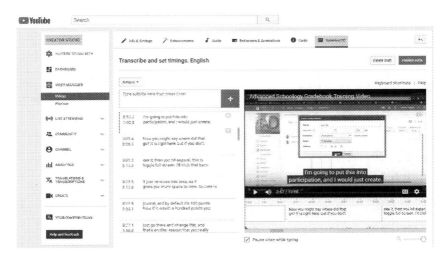

FIGURE 28.1 The YouTube *Creator Studio* Caption Editing Interface

accuracy, engagement, and retention. Moreover, most students in the Theology program were older adults with limited to no technology skills. The department chair noted that embedding YouTube video lectures within courses provided a click-and-play button versus the previous tedious practice of downloading media files and installing media players to watch lectures.

Hosting video lectures on YouTube can be a labor-intensive accessibility solution. The major issues of concern regarding usability in this case included:

- Output lacks punctuation.
- Output may lack appropriate line division and duration.
- The tool often does not recognize context specific words.
- Instructors have difficulty locating their unlisted videos because they are not shown on the main channel.
- Designers must revise supporting material according to platform updates.

These identified areas provide direction for future work in this area. Nevertheless, the YouTube free captioning tool can address media requirements at institutions with limited funding despite being less than accurate—granted that they have technical support and instructors willing and able to take on the challenge.

References

Americans with Disabilities Act. (2008). *ADA amendments act: United States code*. Retrieved from www.dol.gov/oasam/programs/crc/ADA-1990.pdf

Described and Captioned Media Program (DCMP). (2018). *Quality captioning*. Retrieved from www.captioningkey.org/quality_captioning.html

Kolvenbach, P.-H. (1987). *Go forth and teach: The characteristics of Jesuit education*. Washington, DC: Jesuit Secondary Education Association.

Linder, K. (2016). *Student uses and perceptions of closed captions and transcripts: Results from a national study*. Corvallis, OR: Oregon State University. Retrieved from www.3playmedia.com/resources/industry-studies/student-uses-of-closed-captions-and-transcripts/

Section 504, Rehabilitation Act. (1973). *Office of assistant secretary for administration and management*. United States Department of Labor. Retrieved from www.dol.gov/oasam/regs/statutes/sec504.htm

29

SNAPSHOT—A FULLY MOBILE PROFESSIONAL DEVELOPMENT COURSE FOR TEACHERS IN ISRAEL

Shir Boim-Shwartz and Eran Adi Cioban

Background

Smartphone technology offers many capabilities that can be harnessed to obtain authentic customized connected learning experiences (Kearney, Schuck, Burden, & Aubusson, 2012). Crompton (2013, p. 4) defined mobile learning as "learning across multiple contexts, through social and content interactions, using personal electronic devices," where the word *mobile* refers not only to the mobility of the digital learning device but also to the mobility of the learning activity itself. Recognizing the high potential of utilizing smartphones to create accessible and enriched learning processes (Traxler & Wishart, 2011), the authors chose to develop a fully mobile professional development (PD) course. To demonstrate the potential, a challenging subject matter was chosen from the curriculum—*Ceremonies in the Israeli-Jewish Culture*. Since this subject is considered sensitive and controversial on the one hand, and technical and repetitive on the other, the primary goal was to facilitate exploration of the components of ceremonies through various relevant perspectives and demonstrate how teachers can encourage their students to be curious and connected to subject meaning in a respectful way.

Rationale

To achieve this goal, it was determined that conventional e-learning using desktop or laptop computers would not be accessible enough for two reasons. First, traditional e-learning lacks features that enable creation and collaboration in multiple locations and contexts. Mobile devices provide a seamless learning environment, where learning activities can be carried out across different contexts regardless of the location of the users (Song, 2014). Students can continue learning activities through ubiquitous access to learning materials and constant interaction and communication possibilities with other students, teachers, and communities (Sampson & Zervas, 2013). Second, many teachers in Israel do not have ready access to desktop computers, and thus, availability of e-learning through a mobile device would promote greater access to the course.

Highlights

Klopfer, Squire, and Jenkins (2002) listed five main educational affordances that should be considered in order to take full advantage of mobile devices: portability, social interactivity, context sensitivity, connectivity, and individuality. Taking these into account, the PD course was designed to consist of 14 micro-learning units, each dealing with distinct components of the *Ceremonies* topic. Each unit includes three elements:

1. A smartphone-shot video featuring the course instructor. The instructor introduces the broader idea of the unit in a relevant, but not trivial, location. The video serves not only as an interest recruiter but also as an example of how a smartphone camera can be used creatively.
2. A short, multimedia-rich learning resource that is optimized for the smartphone screen. A blend of text, audio, video, and visual symbols were used to create a comprehensible resource with strong links among the components. Based on the UDL framework (CAST, 2018), information should be offered in more than one format (*multiple means of representation*) to provide options for learners to suit their strengths and preferences.
3. An activity that allows the autonomy of choosing how to apply newly acquired knowledge in a personal context. Learners are provided options for what to perform through relevant and engaging assignments (*multiple means of engagement*). Each activity requires the learners to use a recommended digital content-creating method (e.g., video blog, podcast, infographic). The learners interact with the content and show what they have learned in different ways during the course (*multiple means of action and expression*). To keep the learners engaged over time, examples are provided, informing the learners about note-worthy creations by their peers and encouraging them to share unique and distinct creations of their own, and to provide positive constructive feedback.

In conclusion, UDL was chosen as a guiding framework to develop this course, because it focused designer efforts on the *why* (engage the learners), *what* (present information, ideas, and concepts), and *how* (execute learning tasks) of this course. It also helped to accommodate individual learning differences, especially within a heterogeneous group of adult learners.

References

CAST. (2018). *UDL: The UDL guidelines*. Retrieved from http://udlguidelines.cast.org/

Crompton, H. (2013). Mobile learning: New approach, new theory. In Z. L. Berge & L.Y. Muilenburg (Eds.), *Handbook of mobile learning* (pp. 47–58). New York, NY: Routledge.

Kearney, M., Schuck, S., Burden, K., & Aubusson, P. (2012). Viewing mobile learning from a pedagogical perspective. *Research in Learning Technology, 20*(1). https://doi.org/10.3402/rlt.v20i0.14406

Klopfer, E., Squire, K., & Jenkins, H. (2002). *Environmental detectives: PDAs as a window into a virtual simulated world*. Proceedings of the IEEE Wireless and Mobile Technologies in Education Workshop, 95–98.

Sampson, D. G., & Zervas, P. (2013). Context-aware adaptive and personalized mobile learning systems. In D. G. Sampson, P. Isaias, D. Ifenthaler, & J. M. Spector (Eds.), *Ubiquitous and mobile learning in the digital age* (pp. 3–17). New York, NY: Springer.

Song, Y. (2014). "Bring Your Own Device (BYOD)" for seamless science inquiry in a primary school. *Computers & Education, 74*, 50–60.

Traxler, J., & Wishart, J. M. (2011). *Making mobile learning work: Case studies of practice*. (Discussion Papers in Education). Bristol: ESCalate, HEA Subject Centre for Education. Retrieved from http://hdl.handle.net/1983/da728e49-f5b2-45fe-9839-7d5b6ca12ad2

30

SNAPSHOT—EXAMINING THE INTEGRATION OF DIGITAL AND MULTIMODAL RESOURCES IN ONLINE COURSES USING A UNIVERSAL DESIGN FRAMEWORK

Peggy Semingson and Kathryn Pole

Background Information

The authors work at a large public urban university, The University of Texas at Arlington, in a "megacity"—the Dallas-Fort Worth Metroplex. Students are economically diverse and reflect cultural, linguistic, and age diversity. The university is innovative in offering flexible and accelerated online degrees and courses. The Literacy Studies Master's degree program is taught entirely online and focuses on addressing Universal Design for Learning (UDL) principles in the courses. In entirely online courses such as these, and with diverse students, multimodal learning approaches using UDL principles provide helpful structures for learning (Rose & Meyer, 2002, 2006). This snapshot describes using multimodal learning (Fadel, 2008) within a UDL framework.

Rationale for Accessible Multimodal Learning

Multimodal learning uses audio, video, and visual-focused curriculum to provide additional ways to offer flexibility in online courses. Visuals, podcasts, professor-authored videos, curated videos, webinars, and other flexible instructional digital content are used. Student-created multimodal content is accessible through closed captioning, transcription, microlearning, increased use of open content, and other more technical ways to make online learning inclusive. Because students in this program are either planning to be teachers or are seeking advanced teaching certifications, an additional goal is to provide models of inclusive teaching practices that can be taken into pre-K-12 classrooms.

Key Concepts and Design Recommendations

Traditional ways of teaching that use singular ways to present content (e.g., lecture through PowerPoint or text-only readings) and engage students may not allow all

228 Peggy Semingson and Kathryn Pole

students to perform to their highest level. UDL principles and guidelines provide flexible ways of representation and ways to engage with course content and people in the course (Rose & Meyer, 2002).

One of the three UDL principles, *representation*, provides multiple multimodal pathways to present information to students, and gives students opportunities to demonstrate their learning in a variety of ways. Traditional paper and digital readings, asynchronous videos that students can access at any time, podcasts, text-based discussion boards, and synchronous webinars (which are also recorded for later access) are used in the literacy program. Importantly, much of the content is mobile-compatible and provides multiple ways to make content accessible. In one of the instructor's professor-authored SoundCloud podcasts, students can listen to embedded content in the learning management system (LMS) or download the mobile app to access themed playlists on their smartphones/tablets. All podcasts are transcribed. YouTube videos are organized into thematic playlists, kept short, and include closed captions and transcripts using the built-in captioning tool in YouTube along with editing for accuracy (see Figure 30.1).

A different principle relates to *ways to engage* with course content. Students demonstrate their learning using similar tools (described earlier), as they post text, audio, and graphics to discussion boards; create videos, podcasts, and visual artifacts; and use digital formats such as blogs and microblogs that are multimodal

Phonological awareness, phonemic awareness, and phonics

FIGURE 30.1 Screenshot of Captioned Video

by design. For example, in one of the instructor's courses, students build their own professional learning networks (PLNs) using Twitter to discover ways that teachers are using content literacies in their classrooms. This becomes a *meta* way to demonstrate to students ways in which they can provide the same kinds of multimodal opportunities for their own students.

Although this snapshot focuses on an online learning context and UDL-focused course design in literacy teacher preparation, ideas can also apply to blended learning. Technology can foster inclusive teaching and build solidly on universal design principles across a variety of platforms.

References

Fadel, C. (2008). *Multimodal learning through media: What the research says*. San Jose, CA: CiscoSystems.

Rose, D. H., & Meyer, A. (2002). *Teaching every student in the digital age*. Alexandria, VA: Association for Supervision and Curriculum Development. Retrieved from www.cast.org

Rose, D. H., & Meyer, A. (Eds.). (2006). *A practical reader in universal design for learning*. Cambridge, MA: Harvard Education Press.

SECTION 6

Current Research and Evaluation in Inclusive Learning Around the World

31
THE INTERSECTION OF CHINESE PHILOSOPHICAL TRADITIONS AND UDL

Exploring Current Practice in Chinese Early Childhood Classrooms

Janet Arndt and Nili Luo

Historical Context

Over 2,500 years ago Confucius, noted as a historian, philosopher, and educator, contributed to the development of Chinese beliefs and tradition. His ideas, framed in short question and answer format, were written down by his followers in the *Analects* many years after his death. Chinese culture adopted his philosophy, which included the importance of respect for elders, loyalty to family, adherence to rituals, personal responsibility, high regard for education, moral virtues, ethical government, and justice. Although there were periods within Chinese history where Confucianism was buried or distorted amidst philosophy and theories of others, Confucianism permeated society enough to influence and make a lasting mark on the Chinese culture. Confucius promoted the importance of studying to better oneself noted in the *Analects*. He taught virtues through examples, rather than just stating rules of behavior, and supported the importance of establishing rituals. According to Confucius, it's much better to do right for the betterment of all rather than self (China Education Center, 2019).

With the Communist takeover in the mid-twentieth century, education became the means to disseminate the goals of the Communist party. The central idea from Confucius that continued was the importance of study to better oneself for the good of all. Education was the means by which individuals would learn for the good of all. Teachers provided the education; therefore, teachers were respected pillars of morality and their words were expected to be followed. The power and benefits of being educated edified the learner. This respect for scholars supports the common thought in Chinese culture that copying the work of another is seen as honoring that author (Wang, 2014).

Communist Revolution Changes in Education

There are four stages in education that have occurred since the Communist revolution in 1949 and have influenced curriculum in China. Despite drastic changes in education over the years, it is interesting to note that Confucius' philosophy had influence, albeit little at times. The descriptions of the four stages offer a glimpse into the overall changes in Chinese education after the revolution.

First Stage: 1949–1965—Overemphasis on Political Development in Education

In February 1957, the Confucius principles that were once a part of Chinese culture that had been overshadowed by other philosophies were brought back at the beginning of the revolution. Mao Zedong, the Father of the Cultural Revolution, wanted all students to learn what Confucius taught: personal responsibility, love of family, virtues, high regard for education, being erudite, obedience to government, and justice (China Education Center, 2019). The rich heritage of Confucius had been passed down in the culture even though the name of Confucius was not necessarily associated with his philosophy, which made reviving his example of life acceptable. Teachers were treated with respect as the disseminators of communism and stalwarts of morality in the community (Wang, 2014).

Second Stage: 1966–1976—Political Only

The 10-year Great Cultural Revolution occurred in China from May 1966 to October 1976, and the entire nation was in chaos during this time. Teachers were sent to rural areas, and teaching in schools was stopped. The policy that reflected Confucius' teachings vanished. Mao started to feel that Confucian principles should be abandoned, as he now felt that they were incompatible with building a socialist society (Encyclopedia Britannica, 2019). Mao felt that the current education practices needed to be discarded as well. It was thought that Confucius' thinking enslaved people rather than made them productive citizens. Education was seen as discriminating against the students of the working class. During this time, schools were closed so the government could get rid of and destroy the old culture, old ideology, old customs, and old habits. The government wanted to remove the past and start anew. The educational system was completely overhauled, and Confucius' values were removed from education classrooms (Wang, 2014).

In February 1967, the central government reopened schools with new curricula. First through fourth grade students studied Chairman Mao's words, learned how to read some characters and revolutionary songs, and mastered some basic math and science. Fifth and sixth grade students memorized Chairman Mao's words and his articles that were published before 1949 (Mao & Sheng, 2006) along with many revolutionary songs. Soldiers were sent to school to organize the students and helped start the *worship* of Chairman Mao. Confucius' teachings "to be obedient to authority" were an integral part of the culture, so honoring leadership in this way was accepted (Wang, 2014, p. 4).

Third Stage: 1977–2000—Recovering Education

In 1976, Chairman Mao died. The death of this powerful Chinese leader and the overthrow of the *Gang of Four* ended the Great Cultural Revolution. China started to gradually reform and develop an open policy. This is when education began to revive and reorganize. Additional schools were built, and teachers were rehabilitated and returned to classrooms. Teachers once again were honored and revered. A college-accepted student was viewed as a "son or daughter of heaven" (Mao & Sheng, 2006). To be educated became the number one priority in China, and it reflected Confucian thinking that reading and studying knowledge is the priority in a human's life (Mao & Sheng, 2006).

Fourth Stage: 2001–Present—Conforming to the Modern World Educational Trends

During these years, the education system in China recovered and developed dramatically (Mao & Shen, 2006). The new curriculum focused on content instruction. The curriculum emphasized the need for children to actively participate in their own learning. This reflects Confucius' *Ying Cai Shu Jiao*, which means meeting individual students' learning needs and requires teachers to understand students' learning styles. In practice, teachers presented learning materials at different paces or in different formats to customize students' educational experiences. There is a famous Chinese metaphor used to describe this idea, which is that like an experienced gardener, different fertilizers are used for the flowers and trees. Flowers might need less and trees might need more or different types of fertilizer. As the gardener recognizes the variation between trees and flowers, teachers need to recognize the variation that exists amongst diverse learners.

All of the stages affected the Chinese educational system and, in the process, changed the way students were taught. Confucius' philosophy, sometimes more silently at some points in history than at other times, has had impacts on Chinese behavior and thought throughout.

Modern Influences on Education

During the fourth stage, the educational system in China has recovered and changed dramatically, and the Chinese Ministry of Education now regulates the educational system using a standard curriculum (Liu, 2010). The Ministry of Education has refocused the theory of education, changing it from the *dissemination of ideas* to students acquiring knowledge through *interactive learning* (Liu, 2010). There is a greater emphasis on how to meet the diverse learning needs of students rather than focusing only on their acquiring subject matter knowledge. Based upon the authors' reading of Confucius, it seems that many of these reforms emanate from Confucius' teachings that demonstrated working with an individual to promote learning by making content knowledge meaningful and individualized for him or her. Determining what students should learn to be successful in life has become the focus of Chinese education, rather than strict adherence to the curriculum that had been designed.

The Ministry has become more interested in developing lifelong learners, which resonates with Confucius' teaching of learning to improve oneself. There has been a move away from passive and rote styles of learning to more active learning approaches, including problem-solving and cooperative learning. Also within this educational framework is the desire to implement formative assessment to help promote student growth and to provide teachers with information to help improve their instruction. Moving away from a centralized curriculum has provided new pathways to meet individual and cultural needs of diverse students. New textbooks have been written, with faculty, students, and other related personnel participating in the curriculum committees. These are referred to as "democratic meetings for the discussion of teaching and studying" (Chang, 1974).

Inclusion Classrooms

In 2006, China joined with other countries in signing and ratifying the United Nations treaty that addressed the rights of people with disabilities to full participation in life. Article 26 specifically addressed the equal right of persons with disabilities to an "inclusive, quality, and free" education (United Nations, 2006). This step also helped in the curricula changes that continued to occur.

The Ministry of Education's relaxing of the national curriculum framework is helpful in setting the stage to use Universal Design for Learning (UDL). The China Reform policy for 2020 has guided schools on new methods for preparing teachers as well as new strategies of teaching to meet the needs of diverse learners. During the past nine years, there have been some scholarly publications that introduce UDL concepts within higher education communities in China (Gao & Gao, 2009; Hu, 2013; Xu & Wang, 2015). The UDL concepts, though, have not yet trickled down to practice in the field. Although the government has accepted the ideas as outlined in the United Nations treaty, there is still the need for teacher preparation programs and instructors of professional development to more actively teach and promote UDL principles to increase teachers' understanding and practice of implementing UDL.

Another core feature of the reform strategy has been updating curricula to meet real-world needs. For instance, there is a de-emphasis in math instruction in regards to student response speed and memorization of complex and seldom-used formulas. Instead, the curriculum will encourage multiple ways of solving problems and a deeper understanding of concepts relating to larger world problems, such as space development. In science, inauthentic demonstrations, calculations, and drills are being replaced with student experiments in real-world applications, including emphases on new energy, health, and conservation (Asia Society, 2019).

Tan (2015) discusses how Chinese education for many years had a distortion of Confucius' thinking in terms of education focusing only on his idea of the importance of learning that involves rote memorization with the purpose to pass tests. Tan referred to that method used in the Chinese classroom as *surface learning*, but the new curriculum promotes *deeper learning*, characterized by activating prior knowledge, interactively participating with the content, and making learning personalized (p. 429). Tan points out, "What Confucius does not recommend is rote memorization as this will not enable a student to take ownership of her own learning or engage in higher order thinking, and reflectively apply the lessons learnt in her life" (p. 436).

In June 2015, more specific early childhood reforms were provided by the Ministry of Education for the early childhood classrooms (Tan, 2015). The directives included planning for education around the developmental milestones of the children, taking into consideration their likes, dislikes and interests. Teacher education developed and progressed so planning could be developmentally appropriate, interactive, and based on discovery. The directive argued that children should be taught based on their individual needs and be respected as individual beings. They should learn communication skills and how to work together so that they will be prepared for real world experiences. Children should have access to curriculum that captivates their imagination and challenges them in their curiosity.

Confucius' thinking was thus renewed with this curriculum reform. However, many questions still remain about actual changes in teaching methods and responses to diversity in the classroom, as well as pupil choice in the learning process and curricular access. An important question also remains concerning the effects of the reform for early childhood classrooms in particular. Are the UDL principles that purport multiple means of representation, multiple means of action and expression, and multiple means of engagement present in the Chinese early childhood classrooms? The study described next is an effort to answer these questions.

Early Childhood Educator Knowledge and Use of UDL—Survey Research

Methodology

In a large city in northern China, 20 early childhood teachers randomly chosen from five schools completed a researcher-designed survey. The online survey was comprised of 12 fill-in and open-ended questions about the scope of their practices. The questionnaire also collected information about their knowledge and use of Universal Design for Learning (UDL). Questions were constructed to explore the use of UDL in planning and classroom instruction. Answers were coded and analyzed for themes. The teachers who responded to the surveys had taught for a minimum of 10 years and had a minimum of 14 years of education.

In addition, there were two focus group of teachers who were asked the same questions. There were five early childhood teachers, randomly selected, who participated in each focus group. Similar to the survey respondents, the teachers in the focus groups had also taught for a minimum of 10 years and had a minimum of 14 years of education. Each focus group met for two hours, with initial questions regarding UDL starting group discussion and then participants were free to share related experiences. The focus group process provided context and background information to related issues (Morgan, 1996). Answers from the focus group sessions were transcribed, coded, and analyzed for common threads.

Findings

The survey focused mainly on the implementation of UDL principles rather than the terminology associated with UDL. Questions pertained to the *what* and *how* of their classroom teaching experiences. Survey responses yielded interesting results. With inclusion in schools fairly well-established in China due to the signing and ratification of the UN treaty on the Convention of the Rights of Persons with Disabilities (2006), teachers seem to have realized that they must be prepared to teach all students.

One survey question centered on the design of a well-structured lesson that provides explicit instruction for all students but is also inclusively designed to address needs of students with disabilities. When teachers were asked if they started their lesson with a written objective that they then explained orally, more than half of the teachers shared that they do write the goal of the lesson and talk about it to engage students. The remaining teachers shared that while they often discuss what students will be learning prior to the start of a lesson, which does help to capture student attention and prompt their listening, they tend to not have the objectives written for students to see.

Teachers were then asked to define UDL. It was interesting to note that 25% of the respondents had never heard of it; 12% had, and 63% of respondents had used principles of UDL without specific knowledge of the concept. It is interesting to note that even though the terminology of UDL was not widely known or understood, many of the concepts of UDL do seem to be implemented in classrooms, as will be described further later in this section.

Another question focused on the teaching of reading. In China, reading in early childhood classrooms is comprised of memorizing ancient poems, engaging in rhythm and finger songs, and learning the Chinese characters. In most publicly funded classrooms, it is required to read at least 100 books. Reading can be reinforced using various tools. Students may be given different materials based on their reading levels, and readings may be represented in different ways, such as through print books or audio recordings. The survey revealed that many of the teachers helped students who had reading difficulties through varied strategies. About one third of the teachers said they did not use alternative methods for students having difficulties learning to read; but rather, they repeat the same general class strategies with the students in a smaller group.

Survey results also indicated that teachers often start a lesson with the entire class, then break into smaller groups based on individual students' needs. Teachers model for the students using various examples so that students are able to identify and meet the expectations. Teachers reported that they may ask other students to model as an alternative to teacher-directed modeling. Interactive whiteboards are often used to highlight specific skills, reinforce concepts, or add background information in a lesson.

Some respondents indicated that they often gave choices of ways for students to work, such as in partners, alone at their desks, or in locations within the classroom of their choosing. Many of the teachers in this study seemed to have recognized the importance of providing a variety of learning activities when teaching one concept. Teachers shared how they realized that students learn differently and have favorite ways of learning over others. Although they thought that there are times when all students must do one activity, the teachers indicated that they sought to provide alternative activities for reinforcement of skills.

Providing multiple ways for students to show their learning was a theme in the teachers' comments. In the majority of the surveyed classrooms, students seem to have flexibility in how they express what they are learning. Sharing orally about what they have learned was given high priority, as it contributes to the development of students' speaking skills and confidence; but drawing, writing, or completing a project were also options for student expression of learning that respondents mentioned. Using manipulatives to explain concepts was also a strategy reported by over half of the respondents. The rest indicated that they use manipulatives sometimes, depending on the subject area but generally in math and science.

Feedback was mentioned as a key ingredient to success in learning. All of the respondents indicated that they provide feedback to students in their daily work. The majority of teachers were consistent with this practice, while a small number said that they sometimes miss feedback opportunities. All teachers seemed to have recognized the importance of consistent feedback and remarked that they were striving to meet this expectation. In China, it is still customary for teachers to post the students' grades on a wall, and award stickers may be placed on a chart under student names so that families can view their children's progress. To avoid public reporting, teachers should make specific comments to students on their accomplishments and develop individualized methods to let families know their children's progress via a personal communication book or individual emails.

Teachers reported providing options for materials used in the classroom. For instance, many use the Smartboard, as it enables them to enlarge print and show video clips to reinforce skills or provide specific information during a lesson, such as bringing animals from another country to be part of the classroom experience. Students can use the Smartboard to practice different skills or play games. Video books and audiobooks are also being used, and teachers can enlarge the print when students follow along with a book on tape. Teachers reported that there continues to be development in using technology to expand options in learning.

During the focus group discussions, teachers expanded upon how they continue to learn about more ways to provide for all learners in their classrooms. They use different strategies and technology available to them and are eager to increase their repertoires. They talked about ways that they have engaged their students in learning by using technology, manipulatives, and multisensory activities. They also discussed the variety of ways they allowed students to express what they know, including oral and written activities. It would appear from the findings of this study that without specifically naming UDL principles, teachers were implementing some UDL practices. The teachers' philosophies appeared to resonate with Confucian ideals of personal responsibility where they gave children responsibility for making decisions in the classroom and the moral virtue of helping students learn because of the high regard education has within Chinese culture. The idea of individualizing instruction seems to be becoming more popular within the culture as teachers worked to meet the individual needs of students. The teachers in the focus groups discussed similar experiences as were shared in the survey results. The teachers in the focus groups added information about families, noting that families seemed to appreciate the work teachers did with their students because of the families' emphasis and value placed upon education.

According to one of the researchers, the teachers in the focus group had teachable spirits. They were very interested in the strategies other teachers shared. There appears to be a desire to grow in knowledge and develop practices that meet individual students' needs. Professional development to meet the educational needs of teachers should be developed and expanded.

Recently the Chinese government issued "China Education Modernization 2035." Within the objectives for this initiative there are three areas important to the issues outlined in this chapter. The government recommends raising the quality of preschool education, developing and increasing personalized individualized training through updated technology, and providing suitable education for children and adolescents with disabilities. The plan is to form a new pattern of educational governance in which the whole society participates together (Ministry of Education of the People's Republic of China, 2018).

Conclusion

Confucian ideals of personal responsibility, interactive learning, and meeting students' needs blends well with the UDL framework. Many Chinese teachers are interested in continuing their education to become more effective in their teaching and are ready to learn more about UDL. When reviewing the history of China and its rich traditions, it is interesting to see how Confucius' teachings have influenced the Chinese culture through the ages, in spite of political upheaval. It is also important to note how Confucius' teachings lend themselves well to the philosophy behind UDL. Key points of UDL, such as finding ways that meet students' individual needs, seem to readily match with Confucianism. It seems that Confucius' teaching in today's China can help Chinese teachers meet the needs of diverse learners and embrace strategies that seek to give all students access to the curriculum. This is a beginning step, and with more professional development in UDL, teachers will become more adept in how to differentiate for inclusive teaching.

References

Asia Society. (2019). *China's 2020 education reform strategy*. Retrieved from https://asiasociety.org/global-cities-education-network/chinas-2020-education-reform-strategy

Chang, P. H. (1974). The cultural revolution and Chinese higher education: Change and controversy. *The Journal of General Education, 26*(3), 187–194.

China Education Center. (2019). *History of education in China*. Retrieved from www.chinaeducenter.com/en/chistory.php

Encyclopedia Britannica. (2019). *China: Attacks on party members*. Retrieved from www.britannica.com/place/China/Attacks-on-party-members#ref590794

Gao, W., & Gao, Y. (2009). Tong yong xue xi she ji: Shi xian quan na de jiao yu xue [Universal learning design: Achieving inclusive teaching and learning]. *Studies in Foreign Education, 5*, 11–15.

Hu, F. (2013). Tong yong xue xi she ji zai te shu jiao yu ling yu de ying yong [The application of universal learning design in special education]. *China Social Welfare, 3*, 50–52.

Liu, Y. (2010). *Zhongguo xue qian jiao yu shi [The history of Chinese preschool education]*. Beijing: GU Ang Ming Daily Press.

Mao, L., & Sheng, G. (2006). *General history of Chinese education*. China: Shandong Education Press.

Ministry of Education of the People's Republic of China. (2018). *China education*. Retrieved from www.moe.gov.cn/jyb_xwfb/s6052/moe_838/201902/t20190223_370857.html

Morgan, D. L. (1996). *Focus groups as qualitative research* (2nd ed.). Washington, DC: Sage Publications.

Tan, C. (2015). Beyond rote-memorisation: Confucius' concept of thinking. *Educational Philosophy and Theory, 47*(5), 428–439.

United Nations. (2006). *Convention on the rights of persons with disabilities*. Retrieved from www.un.org/development/desa/disabilities/convention-on-the-rights-of-persons-with-disabilities.html

Wang, R. (2014). "Yin cai shi jiao" shijianguan de bianqian [The transition of the practical view of "yin cai shi jiao" in modern China]. *Basic Education Research, 17*, 2–5.

Xu, J., & Wang, Y. (2015). Tong yong xue xi she ji zai rong he jiao yu zhong de ying yong yan jiu [Application research of general learning design in integrated education]. *Journal of Modern Special Education, 7*, 102–106.

32
PROMOTING INCLUSION EDUCATION AND INTERCULTURAL COMPETENCE IN INTERNATIONAL SERVICE-LEARNING PROJECT-BASED COURSE IN ECUADOR

Maria De Freece Lawrence

Background

Sí, se puede (yes, it can be done) became a phrase of solidarity to the rights of workers and resistance to social inequality during the 1972 protests by Arizona's United Farm Workers (2019). It is a phrase that has persisted among the struggles of Latina/o communities in the United States to this day. The slogan is a powerful motivating call to action and to create and sustain social change and achieve *justicia* (justice) (United Farm Workers, 2019). The phrase served as the grounding context for a short-term international service learning (ISL) course in Ecuador offered to students attending a mid-size, northeast US college.

The course is offered in a quasi-rural community south of Quito. The course goals were aligned with the United Nations Sustainable Development Goals ([SDG]; 2019). The 17 SDGs are presented as actions to develop quality education, to challenge poverty, and to achieve social equity while preserving the natural environment for future generations. The ISL course that is described in this chapter is grounded in the Universal Design for Learning (UDL) framework and was developed as an inclusion curriculum that approached the SDGs on an intimate scale at a single school and orphanage in Ecuador.

The ISL course sought to expand the involvement and experiences of higher education students in other communities with the reciprocity goals of a rich intercultural learning experience. This case study addresses the improvement of education, nutrition, and sustainability practices in a high needs population in Ecuador by employing principles of UDL without reproducing "the relations of inequality [we were seeking] to redress" (Johnson, 2004, p. 146). This qualitative research positions UDL as an inclusion education design strategy to achieve equitable sustainability at an ISL site. The project goal was to address food security and nutrition by growing crops using a blend of hydroponic and traditional gardening methods and by promoting positive intercultural (or cross-cultural) communication, skills, relationships, and partnerships.

Rationale

Institutions of higher education have been increasingly focused on the globalization of curricula and making learning more inclusive for students. In addition to the goal to develop global citizens with intercultural competences, there is the legal and instructional responsibility to assure accessibility and inclusion in the design of college curricula. For example, the college students involved in the project described in this chapter reacted very differently to the change in altitude from being at sea level at the college on the Atlantic coast to being at higher elevations at the project site in the Andean mountains. Some became temporarily physically challenged to breathe and walk short distances in the hilly terrain. The initial learning experience for the students was a guided tour of *Museo Ethnohistorico de Artesannias del Ecuador Mindalae* and an open-air market in Quito, which allowed all students to benefit from the initial experiences, even those who were having altitude adjustment difficulties. This curricular design element aligns with universal design principles and facilitated an inclusive setting for learning, as it pursued a central goal of promoting inclusion and access for learners. UDL is applied as the lens through which this case study is described and discussed.

Case Study

UDL is a research-based framework for diversifying pedagogical options by educators for the implementation of an inclusive curriculum. The "instructional activities that allow for multiple means of representation, expression, and engagement" (King-Sears, 2008, as cited in Katz, 2013, p. 155) assure the inclusion of diverse learners. The involvement of higher education students from the US with K-12 learners at the Ecuador service site required planning curriculum to meet the needs of the two learner populations. The Internal Review Board approved qualitative action research to examine how a universally designed college curriculum facilitates (a) meeting the educational, social, and nutritional needs of K-12 Ecuadorian learners while (b) assuring college students develop intercultural competences resulting from learning and teaching in a science and technology, problem-based sustainability project. It also assures that the K-12 children residing in the partnering private orphanage benefit from their intercultural interactions with the US college students. This reciprocal, or *joint*, learning is essential to developing intercultural competences and a culture of sustainability.

The principles of UDL align with dimensions of intercultural competence (IC) in several essential ways. IC measures include a worldview or knowledge about others, awareness of one's cultural identity, and attitudes of openness. The

UDL Guidelines from the Center for Applied Special Technology, or CAST (2018), promote similar attributes, such as advocating for *cross-linguistic understanding*. In the course, the college students developed bilingual curriculum materials in science and engineering that supported using science tools to create physical models and systems. The need for intercultural communication challenged the innovation of multiple means of representation and engagement of the executive functions of all involved. UDL in curriculum design and pedagogical implementation intersects with the social-emotional learning characteristics, as described by Katz (2013), such as empathy, leadership, self-awareness, and belonging to a community of purpose. Throughout this intensive, experiential, short-term, international placement, college students performed across the multiple dimensions of UDL in an intercultural context with a population of learners that had an array of needs.

Project Focus and Design

Ecuador implemented a ten-year plan in 2006 to improve access to education (Blackman, 2016–2017) and has since made significant gains in overall national academic performances. Yet, a gap remains across communities, and there is room for continuing improvement in specific content test scores, such as mathematics and reading. The gap, as measured in 2015–2016, indicated that learners in some less fortunate communities require additional supports during the national education reforms. The service site for the project had struggled to secure stability and quality among its education staff at the school, which serves an orphanage population and learners from the surrounding local community whose families can afford to pay tuition.

The course curriculum project was designed to supplement the school experience, and to take place over multiple years until site sustainability was achieved. The multiple phases were:

- Phase 1: Pre-travel to align the course with community goals and define the project in Ecuador (2014);
- Phase 2: Provide the school children, faculty, and staff with English language learning, informally and formally (2016–2018);
- Phase 3: Identify project goals that required the development of in-country interdisciplinary curricula and activities executed with the community school and site residents (2017); and
- Phase 4: Achieve sustainable production of fresh food from gardens (2017–2018).

The in-country curriculum for the school and orphanage populations required college students to develop a hydroponics classroom wherein the K-12 students and teachers could engage in learning about promoting seed germination, planting seeds, monitoring the growth of plants, and composting organic waste. The college students created games, puzzles, and various community art projects to be completed with the youth learners that would reinforce the science and engineering concepts. The learning activities were designed to assure the inclusion of diverse learners and their needs using elements that were socially interactive and promoted artistic expression.

There were three prominent strands to the universally designed curriculum, portrayed in Figure 32.1. A social-emotional learning (SEL) strand allowed the college students and faculty to learn about each other and the members of the community. This was facilitated by living in the orphanage compound and functioning on the life schedule of the site.

The science, engineering, and art (SEA) learning strand for the college students and the service site facilitated the acquisition and transfer of content knowledge. Art served several functions in achieving the course and project goals, not the least of which was to afford multiple means of representation. Communication in an international setting requires creativity, as language and literacy can be limited between the two communities. Creative expression invites artistic representation. Consistent with experiential learning, the arts combine with the science project-based curricula to motivate all participants, increase the presence of diverse voices, and model knowledge and knowledge systems (Glass, Meyer, & Rose, 2013). Art is an important communicative approach to making and sharing meaning, especially in a multiple language setting with minimal comprehension or skill in speaking or writing proficiently in more than one language. Regardless of facility in formal languages, art facilitated the use of gestures and symbolic representations as alternative ways to convey meaning. The application of SEL and SEA were essential for building the final strand of the experiential project (EP) to ensure that it is culturally respectful and non-colonizing.

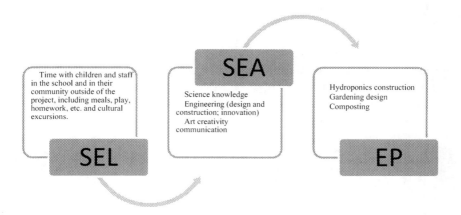

FIGURE 32.1 Course Design Strands

Project Development

This qualitative research relied upon observation of events and the analyses of college students' reflection journals and photographs. Thematic patterns were identified by the individual co-principal investigators employing consistency checking to make meaning from the implementation and outcomes of the curricula. For example, coding of journal entries was performed by each co-principle independent of the other, followed by the identification of emergent themes or patterns. Photographs students posted online at the project website were counted and sorted to determine categories and any correspondence to the themes from the journal entries.

Project planning began in 2014 with a visit to Ecuador to explore service sites. The selected service site's specialized support staff was minimal, such as medical, social, and psychiatric professionals. There was little information about the developmental backgrounds of the residential children that could be shared. What was known about the children was that they had been traumatized by their life circumstances, resulting in their removal from or abandonment by their parents and families. There were overt expressions of anxiety in the children and visible stunting among some of them, suggesting nutritional deficiencies and supporting notions of unassessed needs (both permanent and temporary). The development of special education and associated supports is in its early stages in Ecuador (Villafuerte, Perez, & Boyes, 2018). The lack of family supports for the orphan children at the selected site potentially enhanced the significance of the interactions the children had with service volunteers. Thus, the annual project visits that took place for the three years of the project became quite significant to the overall emotional support provided to the orphanage children.

In the first year of the project, college students were placed in *home-stays* in Quito and traveled daily to and from the service site in Conocoto. The decision was made to house college students at the orphanage compound in subsequent years. The housing compound was situated at the foot of the school, which was located on a hill above the compound. The homes formed a cul-de-sac around a treed grassy common wherein children played with each other and the college students. Each house had a house mother responsible for the daily needs of children of various ages and genders. These house mothers were former orphan residents of the site or high school age orphans.

The college students served as mentors and homework tutors and engaged in learning games and activities to provide individualized attention to the young residents who ranged in age from preschooler to adolescent/young adult. The college students came from a range of academic majors, such as nursing, social work, and education, and they served as supports in the foundation's school by teaching, conducting Body Mass Index (BMI) measurements, and nurturing youth.

An inclusive environment for both populations meant planning with significant flexibility and diversification of methods and materials. Technology was limited to paper, pens, pencils, paint, paint brushes, sand paper, tape, plant seedlings, seeds, and other repurposed items. Table 32.1 shares the alignment of curricula for college and K-12 learners. The table also identifies sample indicators of the UDL principles.

Each year of the project, there was progression in the development of the project goals. In year one, the basics of the project were established. Students spent time with the children, prepared a garden space, and established the idea of hydroponic gardening to grow plants. In year two, the immersion in the compound forged deepened personal relationships with the school faculty, as well as with the youth at the orphanage and the house mothers. For example, holidays or special events were celebrated collaboratively. Since house mothers have no days off or vacations, the college community would cook meals for them and celebrate

TABLE 32.1 Sample Alignment of Content Curriculum and Universal and Intercultural Elements

UDL/IC	College Students	Site and preK-12 School
Intercultural communication with visual/auditory options	Scheduled rotation into classrooms to teach and provide English support. Encourage visual expression (art), allow students to select topic from a generated list.	Students write about what they like in Spanish and translate to English. Assist with proper English pronunciation. Letters in English shared with students in US schools. US students reply in Spanish.
Representation with multiple models; pre-teach vocabulary in multiple languages	Build model hydroponic unit and place essential vocabulary of system components on the board in Spanish and English by labeling an illustration of the model.	Students are given the disassembled components and asked to build their units using the physical model and the conceptual model (illustration) as a guide.
Intercultural learning and communication; high affect; object science (tactile)	Students use beans (seeds) and set up hydroponic germination chambers with children; sprouted seeds are placed in the hydroponics units and/or planted in the soil garden. Bilingual.	Children come with classroom teacher who observes the chamber set-ups. Three days later the germinated seeds have sprouted. Teacher and students discuss the meaning of the results.
Revisit key concepts; action, self-expression, demonstration of critical knowledge	Community art projects (murals) were collaboratively developed and organized by the college students. Arranged for as many children to participate as possible.	Students in the school were included. Students suggested ideas for the project, drew, and painted the murals. Murals reflected their learning about plant life cycle, hydroponics, and the importance of planet Earth.

birthdays. These social-emotional and environmental factors were intentionally incorporated into the planning and implementation of the curriculum. It enabled the college students to learn about the children as individuals and contributing members of a unique community of need.

A critical aspect of the design of this course was that it was project-based, required hands-on activity, and was collaboratively taught to groups of children. This made it both possible and engaging for everyone to participate in some capacity regardless of age and physical or cognitive abilities. Murals, for example, were abstract, realistic, colorful, free-hand, and created by community members. College students guided and modeled within each part of the curriculum. They applied their imaginations to sand down blocks of wood to make picture puzzles of the fruits and vegetables that were planted in the gardens. They employed plastic beverage bottles to design vertically suspended hydroponic units and taught the children and school teachers how to build and maintain them.

The project required *object technology*. The role of objects was powerful due to their sensory accessible features that supported understanding of the properties of matter, such as texture, size, color, malleability, shape, name, and utility. The objects also were used as bilingual language lessons. UNO, in particular, provided practice for the children in learning numbers and colors in English and practice for the college students and faculty in speaking Spanish. Such reciprocal exchanges highlight the co-development of intercultural competences, as all participant groups benefited equally from the UDL design of the curricula.

Conclusions and Recommendations

UDL was a successful approach to the joint curricula for the international competence in a service learning course. College students reported the experiences in Ecuador as life-changing. Areas of growth, as determined from an analysis of reflection journals, were development of effective intercultural communication skills and leadership skills, feelings of empathy, and knowledge about Ecuador's culture, history, and hydroponic gardening. As part of the project, the college students had scheduled time to zipline through a portion of the Amazon forest, visit museums, and go on local tours. These opportunities served to further normalize relationships and enable them to experience daily life outside the service site.

An agronomist from a nearby university has since been working with the site project to help sustain it. Food is being produced for consumption, with potential for selling excess harvested crops to improve the economic opportunity of the site. As it takes about three months for the gardens to go from seed to harvest, the hydroponics system has been expanded to a slanted horizontal system to increase production. This means the nutritional opportunities for the children have improved with the diversification of their diets.

These findings reveal the value of a universally designed, interdisciplinary, mixed ability, project-based curriculum. The children at the service site and the school gained a sense of accomplishment and a strengthened sense of community from their participation in the project. The children and their teachers enhanced their English skills, learned about the life science of plants, and were introduced to two gardening approaches and the value of community projects and their potential for economic viability.

Acknowledgement

Jill Harrison served as co-principle investigator for this study.

References

Blackman, A. (2016–2017). Reorienting education policy to close Ecuador's learning gap. *Latin America Policy Journal, 6*, 52–61. Retrieved from http://lapj.hkspublications.org/wp-content/uploads/sites/19/2017/10/LAPJ_2017-edition.pdf

Center for Applied Special Technology [CAST]. (2018). *Universal design for learning guidelines, version 2.2*. Retrieved from http://udlguidelines.cast.org

Glass, D., Meyer, A., & Rose, D. (2013). Universal design for learning and the arts. *Harvard Review, 83*(1), 98–119.

Johnson, J. (2004). Universal instructional design and critical (communication) pedagogy: Strategies for voice, inclusion, and social justice/change. *Equity & Excellence in Education, 37*(2), 145–153.

Katz, J. (2013). The three-block model of universal design for learning (UDL): Engaging students in inclusive education. *Canadian Journal of Education, 36*(1), 153–194.

United Farm Workers. (2019). *History*. Retrieved from https://ufw.org/research/history/history-si-se-puede/

United Nations. (2019). *Sustainable development goals*. Retrieved from https://sustainabledevelopment.un.org/sdgs

Villafuerte, J., Perez, L., Boyes, E., Mena, L., Pinoargote, J., Riera, A., . . . Delgado, D. (2018). Challenges of the basic education system in Ecuador; the voices of the future teachers. *Arts and Humanities Open Access Journal, 2*(4), 217-224. doi:10.15406/ahoaj.2018.02.00061

33
DESIGNING AN ONLINE GRADUATE ORIENTATION PROGRAM

Informed by UDL and Studied by Design-Based Research

Jennifer Lock, Carol Johnson, Jane Hanson, Yang Liu, and Alicia Adlington

Introduction

Online learning is increasingly seen as a "viable alternative to some forms of face-to-face learning" (Adams Becker et al., 2017, p. 18). Growth in online learning programs allows higher education institutions "to increase flexibility, improve efficiency, and foster engagement in learning" (Hashey & Stahl, 2014, p. 78). With the flexibility and accessibility offered through graduate level online programs, students can advance their own learning by engaging in graduate work without having to leave their employment and/or home communities.

Higher education institutions may want to gauge the preparedness of their students for online learning in order to foster overall success and retention. Adult learners come into graduate programs with diverse experiences and expertise. Some may be advanced users of digital technology, while others may be novice users. It is important not to assume that students in online programs come equipped with confidence and competency in using digital technology for learning.

To address these issues, this chapter discusses the growth of online learning in higher education and the need for inclusive instructional design through the application of Universal Design for Learning (UDL) principles. The authors share their experiences in the design and implementation of an online graduate level orientation program for students in their Faculty of Education that was grounded in UDL principles. The chapter concludes with recommendations for future study.

Design-Based UDL Integration—An Online Study

Background

Current trends in the United States show an increase in the number of online course offerings in higher education. For instance, distance education enrollment saw a "7% increase overall between fall 2012 and fall 2014" (Allen, Seaman, Poulin, & Straut, 2016, p. 13). Furthermore, Allen et al. (2016) reported that "with more than one in four students (28%) taking some of their courses at a distance, these courses seem to have become a common part of the course delivery modality for many students" (p. 13). Canadian institutions are seeing similar trends, with continual growth in the development of online and blended learning opportunities (Bates, 2017). Online learning is evidently appealing to higher education students, as it provides flexibility in participation, accessibility, and convenience (Croxton, 2014).

This reported growth has associated challenges. For example, researchers have found that the dropout rates of online students are significant and linked to factors such as lack of self-regulation, self-determination, and self-efficacy skills (Croxton, 2014; Onah, Sinclair, & Boyatt, 2014; Yang, Sinha, Adamson, & Rosé, 2013). Online orientation programs may assist students in the development of these skills and foster success (Ali & Leeds, 2009; Lee & Choi, 2011). Ali and Leeds (2009) found that students who attended an online orientation program performed significantly better than their peers who did not participate in such a program.

Careful consideration needs to be given to the design of online orientation programs. Designers should recognize and develop programs that consider the varying backgrounds, experiences, skills, and knowledge that students bring to the online learning environment. The UDL framework provides a mechanism for conceptualizing the design and facilitation of online orientation programs. UDL guides educators to design learning based on the varied needs and interests of students (CAST, 2018a). The UDL approach encourages flexible conditions that ensure access and participation by all students while maintaining expectations or standards. UDL emphasizes the importance of creating an inclusive learning environment for students with diverse educational backgrounds and learning abilities through the three core curriculum design principles of multiple means of engagement, representation, and action and expression (Meyer, Rose, & Gordon, 2014). By engaging in these principles, instructional designers and instructors can provide students with an inclusive learning environment that is learner-centered. The students are given opportunities to experience multiple pathways that "diverge from the traditional classroom format . . . and adapt an inclusive curriculum" (Scott, Temple, & Marshall, 2015, p. 101). Gronneberg and Johnston (2015) shared:

> The UDL framework sets high standards for all students and applies flexible means so that each learner finds appropriate learning challenges and

supports. In this way, it helps faculty maximize desirable challenges (such as high achievement standards) and minimize undesirable ones (such as frustration and boredom).

(p. 2)

The ultimate goal is to foster the development of expert learners. An expert learner, according to Meyer et al. (2014), "is purposeful and motivated (the *why* of learning), resourceful and knowledgeable (the *what* of learning), and strategic and goal-directed (the *how* of learning)" (p. 25).

Online Orientation Program Development

Initial informal feedback gathered by design team members indicated there was a need for an orientation program focused on the acquisition of online learning skills for newly admitted graduate students within a Faculty of Education at a western Canadian university. Instructors reported that students were spending valuable time focusing on online learning skills rather than focusing on academic content. The research team saw this real-world problem as an opportunity to create an intervention—an online orientation to support capacity development of graduate students enrolled in the faculty's online programs.

The iterative design process, explained later, was used to create the online orientation program. The program was designed to provide graduate students with active learning opportunities to familiarize themselves with synchronous and asynchronous online learning platforms, to learn effective online learning practices, to prepare for online learning, and to develop the transferable or soft skills required to support their learning.

A design-based research (DBR) methodology (McKenney & Reeves, 2012) was used to develop this orientation initiative. Wang and Hannafin (2005) noted that the purpose of DBR is to "improve educational practices through iterative analysis, design, development, and implementation, based on collaboration among researchers and practitioners in real-world settings, and leading to contextually-sensitive design principles and theories" (pp. 6–7). As such, UDL and DBR provided a harmonious basis for the research team to conduct this study.

Innovation was observed in the design and implementation of the online orientation program over the course of the two-year DBR study. A six-step process was developed and included a needs analysis, the design and assessment of a pilot orientation, and re-design of multiple iterations based on feedback from participants. The design and implementation of each iteration was studied, and evidence-informed decisions were made to refine the design and facilitation of the program.

The research team designed the orientation to align with learning outcomes, signature program pedagogies, and the format and structure of the institution. Key outcomes for the program included community building, goal setting, competence in using the learning management system (LMS), confidence in engaging with multimedia in the online learning environment, and the development of self-regulation practices to enhance effectiveness as online learners.

Application in Practice

The online orientation program offered students a friendly environment where they could learn, practice, and master the skills needed to successfully navigate the online environment (e.g., LMS) used for the graduate program. The overall aim of the program was to familiarize students with strategies for online learning and associated technologies. It also provided pre-program opportunities in which students could experience the academic context and develop their online learning skills before beginning their course work.

UDL principles (Meyer et al., 2014) informed and grounded the design of the orientation program. UDL provided instructors and designers with guidelines to create an inclusive and accessible learning environment for all learners (Hickey, 2013). In the following sections, each of the three principles are discussed in relation to the various strategies that were used in the online orientation program.

Engagement: Affective Network

This UDL principle is focused on the *why of learning*, which includes such items as "interest, effort and persistence, and self-regulation" (CAST, 2018b, p. 1). Various modalities (including synchronous and asynchronous) were used to motivate students' learning in the orientation program. For instance, a synchronous chat activity was offered to initiate an informal community and allow students to develop competency with the synchronous chat tools as they engaged with peers and the instructor. Providing additional synchronous opportunities and offering flexibility around the scheduling enabled greater attendance and increased student engagement.

The program timing and availability was also extended. Initially offered for seven days, the program was extended to 10 days in response to student requests for more active time within the program. Additional collaborative activities and content regarding self-regulation were also prepared by the design team in response to student feedback.

Students were presented with the opportunity to develop strategies regarding time management, self-regulation, and online learning strategies (e.g., note taking). Asynchronous learning activities were designed to be motivating and practical for learners. An example is learning to use the video functions in the discussion area of the LMS.

Outcome

Through the orientation, students experienced various applicable activities to support their engagement in online learning environments.

Representation: Recognition Network

This principle involves the *what of learning* and includes such items as "perception, language and symbols, and comprehension" (CAST, 2018b, p. 1). The orientation program content was presented in a variety of modalities, including text, video, and audio. The opportunity to utilize various means of representation allowed students to experience a number of tools and features within the LMS. For example, students were asked to create a short video as an introductory activity; this replaced traditional text introductions. Students were also asked to create an audio or video response to an assignment.

Outcome

These multimedia activities allowed students to develop familiarity with tools outside of the text context and furthered the development of their confidence and competence in the online learning environment.

Action and Expression: Strategic Network

This principle focuses on the *how of learning* and involves "physical action, expression and communication, and executive function" (CAST, 2018b, p. 1). In the orientation program, students were encouraged to use various methods to express their learnings through synchronous and asynchronous modalities. Text, audio, and video expression were seen in learning activities such as discussion forums and assignment submissions.

Outcome

Students enthusiastically utilized multiple means of communication for the learning activities.

Summary of Applications

Throughout the program, students were encouraged to examine their online learning skills and seek out opportunities for improvement in order to enhance their online learning experiences. Students were asked to reflect on their strengths and identify areas of improvement in order to best prepare themselves for their online graduate program. Areas of time management, self-regulation, and goal setting were addressed. Options for collaboration and group participation were also presented. For example, students engaged in group projects and presentations with their peers. Students were allowed to self-select their groups. One student in particular shared how the course design was motivating and engaging for a person with a learning disability, as it offered a rich learning environment with a high level of instructor presence and support. Students of all levels of expertise were offered a chance to be challenged in their learning.

Instructor Implications

A key finding of the study was the importance of ensuring that instructors of online orientation programs have expert-level knowledge with the technology and the accompanying academic program. This helped students to develop their comfort and confidence with online learning, as instructors were able to provide mentorship, troubleshooting, and expert-level advice. Instructors should also take learner variability into consideration when presenting content and activities. For example, an experienced instructor can provide advanced learners with more challenging activities than those designed for novice users. A strong instructor presence was found to be critical so that students did not feel isolated. Rather, they were being mentored and guided in their learning to become confident and competent online learners. Within the online environment, there can be flexibility in terms of timing of activities (e.g., synchronous and asynchronous), representation of content (e.g., text, image, video), and support for various ways that students can express their learning.

Conclusions and Recommendations

Online orientation programs play a critical role in preparing students for online learning. Skills associated with educational technology and learning strategies are key components to success. These skills position students to be able to more fully engage in academic discourse and activities by equipping them to be able to use the various tools and features within the LMS. Online orientation programs grounded in UDL principles can introduce students to an array of possibilities in terms of how they can engage with the *why*, *what*, and *how* of learning as part of becoming expert learners (Meyer et al., 2014). As noted by Meyer et al. (2014), "Dynamic, flexible learning environments are needed to respond to the natural variability of learners" (p. 47). The UDL framework is well-suited to online orientation programs given the affordances of the technology and the flexibility it can provide in the online environment. Flexibility supports the personalization of learning by embracing the three UDL principles in the design of online environments. As such, there is a need to use UDL for designing online learning environments.

It is important to help students to understand how UDL impacts their learning. Students in online environments that are grounded by UDL principles are empowered and given agency to make decisions around engagement, use, and representation. Consideration needs to be given to how to further grow this capacity.

It should be noted, though, that there is complexity with UDL. Meyer et al. (2014) argued that it is "a broad framework made up of principles, with related guidelines that provide a systematic means by which we move to the practical.

UDL is not a prescriptive checklist or formula with set methods and tools" (p. 87). Instructors need professional development to support their understanding of UDL and how to apply it in the design and facilitation of online courses. Research is needed regarding the impact of UDL practices within online learning environments, both for formal course instruction as well as pre-program activities such as the orientation described in this chapter.

In conclusion, the authors gained a deeper understanding of the richness and the complexity of designing an online orientation environment grounded on UDL. Using the DBR methodology, continuous learning through evidence-informed practice on the nature and impact of the orientation program and enhanced engagement with the UDL framework were experienced. This orientation program reflects only a small portion of what can be learned and applied in the practice and design of using UDL for online learning.

References

Adams Becker, S., Cummins, M., Davis, A., Freeman, A., Hall Giesinger, C., & Ananthanarayanan, V. (2017). *NMC horizon report: 2017 higher education edition*. Austin, TX: The New Media Consortium. Retrieved from http://cdn.nmc.org/media/2017-nmc-horizon-report-he-EN.pdf

Ali, R., & Leeds, E. (2009). The impact of classroom orientation in online student retention. *Online Journal of Distance Learning Administration, 12*(4). Retrieved from www.westga.edu/~distance/ojdla/ winter124/ali124.html

Allen, I. E., Seaman, J., Poulin, R., & Straut, T. T. (2016). *Online report card: Tracking online education in the United States*. Babson Survey Research Group. Retrieved from http://onlinelearningsurvey.com/reports/onlinereportcard.pdf

Bates, T. (Ed.). (2017). *Tracking online and distance education in Canadian universities and colleges: 2017*. Vancouver, BC: The National Survey of Online and Distance Education in Canadian Post-Secondary Education. Retrieved from https://onlinelearningsurveycanada.ca/

CAST. (2018a). *Universal design for learning guidelines*. Retrieved from http://udlguidelines.cast.org/?utm_medium=web&utm_campaign=none&utm_source=cast-about-udl

CAST. (2018b). *UDL and the learning brain*. Wakefield, MA: CAST Professional Publishing. Retrieved from www.cast.org/our-work/publications/2018/udl-learning-brain-neuroscience.html

Croxton, R. A. (2014). The role of interactivity in student satisfaction and persistence in online learning. *Journal of Online Learning and Teaching, 10*(2), 314–325.

Gronneberg, J., & Johnston, S. (2015). *7 Things you should know about universal design for learning*. EDUCAUSE Learning Initiatives (ELI). Received from https://library.educause.edu/~/media/files/library/2015/4/eli7119-pdf.pdf

Hashey, A. I., & Stahl, S. (2014). Making online learning accessible for students with disabilities. *Teaching Exceptional Children, 46*(5), 70–78. doi:10.1177/0040059914528329

Hickey, E. (2013). *Dismantling barriers via multiple representations on grade nine provincial achievement tests in mathematics and social studies* (Doctoral dissertation). University of Calgary (ProQuest Dissertations and Theses). (Accession No. NR96742).

Lee, Y., & Choi, J. (2011). A review of online course dropout research: Implications for practice and future research. *Educational Technology Research and Development, 59*, 593–618.

Meyer, A., Rose, D. H., & Gordon, D. (2014). *Universal design for learning: Theory and practice*. Wakefield, MA: CAST Professional Publishing.

McKenney, S., & Reeves, T. C. (2012). *Conducting educational design research*. New York, NY: Routledge.

Onah, D. F., Sinclair, J., & Boyatt, R. (2014). Dropout rates of massive open online courses: Behavioural patterns. *EDULEARN14 Proceedings*, 5825–5834.

Scott, L. A., Temple, P., & Marshall, D. (2015). UDL in online college coursework: Insights of infusion and educator preparedness. *Online Learning, 19*(5), 99–119.

Wang, F., & Hannafin, M. J. (2005). Design-based research and technology-enhanced learning environments. *Educational Technology Research and Development, 53*(4), 5–23.

Yang, D., Sinha, T., Adamson, D., & Rosé, C. P. (2013). *Turn on, tune in, drop out: Anticipating student dropouts in massive open online courses*. Proceedings of the 2013 NIPS Data-driven education workshop, 11, 14.

34
DEVELOPING INCLUSIVE EDUCATION IN IRELAND

The Case for UDL in Initial Teacher Education

Ellen Reynor

Background

Inclusive Education in Ireland

Since the Salamanca Statement and Framework for Special Educational Needs (UNESCO, 1994), there has been international commitment to more equitable education systems that recognise and respond to the diversity of the population and a focus on educational inclusion for individuals with disabilities (Priestley, 2005). A new framework for action was adopted, with a guiding principle that schools should accommodate all children, regardless of their physical, intellectual, social, emotional, linguistic or other conditions (UNESCO, 1994). It should be noted that the term "special educational needs" or SEN can have many meanings. For the purposes of this chapter, it refers to individuals who experience barriers to learning, whether that is through a physical disability, a learning difficulty or an exceptional learning ability (National Council for Curriculum and Assessment [NCCA], 1999).

The inclusion of children with SEN in mainstream education is relatively new in Ireland compared with many other countries. Throughout the 1970s and 1980s, Ireland operated a multitrack system of education, with children being educated in mainstream schools, special schools or special classes in mainstream schools where available (Kyriazopoulou & Weber, 2009). However, there has been a major policy shift since the early 1990s to move toward a more inclusive education system that is in line with many other countries, and Ireland appears to be in a transition phase currently in its efforts toward this goal (Banks & McCoy, 2011). This is largely due to significant legislation such as the *Education Act* (Government of Ireland, 1998), guaranteeing curricular access for children and young people with SEN and the *Education for Persons with Special Educational Needs Act (EPSEN)* (Government of Ireland, 2004). The latter Act enshrines inclusion as a core value and states explicitly that school provisions should be informed by principles of equality and human rights. It also states that children with SEN are to be educated in an inclusive setting unless this is not in the best interests of the child or if it negatively impacts the effective provision of education for other children in mainstream education. The focus on inclusive education policy in Ireland has resulted in greater numbers of students with SEN attending mainstream schools, with prevalence estimates as high as 25%–28% of the school population with SEN (Banks & McCoy, 2011; McCoy, Banks, & Shevlin, 2016).

The Changing Profile of Mainstream Schools in Ireland

Over the years, educational inclusion has progressed from an initial approach emphasising *integration* or the need for children with SEN to *fit in* with their class level (Meegan & MacPhail, 2006) and follow a *one size fits all* curriculum (Phádraig, 2007, p. 290) to addressing the broader discourse of human rights and social justice which shifts the emphasis from the individual learner to the environment as the site of change (Drudy & Kinsella, 2009; Thomas & Loxley, 2001). In Ireland, this shift has been slow, mainly due to the influence of the psycho-medical model of disabilities that emphasises perceived individual deficits in people labelled as disabled or having SEN, and deterministic thinking embedded in Irish educational policy documents such as the EPSEN Act (Smyth et al., 2014). It is argued that, thus far, the necessary restructuring of the Irish education system to effectively meet the needs of students with SEN has not taken place, nor does there appear to be any consistent model of inclusive practice across schools in Ireland (Kinsella & Senior, 2008). It is a continuing challenge, therefore, for Irish schools to progress toward truly inclusive school cultures and practices.

Universal Design for Learning in Ireland

The Association of Higher Education and Disability (AHEAD) in Ireland has been instrumental in developing inclusive higher education institutions (HEIs) and equality of access for all students in further and higher education (AHEAD, 2017). They stipulate that universal design (UD) and the Universal Design for Learning (UDL) framework are important approaches in supporting the diverse range of learners in HEIs. AHEAD has been instrumental in developing knowledge and understanding of UDL approaches in third level institutions and among administrators, educators and lecturers in colleges and institutions in Ireland. However, the enthusiasm and support for UDL approaches promoted by AHEAD in Ireland has been slow to influence the Initial Teacher Education (ITE) sector. Further, there is no clear UDL model of practice available for pre-service teachers to enable them to develop their planning and instructional skills and prepare them to teach in an education system with a high level of student diversity and students with SEN (Drudy & Kinsella, 2009).

Teacher Education and the Curriculum

Undergraduate teachers in Ireland complete a four-year degree programme culminating in a Bachelor of Education degree (B. Ed.), preparing them to teach in primary schools (junior infants to 6th class, 4 to 12 years old approximately). The Teaching Council of Ireland promotes "the continuing education, training and professional development of teachers" (Government of Ireland, 2001, section 6c, 8) and advocates that ITE programmes should "develop students' understanding and capacity to critically engage with curriculum aims, design, policy, reform, pedagogy and assessment" (Teaching Council, 2011a, p. 13). In the past, the Irish curriculum was viewed as a document to be followed *specifically* by teachers (Gleeson & Donnabháin, 2009), with a narrow focus on the transmission of content with each subject consisting of separate strands and strand units for the different class or grade levels (Gleeson, 2009). Given the importance of the curriculum in conveying ideological positions about inclusion and societal values toward diversity (Apple, 2004), the Teaching Council's view represents a shift from what has been a technicist approach to the curriculum, which views curriculum as a static package to be transmitted by teachers to students (Grundy, 1987), to a view that it involves a set of processes that teachers act on, in the context of the educational environment and teaching (Young, 2013). This is in line with the active view of the curriculum promoted by UDL (Stanford & Reeves, 2009).

In the Irish curriculum, there is no reference to the potential barriers to learning for students or how to address them, and while *access to the highest quality of education* is stated as a right for all children (PSC Introduction, p. 29), it is not clear how it should be operationalised. The diversity of the learners in Irish classrooms is not a focus in the specific aims and objectives of the curriculum, but it is an afternote, stating simply that "the child's stage of development and differences in terms of intellectual and physical ability require consideration" (PCS, 1999, p. 34). In sum, there appears to be little support in the curriculum for teachers to build their understanding of broader student diversity or to address it from a whole-class perspective.

UDL Framework as Inclusive Practice

UDL seeks to provide all students, regardless of ability, with opportunities to learn to the best of their abilities. It argues that the traditional *one-size-fits-all* curriculum ignores the vast individual differences in learning strengths and challenges (Nelson, 2014). As such, it directly addresses the instructional challenges that teachers face in their classrooms and attempts to support their pedagogical choices in meeting the needs of all learners. UDL is seen as an educational

Developing Inclusive Education in Ireland   **261**

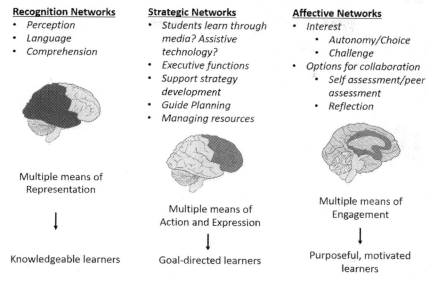

FIGURE 34.1   Simplified Version of UDL Guidelines

approach that facilitates inclusion and caters to diversity (Coyne et al., 2006) as intentional aspects of instructional design, as addressing the "divergent needs of *special* populations increase usability for everyone" (p. 39). The three UDL principles (see Figure 34.1) are based on: how educators represent the learning to pupils (recognition), how students engage with the learning and stay engaged as learners (engagement), and how students express their learning (expression). Each of the principles has accompanying guidelines, providing options that underpin the UDL framework.

The framework is a "blueprint for creating flexible goals, methods, materials and assessments that work for everyone" (CAST, 1998, para. 2). The concept and framework of UDL are based on research in the areas of developmental psychology, cognitive neuroscience and education, guiding the design of flexible learning environments, materials and instruction (Hitchcock, Meyer, & Rose, 2005) in a proactive way, improving expected outcomes for all learners (Pisha & Coyne, 2001).

The B. Ed. Research Project

Fourth year students on the B. Ed. degree programme in Dublin City University must complete a research project as part of their final year coursework. The project introduces students to action research and reflective inquiry as part of their professional development (Teaching Council, 2011a) and allows them to explore an area of education of interest to them. In this context, the author developed a research project with 25 student teachers using the UDL framework to support student teachers to improve their planning and teaching for inclusion. The purpose of the project was to investigate how student teachers make meaning of the concept of *inclusive education* through their planning and instruction. A further aim was to support the students to develop their planning and teaching in inclusive ways, to reduce their bias in using a one-size-fits-all approach to planning and teaching and to increase their awareness of *bell-curve thinking* (Florian & Black-Hawkins, 2011). Although UDL is underpinned by a strong body of research in neuroscience (Meyer, Rose, & Gordon, 2014), there is a lack of research in how to prepare teachers to implement universally designed lessons (McGuire-Schwartz & Arndt, 2007) and on the advantages and limitations of UDL in practice for teachers and learners (Edyburn, 2010). This is especially important at early childhood and primary school levels, which are the foundation levels of learning and development. The research project required students to plan and teach some lessons that incorporated the UDL framework (CAST, 2011) as a decision-making approach. Students used a reflective diary throughout and identified key observations and reflections from their field notes, findings and reflections on the project. Data on their knowledge and use of inclusive approaches, their interactions with UDL as a process, as well as their reflections on UDL approaches in planning and teaching were gathered using semi-structured interviews, student lesson plan reflections, field notes, as well as their key findings.

Findings

Planning and Teaching for All Learners

During one of the UDL preparation sessions, students discussed their understanding of the diversity of learners they may be teaching in their practicum placements. They agreed that meeting the class teacher usually consisted of an informal discussion about the children with SEN in the class. When questioned about the need to consider the range of learners in their classes when planning, some students said they used differentiation to achieve this, but many students felt that although they knew what differentiation was, they did not know how to use it in practice. Students admitted that their lesson goals were often very broad and weren't linked to pupil outcomes. When asked if it was important that all children achieved the lesson goals, the students agreed that it was, but admitted that they did not focus on assessment of learning. Students viewed resources as key elements of their lessons. The most popular ones were YouTube clips, pictures, homemade charts, objects and artefacts, and DVDs of music and songs. Interestingly, when asked about the purpose of these resources, the students agreed that they were primarily used to make lessons interesting for the pupils rather than to diversify representation of the content.

Student Reflections on UDL

Planning Using UDL Templates

A number of different lesson plan templates were provided for the students to plan their UDL lessons. Students reacted very positively to these templates in their reflections. For instance, they noted how it was necessary to have in-depth knowledge of their pupils' strengths and needs in order to recognise the barriers to learning and offer solutions. Unlike previous placements, *all* students spoke with the learning support teacher and read pupil profiles prior to their placement. They found these added to their knowledge and understanding of the children's needs from the viewpoint of planning and teaching. One student noted how using UDL forced her to shift focus from herself as the centre of the lesson to closer observation of the pupils during lessons. Another student noted that the UDL planning process made her more aware of pupils who are high achievers in the class and how she may not be challenging these learners in her teaching.

Disadvantages and Difficulties with UDL Approaches

Reflections indicated that the UDL framework was difficult to negotiate at times, and some felt it was difficult to process in a short time. This is something that has been noted by Nelson (2014) in her characterization of the "unwieldiness of the UDL framework" (p. 15). As there is no right way to use the framework, it is necessary to practice using it over time, reflect on that practice and return to it again with new insights. Several students also felt confused by the representation and expression principles at times. Additionally, students found it difficult to differentiate in their planning at times and felt that they would not be able to do this for all lessons every day, as resources were at times limited by what was available in the school.

Time was a recurring issue for the students when planning their UDL lessons. Students documented how it required much more time to plan UDL lessons, as it could involve additional steps of checking the environment and availability of technology and planning of multiple options. Students argued that it would be helpful to have guidance from teachers in the school, but they noted that teachers were not using UDL in any organised way. Students felt that it would make planning easier if teachers already had a selection of resources that were UDL friendly, and that the sharing of knowledge and resources for UDL would have been a great support for them. Use of technology was problematic at times, as Internet connectivity was not consistently available, especially in rural schools.

Several students found it difficult to find solutions to some of the learning barriers experienced by pupils with ADHD and dyslexia. Barriers mainly related to reading and writing components of lessons. One student expressed that her planning and teaching had become more pupil-centred. Students felt that they came to know their pupils better because of the UDL project, and it made them question their views of disability and SEN. They also found it to be a very positive experience.

Conclusion and Recommendations

The UDL project described in this chapter highlights some of the difficulties in policy, curriculum and educational practice at the primary school level (e.g., grades 1–8) in Ireland that may be inhibiting the progress of inclusion and UDL approaches. One of the difficulties evident from the findings was the student teachers' view of the curriculum as a body of information (e.g., strand units and objectives) that needed to be transferred to the pupils they teach. The UDL framework allowed the student teachers to take an active rather than a passive approach to the curriculum and reflect on ways that they could alter, develop and improve it for the purposes of addressing the diverse needs of their pupils.

The effectiveness of UDL as an inclusive approach will largely be dependent on how teachers and educators use it. There appears to be a need to embed UDL approaches in all four years of the B. Ed. degree course if it is to be an effective tool as part of inclusive practices. As many students noted, it does require time to understand and use the framework and the approaches. Embedding UDL, though, would likely result in student teachers being less reliant on textbooks when planning and teaching and systematically considering the strengths and needs of all pupils in their classrooms.

More research on UDL is needed around its development and effectiveness for students with additional needs (Edyburn, 2010). Additionally, it has been noted that the UDL framework does not include a component associated with meaningful student outcomes, and it does not provide a means of measuring the effectiveness of specific student interventions (Edyburn, 2010). However, adherence to the UDL principles can make the curriculum accessible to as wide an extent of learners as possible (Meo, 2008). Suitable structures (e.g., community of learners) and supports could help teachers in their learning and use of UDL approaches (Novak, 2016). The student teachers involved in this project appeared to be using a one-size-fits-all model for planning and teaching, of which they were totally unaware until questioned about it. The diversity of classrooms and learners is slowly eroding the usefulness of that approach, as *inclusive education* calls for schools to celebrate diversity, provide equal opportunities and reconstruct schooling (Slee, 2010). The application of the UDL framework and approaches at the preservice level must be a first step in this direction.

References

Apple, M. (2004). *Ideology and curriculum* (3rd ed.). New York: Routledge.
Association for Higher Education Access and Disability (AHEAD). (2017). *The UDL framework explained*. Retrieved from https://ahead.ie/udl-framework

Banks, J., & McCoy, S. (2011). *A study on the prevalence of special educational needs: National council for special education research report No. 9*. Trim, Ireland: NCSE.

Center for Applied Learning and Technology (CAST). (1998). *What is universal design for learning?* Wakefield, MA: CAST Professional Publishing. Retrieved from www.cast.org/udl/index

Center for Applied Learning and Technology (CAST). (2011). *Universal design for learning guidelines* (version 2.0). Wakefield, MA: CAST Professional Publishing.

Coyne, P., Ganley, P., Hall, T., Meo, G., Murray, E., & Gordon, D. (2006). Applying universal design for learning in the classroom. In D. Rose & A. Meyers (Eds.), *A practical reader in universal design for learning* (pp. 1–14). Cambridge, MA: Harvard Education Press.

Drudy, S., & Kinsella, W. (2009). Developing an inclusive system in a rapidly changing European society. *International Journal of Inclusive Education, 13*(6), 647–663.

Edyburn, D. L. (2010). Would you recognize universal design for learning if you saw it? Ten propositions for new directions for the second decade of UDL. *Learning Disability Quarterly, 33*, 33–41.

Florian, L., & Black-Hawkins, K. (2011). Exploring inclusive pedagogy. *British Educational Research Journal, 37*(5), 813–828.

Gleeson, J. (2009). *Curriculum in context: Partnership, power and praxis in Ireland*. Berlin: Peter Lang.

Gleeson, J., & Donnabháin, D. Ó. (2009). Strategic planning and accountability in Irish education. *Irish Educational Studies, 28*(1), 27–46.

Government of Ireland. (1998). *Education act 1998 (Ireland)*. Dublin: Stationary Office.

Government of Ireland. (2001). *The teaching council act*. Dublin: Stationery Office.

Government of Ireland. (2004). *Education for persons with special educational needs act 2004 (Ireland)*. Dublin: Stationary Office.

Grundy, S. (1987). *Curriculum: Product or praxis*. Lewes: Falmer.

Hitchcock, C. H., Meyer, A., & Rose, D. H. (2005). *The universally designed classroom: Accessible curriculum and digital technologies*. Cambridge, MA: Harvard Education Press.

Kinsella, W., & Senior, J. (2008). Developing inclusive schools: A systemic approach. *International Journal of Inclusive Education, 12*(5–6), 651–665.

Kyriazopoulou, M., & Weber, H. (Eds.). (2009). *Development of a set of indicators—For inclusive education in Europe*. Odense, Denmark: European Agency for Development in Special Needs Education (EADSNE).

McCoy, S., Banks, J., & Shevlin, M. (2016). Insights into the prevalence of special educational needs. In J. Williams, E. Nixon, E. Smyth, & D. Watson (Eds.), *Cherishing all the children equally? Ireland 100 years on from the rising* (pp. 153–174). Cork, Ireland: Oak Tree Press.

McGuire-Schwartz, M., & Arndt, J. S. (2007). Transforming universal design for learning in early childhood teacher education from college classroom to early childhood classroom. *Journal of Early Childhood Teacher Education, 28*(2), 127–139.

Meegan, S., & MacPhail, A. (2006). Inclusive education: Ireland's provision for children with special educational needs. *Irish Educational Studies, 25*, 53–62.

Meo, G. (2008). Curriculum planning for all learners: Applying universal design for learning (UDL) to a high school reading comprehension programme. *Preventing School Failure, 52*(2), 21–30.

Meyer, A., Rose, D. H., & Gordon, D. (2014). *Universal design for learning: Theory & practice*. Wakefield, MA: CAST Professional Publishing.

National Council for Curriculum and Assessment (NCCA). (1999). *Curriculum issues, discussion document*. Dublin, Ireland: NCCA.

Nelson, L. (2014). *Design and deliver: Planning and teaching using universal design for learning*. Baltimore, MA: Brookes Publishing.

Novak, K. (2016). *UDL now: A teacher's guide to applying universal design for learning in today's classrooms*. Wakefield, MA: CAST Professional Publishing.

Phádraig, B. M. (2007). Towards inclusion: The development of provision for children with special educational needs in Ireland from 1991–2004. *Irish Educational Studies, 26*, 289–300.

Pisha, B., & Coyne, P. (2001). Smart from the start: The promise of universal design for learning. *Remedial and Special Education, 22*(4), 197–203.

Priestley, M. (2005). We're all Europeans now! The social model of disability and European social policy. In C. Barnes & G. Mercer (Eds.), *The social model of disability: Europe and the majority world* (pp. 17–31). Leeds: Disability Press.

Slee, R. (2010). How do we make inclusive education happen when exclusion is a political disposition. *International Journal of Inclusive Education, 17*(8), 895–907.

Smyth, F., Shevlin, M., Buchner, T., Biewer, G., Flynn, P., Latimier, C., . . . Ferreira, M. A. V. (2014). Inclusive education in progress: Policy evolution in four European countries. *European Journal of Special Needs Education, 29*(4), 1–13.

Stanford, B., & Reeves, S. (2009). Making it happen: Using differentiated instruction, retrofit framework, and universal design for learning. *Teaching Exceptional Children Plus, 5*(6), 1–9.

Teaching Council. (2011a). *Initial teacher education: Criteria and guidelines for programme providers*. Maynooth: Teaching Council of Ireland.

Thomas, G., & Loxley, A. (2001). *Deconstructing special education and constructing inclusion*. Buckingham: Open University Press.

UNESCO. (1994). *The Salamanca statement and framework for action on special needs education*. New York: UNESCO.

Young, M. (2013). Overcoming the crisis in curriculum theory: A knowledge-based approach. *Journal of Curriculum Studies, 45*(2), 101–118.

35

SNAPSHOT—UNDERSTANDING HOW UDL CAN SERVE AS A FRAMEWORK FOR INSTRUCTIONAL DECISIONS

Lisa Harris and Lindsay Yearta

Background

This snapshot focuses on the second phase of a longitudinal study. In the first phase, year one of the study, teacher candidates were enrolled in a technology-integration course with a field-based component. Candidates learned how to use the Universal Design for Learning (UDL) framework (CAST, 2018) to inform instructional decisions and were given opportunities to practice these skills in a P-12 classroom. The second phase, year two of the study, featured the same teacher candidates enrolled in a full-time internship. A qualitative case study research design was used to explore the extent to which teacher candidates integrated technology and content during the internship experience. After completing the internship experience, ten teacher candidates participated in semi-structured interviews regarding how they integrated technology into their internship classroom. The ten teacher candidates interviewed had a range of elementary to high school internship placements and described examples from the content areas of English Language Arts, social studies, mathematics, art, and science. Their statements regarding technology use in the classroom were coded and categorized by the three UDL principles of multiple means of engagement, representation, and action and expression.

UDL in Teacher Preparation

Providing teacher candidates with opportunities to design, implement, and evaluate technology-integrated lessons in a P-12 classroom setting, using UDL as a framework, better enables teacher candidates to develop skills in technological, pedagogical, and content knowledge, or TPACK (Haley-Mize & Walker, 2014; Muilenburg & Berge, 2015). The TPACK framework outlines these three forms of knowledge and the interactions between those three forms (Muilenburg & Berge, 2015). More information on TPACK is available at http://tpack.org/. When teacher candidates experience firsthand what it looks and feels like to teach with technology, they are able to move beyond a theoretical understanding of why and how to integrate technology to provide multiple means of engagement, representation, and action and expression. As teacher candidates gain experience in a safe internship environment, under the direction of veteran teachers, they learn to be more reflective and subsequently are able to remove barriers so that all learners may excel in the learning process (Novak, 2016).

Study Highlights

After coding the interviews, the researchers noticed a strong connection between the technology examples provided by the teacher candidates and the UDL principles and guidelines. Specifically, without any prompting to identify UDL, interviewed teacher candidates noted 35 examples of multiple means of representation, 30 examples of multiple means of engagement, and 21 examples of multiple means of action and expression. Examples included third graders choosing to use Prezi, ChatterPix, Shadow Puppet, PowerPoint, or iMovie to demonstrate what they learned about severe weather; tenth graders reading a play on an online textbook and having the option to read the words or listen to the audio recording; and art students creating e-portfolios in which they posted images of their work and reflections about their process and received guiding feedback from their teacher, peers, and other stakeholders.

The findings support the assertion that combining the use of UDL and TPACK frameworks in teacher training programs can be an effective way to increase teacher candidates' abilities to effectively design and implement technology-infused lessons to meet the needs of all P-12 students (Benton-Borghi, 2013).

References

Benton-Borghi, B. H. (2013). A universally designed for learning (UDL) infused technological pedagogical content knowledge (TPACK) practitioners' model essential for teacher preparation in the 21st century. *Journal of Educational Computing Research*, 48(2), 245–265.

CAST. (2018). *The UDL guidelines*. Wakefield, MA: CAST Professional Publishing. Retrieved from http://udlguidelines.cast.org/

Haley-Mize, S., & Walker, D. (2014). The effect of instructional methodology on preservice educators' technological, pedagogical, and content knowledge. *International Journal of Learning in Higher Education*, 20(3), 13–25.

Muilenburg, L. Y., & Berge, Z. L. (2015). Revisiting teacher preparation: Responding to technology transience in the educational setting. *The Quarterly Review of Distance Education*, 16(2), 93–105.

Novak, K. (2016). *UDL now! A teacher's guide to applying universal design for learning in today's classrooms*. Wakefield, MA: CAST Professional Publishing.

36

SNAPSHOT—IMPORTANCE OF CLASSROOM ATMOSPHERE IN ELEMENTARY SCHOOLS TO IMPROVE THE INCLUSIVE EDUCATION SYSTEM IN JAPAN

Honami Okabe and Masayoshi Tsuge

Inclusive Education in Japan

In recent years, developmental disabilities, including learning disabilities (LD), Attention Deficit Hyperactivity Disorder (ADHD), and Autism Spectrum Disorder (ASD), have been included in services provided through Special Needs Education (SNE) in Japan. In 2012, a survey conducted by the Ministry of Education, Culture, Sports, Science, and Technology (MEXT, 2012a) in Japan reported that about 6.5% of students with a possible diagnosis of a developmental disability are enrolled in mainstream classes. In 2014, Japan ratified the "Convention on the Rights of Persons with Disabilities" and began constructing an inclusive education system that enables students with disabilities and typically developing students to study together (MEXT, 2012b). Due to this increased governmental focus, research in SNE within mainstream Japanese classrooms has been rapidly increasing.

In mainstream classes, there have been efforts to adopt the view of universal design in education that aims toward inclusive educational practices. The concept of *educational universal design* in Japan is based on specific views of the *students in a class*, *classroom environment*, and *human environment*. Improvements in the educational system are intended not only for students with developmental disabilities, but for *all* students.

Schools focus on subject-based teaching and human education. Therefore, an inclusive education system should provide the opportunity for all students to understand and be aware of the needs and abilities of students with disabilities. Such student interactions can be beneficial for the entire class. However, students with developmental disabilities, when not supported appropriately, may have difficulty positively engaging in the class environment, which can have unexpected effects. For example, Ohkubo, Takahashi, and Noro (2011) assert that if some students have behavioral problems, their peers could begin to imitate these problematic behaviors. There is a limit to a teacher's ability to resolve the issues faced by students with developmental disabilities due to little training or supports in this area; therefore, many teachers are concerned about their ability to manage these challenges. To better support students with developmental disabilities, and to further improve the existing system, improvements are needed that lead to increasing the understanding of and growing the support provided by typically developing students who share classes with students with developmental disabilities. Japanese schools have fixed member classes for at least one year, and together students work on everyday learning, cleaning activities, school lunch, and events. Therefore, since Japanese schools spend most of their time *in classroom* and conduct various activities with members of the class, maintaining a *classroom atmosphere* that is comfortable for children with disabilities becomes important.

Study Highlights

In this study, the authors conducted a survey of elementary school students (ages 9–12) on classroom atmosphere of regular education classrooms that had students with developmental disabilities enrolled. In this survey, class conditions were identified that promoted an affinity atmosphere that helped create a cheerful classroom with good relationships and maintained class discipline. Survey results revealed that:

1. A well-managed classroom was viewed as an environment wherein it is easy for the students with developmental disabilities to adapt. This appears to be due to teacher instructions being easy to follow and students working and learning in a calm atmosphere.
2. In a class with an *affinity atmosphere* (e.g., a warm atmosphere, a calm atmosphere, a friendly atmosphere), there are frequent activities to help and encourage classmates. Such classes were comfortable, and positive attitudes toward peers were established.
3. The children's relationship with the class teacher was shown to be positive.

Conclusion

From the results obtained in this study, several conclusions were reached. In a classroom with an affinity atmosphere, it can be expected that the merit of an inclusive education system can be maximized. For students with and those without disabilities to learn together in an inclusive class, an affinity in the classroom atmosphere, classroom discipline, and mutual respect are needed. These findings indicate the necessary conditions for an inclusive education system wherein students with and without disabilities can learn together. In addition to preparing the physical environment, the findings of this survey supported the results of Torii et al. (2015), indicating that it is important to enrich the classroom atmosphere in a manner that supports students' mutual acknowledgment and support of each other. Therefore, in addition to pursuing redesigned and scaffolded instruction through the Universal Design for Learning (UDL) framework, making it more accessible, and through this accessibility easier to learn, it is important to facilitate a steady classroom atmosphere, which is the human environment surrounding students with disabilities, supported by *all* students in the classroom through understanding and cooperation.

References

MEXT. (2012a). *Tsūjō no gakkyū ni zaiseki suru hattatsu shōgai no kanōsei no aru tokubetsuna kyōiku-teki shien wo hitsuyō to suru jidō seito ni kansuru chōsa kekka ni tsuite* [in Japanese]. Retrieved from www.mext.go.jp/a_menu/shotou/tokubetu/material/__icsFiles/afieldfile/2012/12/10/1328729_01.pdf

MEXT. (2012b). *Kyōsei shakai no keisei ni muketa inkurūshibu kyōiku shisutemu kōchiku no tame no tokubetsu shien kyōiku no suishin (hōkoku)* [in Japanese]. Retrieved from www.mext.go.jp/b_menu/shingi/chukyo/chukyo0/gijiroku/__icsFiles/afieldfile/2012/07/24/1323733_8.pdf

Ohkubo, K., Takahashi, N., & Noro, F. (2011). Effects of behavioral support on participation in routine classroom activities: Support for an individual pupil and for the class as a whole [in Japanese]. *The Japanese Association of Special Education, 48*(2), 383–394. Retrieved from www.jstage.jst.go.jp/article/tokkyou/48/5/48_KJ00007226327/_pdf/-char/ja

Torii, M., Kawasaki, Y., Kaizu, A., Sato, K., Torigoe, T., & Inoue, M. (2015). The prospect of the Special Needs Education: The goal of inclusive education system, universal design for learning and specialized education for children with disabilities [in Japanese]. *The Annual Report of Educational Psychology in Japan, 54*, 173–180. Retrieved from www.jstage.jst.go.jp/article/arepj/54/0/54_173/_pdf/-char/ja

SECTION 7
Inclusive Instructional Design Cases

37

INNOVATIVE APPROACH

Using Legos in a Hands-On Activity to Teach Educators the Foundations of UDL

Amir Bar and Betty Shrieber

Introduction

The State of Israel passed several new laws and regulations to protect the rights of people with disabilities, including those with learning disabilities, to enjoy equal opportunities in all aspects of life, including leisure, daily management, employment, and learning (Israel Commission for Equal Rights of Persons with Disabilities, 2019a). The 1998 Equal Rights for Persons with Disabilities Law was amended in 2005 by adding an accessibility section stating that "all public places and public services must be accessible to people of all disabilities" (Commission for Equal Rights of Persons with Disabilities, 2019b, p. 14). Regulations regarding accessibility of services, including Internet accessibility, came into effect on October 25, 2013, including Section 35, which specifically addresses the accessibility of websites and what is required of website owners to meet their obligations by law (Access Israel, 2019).

Learning accessibility is a major area that should, as indicated by equal rights law, be delivered in each classroom. Universal Design for Learning (UDL) is a potential means to support learner accessibility; however, UDL is not solely about accessibility. By providing multiple means of learning and assessment, UDL allows all students, especially those with special needs, to compensate for their learning difficulties and to show their mastery of material.

Why UDL?

While UDL principles can be applied to design instruction without the use of technology, at its root UDL is strongly associated with technology. The creator of UDL, David Rose, stated in a personal discussion (D. Rose, personal communication, 2012) that one of the triggers for developing the UDL framework was the development of computer technology, particularly the demonstration in the mid-80s of the Apple Macintosh with speech capability.

When UDL was first invented in the early 1990s, creating, curating, and publishing content, particularly digital content, was quite challenging. Since then, much has changed. By leveraging digital tools, which today are widely available and inexpensive, teachers can create multiple paths to the same learning objectives, allowing their students to select the paths that work best for them. While the power of a teacher today to create content is greater than any previous time in history, the challenges are not just with exposing teachers to theories like UDL, but also teaching them digital instructional design. Often teachers who have a lot of experience with designing and delivering traditional face-to-face class activities do not have the foundations and knowledge to design and create online content. While the value of UDL is already established (Cosden, Gannon, & Haring, 1995), UDL cannot be practiced in the classroom without the teacher knowing about it, understanding it, and being motivated to apply it. In this chapter, the final project activity from a graduate class is presented, as it provided meaningful professional development for educators in how to take a traditional class activity, look at it from the UDL point of view, and enhance it with digital tools. This course experience offered a number of benefits through the practical application of the UDL principles in practice.

UDL for Technology in Education Studies

The exercise described in this chapter is part of a course, Principles of Universal Design for Learning, delivered to graduate students, many of whom are already special education teachers employed in regular or special education schools in Israel and who are studying for their M.Ed. in the Kibbutzim College Technology in Education program. Their own students' backgrounds included Autism Spectrum Disorder (ASD) ranging from high to low functioning levels, hard of hearing and deaf, visual impairments, moderate to severe intellectual disabilities, and attention and learning disorders. The program incorporates a number of key institutional design competencies, including producing and editing videos, recording and editing audio, creating and editing images, writing, and using an online platform to post digital materials.

Course Description

The goal of the course is to present graduate students with the UDL perspective on instructional design and to enable them to experience UDL hands-on through building and delivering UDL-based class activities for their own pupils. It is grounded in the premise that enabling special educators to use UDL can potentially improve significantly the performance of pupils with unique needs.

The development of this course aimed to provide real-life examples of how UDL can be leveraged to impact diverse learners.

An in-class experience using UDL helps teachers to understand the principles of UDL as they apply them to a particular instructional task. Graduate students, many of whom are working teachers, are inundated with new education theories and methods. It is therefore essential to introduce UDL in a way that not only excites them about its use but makes them believe that they can implement it with their students. As part of the final project for this experience, students design their own UDL-based activity for their classroom in which their own students access, engage with, and show their comprehension of new material through multiple means. The goal of the class is not just to *sell* the value of UDL to teachers but also to encourage them to develop and improve their instructional design competencies.

Activity Description

The innovative two-hour classroom activity leverages the use of Lego building blocks and digital tools to introduce education students to UDL. The activity starts with a pre-class online survey assignment (delivered via SurveyGizmo) which maps the digital instructional design competencies of each student that will be described in detail later. Students are then placed into groups of about five members each, with the intention of having at least one member who is strong in each of the five competencies.

When students arrive to class for the activity, each group is given a small Lego model of a motorcycle (Model #2544). Following this, there is a short lecture about the three principles of UDL, and they are informed that for the next two hours they will practice applying these principles. Each group is given the original 10-step instructions that come with the Legos and is directed to create new instructions on how to build the motorcycle by applying the UDL representation principle to present the instructions in multiple ways. The teams are directed to create four deliverables and upload them into an online digital tool such as Wizer.me or similar platforms. The deliverables include:

1. text instructions on how to build the motorcycle,
2. an audio recording with instructions on how to build the motorcycle,
3. an image with the steps for building the model, and
4. a video with visual and audio instructions on how to build the model.

Past experiences with this activity indicate that the activity is one of the key highlights of the course, and students often report that they finally understood UDL only after participating in the Lego assignment. When the students are struggling with creating one of the deliverables, they gain insight into the experience of their own students who benefit from flexibility in differing ways of learning.

Further, the activity fosters in the teachers a breadth of varied approaches that they can incorporate into the design of learning activities. They come to see that a teacher is like an *orchestra* of one person in that he or she needs to master many different *instruments* (educational tools and competencies) and at the same time know how to combine them all into a pleasant symphony. While understanding UDL can certainly help with conducting different educational approaches, even the best conductor cannot make music sound good if the individual instruments cannot produce quality sound.

Guidelines for Applying UDL in the Course Project

At the core of this case study is the course project that promotes the development of digital instructional design skills and understanding of how to apply UDL in their classrooms. The key components of the process for the course project are summarized in Table 37.1.

Why Legos?

From the pedagogical point of view, Legos were selected for this activity for multiple reasons. First, most of the learners were familiar with Legos and had experience with using them. Second, it is a material generally associated with playfulness, making it a great anchor for a group activity. This activity leverages the contrast between how much fun it is to work with Legos and how difficult it can be to place oneself in the shoes of other learners, particularly those with learning differences. The activity emphasizes that something that is easy for some learners can be nearly impossible for others. These two aspects merge into an activity in which parts are fun, easy, and social, and other parts are quite challenging—a comparison that can stay with the learners for a long time. Based on feedback from learners over several years, using Legos is a leading reason that students enjoy this activity.

TABLE 37.1 Components of Process to Apply UDL in the Course Project

Project Goals for Course Instructors	*Project Goals for Course Students*
Evaluate the digital instructional design skills of the students.	Write text instructions on how to build the motorcycle.
Group students so that they can learn from each other.	Create an audio recording with instructions on how to build the motorcycle.
Deliver an overview of UDL.	Generate an image with the multiple steps of building the model.
Deliver a hands-on activity where students get to practice UDL within a defined timeline.	Make a video with visual and audio instructions on how to build the model.
Provide feedback.	Upload instructions to educational platform.

How to Deliver the UDL Activity—Step by Step Instructions

The course instructor and student goals for the UDL project, as described in Table 37.1, provide the organizational focus for the specific activity step instructions.

Step 1

About two weeks prior to the activity date, instructors should evaluate the technical skills of class members and assign them to one of five teams that will complement their digital competencies. At least one individual who is strong in the particular mode of presentation featured (e.g., writing text, recording audio instructions, and producing a video presentation) should be included in each group.

This assignment requires technical knowledge and is carried out in groups; therefore, it is very important to make sure that each group has enough technical capability to complete the activity. To evaluate the level of technical skills for each student, an online survey is sent to the class about two weeks before the activity (see link in Resources section). The survey includes questions regarding name, background, and teaching experience as well as technical questions, such as:

- Question #1: How comfortable are you with taking a picture via mobile phone or via digital camera?
    1. I don't think I can do it.
    2. I have never done it, but I think I might be able to learn quickly.
    3. I've done it a few times, but I'm not an expert.
    4. I've done it many times; I'm very good at it.
    5. I'm very good at it; I can even teach other people how to do it.

The questions are structured so that students can indicate their experience level from minimal to extensive. It is important to create a survey appropriate for those with advanced skills as well as inexperienced students. Educators should ensure that students are aware that they will need to show that they can use the skills they claim to have. Other technical questions included:

- Question #2: How comfortable are you in adding information to an image (by using software like Photoshop, Pages, Pixelmator, etc.)? For example, adding an arrow on an image to emphasize a specific area in the picture.
- Question #3: How comfortable are you with saving an image as a PDF file?
- Question #4: How comfortable are you with capturing video via your phone or digital camera?
- Question #5: How comfortable are you with uploading a video to YouTube (or similar service)?

- Question #6: How comfortable are you with creating (recording) an audio file (MP3) on your computer?
- Question #7: How comfortable are you with writing without grammar or spelling mistakes?
- Question #8: Are you familiar with SoundCloud?
- Question #9: Are you familiar with a service named Voki (Voki.com)?

After the students take the survey, responses are exported into Excel. Using SurveyGizmo offers the ability to download all the data into an Excel file. Answers are color coded with a different color (1=red, 2=orange, 3=gray, 4=light green, 5=dark green). This visual representation helps instructors quickly assess the strengths of each student and use that information to create groups. One unintended consequence of using a survey to create the groups rather than letting students form their own groups is that students who have never worked together may be teamed together to collaborate. The typical feedback about taking this approach thus far has been positive.

Step 2

Review the UDL principles (length: 10 minutes). Instructors can start each of the first few classes of the semester (prior to the UDL Lego activity) by doing a quick review of the UDL principles. A slide can be displayed with the list of principles, and the definitions can be reviewed and discussed.

Step 3

Explain the Lego assignment (length: 10 minutes). A slide can then be displayed that identifies the groupings, and students can move around the classroom to form their teams. Each group is then given two models of a Lego motorcycle★ (Model #2544) and two original Lego instruction pages. The instruction page shows how to build the motorcycle in 10 steps, and each team is assigned to two steps (i.e., Team 1 is in charge of steps 1 & 2, Team 2 is in charge of steps 3 & 4, and so on). ★Please note that the activity can be done with any small Lego model.

Each team will create four types of instructions on how to complete the two assigned steps (out of 10, in all). The four types of instructions expected are:

1. Create a written set of instructions on how to connect the Lego blocks. In this part, they can only use plain text.
2. Create a set of images with visual instructions on how to complete the steps. Pictures, arrows, and numbers can be used, but text cannot. Instructors can inform students that their audience has a particular relevant characteristic, such as speaks different languages. This step is usually done by taking several pictures of each block addition and combining all of them into one page of PowerPoint by using arrows or numbers.

3. Create a one-minute audio recording explaining how to complete the steps. For additional challenge, students can be told that their audience has specific barriers, such as color-blindness.
4. Create a video that demonstrates how to build the respective steps with visual images, text, and audio. The instructions to the students for the video are to be as creative as possible, adding music and editing effects to their video. The only limitation is to keep the video less than two minutes in length.

Step 4

Students complete the assignment in their groups (length: 55 minutes). When the groups are organized based on individual students' skills, the information about individual strengths and weaknesses is not shared with the students. Instead, each group is charged to decide what part of the assignment each member will do. The authors found that most teams tended to divide the group into two sub-teams of two or three students. One of the reasons to provide each team with two identical Lego models of the motorcycle is to allow each team to have enough Lego parts for the two sub-teams to work in parallel without the need to wait for the parts. It usually takes about 10 minutes for everyone to figure out a plan. The instructors should constantly walk among the tables, answering any questions students might have.

To make sure students have access to the assignment objectives during the activity, a mobile app (accessible via a QR code that displays on the screen) with instructions and examples of work from previous semesters was created. The app is hosted on SurveyGizmo, which allows the upload of text, images, audio, and videos, to create step-by-step instructional guides. By using the app, time is saved showing each team how the final product should look. At the same time, it provides only small examples so the teams can still be creative with each deliverable and not try to just copy the work that is shown in the app (see link in Resources section).

It is important to not restrict any type of digital tools. Instructors should encourage exploration of free software and apps that can help edit videos, audio, and images and publish them, as well as various platforms on which students can post their content. Specific options (i.e., Wizer.me, YouTube, Voki, etc.) can be offered, but students can be free to use whatever tools they want as long as they can achieve the assignment's objectives.

This step should be completed about 15 minutes before the end of the class. Typically, about half of the teams will have completed the assignment, and the other half will have completed creating content but will not yet have published it. Teams can be provided a few extra days to complete the assignment before sending in the link for grading. It seems that the optimal time for completing the assignment in class is around two hours; but given that some classes are not that long, students can be allowed to complete it at home. The quality of the deliverable can be limited when students need to work in class and under time constraints. For example, making videos in the noisy environment of the class invites background sounds. However, the benefits of being able to deliver this entire experience in one class period instead of two may be worth the cost to the overall quality of the deliverables.

Step 5

Conclude the activity and lead students in reflection (length: 15 minutes). The last 15 minutes of the class can be used to share conclusions and reflections. At this stage, the authors have found that students are usually excited and want to share their experiences with the rest of the class. Representatives of each team can tell a little bit about the experiences of their team and talk about the challenges they faced and how they solved them.

Step 6

Projects are graded and written feedback provided. Because the groups do not have much time to create high quality content and to do advanced editing, grading can be based on the level of accomplishment and how well they have followed the instructions. The grading guide (see Table 37.2) provides more detail for the grading of the assignment.

TABLE 37.2 Assignment Grading Guide

Assignment part	Maximum score	Grading guidelines
Image	20	- The image cannot have any words in it. - The image should be of good quality and easy to understand. - The group must use one image only.
Audio	20	- Audio cannot be longer than two minutes. - Recording must be clear and at a normal speed.
Video	20	- Video must be easy to understand. - It should not be too long. - Instructions cannot include any color reference. - Instructions should be written as if they were for a blind person.
Writing	20	- Clear writing.
Delivery	20	- All the content must be uploaded to the wiser. me page.
Total:	100	Other aspects that can affect the overall score - Not submitted on time

Conclusions

As mentioned earlier in this chapter, this UDL Lego activity is delivered at the beginning of a graduate class and challenges and requires a deep understanding of the UDL principles and capability for designing online content by applying instructional design skills. In order for students to achieve these goals, it is essential to create an impactful introduction to UDL early in the semester. This Lego assignment delivers an impactful experience, one that motivates and enables students to be able to apply the UDL principles in their own classrooms. In feedback collected at the end of the semester, student comments have identified the significance of the Lego assignment in developing their understanding of UDL. The activity can be modified to incorporate other building materials; but following similar steps, it can increase hands-on experiences for teachers in UDL applications.

Resources

The content used in this class is in Hebrew. To better address the international audience of this book, we share links to the activity app and documentation we created for a similar activity that was delivered by Amir Bar at the University of Houston (where he attended graduate school and first created the assignment).

- Link to UDL Lego assignment cards (as was used in an activity in the US at the University of Houston for an undergraduate class in instructional design): http://bit.ly/2TC0zjr
- Link to the UDL Lego assignment app (as was used in an activity in the US at the University of Houston): http://bit.ly/2HJkYBx
- Link to the UDL Lego assignment submission app (for demonstration purposes only): http://bit.ly/2Ww6aK2

References

Access Israel. (2019). *About access Israel*. Retrieved from www.aisrael.org/?CategoryID=21 10&ArticleID=49527

Commission for Equal Rights of Persons with Disabilities. (2019a). *About the commission for equal rights of persons with disabilities*. Israel: Ministry of Justice. Retrieved from www.justice.gov.il/En/Units/CommissionEqualRightsPersonsDisabilities/Pages/About-the-Commission-for-Equal-Rights-of-Persons-With-Disablties.aspx

Commission for Equal Rights of Persons with Disabilities. (2019b). *Equal rights for persons with disabilities law 5758–1998*. Retrieved from www.justice.gov.il/En/Units/CommissionEqualRightsPersonsDisabilities/Equal-Rights-For-Persons-With-Disabilities-Law/Pages/Equal-Rights-For-Persons-With-Disabilities-Law.aspx

Cosden, M., Gannon, C., & Haring, T. G. (1995). Teacher-control versus student-control over choice of task and reinforcement for students with severe behavior problems. *Journal of Behavioral Education*, 5(1), 11–27.

38

SPREADING THE WORD ABOUT ASSISTIVE TECHNOLOGY AND UNIVERSAL DESIGN FOR LEARNING

A Model for Professional Teacher Learning

Jennifer Edge-Savage and Mike Marotta

Introduction and Course Summary

Problem

Educational technology has been available in classrooms for decades. Despite this, educators are still struggling to effectively leverage the power of technology to transform teaching and learning in active or creative ways. Assistive technology (AT) is defined as "any item, piece of equipment, or product system, whether acquired commercially off the shelf, modified, or customized, that is used to increase, maintain, or improve functional capabilities of a child with a disability" (IDEA, 1997). Legally in the United States, educators are required to consider AT for every student with an individualized education program (IEP) or 504 Plan since 1997's reauthorization of the *Individuals with Disabilities Education Act (IDEA)*. Inclusion of AT in the IEP/504 plans has led to increased conversations about the potential for educating *all* students by applying the Universal Design for Learning (UDL) lens (Hehir, 2009). Although developed in the early 1990s, UDL has now been formally defined and included in Federal Education Law with the *Every Student Succeeds Act of 2015* (US Department of Education, 2019). UDL provides a framework for teaching and learning that considers learner voice and choice and the variability of learners. The authors strongly believe in the interconnectedness of UDL and AT, specifically applying UDL to intentional design for all learners and applying AT to support specific learners. Based on their years of experience in the field, the authors believe a UDL lens that includes the appropriate AT tools to provide equitable access to curriculum can truly make a difference in the educational access and success of *all* learners.

Are educators prepared to think about and apply an AT-UDL lens? To do so, educators need support in basic technological skill development, need to build an awareness of general and specialized technology tools, and need to experience how these tools can transform student learning. They need ongoing support for implementation as well. However, teacher candidates are sometimes graduating teacher preparation programs with little more than a singular course in technology and limited modeling of the actual use of technology by faculty in their program (Stokes-Beverly & Samoy, 2016). This calls into question the true preparedness of teachers to implement technology in the classroom upon graduation. Once working in a school district, effective professional development opportunities available to teachers may also be lacking (Stokes-Beverly & Samoy, 2016). From the authors' experiences in the field, both new and experienced educators are actively seeking practical and meaningful professional development opportunities to better utilize the technology available to them and identify new tools and strategies to introduce in their practice.

The authors were faced with the following questions:

- How might UDL and AT be introduced to educators who are not proficient with technology?
- How can practical application of technology for learning be ensured?

Solution

To address these concerns, the authors developed a blended course model for learning, applying, and sharing skills in the areas of UDL and AT. *Spreading the Word about AT and UDL: Tools and Strategies for ALL Students* is a grant-funded project that provided professional learning including multiple face-to-face and online learning activities, professional sharing in a safe environment, practical meaningful projects, and active use of social media over a seven month period.

The course design was based on decades of professional experience by the authors in providing AT services to individual learners and professional development to K-12 educators. This blended professional development model was developed with a combination of online and classroom-based interventions. The combination of tech-based and person-to-person instruction, with practical application and ongoing support, shows the greatest potential benefits for adult learners (Means, Toyama, Murphy, Bakia, & Jones, 2010; Pregot, 2013). All course participants received a toolkit with a Chromebook, iPad, Chrome extensions, apps, and online subscriptions. This encouraged self-directed hands-on learning and practical application of technology. Inclusive instructional design and principles of UDL (engagement, representation, and expression) were embedded throughout all learning experiences.

The content of the course and connected assignments included an overview of the laws pertaining to AT, UDL, and accessible education materials (AEM), explicit instruction and practice with Quality Indicators for Assistive Technology (QIAT) and SETT (Student, Environment, Task, Tools) processes, hands-on learning and application of a variety of educational technology tools, development of resources to share with others, and supported use of social media. The growth in knowledge and confidence of all participants was remarkable, as evidenced by performance on pre- and post-tests, projects, and participant video testimonials. The #ATUDL Twitter topic was born and continues to connect the professional community by *spreading the word* about AT and UDL.

Details of the *Spreading the Word About AT and UDL* Course

Spreading the Word about AT and UDL: Tools and Strategies for ALL Students was originally funded by the Massachusetts Department of Elementary and Secondary Education in the 2016–2017 school year and was replicated the following year with similar results. The purpose of this seven-month course was to provide professional educators with foundational and practical knowledge in the areas of UDL and AT, provide explicit instruction on specific tools, offer a supportive environment for learners to explore areas of their choosing, and empower participants to continue to *spread the word about AT and UDL* in their districts and across the state.

Principles of UDL were embedded in the design of the course. Information was co-created with participants through explicit instruction, hands-on activities, collaborative projects, multimedia and print-based tutorials, interactive videos, models and examples, live and online discussions, Twitter chats, and active use of online resources for sharing and discussion during the course and beyond. All online sessions were recorded, and resources, materials, and projects were shared in an accessible online learning environment (see Figure 38.1).

FIGURE 38.1 Course Website

The blended course design consisted of face-to-face and online activities. Face-to-face meetings occurred at three points in time: beginning, middle, and end of the course. Online components included synchronous (webinars, Twitter social media chats) and asynchronous (tech tool tutorials, school-based implementation projects) learning experiences. Course assignments offered a variety of opportunities for expression, reflection, and sharing and were designed to ensure practical application of course concepts.

A core component of the course was the *Assistive Technology Toolkit*. Each participant was provided with their own technology tools so that they could immediately practice newly learned skills. The toolkit included an iPad with keyboard case, a Chromebook, a variety of iOS apps, Chrome extensions, and a $25 Apple gift card to purchase apps specific to their classroom needs (see Addendum 3 for toolkit). These technology tools served multiple purposes. First, the facilitators modeled uses of these technology tools to provide interactive instruction. Second, the immediate availability of the tools ensured opportunities for self-directed exploration. Third, the tools could be readily applied in the classroom to promote UDL learning environments, practice skills and strategies, and reflect on practices to be shared with colleagues.

Participants were not only exposed to new techniques and tools, they were also exposed to new ways of learning in a safe, fun, and professional environment with multiple opportunities to engage in learning. Interactive polling and game tools, small and large group activities, and projects were used to assess understanding throughout the course and served as models for the participants to then replicate in their own classrooms.

Course Participants

Course participants were comprised of 40 PreK-12 educators with varying years of experience from over 20 different school districts in Massachusetts. The cohort was co-located, with one group in Eastern Massachusetts and the other in Western Massachusetts, and both groups participated together for the online activities. Participants included special education teachers, general education teachers, instructional technology specialists, speech-language pathologists (SLP), reading specialists, administrators, occupational therapists (OT), and English language learner (ELL) educators. All but one of the initial participants completed the entire course.

Course Content

The course goals included developing a foundational knowledge of *why* learning about AT and UDL is important in educational practice, understanding procedures for *how* to assess and implement, engaging in practical experience with *what* to do with the technology they were given, and maintaining ongoing support in sharing these newly learned skills with others (see Addendum 1 for detailed course goals). Course assignments were designed to ensure practical application of course concepts. The course intentionally began with a pre-test of skills. This was followed by an online webinar, which tossed educators out of their comfort zones and immediately into new technology and set the stage for the entire course. The intent was to show the power of connecting beyond face-to-face and the value of the vast resources available to *lone educators* when they do become connected.

The use of social media was an important part of the course. Participants were introduced to Twitter and Tweetdeck, supported through the process of account creation, and led in engaging in a weekly #atchat. After discussion with course participants, a Facebook group was added later in the course, which presented an opportunity to discuss different learning needs and the importance of providing *choice* to learners. Many of the participants continue to *lurk* on social media, and several have become active users of it as part of their professional learning community.

It was important to develop a foundation in the processes of AT consideration, implementation, and feature-matching, as well as the principles of UDL, before diving into tools. Assignments included opportunities to experience the processes of AT, as well as UDL lesson planning. Participants were tasked with using the SETT Framework (Zabala, 2005) to become familiar with best practices for AT consideration, assessment, and implementation with a team approach. This framework, a cornerstone of AT consideration, had previously been unknown to the majority of participants. Participants also took an *eagle's eye* view of their districts by using the Quality Indicators for Assistive Technology (QIAT, 2000) to assess their district's performance in regards to AT best practices. Practical application of technology tools was expected after a combination of explicit instruction, multiple hands-on opportunities in individual and group arrangements, and self-exploration of technology. Once participants became more comfortable with the basics of technology, they were ready to design sample lessons using UDL principles. Given the intentional long-term timing of the course, participants were able to pilot their technology-infused lessons with their students and report back to the group for support and feedback.

Additional assignments included opportunities to deepen technical skills and technology integration skills. One assignment, the transformation of the Massachusetts Department of Elementary and Secondary Education (2012) policy brief, *Access to Learning: Assistive Technology and Accessible Instructional Materials*, provided an opportunity to develop content knowledge as well as technical knowledge in creating a collaborative presentation by *app-smashing* several multimedia tools. Final projects included creations of multiple tutorials in the practical use of technology to support all learners. Concluding testimonials from educators and their students were submitted via video or text. The authors *walked the walk* of UDL by providing flexibility and choice in developing and creating final projects that were meaningful to each participant (see Addendum 2 for detailed course assignments).

Results

Remarkable growth was evident in the knowledge and confidence of *all* participants, as indicated by performance on pre- and post-tests, projects, and participant video testimonials. The majority of participants entered the course with limited awareness of tools and processes for AT and UDL and completed it with greater knowledge of what AT and UDL mean. All participants had practice in implementing UDL principles and AT in the classroom, as well as finding and developing AEM. All participants greatly expanded their skills in using both general and AT tools, including Google applications, Chrome extensions, built-in accessibility features, text-to-speech, speech-to-text, cloud storage, iOS apps, online resources, social media, low-tech and higher technologies, and multimedia tools. Participants either met (27%) or exceeded (73%) their self-developed professional goals for the course (see Table 38.1).

Teacher Testimonials

In the concluding course reflections, teachers remarked how the course impacted their teaching practices:

> "Being part of this grant has helped me become a better teacher. I've learned how to use the technology I had at my fingertips but didn't know how to implement."—SDL
>
> "Getting them (students) collaborating on writing together has been absolutely fantastic!"—MH
>
> "This course has sparked a big interest in this field for me. I find myself asking tons of questions from my district and expecting more from them as far as putting procedures in place and really getting the word out."—JB
>
> "Prior to this class, I had never heard of SETT or QIAT . . . we are going to use them in professional development plans for next year."—LD
>
> "It is so simple to take an everyday vanilla lesson, and add a simple tool to engage the kids and take it to a different level."—MH
>
> "I have developed my PLN through Twitter and Facebook, I didn't realize how relevant they are."—LD

Student Testimonials

Participants also shared how their learning directly impacted student learning through text and multimedia (see Figure 38.2 for an example) testimonials.

> I like school so much better this year. School is easier because I get to use (technology). It reads for me, corrects words, and makes it easier for me to

TABLE 38.1 Pre-/Post-Test Results

Question	Pre-Test	Post-Test
1. Do you know the IDEA definition of Assistive Technology?	32%	100%
2. Does your school have a process in place to determine need for Assistive Technology?	33%	66%
3. What AT Tools are currently being used by your classroom/school/district?	Limited variety	Global increase in use of a wide variety of tools
4. Do you know what UDL means?	54%	100%
5. What are the 3 principles of UDL?	23% know	100% know
6. Have you ever implemented UDL principles in your lesson plans?	52%	98%
7. Do you know what AEM means?	13%	98%
8. What is AEM?	18% know	98% know
9. Do you know the name of your district contact for AEM?	10%	93%
10. Are you familiar with the built in accessibility features of iOS?	41%	95%
11. Do you know how to install an app on iOS?	71%	98%
12. Are you familiar with the built-in accessibility features of Google Chrome?	25%	100%
13. Do you know how to add an extension to the Chrome Browser?	25%	95%
14. Do you use cloud storage for file management?	44%	95%
15. Have you ever collaborated on a Google Doc?	83%	100%
16. Have you ever shared a file or folder in Google Drive?	86%	100%
17. Do you use social media professionally?	49%	98%
18. What social media tools are you using for your PLN to keep up to date in your field?	33% know	98% know
19. Which of the following tools/resources are you familiar with? (see addendum for detailed list)	Limited	Global increase in awareness of a wide variety of tools.
20. What are your personal/professional goals for this Institute? Have you Met/Exceeded your goals?	Varied/personalized	27% met; 73% exceeded

FIGURE 38.2 Screenshots from Student Multimedia Testimonial

see my worksheets. I can see them better because I can zoom in. Last year school was hard and I hated it. This year school is fun and I love it!

—*Student A*

Conclusion

This blended model of professional development was successful in providing professional educators with foundational and practical knowledge in the areas of UDL and AT. Participants felt supported in their skill development and empowered to apply their skills and continue to *spread the word about AT and UDL* in their districts and beyond. The combination of face-to-face, synchronous, and asynchronous online learning activities, recorded lessons, discussions, and social media support ultimately provided multiple methods that worked for everyone, thus supporting the varied learner preferences and needs of busy educational professionals.

The time spent on processes for AT and UDL proved very productive. The participants needed support in understanding the frameworks for considering, assessing, and implementing AT, and the frameworks for intentionally considering learner variability in UDL Lesson Design (SETT, QIAT, uPAR, etc.), which made the exploration and integration of tools very meaningful. Professional development in this field *must* be more than just about *tools*; it should recognize the importance of supporting educators in *overcoming fear and barriers* to using technology and provide them with the *time and space* to master it.

Resources/Addendums

http://bit.ly/ATUDLcoursegoals
http://bit.ly/ATUDLcourseassignments
http://bit.ly/ATUDLtoolkit

References

Hehir, T. (2009). Policy foundations of universal design for learning. In D. T. Gordon, J. W. Gravel, & L. A. Schifter (Eds.), *A policy reader in universal design for learning* (pp. 35–45). Cambridge, MA: Harvard Education Press.

Individuals with Disabilities Education Act (IDEA). (1997). U.S.C. section 34. C.F.R. 300.5.

Massachusetts Department of Elementary and Secondary Education. (2012). *Access to learning: Assistive technology and accessible instructional materials.* Retrieved from www.doe.mass.edu/sped/assistive/AccessToLearning.pdf

Means, B., Toyama, Y., Murphy, R., Bakia, M., & Jones, K. (2010). *Evaluation of evidence-based practices in online learning: A meta-analysis and review of online learning studies.* Retrieved from https://www2.ed.gov/rschstat/eval/tech/evidence-based-practices/finalreport.pdf

Pregot, M. V. (2013). The case for blended instruction: Is it a proven better way to teach? *US-China Education Review A, 3*(5), 320–324.

QIAT. (2000). *Quality indicators.* Retrieved from https://qiat.org/indicators.html
Stokes-Beverly, C., & Samoy, I. (2016). *Advancing educational technology in teacher preparation: Policy brief.* Retrieved from https://tech.ed.gov/files/2016/12/Ed-Tech-in-Teacher-Preparation-Brief.pdf
U.S. Department of Education. (2019). *Every student succeeds act (ESSA) of 2015.* Retrieved from www.ed.gov/essa
Zabala, J. (2005). *Using the SETT framework to level the learning field for students with disabilities.* Retrieved from www.joyzabala.com/uploads/Zabala_SETT_Leveling_the_Learning_Field.pdf

39
UNIVERSAL DESIGN FOR LEARNING IN AUGMENTED AND VIRTUAL REALITY TRAININGS

Katharina Menke, Jennifer Beckmann, and Peter Weber

Introduction

At first, virtual reality was mainly used for military training, for product engineering, and for entertainment purposes. The range of applications has drastically grown since then, as devices with head-mounted displays (HMD) now provide affordable mobile settings of high quality. Today, the private sector is highly interested in augmented reality (AR) and virtual reality (VR) (Sag, 2018). In education and training, the immersive and contextual learning processes of AR/VR are considered very promising with regard to authentic learning environments (Johnson, Adams Becker, & Cummins, 2016).

Although often addressed together, AR and VR promise different advantages. AR enhances reality with virtual objects. The AR systems use existing environments and overlay them with multimedia content. VR, in contrast, creates a completely separate and very flexible virtual environment for users and locks out reality by creating a fully immersive simulation. Thus, physical laws can be suspended, extreme situations can be approached in a risk-free manner, and space and time can be manipulated (Akçayır & Akçayır, 2017; Jerald, 2016; Olmos, Cavalcanti, Soler, Contero, & Alcañiz, 2018; Saltan, 2017). VR enables people to experience situations that they cannot experience in reality. Figure 39.1 shows the Reality-Virtuality Continuum (Milgram, Takemura, Utsumi, & Kishino, 1994), on which the left side defines real-world environments. Virtual environments (VE), classified on the right side, are completely composed of virtual objects. In mixed reality (MR) environments, real and virtual objects are combined in various ways. In AR, real objects predominate; in augmented virtuality (AV), virtual objects prevail.

As VR/AR offer new opportunities for the educational field and as Universal Design for Learning (UDL) tries to overcome the "one-size-fits-all" approach, a

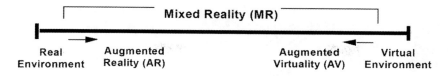

FIGURE 39.1 The Reality-Virtuality Continuum (Milgram et al., 1994)

combination of both seems to be promising—especially for heterogeneous target groups.

In the 1990s, Meyer, Rose, and Gordon introduced UDL as a framework to improve teaching and learning by reducing or avoiding barriers in teaching methods and materials. Reflecting the three fundamental brain processing networks of recognition, strategy, and affect, the framework provides guidelines and checklists for three UDL principles—1) *representation*, 2) *action and expression*, and 3) *engagement*—to guide the design, selection, and application of learning tools, methods, and environments (Meyer et al., 2014).

This chapter sheds light on the interrelationship of AR/VR learning and UDL. It provides the results of a structured literature review, proving that there is still very little research on UDL in AR and VR trainings. Furthermore, an exemplary AR/VR learning scenario for craftsmen is presented, developed as part of the federal research project ARSuL in Germany (Beckmann, Menke, & Weber, 2018). The chapter reflects selected design elements behind the first AR and VR prototypes of the ARSuL project through the lens of UDL, in order to identify weaknesses and improvement options.

The ARSuL Project

The ARSuL Project (Augmented Reality Based Support for Learning in the HVAC Industry), funded by the Federal Ministry of Education and Research of the Federal Republic of Germany, focuses on lifelong learning. The overall aim of the project is to develop a system that assists craftsmen in the heating, ventilation, and air conditioning industry (HVAC) at their workplace and during their vocational and further education by means of E-Learning, AR, and VR.

Beckmann et al. (2018) describe the user-centered design approach applied in the project to understand the target group with its specific needs. First, a requirements analysis for AR/VR was conducted by means of a methodological triangulation, combining 1) job shadowing visits in HVAC companies, 2) a guided interview with a training engineer, and 3) a workshop with HVAC craftsmen. The project team discussed the identified requirements and derived a set of 31 design elements for AR/VR, which they then used to develop first prototypes of AR and VR trainings. These trainings are currently being tested and evaluated to derive potential weaknesses and necessary improvements.

As the German HVAC industry lacks skilled workers and young talents, the companies need to address a broadening range of people and enable them to fulfill the technical workflows. They not only accept a growing number of apprentices with non-standard educational backgrounds to fill vacant positions, but they also try to better understand what physical or other disabilities do or do not hinder a person's proficiency in their businesses. Considering this development and that the UDL framework was not taken into consideration in the initial ARSuL development process, a reflection of the ARSuL design elements with regards to UDL is a promising option to improve the usability of the developed prototypes.

The Interrelationship of AR/VR and UDL

To assess the current state of the discussion on the interrelationship of AR/VR and UDL, a structured literature review in accordance with Webster and Watson (2002) was carried out. Full-text searches in journals and conference contributions (only full papers) in the online databases of ScienceDirect, IEEE, ACM, LearnTechLib, SpringerLink, JSTOR, SAGEPub, Wiley, and Taylor and Francis were conducted without any constraints for publication dates. Duplicates were eliminated.

During the search process, the keywords *virtual reality* and *augmented reality* were each combined with *universal design for learning* (two searches per database). This resulted in a corpus of 55 papers. After analyzing the titles and the abstracts of these papers, eight were assessed in depth, leading to only two matching papers (see Table 39.1).

When reviewing the eight full papers, it became clear that most of them describe how AR and VR can serve as tools to implement UDL, providing for

TABLE 39.1 Literature Review Process

	Total	Science-Direct	IEEE	ACM	Learn-TechLib	Springer-Link	JSTOR	SAGE-Pub	Wiley	Taylor & Francis
Total papers	55	3	7	0	13	8	5	13	2	4
After analyzing title & abstract	8	1	2	0	0	2	0	1	0	1
After detailed analysis	2	1	0	0	0	0	0	0	0	1

multiple means of representation within a greater learning environment. Only the two papers by McMahon, Cihak, Wright, and Bell (2016) and Bacca, Baldiris, Fabregat, Kinshuk, and Graf (2015) contain sections in which they address UDL integration within their AR/VR learning environments. McMahon et al. (2016) created an AR-App to teach science vocabulary to college students with intellectual disabilities. They implemented UDL by displaying both audio and video representations of the science vocabulary (*representation*), through the "students' physical interaction with the device and the environment to learn and find the information" (McMahon et al., 2016, p. 53) (*action and expression*), and by providing explanations for vocabulary that users can trigger when not understanding specific terms (*engagement*). Bacca et al. (2015) describe a marker-based mobile AR application named Paint-cAR in the context of vocational education, supporting the learning process of repairing paint on a car. The authors claim that during the user-centered and collaborative design process UDL guidelines were considered. Information is presented by using icons, images, texts, and videos with subtitles (*representation*). Furthermore, learners are provided with different options to express their knowledge and to keep in touch with their teachers. They can also take personal notes (*expression*). In addition, students are challenged in each step of the repair process by being shown how other students or experts carry out the repair process, and also with the help of puzzle tasks (*engagement*).

Summarizing the reviewed literature dealing with both AR/VR and UDL at the same time, AR/VR are currently mostly seen as enablers of UDL. On the other hand, the growing relevance of the technology makes it necessary to assess the UDL integration of AR/VR settings. Figure 39.2 depicts the interrelationship of AR/VR and UDL.

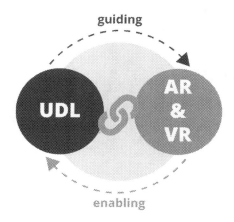

FIGURE 39.2 Interrelationship of AR/VR and UDL

UDL Improvements for the ARSuL Training Prototypes

Within the ARSuL project, first prototypes of AR and VR trainings were developed with the help of a requirements analysis. The identified requirements were processed into a set of 31 design elements to guide the development of the overall learning scenario and the specific trainings. Currently, tests and evaluations are accomplished with apprentices and experienced craftsmen to test the prototypes regarding learning success and learning satisfaction, and to compare them with a traditional face-to-face training. The learning content of all three trainings (AR, VR, and classical) is the replacement of a blower in a heating model as a standard activity that HVAC apprentices need to master with confidence in their everyday work. The learning scenario behind all three trainings (AR, VR, classical) is depicted in Figure 39.3. The learning environments of *exploration*, *exposition*, and *training* structure the scenario into three phases, implying different learning objectives and thus also different levels of user guidance and interactivity (Schwan & Buder, 2002; Weise & Zender, 2017). For details regarding the addressed knowledge dimensions, cognitive processes, and interactions, see Beckmann et al. (2018). Figure 39.4 depicts the three settings tested against each other.

Fifteen of the overall 31 design elements were considered in the development of these first AR and VR prototypes (see Beckmann et al., 2018). After cross-checking their implementation with the principles, guidelines, and checklists of

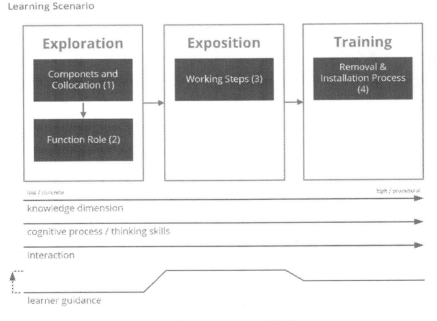

FIGURE 39.3 ARSuL Test Setting (Beckmann et al., 2018)

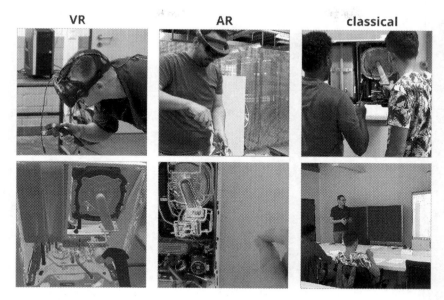

FIGURE 39.4 VR, AR, and Classical Training

the UDL framework (Version 2.0), the following set appears sufficiently fulfilled. Guideline notations refer to the UDL guidelines.

- Tasks/problems for scenario derived from real world (*guidelines 7, 9*);
- Realistic visualization of models/components (*guideline 9*);
- Short learning units (*guideline 3*);
- Constant interactions (*guideline 7*);
- Simple explanations (visual/auditory) using common technical terms (*guideline 2*);
- Casual way of addressing users (on first-name basis) (*guideline 7*);
- Personalized way of addressing users (*guideline 7*).

When the design team analyzed the remaining design elements through the lens of UDL, areas in which the design could be further improved emerged (see Table 39.2). The design team implemented corresponding changes that were grounded in the UDL principles, guidelines, and checklists (CAST, 2011). These changes are described in the next section.

When checking the design elements for their compatibility with UDL, it turned out that the avatar, the navigation, the interaction features, and the presentation of the learning content within the prototypes need improvement. Furthermore, applying the UDL checklists to the prototypes helped to identify lacking feedback within the AR and the VR simulations as a major flaw.

● = already implemented elements   ▲ = needed improvements

TABLE 39.2 Design Elements, Their Allocation to UDL Principles, Their Actual Implementation, and Possible Improvements

Derived Design Elements	Representation			Action & Expression			Engagement			Actual Implementation & Improvements	Checkpoints from UDL framework Version 2.0 (CAST, 2011)
	Recruiting Interest	Sustaining Effort & Persistence	Self-Regulation	Perception	Language & Symbols	Compre-hension	Physical Action	Expression & Communication	Executive Functions		
"Craftsman" (Avatar) guides through the setting	●		●							● Avatar with tool belt	● Provide differentiated models, scaffolds, and feedback for seeking external emotional support
	▲1 ▲3 ▲4			▲2	▲2					▲1: Modifiable avatar (e.g., color, voice) ▲2: Avatar speaks/reads with human voice ▲3: Specific feedback from avatar ▲4: Demand in scenario to ask for help or insertion of questions/hints of the avatar (e.g., "If you need help, ask...")	▲1: Provide learners with as much discretion and autonomy as possible by providing choices in such things as the color, design, or graphics of layouts, etc. ▲2: Allow for a competent aide, partner, or "intervener" to read text aloud & use digital text with an accompanying human voice recording ▲3: Provide feedback that is frequent, timely, and specific ▲4: Provide prompts that guide learners in when and how to ask peers and/or teachers for help
• Simple navigation • Voice control				●1		●2				●1: Simple menu ●2: No unnecessary interactions	●1: Allow for flexibility and easy access to multiple representations of notation where appropriate ●2: Remove unnecessary distractions unless they are essential to the instructional goal
							▲1 ▲2			▲1: Voice control ▲2: Simple physical interaction with controllers	▲1/2: Provide alternatives for physically interacting with materials by hand, voice, single switch, joystick, keyboard, or adapted keyboard

• Introducing users to the system stepwise	•1 •2	•3	•1: Tutorial "How to interact/navigate" •2: Simple menu •3: No unnecessary interactions	•1/2: Allow for flexibility and easy access to multiple representations of notation where appropriate •3: Remove unnecessary distractions unless they are essential to the instructional goal
• Plain interface				
• Simple navigation/ interaction	▲1 ▲2		▲1: Voice control ▲2: Simple physical interaction with controllers	▲1/2: It is important to provide materials with which all learners can interact. Properly designed curricular materials provide a seamless interface with common assistive technologies through which individuals with movement impairments can navigate and express what they know—to allow navigation or interaction with a single switch, through voice-activated switches, expanded keyboards and others. ▲1/2: Provide alternatives for physically interacting with materials by hand, voice, single switch, joystick, keyboard, or adapted keyboard
• Multimedia presentation of content	•		• Highlighting of relevant physical components to link them with textual information	• Make explicit links between information provided in texts and any accompanying representation of that information in illustrations, equations, charts, or diagrams
• Alternative presentations for different types of learners	▲		▲: Alternative presentations of same information (text, animation, speech)	▲: Provide written transcripts for videos or auditory clips ▲: Provide descriptions (text or spoken) for all images, graphics, video, or animations ▲: Compose in multiple media such as text, speech, drawing, illustration, comics, storyboards, design, film, music, visual art, sculpture, or video

The current implementation of the avatar is simple, monomedial, and static. Factoring in the various guidelines and checkpoints of the UDL framework, the following improvements will be pursued in the upcoming development iteration:

- Besides providing textual information, the avatar will be enabled to read out text (*guideline 1*) using a human voice (*guideline 2*).
- The avatar will get a modifiable appearance (color, voice, etc.) to get the learners more involved (*guideline 7*).
- The avatar will be developed into a flexible and context-sensitive contact point. Depending on a user's preferences (e.g., regarding the level of difficulty), it will offer help (*guideline 8*), either automatically or on request.
- The avatar will hold available redundant multimedia representations of the same content to provide the learners with flexible learning options (*guideline 1*).

With these improvements, the avatar will help strengthen the communication with the learners by providing various types of feedback, such as operating feedback in case of handling errors, and process feedback with recommendations for the learning process. Considering the UDL guidelines and checklists, the avatar thereby needs to offer specific (*guideline 8*) and differentiated (*guideline 5*) feedback in a positive language (*guideline 8*), helping to avoid or manage frustration by pointing at solutions to problems (*guideline 9*).

In addition, on the level of learning management, visualized feedback on the individual learner's progress could be added in a later development stage, such as badges on a learning dashboard (*guideline 8*). The dashboard should then not only show achievements but also provide recommendations for the learners to extend their view and to help them develop their individual knowledge and skills (*guideline 9*).

The current prototypes do not include voice control. As during requirements analysis the target group communicated a wish for voice control and as also the UDL principles suggest provision of alternative control options (*guideline 4*), voice control will be a high priority improvement in the next development iteration.

The current prototypes use tutorials to get the users started. However, the current tests and evaluations show that many users still experience problems interacting with and controlling the environment with the help of the AR and VR devices. Examples include the air tap gesture in AR and the unclear allocation of functions to the various buttons on the VR-controllers that caused users many problems and delays. Considering *guideline 4* (provide options for physical actions), such navigation and interaction problems need to be resolved. To do so, the controller handling could be simplified (use of only one instead of three buttons) and the voice control could help users bypass the air tap gesture in case of problems.

Finally, UDL emphasizes the need for different means of representations, matching the ARSuL design element of different forms of media representation of the learning content. While the current prototypes contain only one version and only single representations of content, the project aims to provide alternative versions for different learner types (e.g., apprentices and experienced craftsmen) and also redundant content representations in different media formats (*guidelines 2 and 5*). Considering the complex development of the still very limited AR and VR prototypes, the project budget and duration may be the limiting factors for this effort.

Conclusion

This chapter focuses on the interrelationship between AR/VR and UDL. There are many opportunities for further research on how the UDL principles and guidelines can be implemented in AR/VR environments. Thus far, AR and VR have generally been treated as tools to facilitate UDL in larger learning environments; while in the design process of AR and VR trainings, UDL seems not yet to be a focus.

Using the example of the ARSuL project and the AR and VR prototypes developed for a first test setting within the project, the chapter illustrates the value of reflecting upon the design of AR and VR trainings in relation to UDL. Working from the UDL framework, improvements were developed and implemented for the rudimentary avatar of the AR and VR trainings, upgrading it to a motivating, flexible, and context-sensitive contact point. Furthermore, improvements for navigation and interaction, and also for content representation within the trainings, were derived in order to reduce barriers and to make the trainings more accessible and fluent.

Currently, the development of AR and VR trainings is still very complex and laborious, limiting their use in education. Considering the dynamics of the technological advancements and the potential didactic benefits of AR and VR, a growing relevance in the near future seems most likely. Therefore, now is the right time to develop, test, and evaluate fundamental and reusable solutions for effective UDL implementation in AR and VR settings. Questions for further research still remain: How can the typical AR and VR navigation and interaction patterns be improved? How can content be represented in redundant, multimedia formats in AR and VR? How can AR and VR trainings incorporate flexible learner guidance, matching the preferences of the individual learner? In conclusion, the interrelationship of AR/VR and UDL deserves heightened attention, as emerging technological innovations like AR and VR can otherwise easily lead to a loss of didactic achievements if the diverse needs and interests of learners are not adequately addressed.

References

Akçayır, M., & Akçayır, G. (2017). Advantages and challenges associated with augmented reality for education: A systematic review of the literature. *Educational Research Review, 20*, 1–11. https://doi.org/10.1016/j.edurev.2016.11.002

Bacca, J., Baldiris, S., Fabregat, R., Kinshuk, & Graf, S. (2015). Mobile augmented reality in vocational education and training. *Procedia Computer Science, 75*, 49–58. https://doi.org/10.1016/j.procs.2015.12.203

Beckmann, J., Menke, K., & Weber, P. (2018). AR and VR meet boiler suits: Deriving design elements for AR/VR trainings in the HVAC industry. *Proceedings of EdMedia + Innovate Learning*, 1533–1542.

CAST. (2011). *Universal design for learning guidelines version 2.0 [graphic organizer]*. Wakefield, MA: CAST Professional Publishing.

Jerald, J. (2016). *The VR book: Human-centered design for virtual reality*. New York: Morgan & Claypool Publishers.

Johnson, L., Adams Becker, S., & Cummins, M. (2016). *The NMC horizon report: 2016 higher education edition*. Toronto, ON: New Media Consortium.

McMahon, D. D., Cihak, D. F., Wright, R. E., & Bell, S. M. (2016). Augmented reality for teaching science vocabulary to postsecondary education students with intellectual disabilities and autism. *Journal of Research on Technology in Education, 48*, 38–56. https://doi.org/10.1080/15391523.2015.1103149

Meyer, A., Rose, D. H., & Gordon, D. (2014). *Universal design for learning: Theory and practice*. Wakefield, MA: CAST Professional Publishing.

Milgram, P., Takemura, H., Utsumi, A., & Kishino, F. (1994). Augmented reality: A class of displays on the reality-virtuality continuum. *Telemanipulator and Telepresence Technologies, 2351*, 282–293. https://doi.org/10.1117/12.197321

Olmos, E., Cavalcanti, J. F., Soler, J-L., Contero, M., & Alcañiz, M. (2018). Mobile virtual reality: A promising technology to change the way we learn and teach. In S. Yu, M. Ally, & A. Tsinakos (Eds.), *Perspectives on rethinking and reforming education: Mobile and ubiquitous learning* (pp. 95–106). Singapore: Springer.

Sag, A. (2018). *CES 2018: Virtual reality and augmented reality get another shot*. Retrieved from www.forbes.com/sites/moorinsights/2018/01/25/ces-2018-virtual-reality-and-augmented-reality-get-another-shot/#45983c5aab04

Saltan, F. (2017). The use of augmented reality in formal education: A scoping review. *EURASIA Journal of Mathematics, Science and Technology Education, 13*, 503–520. https://doi.org/10.12973/eurasia.2017.00628a

Schwan, S., & Buder, J. (2002). Lernen und Wissenserwerb in virtuellen Realitäten. In G. Bente (Ed.), *Internet und Psychologie: Vol. 5. Virtuelle Realitäten* (pp. 109–132). Göttingen: Hogrefe Verl. für Psychologie.

Webster, J., & Watson, R. T. (2002). Analyzing the past to prepare for the future: Writing a literature review. *MIS Quarterly, 26*, xiii–xxiii.

Weise, M., & Zender, R. (2017). Interaktionstechniken in VR-Lernwelten. In C. Ullrich & M. Wessner (Eds.), *Proceedings of DeLFI and GMW workshops 2017*. Retrieved from http://ceur-ws.org/Vol-2092/paper13.pdf

40
RAISING THE BAR WITH UDL
A Case for Change

Leanne Woodley

Introduction

Student engagement, defined as students' involvement with activities and conditions likely to generate high-quality learning (Coates, 2009), has been closely linked as a predictor of school and post-school success (Connell & Klem, 2009). Improving and maintaining student engagement in the classroom is critical to positive student outcomes.

The Case for Change

Working in alternative educational settings for disengaged, at-risk youth aged between 15–18 years of age presents many challenges. Students who enrol in such settings typically face barriers to complete their education in their local secondary school, including mental health issues, learning difficulties, social disadvantages, and behavioural issues (McGregor & Mills, 2012). These manifest as low attendance rates, lack of motivation or interest in school, and risk-taking behaviours (Wierenga & Taylor, 2015).

This chapter will describe action research undertaken in one such setting, an alternative education school located in New South Wales, Australia. The school-based action research project was part of a larger action research effort designed to enable, assist, and support independent schools to achieve the key objectives of the Australian Government's *Students First* reform agenda and the *New South Wales Government's Great Teaching, Inspired Learning* initiative. The initiative provided resources for teacher release to engage in regular meetings with consultants and instructional coaches.

The action research was led by a science teacher who identified low student attendance and engagement in her Year 10 class as pressing issues to be addressed. Prior to the project, many students were present on school grounds, however, they were not attending all science classes. Using an action research process, the research question posed was: *Could the development of a comprehensive understanding of the UDL framework impact teacher practice to positively affect student engagement and student attendance in science classes?*

Implementation of the UDL School-Based Action Research

The spirals of inquiry framework (Halbert & Kaser, 2007) was used as the methodology in reporting the process of the project and formed the basis of instructional coaching sessions. Spirals of inquiry is an action research cycle that supports teachers to become open to new learning and take informed action. It consists of six interconnected phases and associated key questions, which guide teachers to reflect, undertake new learning, and embark on new actions to improve student learning outcomes.

Spiral of Inquiry: Cycle One

Phase 1: Scanning

The school collected a variety of data and evidence. All student science workbooks showing little recorded work were collected alongside the class attendance data. Observations were recorded when students attended school but chose not to enter science classes, rather gathering on the playground to socialise. The class teacher also collected baseline data for later comparison, including use of an online *UDL Educators Checklist* available on the CAST.org website, to reflect on her teaching program. The checklist showed that while some of the UDL principles were being addressed in the current teaching program, most guidelines and checkpoints of the framework were either not in place or only partially addressed.

Phase 2: Focusing

The teacher used the checklist to decide where to concentrate her professional energies for the greatest impact of change. She identified aspects of her teaching that she wanted to change and reflected on the research question to enhance her focus.

Phase 3: Developing a Hunch

The teacher asked questions about how her pedagogical practices may have been a contributor to low attendance and engagement, and then she generated possible solutions as a starting point to set a direction for change in practice. It was hypothesised that if the science class became more practical and skills-focused rather than content-driven, students might begin to choose to attend science classes despite the other barriers they had in their lives.

Phase 4: New Learning

The school leaders were supportive of structuring targeted professional learning initiatives into the teacher's planning time. The professional learning consisted of:

- *Professional learning on lesson design and programming units of work using the UDL framework.* All staff in the school were introduced to the UDL framework to enable a common language to develop amongst staff when discussing program design and lesson implementation. While all staff began to design programs using the UDL principles, the science teacher delved deeply into the guidelines and checkpoints. The science teacher also attended a two-day conference where international UDL experts provided insights into implementing UDL in the classroom.
- *Planning days using the New South Wales Standards Authority (NESA) Science Syllabus for the Australian Curriculum and the UDL framework.* This was an important step in the process, as there were many misconceptions about what was required by NESA versus the school expectations. Spending time studying the support documents available through NESA enabled the teacher to move forward in a new and different direction.

Phase 5: Taking Action

The new learnings were implemented with systematic action to develop new practices. Planning activities involved teacher observations and professional discourse to discern and reflect on practice, repeated visits from an instructional coach, and release time from class to begin planning lessons and assessment tasks using the NESA Science Syllabus for the Australian Curriculum and the UDL framework. Potential student learning barriers were identified, as the UDL framework encouraged the teacher to proactively plan with student variability in mind from the outset.

A unit of work for Year 10 students was developed, entitled *Made for Space*, using the outcomes and content from the Earth and Space strand of the New South Wales Standards Authority (NESA) Science Syllabus. The UDL guidelines and checkpoints were intentionally used from the engagement principle, in conjunction with Wiggins' and McTighe's (2005) Understanding by Design (UbD) framework. UbD is an educational planning approach used by many teachers to design units of work, assessment tasks, and classroom instruction. The design process involved the following:

- The teacher purposefully selected the desired syllabus outcomes and learning goals. The skills, knowledge, and essential content of the syllabus outcomes were identified.

- The teacher made decisions on what evidence and types of assessments would be collected to determine student achievement toward the syllabus outcomes. The assessments were designed to allow for multiple means of action and expression and for multiple means of engagement, providing student choice and autonomy.
- The skills and knowledge required by students to complete the assessments were discussed and then opportunities for students to develop and practice these were incorporated into the learning experiences and instruction. Syllabus outcomes and content were frequently referenced in order to maintain curricular focus. While the science syllabus required only 50% practical investigations within the course, the teacher planned a practical component to every lesson. The UDL framework was referenced to ensure that multiple means of representation of content and multiple means of engagement were evident.
- A wide variety of resources were gathered to support student engagement and variability in learners. There was no traditional science textbook used. A wide variety of graphic organisers, video clips, and thinking routines were utilised.

It was found that other guidelines from the representation and the action and expression principles were included as a matter of course. For example, while deliberately building in student choice and autonomy as part of multiple means of engagement: options for recruiting interest, this element of the program design flowed over into multiple means of action and expression: use of multiple tools for construction and composition. Using the UDL guidelines and checkpoints (CAST, 2011), a numeric coding system was used in the teaching program to highlight the intentional use of the UDL framework (see Figure 40.1).

Further reflection led to the refinement of learning experiences and the addition of tiered group tasks. As the class teacher began to deliver the lessons within the program, changes to practice and student responses were recorded in a chronicle. Instructional coaching was provided by an educational consultant with expertise in the UDL framework. This entailed regular school visits to work one-to-one with the teacher and to model and observe classroom practice. The teacher was encouraged to take teaching risks, try new things, and find ways to make changed pedagogy part of the norm. Reflections were recorded in a coaching journal and were used to inform professional conversations.

Phase 6: Checking

To monitor student attendance and engagement, data continued to be collected over the 10-week term. This included class attendance data, student comments, workbook samples, assessment products, and lesson exit cards. The teacher also taught the same class of students for history/geography. In this class, there was not any intentional application of the UDL framework in lesson planning. Data collected showed that for the same group of students with the same teacher for

Science Program: Earth and Space Strand   Unit of Work: Made for Space: Year 10: Duration of 5 weeks

Target outcomes from the NSW Science Syllabus

Working Scientifically

SCS-6WS   undertake first-hand investigations to collect valid and reliable data and information, individually and collaboratively

SCS-7WS   processes, analyses, and evaluates data from first-hand investigations and secondary sources to develop evidence-based arguments and conclusions

SCS-9WS   presents science ideas and evidence for a particular purpose and to a specific audience, using appropriate scientific language, conventions, and representations

Knowledge and Understanding

SCS-12ES   describes changing ideas about the structure of the Earth and the universe to illustrate how models, theories, and laws are refined over time by the scientific community

Content from the NSW Science Syllabus	Planned teaching, learning, and assessment experiences
WS7.1 a. Selecting and using a variety of methods to organise data and information, including diagrams, tables, models, spreadsheets, and databases b. selecting and extracting information from tables, flow diagrams, other texts, audio-visual resources, and graphs, including histograms and column sector or line graphs c. accessing data and information by using a range of appropriate digital technologies	Lesson 1: Unit introduction: Activate prior knowledge using image from Hubble's Twelve Best Photos on the 25th Anniversary. (3.1) Students answer questions and then have a discussion based on Harvard Thinking Routine: I see ... I think ... I wonder... (3.3) Show a Richard Branson clip on Space Exploration and Travel for the Future (1.2). Discuss the implications. Introduce students to the outcomes and goals for the unit of work: 1. Describe ideas about the changing universe including its structure. 2. Show how models and theories have changed over time by the scientific community and familiarise them with the assessment task—a space travel itinerary. (8.1) To support self-monitoring and assessment, students will monitor their progress using a self-monitoring rating scale (9.3).

FIGURE 40.1   Sample of UDL Coded Teaching Program

both subjects, their attendance in science lessons was higher for almost all students (see Figure 40.2).

Figure 40.2 shows the majority of students had a higher attendance rate in science (dark grey) than in history/geography (light grey). Students 15, 18, and 4 were exceptions, as they had a higher attendance rate in history/geography due to their interest in the topic being studied at the time. The graph highlights a large range in attendance, with Student 2 having 84% attendance in science and Student 6 having 2% attendance in history/geography.

Student comments showed an eagerness to attend class, as well as engagement with the lesson content and learning activities:

> "I'm only staying (at school) if we have science next."
> "I only came to school today so I could do the science work."
> "It is so much easier to do research with the graphic organisers. I really like using them. Can we use them for this task too?"
> "I was able to find out so much information for my Space project from our excursion to the science centre."
> "I think I need to add to my brochure. I think it needs more detail."

The impact on teacher practice was also evident in comments recorded in her chronicle:

> "With the UDL guidelines and checklist, I found it easier to stay focused on the syllabus outcomes and cater for all students in a meaningful and engaging way."

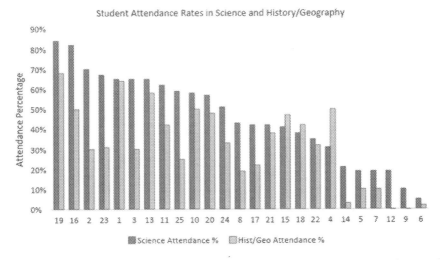

FIGURE 40.2 Attendance in Science (UDL-Dark Grey) Compared to Attendance in History/ Geography (Non-UDL-Light Grey)

"This is the first week of science teaching I have felt so prepared and the kids have embraced the learning. I have not had any behaviour problems!"

Spiral of Inquiry: Cycle Two and Scaling Up

After the first cycle of school-based action research inquiry, where positive impacts had been evident on student achievement toward the learning outcomes, it was decided to scale up the UDL implementation to focus on whether improvements to student attendance and engagement were due to applications of the UDL framework or specific content.

The phases of spirals of inquiry were thus repeated. A second science unit of work on *Evolution and Natural Selection* from the Living World strand of the New South Wales Standards Authority (NESA) Science Syllabus was planned using the same process of understanding by design and the intentional use of the UDL framework, coding the checkpoints to highlight their implementation. Teacher reflections and student feedback were considered and incorporated to strengthen the learning experiences and instruction included in the unit of work, making it more responsive to student needs.

Elements of the *Made for Space* unit of work that were not as effective were adjusted to better meet the needs and interests of students. For example, the options for self-regulation: developing self-assessment and reflection in the engagement principle was changed so that students were able to privately share their self-assessment with the teacher, rather than as a whole class. Also within the engagement principle, the options for self-regulation: facilitating personal coping skills and strategies, a lesson menu was available on the classroom noticeboard for students to access lesson summaries and work from labelled pockets, if they were absent. Options for sustaining effort and persistence: heighten salience of goals and objectives was enhanced by students recording the lesson intentions at the start of each lesson, creating a summary over the unit of key learnings. Previously, the teacher wrote the lesson intention on the board and referred to it only at the start of the lesson.

Another area strengthened was the representation principle. The options for comprehension: activating background knowledge was strengthened by the use of an anticipation guide at the beginning of the unit, serving also as a student self-reflection tool at the conclusion of the unit. Options for language: clarifying vocabulary was enhanced by adding a review of key terms at the beginning of each lesson, rather than just being addressed at the beginning of the unit.

In the principle of action and expression, the teacher focused on options for expression and communication: multiple use of media for communication. Students could demonstrate their understanding of concepts by the use of manipulatives or graphics, rather than a written record in their science workbooks. Photographs and video snippets of students completing practical investigations were used as work samples to record student learning.

The assessment experiences for this unit were considered. Smaller informal experiences were used to gather evidence of student achievement toward the outcomes, which included a picture book task, thinking routines such as *I used to think ... but now I think ...*, and *Compass points*, which is a scaffold to explore various sides of an idea before expressing an opinion.

As with the first unit of work, *Made for Space*, the unit on *Evolution and Natural Selection* required little to no individual curriculum adjustments as students' potential learning barriers were considered as part of design and planning. Science class attendance continued to increase (see Figure 40.3).

Figure 40.3 shows the majority of students had a significantly improved attendance in Term 2 (dark grey) compared to Term 1 (light grey). Students 4 and 9 were exceptions as they had a higher attendance in Term 1 than Term 2. The graph shows 28% of the students (Students 23, 3, 25, 24, 17, 12, and 5) had 0% attendance in Term 1. The reason for this occurrence were student mental health issues and difficulties transitioning back into a school setting.

Teacher and students were interviewed to gather further data on change in practice and increased attendance, engagement, and, ultimately, student learning outcomes. Student comments clearly indicated that they were engaging with the lessons:

> "That is going to be the best lesson all term."
> "I am going to go home and tell my mum about this."
> "Can you take a picture of me doing Ice Fossils and put it on the board? Can you give me a copy to take home too?"

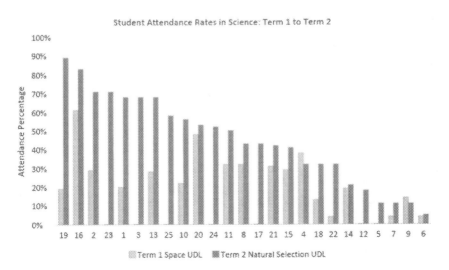

FIGURE 40.3 Attendance in Science for Unit 1: Space Compared to Unit 2: Natural Selection

These comments provided an important insight into increased student engagement, as many students did not live with their parents, so for them to want to share a positive school experience with their family was a measure of success. Student work samples and science workbooks also indicated a high level of class engagement with some students moving from empty books to science books filled with work, photographs, science experiments, and completed graphic organisers. Students were proud of the work they had completed and delighted in showing it to school visitors.

The teacher's comments reflected the observable change in student behaviour and personal professional growth:

> "This has been a learning process for my students. They now have options to access content and present their new knowledge and understandings in different ways."
>
> "This has been a learning curve for me. I won't be able to program any other way now. Seeing the difference in student learning is amazing."
>
> "Seeing the success this has had in Year 10, I have begun to use the same planning process in my senior Food Technology class. Again, I am noticing changes to the way my students are engaging."

Contributors to Success

An external professional evaluating the project noted that the class teacher had a concentrated focus on the use of the UDL framework, allowing for better understanding of its components and opportunities to trial a number of differing framework-grounded approaches. This was reflected in how learning materials were represented and how students were able to demonstrate their learning. A student interviewed during the evaluation process articulated that he liked how he could choose different ways to show his learning (e.g., use of graphic organisers to show understanding of science concepts and applying the science concepts using everyday environmental materials). Being provided with choice was a motivator for many of the students. The evaluation noted that this impact on students did not come immediately, but it drew students into learning through the flexibility of the UDL framework.

One of the main contributors to the successful implementation of the UDL framework was the disposition and growth mindset of the teacher. The teacher was open and willing to try new approaches, persisted through the challenges, reflected and refined teaching practices, and was willing to share experiences and celebrate success with others. The role of the instructional coach and the regular, ongoing meetings were also important, as they provided necessary opportunities for discussion about how to apply the UDL principles in practice. Collecting data was key to making informed decisions about student learning and growth.

Conclusion

This single class case study demonstrates that intentional use of the UDL framework as an approach to design units of work for the New South Wales Standards Authority (NESA) Syllabi for the Australian Curriculum can enhance student engagement, increase attendance, and improve student learning toward the achievement of syllabus outcomes, as well as significantly impact teacher practice. For many other Australian schools who have begun to explore the UDL principles and guidelines, the framework offers a supportive, proactive approach to curriculum design that caters to the diversity of all students.

References

CAST. (2011). *Universal design for learning guidelines version 2.0 [graphic organizer]*. Wakefield, MA: CAST Professional Publishing.

Coates, H. B. (2009). *Engaging students for success: Australasian student engagement report*. ACER. Retrieved from https://research.acer.edu.au/higher_education/17

Connell, J. P., & Klem, A. M. (2009). Relationships matter: Linking teacher support to student engagement and achievement. *Journal of School Health*, 74(7), 262–273. https://doi.org/10.1111/j.1746-1561.2004.tb08283.x

Halbert, J., & Kaser, L. (2007). *Spirals of inquiry: For equality and quality*. Vancouver, BC: BC Principals and Vice Principals Association.

McGregor, G., & Mills, M. (2012). Alternative education sites and marginal young people: I wish there were more schools like this one. *International Journal of Inclusive Education*, 16(8), 843–862. https://doi.org/10.1080/13603116.2010.529467

Weirenga, A., & Taylor, J. (2015). *The case for inclusive learning systems: Building more inclusive learning systems in Australia*. Sydney: Dusseldorp Forum.

Wiggins, G., & McTighe, J. (2005). *Understanding by design* (2nd ed.). Alexandria, VA: Association for Supervision and Curriculum Development.

41

SNAPSHOT—DESIGNING FOR OPEN EDUCATIONAL ENVIRONMENTS

Balancing Access, Equity, and Engagement

Elizabeth Childs and Jo Axe

Background

A redesigned program is currently offered at a university in western Canada with a mandate to provide programs that are applied and professional, responsive to the local community needs, as well as supportive to the more expansive needs of the British Columbia labour market (Royal Roads University Act, Royal Roads University Act [RSBC 1996] Chapter 409 Subsection 2 1996). In addition, the university has an institutional learning, teaching, and research model (LTRM) (Royal Roads University, 2017) that promotes applied and authentic learning that is community-based, caring, and transformational, and meets the needs of students from a variety of backgrounds with diverse abilities and experiences (Al-Azawei et al., 2016). The university offers courses on-campus, online, and in blended formats to mid-career adult learners, with approximately 80% of these courses being in the online format. Currently, the university has no formal open education policy in place.

Rationale

The redesign of a graduate program in learning and technology was informed by the cross-curricular themes of openness, networked learning, and digital mindset in order to create an inclusive, personalized, and flexible learning experience for mid-career adult learners. Inclusivity in this context refers to equity and access to educational opportunities, as the university has a flexible admissions approach.

Designing for personalization of the learning experience resulted in learners participating in open courses as part of graduate course requirements, the ability to customize summative assessment activities to align with workplace problems, and learner agency in exit pathway choice and research question(s) focus. Learner flexibility was designed into the program at the program, course, and assessment levels. This resulted in design decisions that supported learner choice and agency over (1) their blogs, activities, and assignments, (2) exit pathways and associated research question(s), and (3) access to the course and related materials free of geographic constraints and paywalls.

Program Highlights

The graduate program under study approached openness as a dynamic and negotiated space that encompasses "collaborative practices [including] ... the creation, use and reuse of OER, as well as pedagogical practices employing participatory technologies and social networks for interaction, peer-learning, knowledge creation and empowerment of learners" (Cronin, 2017, 10). In the context of a blended and online learning higher education institution, the five Rs of openness—*retain, reuse, revise, remix, and redistribute* (Wiley, 2014)—have been applied at program and course level. The institutional LTRM, and some of the principles of universal design, were used in conceptualizing the program. Specifically, the principles of access and inclusion, recognition of personal biases, multiple ways of engagement, and engagement with a broader network (Steinfeld et al., 2012) apply to this work.

Research on how embodying this view of openness impacted the experience of faculty and students in designing for and facilitating in these more open learning spaces was conducted. The initial findings included the impact of institutional norms, leadership, relationships, humility, and criticality on fostering a culture of openness at multiple levels in the institution. They also pointed to conceptual, practical, and technical challenges. Some of the conceptual issues were lack of understanding of terms, and the varied perceptions relating to openness. The practical challenges uncovered were risk of reputation, potential for copyright violation, and lack of resources. The technical challenges were identified as selection of platform for delivery, privacy issues, and the need for design assistance.

This ongoing research continues to inform our collective understanding of the complexities of open educational environments that have attempted to incorporate some of the principles of universal design for learning. As a result, there is a greater appreciation of how openness can be implemented at the graduate level, and an increased comprehension of the key considerations for designers, faculty, and students moving from a closed learning management system to a more open educational environment as one way to promote universal access and inclusion.

References

Al-Azawei, A., Serenelli, F., & Lundqvist, K. (2016). Universal design for learning (UDL): A content analysis of peer reviewed journals from 2012 to 2015. *Journal of the Scholarship of Teaching and Learning, 16*(3), 39–39. doi:10.14434/josotl.v16i3.19295

Cronin, C. (2017, April 20). *Open culture, open education, open questions*. Session presented at the MALAT Virtual Symposium. Retrieved from http://ow.ly/L9ch30b2f41

Royal Roads University. (2017). *Royal roads learning and teaching model*. Retrieved from http://ctet.royalroads.ca/rru-learning-and-teaching-model

Royal Roads University Act Royal Roads University Act [RSBC 1996] Chapter 409 Subsection 2 (2010). Retrieved from www.bclaws.ca/civix/document/id/consol21/consol21/00_96409_01#section2

Steinfeld, E., Maisel, J., & Levine, D. (2012). *Universal design: Creating inclusive environments*. Hoboken, NJ: Wiley.

Wiley, D. (2014, March 5). *The access compromise and the 5th R*. [Blog post]. Retrieved from https://opencontent.org/blog/archives/3221

42

SNAPSHOT—SUPPORT FOR STUDENTS WITH DEVELOPMENTAL DISABILITIES IN A REGULAR ELEMENTARY SCHOOL CLASS IN JAPAN

Shintaro Nagayama and Masayoshi Tsuge

According to a 2012 survey of teachers of elementary and junior high schools by the Ministry of Education, Culture, Sports, Science and Technology of Japan (MEXT, 2012), about 6.5% of students enrolled in general education classes are students with the possibility of developmental disabilities. The survey had a 97% response rate and reported 53,882 students with developmental disabilities enrolled in regular classes in public elementary and junior high schools in all prefectures except Iwate, Miyagi and Fukushima prefectures.

There are many studies and practices related to support for students with developmental disabilities. In Japan, specific methods and teaching materials have been developed to provide individual support within the group to students with developmental disabilities (Baba, Sato, & Matsumi, 2013). In particular, SST (social skill training) and functional assessment based on applied behavior analysis (ABA) are gaining attention as support methods in general education classes. However, the enrichment of effective individual support for students with developmental disabilities in a regular class faces budgetary problems, requiring training for teachers to obtain specialized skills as well as additional assistance. There are 30 to 40 students enrolled in typical elementary or junior high school classes in Japan, and some classes experience interpersonal relationship and/or behavioral problems. In response to this trend, research and practice on the effectiveness of assisting techniques such as CSST (class-wide social skill training), which conducts SST with the whole class, and GOC (group contingency or group-oriented contingency) based on applied behavior analytics have been suggested.

A literature survey on CSST and GOC in regular elementary school classes in Japan was conducted from 2000 to 2017 (Ngayama & Tsuge, 2017). A total of 18 papers were extracted in CSST and 12 in GOC, showing many papers covering second, third, and fourth grades. However, in Japan, this reveals a need to conduct

CSST and GOC studies for fifth and sixth graders. By showing the effects of CSST and GOC at each grade of elementary school, we can determine the kind of support needed for interpersonal relations and behavioral problems related to learning for each grade.

Recently, research and practice on consultation that external experts have provided to teachers, including information about how to support the unique needs of individuals with developmental disabilities in regular classes and how to support classes as a whole, have been gathering attention. In consultations, rather than just offering effective teaching methods to teachers, there is a growing need to consider proposing support methods according to the unique situations of individual classrooms as well as the needs of teachers.

A major premise of current research is to understand not only the needs of students, but also those of teachers. Teachers have a variety of teaching styles, and in some cases, the support methods being applied in classrooms may not make sense, considering the characteristics of the students or the needs of the teacher. The UDL framework has been shown to give flexibility to the students' efforts and to reduce barriers in instruction (CAST, 2011). In doing so, accessibility of all students, including students with special educational needs, is promoted. Recently, measures for equipping new teachers with UDL practices have been effective in promoting academic achievement and motivation for learning of students of the teacher's entire class, including students who need special educational supports (Ozeki & Notomi, 2018). Of course, in order to optimize these, the needs of the students as well as those of the teacher must be taken into account. Support that meets diverse needs begins with a thorough understanding of the needs of individuals; they can be realized by comprehensively examining classroom situations and the needs of the teacher.

References

BaBa, C., Sato, M., & Matsumi, J. (2013). Review of functional behavioral assessment studies conducted in regular classrooms. *Japanese Journal of Behavior Analysis*, 28(1), 26–42.

CAST. (2011). *Universal design for learning guidelines version 2.0 [graphic organizer]*. Wakefield, MA: CAST Professional Publishing. Retrieved from http://udlguidelines.cast.org/binaries/content/assets/udlguidelines/udlg-v2-0/udlg_graphicorganizer_v2-0.pdf

MEXT. (2012). *Survey results on students with developmental disabilities needing special educational support in regular classes* [in Japanese]. Retrieved from www.mext.go.jp/a_menu/shotou/tokubetu/material/__icsFiles/afieldfile/2012/12/10/1328729_01.pdf

Ngayama, S., & Tsuge, M. (2017). *Research trend of support for CSST and group-oriented contingency to children enrolled in regular class*. Paper presented at the Japan Academy of Learning Disabilities.

Ozeki, K., & Notomi, K. (2018). Improvement of lesson by UDL aiming at improvement of academic ability consultation in the science of medium-sized junior high school. *Bulletin of University of Teacher Education Fukuoka: Part IV, Education and Psychology*, 67, 231–239.

SECTION 8
Future Directions

43

THE POTENTIAL EVOLUTION OF UNIVERSAL DESIGN FOR LEARNING (UDL) THROUGH THE LENS OF TECHNOLOGY INNOVATION

David Banes and Kirk Behnke

Introduction

UDL is an approach for designing instruction that aims to meet the needs of all participants in a learning environment. The three principles—providing multiple means of engagement, representation, and action/expression—lay the foundation for developing curriculum and teaching strategies that address varied learner needs. Though UDL does not require the use of instructional technologies (Rose, Gavel, & Domings, 2010), digital tools often enhance and expand flexibility in content delivery and learner engagement. Accessible technology within a UDL-grounded curriculum involves digital tools that support the principles and corresponding guidelines and goals.

Traditional examples of the integration of technology into UDL include use of assistive technology as a means to offer options for action (Meyer, Rose, & Gordon, 2014). Traditional technology might include screen readers for those with visual impairments or other reading difficulties and magnification/zoom features in operating systems and devices. However, the pace of change in accessible and assistive technologies has accelerated in recent years (Bhowmick & Hazarika, 2017), which has contributed to disruptive innovation in education that can impact the delivery and implementation of UDL.

Emerging Technologies and UDL

UDL principles may be applied without digital technologies to teach all students, but technology can be part of the means, rather than a goal of UDL (Rose et al., 2010). When technology is used, the design of the curriculum and the learning environment should be the focus. For example, Bartholomew Consolidated School Corporation (BCSC) in Columbus, Indiana, has developed procedures, goals, methodology, materials, resources, and assessments to measure progress and uses technology to support access for all, rather than as a means of making accommodations for a select few (BCSC, 2018).

When designing a lesson through a UDL lens, the latest apps or technologies are not essential, although there are many examples of ways that educators have implemented technology to support UDL. A UDL environment seeks to stimulate every learner, regardless of any personalized support they require (Rose et al., 2010). Luis Pérez has suggested that UDL is first and foremost about pedagogy, but "technology gives you a richer palette of tools to choose from" (Noonoo, 2014). If a student feels more comfortable hearing text read aloud, s/he can use text-to-speech, which is built-in to most operating systems or available as freeware; similarly, display modifications for inverting screen colors and highlighting and magnifying text can also support greater accessibility (ibid.).

Innovation has historically been at the heart of assistive technologies; however, the authors observe that the market has seen significant growth in innovations since 2010. The implications are pervasive across all aspects of life, including the delivery of inclusive education and application of Universal Design for Learning in the classroom (Rose et al., 2010). Curran (2016) identifies specific technologies that he believes will have the greatest future impact, including internet of things (IoT), artificial intelligence (AI), robotics, drones, augmented reality (AR), virtual reality (VR), and 3D printing. In addition, the authors would like to acknowledge location-based technologies and wearables, as they pertain directly to persons with disabilities. These technologies are at varying stages of emergence, with early indications for education, particularly for those with special learning needs (Emiliani & Stephanidis, 2005).

Internet of Things (IoT)

IoT connects devices together, enabling data sharing and remote control across networks (Atzori, Iera, & Morabito, 2017). IoT forms the basis of smart homes and facilitates home automation. Combined with natural interfaces, individuals with disabilities can control elements in their environment, enhancing independence in home, school, workplace, and community settings. In the classroom, smart speakers, such as Amazon Echo and Google Home, are comparatively low-cost and feature voice control. Learners can use audible commands to search for information online and control environmental elements such as lighting, entrance doors, heating, and entertainment. The devices can be extended to remote control other technologies for use in the arts or sciences, such as sound and light mixing boards, kilns, or paint sprays.

Location-Based Technology

Location-based technology uses information service to provide information, entertainment, or security that is accessible via devices through a network and uses information on the geographical position of the user or device (Steiniger, Neun, Edwardes, & Lenz, 2008). These can offer increased independence through navigation and orientation. For those with visual impairment or a learning difficulty, the use of GPS in outdoor spaces and beacons in indoor spaces allow for independent navigation facilitated through smartphone apps and wearable technologies (Meliones & Sampson, 2018), which may support independent movement between classrooms, boosting learner confidence and self-esteem. In addition, for persons with memory or cognitive disabilities, location-based security allows caregivers more flexibility in keeping their clients on property and safe.

Artificial Intelligence (AI)

Data generated by IoT and location-based technologies is essential for the application of AI, as AI enhances the capacity to interpret and present data in a variety of formats. Recent reviews identify how AI can support diverse learning needs by transforming information such as text from one format to another, such as voice (Abou-Zahra, Brewer, & Cooper, 2018), and other developments include auto captioning on YouTube and facial recognition on Facebook. Facial recognition technology may be beneficial to persons with autism to help them match facial expressions to emotions and provide context clues. This may enable learners to better work with other students in group-facilitated lessons to provide flexible learning options.

AI can also facilitate content clarification, presentation of text in simple to complex versions, and selection of supports based on learner profiles and behaviors (Marr, 2018). The record of interactions and behaviors of learners accessing technology can be used to anticipate preferences through machine learning and AI, anticipating choices based upon location, time, or activity. Such prediction could speed up communication within the classroom for those using voice output devices to interact with the teacher or peers by providing specific content and context information.

Robotics and Drones

Robots and drones are more than simply remote-controlled devices. Rouse (2018) describes a drone as a flying robot that can be both remotely controlled and flown autonomously through software-controlled flight plans in their embedded systems, working in conjunction with onboard sensors and GPS. It is this combination of control and autonomous systems that distinguishes robots and drones from devices controlled entirely manually.

A variety of such devices can support learners, including:

- Humanoid robots that facilitate communication and interaction for children with autism (Short, Deng, Feil-Seifer, & Matarić, 2017).
- Mechanical robotic *arms* to control a range of tools for those without the physical dexterity to do so manually (Al-Halimi & Moussa, 2017).

- Robotic-enhanced prosthetics for physical needs, including sports and healthy exercise by increasing ease of use and comfort (Ferris & Schlink, 2017).
- Telepresence robots that provide physical presence in locations that are difficult to access, including for those with a disability who are unable to interact with peers due to a health crisis, and have value for those who are excluded because of conditions such as chronic fatigue or pain.

All the tools listed enable the learner to participate in educational activities in an increasingly independent manner. The use of sensors and semi-autonomous actions by the device allows learners to participate in locations and settings that otherwise would be inaccessible, for instance, on field trips to study geology, or when using tools that would present a safety hazard in chemistry labs. Equally for those students who cannot attend school, telepresence robots can be used to remotely attend classes through the control of the robot from their home or hospital location.

Wearables

Wearable technology includes fashion technology and wearable devices. It involves smart devices with controls and sensors that can be incorporated or even woven into clothing or worn on the body as implants or accessories (Rodrigues et al., 2018). Wearables can also include devices that communicate information to the wearer, such as through glasses, audio devices, and tactile alerts. Wearable design features the convergence of functionality, previously available on multiple separate devices to be converged into singular, ready-to-access devices (Kim & Shin, 2015). Wearables include fitness trackers and smartwatches, and they are increasingly available in many parts of the world (Blackman, 2016). Wearables can have haptic and tactile features that facilitate communication, information access, navigation, reminder capabilities, and alert notification. Within the classroom, wearables have many potential uses, such as discrete communication between a student and teacher in which assistance requests can be made privately (Schlosser et al., 2017). Devices such as the Apple Watch can be used by pupils to send messages to a phone or tablet held by the teacher, as a means to respond to a question or to promote increased attention.

Augmented Reality (AR) and Virtual Reality (VR)

AR and VR are closely related, with each involving computer-generated simulations that integrate the real world (AR) or are entirely self-contained (VR) (Computer Language Co., 2018). AR applications allow the user to move around in the real world; but in VR environments, the user remains in a single physical location as they are viewing a virtual setting. Wearable displays, used with AR and VR, are becoming popular items available both for game consoles and as standalone devices. VR has been used for those who have experienced strokes to facilitate rehabilitation through virtual instruction and practice on how to drive powered wheelchairs (Archambault, Routhier, Gagnon, & Miller, 2018). AR and VR can be used to reinforce skills and learning and provide additional opportunities for practice. Pokémon Go was an early AR game that featured 3D navigation and integration of AR overlays, prompting many people to be more active whilst searching for Pokémon (Gabbiadini, Sagioglou, & Greitemeyer, 2018) and combining exercise with map-reading. Other applications of these technologies include low-cost virtual environments for those with complex needs (Brooks, 2017) and mobility training with gamification to practice skills and explore settings that would otherwise be unreachable.

Facilitators of instruction can use free and simple-to-use types of AR and VR in their classrooms within the engagement principle of UDL as well as provide flexible options for learners to gain a different perspective of information gathering. For example, Merge Cubes (https://miniverse.io/cube) and Google Cardboard (https://vr.google.com/cardboard/) have learning experiences that can engage and sustain student learning in a VR environment. One example is the use of AR to help students recognize stars and planets in science lessons. By pointing the app at the sky, bodies are shown, named, and linked to further information. The technology is helpful to those with low vision, as it augments the quality of what is seen in the sky unaided.

3D printing

3D printing offers a new model for the distribution of assistive technologies, including hardware devices, aids, and appliances. In the past, traditional provision of even small aids for access has largely depended on vendor availability and procurement (MacLachlan & Scherer, 2018). 3D printing allows rapid provision of these aids. Coupled with maker communities, like ATMakers (2019), there is capacity to store and share designs online, and simple technologies, such as switch adapted toys, can be readily distributed in this way. Collections of designs and instructions can be shared on social media and maker websites (e.g., Instructables and Thingiverse). Such technologies have the potential to empower classrooms and schools to be able to print aids and devices that support learning and interaction locally and on demand, reducing dependency on specialist services (Buehler, Kane, & Hurst, 2014). Some examples from the classroom include adapted pen grips to help with manipulating a pen, reading rulers to isolate lines of text, and 3D printed art works allowing tactile exploration of an image (Anderson, 2017).

Applying Emerging Technologies to UDL

The emerging technologies described support greater inclusive instruction in different ways. The authors contend that collectively they offer benefits of automating processes and supporting learner independence and self-regulation (Herro,

2015). There are numerous factors that influence successful implementation of emerging technologies, including the need to raise awareness of the application of tools and training teachers to make best use of them. For those engaged in creating UDL-grounded classrooms, the following recommendations are offered:

- Apply AI tools to predict need and accommodations through voice searches and spoken results, such as including location-aware core and extended vocabulary for written and spoken communication and voice interfaces for independent research.
- Facilitate the transformation of materials into accessible formats by producing automated alternative formats, including text-to-speech, braille, or captioning, and the use of content clarification using AI to simplify and clarify content to specific reading levels.
- Increase opportunities for diverse forms of expression through technologies that support learners to use alternative forms of presentation and literacy, including audio and video, which can be integrated into virtual layers in AR environments.
- Ease personal mobility and activity presence by increasing the capacity for learners to participate in activities that may otherwise be inaccessible. The use of telepresence technologies can help those with severe health needs remain in school, and autonomous mobility technologies may allow students to participate with peers in social groups without having an aide available who may not be a member of the group.
- Increase safe control of devices and appliances in an inclusive environment through modern robotic technologies and remote access solutions that support learners to manipulate specific tools and devices essential in specialist subjects such as the sciences and arts. Increasingly, remotely controlled drones facilitate access to areas that would otherwise be physically inaccessible.

Such implementation expands and enhances the application of the UDL principles (see Table 43.1). Each of the principles can be further facilitated by the emerging technologies in order to reduce the *strain* upon personnel.

Conclusion

The emerging technologies described in this chapter support inclusive learning in a variety of ways. Driven by ease of use and implementation, they can reduce learner barriers and requirements for teacher-driven individual accommodations of need by automating many forms of support. They offer benefits for all learners, beyond those with disabilities or special needs. Implementing new technologies into classrooms is concerned with more than providing new tools to teach the same way, as technologies such as these have the capacity to bring about

TABLE 43.1 Example Applications of Emerging Technologies Within the UDL Framework

Providing Multiple Means of Engagement is enhanced by

Robotics	Including learners who are unable to be physically located in the classroom due to illnesses
Internet of Things	Newsela—connecting to other outside sources to engage in content specifically designed for their own reading level
3D Printing	Engaged in designing and fabricating actual pieces from a lesson
Autonomous mobility	Increasing capacity to be present in real time and to engage at locations which may not be physically accessible
Location-based technologies	Predicting context and setting aware vocabulary to support written and spoken communication
Wearables	Use of timers, biofeedback, and reminders to enhance engagement and support self-regulation

Providing Multiple Means of Representation is enhanced by

Artificial Intelligence (AI)	Analyzing content and presenting meaning at the comprehension level of the learner
Augmented Reality (AR)	Integrating learning content with real work settings to support generalization
Virtual Reality (VR)	Reducing superfluous data and increasing distraction-free content
Smart Speakers	Utilizing voice commands to conduct quick research on a specific item
Wearables	Interpreting alerts and reminders into tactile, visual, and audible formats

Providing Multiple Means of Action and Expression is enhanced by

Internet of Things	Using natural interfaces such as voice or gesture to increase modes of expression to collaborative activities
3D Printing	Low cost production of prototypes and producing physical evidence of understanding through models
AR and VR	Communicating with others, not in the shared educational environment; museum tours and activities that simply cannot be done in the classroom
Robotics	Using robotic aids to control tools required in experiments and the creative process
Location and Context aware technology	Increasing communication, including directing the movements and actions of others by linking communication boards to settings and context identified by location sensors

fundamental changes in pedagogy, such as that envisaged in flipped classrooms (DeLozier & Rhodes, 2017). Through the lens of the UDL framework, they can bring about an increased capacity for inclusive education. This will involve consideration of building capacity within schools and districts, alongside greater integration with post-school transition.

References

Abou-Zahra, S., Brewer, J., & Cooper, M. (2018). *Artificial intelligence (AI) for web accessibility: Is conformance evaluation a way forward?* Proceedings of the ACM Internet of Accessible Things, Lyon, France.

Al-Halimi, R. K., & Moussa, M. (2017). Performing complex tasks by users with upper-extremity disabilities using a 6-DOF robotic arm: A study. *IEEE Transactions on Neural Systems and Rehabilitation Engineering, 25*(6), 686–693.

Anderson, K. (2017). *With 3D technology, special education students can focus on content—not access.* Retrieved from www.edsurge.com/news/2017-08-14-with-3d-technology-special-education-students-can-focus-on-content-not-access

Archambault, P., Routhier, F., Gagnon, D., & Miller, W. (2018). Usability and efficacy of a virtual reality simulator for power wheelchair training. *Annals of Physical and Rehabilitation Medicine, 61*, e90.

ATMakers. (2019). *About us.* Retrieved from http://atmakers.org/about-us/

Atzori, L., Iera, A., & Morabito, G. (2017). Understanding the Internet of things: Definition, potentials, and societal role of a fast evolving paradigm. *Ad Hoc Networks, 56*, 122–140.

Bartholomew Consolidated School Corporation (BCSC). (2018). *Universal design for learning at BSBC.* Retrieved from www.bcsc.k12.in.us/Page/341

Bhowmick, A., & Hazarika, S. (2017). An insight into assistive technology for the visually impaired and blind people: State-of-the-art and future trends. *Journal on Multimodal User Interfaces, 11*(2), 149–172.

Blackman, N. M. D. (2016). *The growing availability of wearable devices: A perspective on current applications in clinical trials.* Retrieved November 5, 2018, from www.appliedclinicaltrialsonline.com/growing-availability-wearable-devices-perspective-current-applications-clinical-trials

Brooks, A. (2017). Digital ethics: "Ethical" considerations of post-research ICT impact. In A. Brooks, S. Brahnam, B. Kapralos, & L. C. Jain (Eds.), *Recent advances in technologies for inclusive well-being* (pp. 273–282). Cham, Switzerland: Springer International Publishing.

Buehler, E., Kane, S. K., & Hurst, A. (2014). ABC and 3D: Opportunities and obstacles to 3D printing in special education environments. ACM Proceedings of the 16th international ACM SIGACCESS conference on Computers & accessibility, 107–114.

Computer Language Co. (2018). *Definition of AR/VR.* Retrieved from www.pcmag.com/encyclopedia/term/69784/ar-vr

Curran, C. (2016). *A guide to the "essential eight" emerging technologies* [Blog post]. Retrieved from https://pwc.blogs.com/ceoinsights/2016/08/a-guide-to-the-essential-eight-emerging-technologies.html

DeLozier, S. J., & Rhodes, M. G. (2017). Flipped classrooms: A review of key ideas and recommendations for practice. *Educational Psychology Review, 29*(1), 141–151.

Emiliani, P. L., & Stephanidis, C. (2005). Universal access to ambient intelligence environments: Opportunities and challenges for people with disabilities. *IBM Systems Journal, 44*(3), 605–619.

Ferris, D. P., & Schlink, B. R. (2017). Robotic devices to enhance human movement performance. *Kinesiology Review, 6*(1), 70–77.

Gabbiadini, A., Sagioglou, C., & Greitemeyer, T. (2018). Does Pokémon GO lead to a more physically active life style? *Computers in Human Behavior, 84*, 258–263.

Herro, D. (2015). Sustainable innovations: Bringing digital media and emerging technologies to the classroom. *Theory into Practice, 54*(2), 117–127.

Kim, K. J., & Shin, D. H. (2015). An acceptance model for smart watches: Implications for the adoption of future wearable technology. *Internet Research, 25*(4), 527–541.

MacLachlan, M., & Scherer, M. (2018). Systems thinking for assistive technology: A commentary on the GREAT summit. *Disability and Rehabilitation: Assistive Technology, 13*(5), 492–496.

Marr, B. (2018). How is AI used in education—real world examples of today and a peek into the future. *Forbes.* Retrieved from www.forbes.com/sites/bernardmarr/2018/07/25/how-is-ai-used-in-education-real-world-examples-of-today-and-a-peek-into-the-future/

Meliones, A., & Sampson, D. (2018). Blind museum tourer: A system for self-guided tours in museums and blind indoor navigation. *Technologies, 6*(1), 1–31.

Meyer, A., Rose, D. H., & Gordon, D. (2014). *Universal design for learning: Theory & practice.* Wakefield, MA: CAST Professional Publishing.

Noonoo, S. (2014). Six ways to engage every learner using UDL. *THE Journal.* Retrieved from https://thejournal.com/articles/2014/12/03/6-ways-to-engage-every-learner-using-udl.aspx

Rodrigues, J. J., Segundo, D. B. D. R., Junqueira, H. A., Sabino, M. H., Prince, R. M., Al-Muhtadi, J., & De Albuquerque, V. H. C. (2018). Enabling technologies for the Internet of health things. *IEEE Access, 6*, 13129–13141.

Rose, D., Gavel, J., & Domings, Y. (2010). *UDL unplugged: The role of technology in UDL.* Retrieved from www.cast.org/our-work/publications/2012/udl-unplugged-role-technology.html

Rouse, M. (2018). *What is a drone or UAV?* Retrieved from https://internetofthingsagenda.techtarget.com/definition/drone

Schlosser, R. W., O'Brien, A., Yu, C., Abramson, J., Allen, A. A., Flynn, S., & Shane, H. C. (2017). Repurposing everyday technologies to provide just-in-time visual supports to children with intellectual disability and autism: A pilot feasibility study with the Apple Watch®. *International Journal of Developmental Disabilities, 63*(4), 221–227.

Short, E. S., Deng, E. C., Feil-Seifer, D., & Matarić, M. J. (2017). Understanding agency in interactions between children with autism and socially assistive robots. *Journal of Human-Robot Interaction, 6*(3), 21–47.

Steiniger, S., Neun, M., Edwardes, A., & Lenz, B. (2008). *Foundations of LBS. Module in CartouCHe-cartography for Swiss higher education.* Retrieved from www.e-cartouche.ch/content_reg/cartouche/LBSbasics/en/text/LBSbasics.pdf

44
UNIVERSAL DESIGN FOR LEARNING AND THE LANDFILL OF REVOLUTIONARY EDUCATIONAL INNOVATIONS

Dave L. Edyburn

Introduction

Paul and Elder (2007) define an educational fad as a "short-lived emphasis on a seemingly wonderful new idea that will transform teaching and learning without much effort on anyone's part" (p. 4). Fullan (1991) argued that educational fads are common in the field of education because of the short-term perspective of policy-makers and educators. Maddux (1986) described a repetitive and descriptive cycle that he termed the *pendulum syndrome*, and later offered the following summary:

> This phenomenon begins with unrealistically optimistic claims and expectations for each emerging educational innovation followed by too-hasty, wide adoption in schools. Inevitably, the innovation fails to live up to the initial, over-inflated expectations, resulting in disillusionment by teachers, parents, and policy-makers. This causes pre-mature abandonment of the innovation before it receives either a fair field trial or formal research validation.
>
> *(Maddux & Cummings, 2004, p. 512)*

Maddux and Cummings (2004) observed that

> Fad and fashion are facts of professional life in most disciplines. However, education has always been particularly susceptible to short-lived, fashionable movements that come suddenly into vogue, generate brief but intense enthusiasm and optimism, and fall quickly into disrepute and abandonment.
>
> *(p. 511)*

Experienced educators will be familiar with a litany of educational fads:

> Only a few of these [fads] in general education include programmed learning, teaching machines, controlled readers and other "reading machines," reality therapy, assertive discipline, new mathematics, new grammar, open education, the "back to basics" movement, outcome-based education, the Madeline Hunter model, and right brain-left brain instruction. The syndrome has also claimed its share of casualties in the field of special education. A few of the better-known ones include balance beams to treat learning disabilities, colored lenses or plastic overlays to treat reading problems, eye movement therapy, the non-stimulating environment, and facilitated communication.
>
> *(Maddux & Cummings, 2004, pp. 512–513)*

In a classic article about the pre-adolescent evolution of Universal Design for Learning (UDL), Edyburn (2010) warned that "unless serious intellectual energy is devoted to addressing the current shortcomings of the UDL construct, within the next 10 years we may be commemorating the passing of another education fad" (p. 40). As the decade comes to a close, this chapter seeks to address the question: Is there any merit to Edyburn's forecast that UDL was on a pathway to becoming another educational fad?

In the sections that follow, a quantifiable profile of an educational fad is constructed in order to compare and contrast the evolution of UDL in order to determine if its trajectory is similar to, or different from, other selected educational fads. Secondly, three lenses are applied to a body of recent UDL literature syntheses to assess three characteristics of his forecast: (a) difficulty in operationally defining UDL, (b) inability to identify the active ingredients in UDL intervention claims, and (c) insufficient attention to measuring the outcomes of UDL interventions.

Quantifiable Profile of an Educational Fad

Google Books Ngram Viewer

Google Books Ngram Viewer (https://books.google.com/ngrams) was created to give linguistic scholars a tool for studying word usage over time. The database of English words was built as part of the Google Books project (Weingarten, 2013) in which the contents of print books were scanned to provide full-text searching. Public access to this dataset offered inspiration for the following research questions:

1. What does the profile of an educational fad look like over time relative to its word frequency?

334 Dave L. Edyburn

2. If there is a pattern to the diminishing use of an educational fad over time, would the pattern for word frequency for the term *UDL* be similar or different?

After reviewing the Maddux and Cummings (2004) list of recent education fads, four terms were selected by the author to enter into Ngram in order to establish a baseline profile: *programmed learning, teaching machines, open education*, and *assertive discipline*. The period of analysis was set to the range of 1960 to 2008. The visual results are presented in Figure 44.1. Three terms (*programmed learning, teaching machines*, and *open education*) illustrate a pattern of modest growth in usage over time culminating in a spike before a steady and gradual decline. The term *assertive discipline* stays consistently flat and minimally used over time.

Following the establishment of the baseline illustrated in Figure 44.1, four terms related to inclusive instructional design were subsequently entered into Ngram: *assistive technology, educational technology, personalized learning*, and *universal design for learning*. Again, the period of analysis was set from 1960 to 2008. The results are presented visually in Figure 44.2 and illustrate strikingly different patterns from the educational fads illustrated in Figure 44.1. However, the term *UDL* does appear similar to the pattern associated with a*ssertive discipline*, which may suggest that the use of these two terms has been limited to special education, a small subpopulation within the entire educational profession.

Figure 44.2 therefore offers some evidence that patterns of educational fads can be identified by using Google Ngram. However, a fundamental limitation of this analysis is that Google stopped adding words to the corpus in 2008 as book scanning efforts were targeted to specific niches and Google project leaders believed that the data set was sufficiently large and general usage patterns were stable (Weingarten, 2013). Unfortunately, the word frequency of UDL is inconclusive in the Google Ngram analysis, because the term was still within an emergent phase pre-2009. To overcome this methodological limitation, a second quantitative analysis was conducted.

Google Trends

To mitigate the limitation discovered in Google Ngram, a second tactic was used to quantify search term usage. Google Trends (https://trends.google.com/trends/?geo=US) is a tool that allows users to view the results of Google search terms over time as a metric for understanding the frequency of words and phrases used in web searches. The four educational fad terms were initially searched to provide a comparative baseline (see Figure 44.3). Combined with the pattern observed in the Google Ngram search, there does seem to be a visible trend produced by this quantitative evidence for short-term educational fads during the 58-year period (1960 through 2018) for three terms: *programmed learning, teaching*

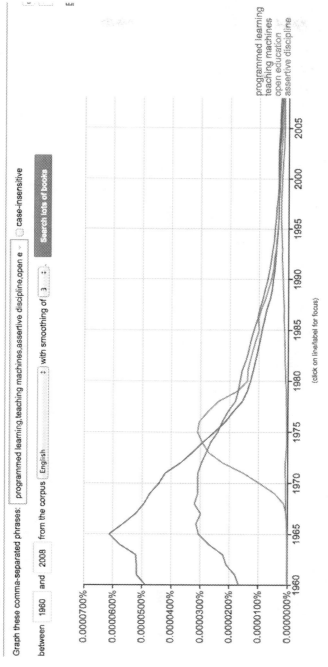

FIGURE 44.1 Ngram of the Frequency of Four Terms Frequently Recognized as an Educational Fad: *Programmed Learning, Teaching Machines, Open Education,* and *Assertive Discipline* from the Period 1960 to 2008

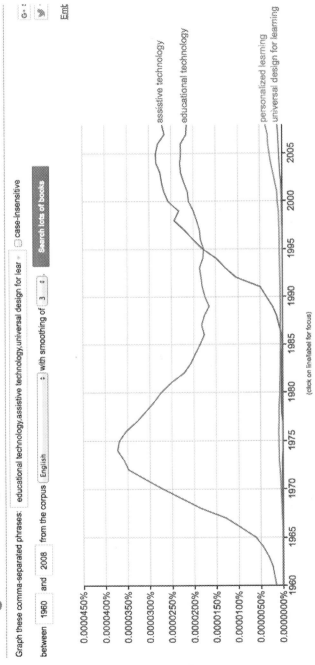

FIGURE 44.2 Ngram of the Frequency of Four Technology Terms: *Assistive Technology*, *Educational Technology*, *Personalized Learning*, and *Universal Design for Learning* from the Period 1960 to 2008

The Landfill of Educational Innovations   337

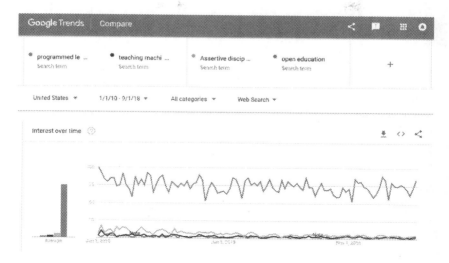

FIGURE 44.3   Google Trends of the Frequency of *Programmed Learning, Teaching Machines, Open Education*, and *Assertive Discipline* from the Period January 1, 2006 Through September 1, 2018

*machine*s, and *assertive discipline*. The exception is *open education*, with a consistent and very high search pattern over time.

Replicating the two-step process used earlier with Google Ngram, the four inclusive instructional design terms (*assistive technology, educational technology, personalized learning*, and *universal design for learning*) were searched in Google Trends for the time period of January 1, 2006 through September 1, 2018. As illustrated in Figure 44.4, the terms *assistive technology* and *educational technology* show robust use but slow declines over time. Web searches of the term *universal design for learning* were consistently low; and in 2016, this term was surpassed by *personalized learning*.

Google Ngram and Google Trends provide quantitative evidence for use of terms labeled as education fads, visualizing distinct patterns of these words used over time. As a result of the analyses in this study, it appears that more confidence can be placed in word profiles that exceed 50 years than word profiles that involve periods of less than 10 years. Whereas, the term *UDL* has some shared characteristics with terms that have been identified as educational fads, the findings are inconclusive as to whether or not usage of the term *Universal Design for Learning* is on the same pathway as previous educational innovations that turned out to be fads. As a result, attention will be given to another characteristic of an educational fad that Maddux and Cummings (2004) call into question, whether or not premature "abandonment of the innovation before it receives either a fair field trial or formal research validation" (p. 512) occurs.

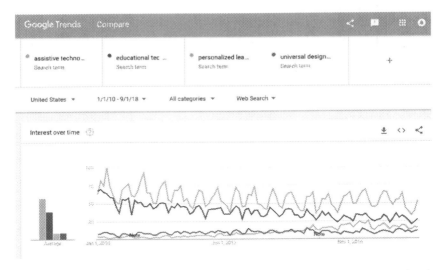

FIGURE 44.4 Google Trends of the Frequency of *Assistive Technology, Educational Technology, Personalized Learning,* and *Universal Design for Learning* from the Period January 1, 2006 Through September 1, 2018

The Emergence of the UDL Research Base

As part of his argument that UDL was on an educational fad pathway, Edyburn (2010) argued that there was an inadequate base of primary research, with most literature largely based on philosophical support, rather than studies that empirically assessed UDL interventions. As a result, he concluded that the "claim that UDL has been scientifically validated through research cannot be substantiated at this time" (p. 34).

Space limitations prevent a comprehensive review of UDL literature and synthesis of recent research since 2010. However, the author discovered six recent comprehensive UDL literature reviews/syntheses/meta-analyses (Capp, 2017; Crevecoeur, Sorenson, Mayorga, & Gonzalez, 2014; Kennedy et al., 2018; McGuire, 2014; Ok, Rao, Bryant, & McDougall, 2017; Rao, Ok, & Bryant, 2014). These works provide a lens for examining three main concerns Edyburn argued had impaired the field's ability to establish a research base supporting the efficacy of UDL: (a) difficulty in operationally defining UDL, (b) inability to identify the active ingredients in UDL intervention claims, and (c) insufficient attention to measuring the outcomes of UDL interventions.

Corpus of UDL Research Evidence

As summarized in Table 44.1, varied methodological approaches have been used when conducting reviews of empirical peer-reviewed articles describing

TABLE 44.1 Characteristics of Six Recent UDL Research Reviews

	Capp	Crevecoeur	Kennedy	McGuire	Ok	Rao
Year	2017	2014	2018	2014	2017	2014
Type of Review	Meta-Analysis	Methodological	Scoping Review	Frameworks	Lit Review	Lit Review
Focus	PreK-College	K-12	Rehab in Schools	Higher Education	PreK -12	PreK-College
# of articles	18	5	45	6	13	13

interventions grounded in UDL principles. Hence the discovery of six literature reviews/syntheses assuage Maddux and Cummings' (2004) concern about an innovation failing before research could be conducted to establish efficacy. Across the six research syntheses, there were a total of 69 articles; but after removing duplicate citations, the 2014–2018 empirical base for UDL can be evaluated through a corpus of 53 studies. Authorship of this set of syntheses reflect the US-centric nature of UDL and the international adoption in English-speaking countries: Australia (n=1), Canada (n=1), and USA (n=4).

Operationally Defining UDL

Five of the six reviews noted the intrinsic problem of defining UDL wherein many authors used the term but did not provide an operational definition in their study (Capp, 2017; Crevecoeur et al., 2014; Kennedy et al., 2018; Ok et al., 2017; Rao et al., 2014). In addition, problems were noted concerning research designs that did not have sufficient power or control. However, it is very curious to discover an extensive number of UDL studies that only involved students with disabilities. Perhaps most striking about the UDL definitional problem Edyburn (2010) raised is that only 23% of the studies (16 of 69) were identified by more than one of the six independent researchers engaged in conducting comprehensive literature reviews. Clearly, there is a problem with our scientific methodology or the ability to define the construct when multiple reviews produce an overlap of only 23%.

Identification of the Active Ingredients in Claims of UDL Interventions

A companion problem to the lack of a measurable definition of UDL involves what Edyburn (2010) referred to as *active ingredients* (i.e., the design features that must be present in a claim of a UDL intervention) and *dosage* (i.e., the amount [time, duration] of UDL intervention provided). Four reviews raised these concerns as a limitation of current research or as a suggestion for future research (Capp, 2017; Crevecoeur et al., 2014; Ok et al., 2017; Rao et al., 2014). However, in several of the literature reviews it is not clear that analysis of the UDL principles, guidelines, and checkpoints was a fruitful tactic to answer questions about the active ingredients and dosage of UDL. As a result, without this information there is little empirical evidence about what it means to design, implement, and measure the outcome of a UDL claim.

Measuring the Outcomes of UDL Interventions

The body of UDL research has grown considerably since 2010, and the analytic lenses have expanded as a means for understanding the potential impact of UDL (descriptive review, McGuire, 2014; analytic reviews, Ok et al., 2017; Rao et al., 2014; meta-analysis, Capp, 2017; single-subject case design, Crevecoeur et al., 2014; and a scoping review, Kennedy et al., 2018). Yet, the tenets of science remain missing in the field of UDL relevant to the standard of evidence-based practice, in particular:

1. Definitional clarity of what it means to create a UDL intervention,
2. An ability to isolate the active ingredients that are thought to make UDL work,
3. Guidelines about the dosage of a UDL intervention needed to achieve access, engagement, and success in demonstrating a learning outcome, and
4. Appropriate research methodologies that measure the impact of the intervention on the targeted population (i.e., primary beneficiary) as well as the population as a whole (i.e., secondary beneficiary).

Conclusions and Recommendations

When Edyburn (2010) wrote his classic article, the field of UDL was approximately 10 years old. Over the past decade, considerable effort has focused on implementing UDL at scale given the political support provided for the construct in the Higher Education Act of 2008 and the National Technology Plan (https://tech.ed.gov/netp/). This is consistent with Maddux's (1986) assessment of an education fad, that is, the tendency for educators, administrators, and policymakers to adopt innovations before they have been empirically tested through research. However, as the field looks to the third decade of UDL, questions must be raised about whether UDL will fade as its impact is absorbed within other domains such as personalized learning.

To alter such a trajectory, the following initiatives are proposed:

- Develop academic diversity blueprints to facilitate designers' understanding of the meaningful ways learners are different (learner variance) in order to

embed supports. If UDL is a design intervention, why must educators wait to meet their diverse students before proactively designing curricula to support student success?
- Re-examine the role of accessibility in universal design. This can be initiated by considering questions of "What are the inherent barriers associated with standard learning environments and instructional materials?" and "How can inclusive technologies improve access, engagement, and outcomes for all?"
- Enhance the quality and scope of the research methods needed to study UDL in order to isolate the active ingredients in a UDL intervention. How might UDL researchers and developers use technology to gather data about what works, for whom, and under what conditions to advance the field as a data-based profession?
- Measure the use and benefit of UDL interventions by both the primary beneficiaries (individuals who typically experience poor learning outcomes) and the secondary beneficiaries (individuals who can use and benefit from the same interventions but who are not identified in advance). Can the profession discover inclusive solutions for students that need support and assistance while simultaneously offering benefits to others that are not known in advance?

Perhaps 10 years from now, there will be sufficient research evidence or Ngram-type tools that will quantitatively reveal whether or not UDL enters the landfill of revolutionary educational innovations. In the meantime, as UDL matures into its third decade, there is urgent and important work to do to capture the potential of UDL in meaningful applications to help all students access, engage, and succeed in meeting grade-level expectations in a global society.

References

Capp, M. J. (2017). The effectiveness of universal design for learning: A meta-analysis of literature between 2013 and 2016. *International Journal of Inclusive Education*, 21(8), 791–807.

Crevecoeur, Y. C., Sorenson, S. E., Mayorga, V., & Gonzalez, A. P. (2014). Universal design for learning in K-12 educational settings: A review of group comparison and single-subject intervention studies. *Journal of Special Education Apprenticeship*, 3(2), 1–23.

Edyburn, D. L. (2010). Would you recognize universal design for learning if you saw it? Ten propositions for new directions for the second decade of UDL. *Learning Disability Quarterly*, 33(1), 33–41.

Fullan, M. G. (1991). *The new meaning of educational change* (2nd ed.). New York: Teachers College Press.

Kennedy, J., Missiuna, C., Pollock, N., Wu, S., Yost, J., & Campbell, W. (2018). A scoping review to explore how universal design for learning is described and implemented by rehabilitation health professionals in school settings. *Child: Care, Health and Development*, 44(5), 670–688.

Maddux, C. D. (1986). The educational computing backlash: Can the swing of the pendulum be halted? *Computers in the Schools*, 3(2), 27–30.

Maddux, C. D., & Cummings, R. (2004). Fad, fashion, and the weak role of theory and research in information technology in education. *Journal of Technology and Teacher Education, 12*(4), 511–533.

McGuire, J. M. (2014). Universally accessible instruction: Oxymoron or opportunity? *Journal of Postsecondary Education and Disability, 27*(4), 387–398.

Ok, M. W., Rao, K., Bryant, B. R., & McDougall, D. (2017). Universal design for learning in pre-K to grade 12 classrooms: A systematic review of research. *Exceptionality, 25*(2), 116–138.

Paul, R., & Elder, L. (2007). *A critical thinker's guide to educational fads: How to get beyond educational glitz and glitter.* Tomales, CA: Foundation for Critical Thinking.

Rao, K., Ok, M. W., & Bryant, B. R. (2014). A review of research on universal design educational models. *Remedial and Special Education, 35*(3), 153–166.

Weingarten, E. (2013, September 9). The language time machine. *Slate.* Retrieved from www.slate.com/articles/technology/future_tense/2013/09/google_ngram_viewer_a_language_time_machine.html

45

SNAPSHOT—THE PRECARIOUS PROMISE OF EMERGENT TECH AND UNIVERSAL DESIGN FOR LEARNING

A Pivotal Point

Susan Molnar

Rationale

For the successful application of emergent technologies, the *universal* factor needs to be accounted for in its development. Many of these technological advances are designed by and for a specific subset of humanity that often has a certain degree of privilege and tend to be standard English speakers with westernized points of view. Thus, users beyond this demographic may have to resort to modifying inputs and hacking to adjust pre-existing constraints to their needs.

Examples

Such is the case with emergent technologies, including voice-controlled devices like the Microsoft Hololens. To use the Hololens, one must say "Next" with a pronounced *T* sound. With such a structural default, this can be challenging for non-native English speakers and inherently exclude them from being able to use and participate in this branch of new technology. Similarly, gestural functions such as the *air tap* (see Figure 45.1) require exact movements to perform an action recognizable by the device (Microsoft, 2019). Users with disability issues that impair motor functions are thus limited in interactions with this technology and its potential. Failure to address issues of this nature closes the door to equal access and stifles diversity, a key component to innovation (Page, 2008).

This can also be seen in the rise of artificial intelligence (AI) neural networks. As Cummings (2017, para. 2) asserts, "It's a misconception that AI is objective because it relies on mathematical computations; the construction of an AI system is an inherently human-driven process. It is unavoidable that such systems will contain bias." The construction of these networks relies on data that is chosen by

1. Finger in the ready position   2. Press finger down to tap or click

FIGURE 45.1   Gestural Air Tap Function

humans, the majority of which are white, cisgender male, affluent programmers (Crawford, 2018). Having greater diversity among programmers and their support teams would be beneficial and therefore likely reflect the types of user data that would be considered in product development. Further, homogeneous group factors may influence data based on socio-economic structures, gender and race, and they need to be checked and mitigated.

Emergent technology may seem to support humanity's evolution in a dynamic world using agile and sophisticated means generated through global understandings of learning and communication. New technologies can be modified to accommodate speech patterns, motion patterns and cultural localizations, but are in a critical moment. For example, an advance that could benefit by diversification in technology could be as simple as enabling customization of Hololens input words and gestures that are more natural to the end user's patterns. Such a user-centered improvement would allow the technology to address the needs of a broader set of users. These types of redesigns allow diverse users to learn them in ways that are specific to their needs.

User-centered design is not a new concept, as artists and hackers have been doing this for years, with projects such as the EyeWriter, a device constructed by members of Free Art and Technology (FAT), OpenFrameworks and the Graffiti Research Lab for the American graffiti artist Tony Quan (tag name Tempt One or Tempt1), who has the degenerative nerve disorder ALS (EyeWriter, 2009). The EyeWriter was constructed with the needs of this user in mind to allow control of the device through eye tracking in order to continue practice as an artist from the hospital bed (see Figure 45.2). By designing a device that removed barriers of operation with direct feedback from the user, a new and better device was created. With this device, Tempt1 was able to continue his art as his ALS progressed.

Designing devices and systems that allow for universal access is essential. The peril, though, is that often those with the access and ability to do so are segregated from the populations with diverse abilities who need to or could be the systems'

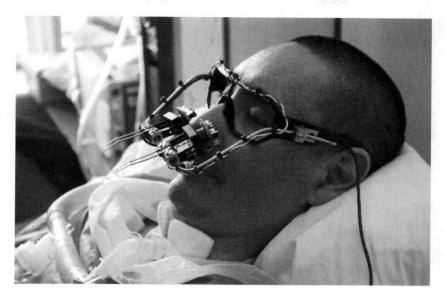

FIGURE 45.2 EyeWriter Created for Tempt1

potential users and could help push further innovation for needs that may not otherwise be accounted for in the design. In order for emergent technologies to support universal access, they must have a focus on the inclusion of varied users and incorporate this variability into the design, prototyping and development stages. This is especially true for mainstream commercial technologies. The potential of what's possible can be seen in independent projects like the EyeWriter that empower access through collaboration. The contrast between what is possible and what is mass produced highlights how crucial it is to have greater commitment from mainstream manufacturers and research labs for inclusion and diversity. Failure to do so is likely to continue to propagate structural inequities into the future technology landscape that are all too common in those existing today.

References

Crawford, K. (2018, January 20). *Opinion | artificial intelligence's white guy problem*. Retrieved from www.nytimes.com/2016/06/26/opinion/sunday/artificial-intelligences-white-guy-problem.html

Cummings, M. (2017). *We need to overcome AI's inherent human bias*. Retrieved from www.weforum.org/agenda/2017/10/we-need-to-overcome-ais-inherent-human-bias/

EyeWriter. (2009). *About the EyeWriter*. Retrieved from www.eyewriter.org/

Microsoft. (2019). *Mixed reality: Gestures*. Retrieved from https://docs.microsoft.com/en-us/windows/mixed-reality/gestures

Page, S. E. (2008). *The difference: How the power of diversity creates better groups, firms, schools, and societies*. Princeton, NJ: Princeton University Press.

46
SNAPSHOT—A VISION FOR PRE-SERVICE AND IN-SERVICE LEARNER-CENTERED TEACHING THROUGH THE ARTS

Susan Trostle Brand and Laurie J. DeRosa

Background

As societal attitudes and expectations change, the arts have been included and removed, in various degrees, from curriculums around the world. Arts integration, which blends artistic skills with the content of various disciplines, continues to move along a continuum of practice in classrooms. Past and present factors that have influenced this fluctuation in the United States include education reform, such as the No Child Left Behind Act, the Common Core Standards, and the focus on standardized testing and national assessment, including the overhaul of educator evaluation systems. With the advent of Universal Design for Learning (UDL) (Orkwis, 1999) and expanding STEM to STEAM (Science, Technology, Engineering, Art, and Math), many natural, innovative, and convenient pathways for integrating the arts into instruction have emerged. However, the integration of UDL and the arts into the standards-based curriculum is far from common practice in many public schools today.

Rationale

Teachers and teacher-trainers often struggle with the rigid, standards-based curriculum. The current state of curriculum in public schools is assessment-driven and limited in arts integration. Some teachers, against their better judgment, believe that they must accept the curriculum at *face value*. According to Egbert and Roe (2014, p. 251), "Student disengagement can be a major impediment to effective student learning. When parents and educators cannot provide adequate reasoning to explain the value of what is taught at home and school, students can lose their motivation to learn and be engaged in classroom activities." Perhaps the ultimate, ideal outcome of curriculum reform would emphasize the development of critical thinking and problem solving that leads to contributions as active and engaged citizens.

Teaching through an arts-integrated curriculum using the tenants of UDL offers a tangible vehicle for developing students' problem-solving abilities, communication skills, and active, meaningful participation in learning. Yet the value of arts integration, including the visual arts, storytelling, and drama, into today's schools is not fully realized by educators and administrators. "The arts need a voice in power, say people in the field, someone in the corridors of influence to argue the benefits of teaching students about classical and jazz music, ballet, and sculpture" (Bauerlein, 2010, p. 42) as well as visual arts, storytelling, and drama. Through teacher training in the arts, at both pre-service and in-service levels, educators can discover how state and national standards can be addressed in learner-centered ways. With an arts-integrated curriculum, standards-based, learner-centered arts are infused into all content areas by trained and enlightened educators. Gardner's theory of multiple intelligences (1983, 2006) suggests that students' learning is best facilitated when educators teach the way that students learn. Likewise, multiple intelligence-based activities, tailored to individual learners' needs, can be transformed from passive to active by applying the UDL framework through an arts-integrated curriculum. Table 46.1 illustrates the three principles of UDL and

TABLE 46.1 UDL Applications Through Arts-Integrated Curricula

Move From Passive:	To Active (Multiple Means of Representation and Expression):	Using (Multiple Means of Expression and Engagement):
Reading Textbooks	Seeking information from a variety of sources	Technology, Group Work, Demonstrations, Field Trips, Expressive Arts; *linguistic, intrapersonal, and interpersonal intelligences*
Listening Passively	Relating and connecting previous information and prior knowledge with new information	Audio, Visual, Tactile, Multisensory Media, Expressive Arts; *linguistic, visual-spatial, existential/spiritual, and interpersonal intelligences*
Writing Notes, Essays, and Reports	Demonstrating understanding of facts, concepts, and ideas acquired from multiple sources	Auditory, Visual, Tactile, Multisensory Media, Expressive Arts; *linguistic and visual-spatial intelligences*
Oral Reports	Sharing knowledge about facts, concepts, and ideas; weaving concepts together to draw conclusions	Computers, Auditory, Visual, Tactile, Multisensory Media, Expressive Arts; *logical-mathematical, linguistic, bodily-kinesthetic, musical, and interpersonal intelligences*

(Continued)

TABLE 46.1 (Continued)

Move From Passive:	To Active (Multiple Means of Representation and Expression):	Using (Multiple Means of Expression and Engagement):
Manipulating Calculations	Demonstrating steps in the process as well as the product	Technology; *logical-mathematical and interpersonal intelligences*
Remembering Concepts	Demonstrating understanding of concepts and ideas	Outlines and other graphic organizers; *visual spatial and linguistic multiple intelligences*
Remembering Procedures	Demonstrating procedures	Auditory, Visual (charts, tables, graphs); *naturalistic, linguistic, bodily-kinesthetic, and visual-spatial multiple intelligences*
Solving Paper and Pencil Problems	Showing ability and skills through personally accessible formats	Computers, Calculators, iPads, Expressive Arts; *linguistic and logical-mathematical intelligences*
Reciting Facts	Weaving sources and information together to make connections and draw conclusions	Reference materials, Computers, iPads, Expressive Arts; *existential/spiritual, musical, naturalistic, bodily-kinesthetic, and linguistic intelligences*

the transformation of the classroom from passive to active learning for students at all levels and all abilities. It illustrates the connections between the expressive arts of music, drama, graphic arts, media arts, and dance and the multiple intelligences of naturalistic, interpersonal, intrapersonal, visual-spatial, mathematical, linguistic, musical, bodily-kinesthetic, and (more recently) existential (Gardner, 2006).

Application

As an example, an integrated arts lesson could involve elementary school students in creating a tissue paper collage of animals from A-Z. Students research their animals, investigating key animal traits, characteristics, and habitats. All of the animal images and descriptions are then collated to create a book representing animals from a representative state, such as Massachusetts (see Figure 46.1). Using a formative assessment process, educators and learners can work through establishing criteria, observing (behaviors, conversations, and products), clarifying (questioning and feedback), and directing (going back, remaining, or moving on).

The books can be shared with children from different countries through the ePals program (Cricket Media, 2017). In another example, books created by pre-K to grade 12 students included *Weather Throughout the Seasons, Cultural Areas of Interest in Our Region,* and *The History of Our Region.* This type of integrated, learner-centered project enlists tenets of UDL by incorporating multiple means of representation (locating state information from various sources), multiple means

A Vision for Learner-Centered Teaching **349**

FIGURE 46.1 A to Z Animals from Massachusetts Example Student Book

of expression (typing descriptions and orally and visually sharing), and multiple means of engagement (creating artistic collages of animals of students' choice at their unique levels).

References

Bauerlein, M. (2010, Fall). Advocating for arts in the classroom. *Education Next Institute, Inc.*, *10*(4).

Cricket Media. (2017). *ePals: Find connections*. Retrieved from www.epals.com/

Egbert, J., & Roe, M. (2014). The power of why: Connecting curriculum to students' lives. *Childhood Education, 90*(4), 251–258.

Gardner, H. (1983). *Frames of mind: The theory of multiple intelligence.* New York: Basic Books.

Gardner, H. (2006). *Multiple intelligences: New horizons in theory and practice.* New York: Basic Books.

Orkwis, R. (1999). *Curriculum access and universal design for learning (Digest No. E586).* Reston, VA: ERIC Clearinghouse on Disabilities and Gifted Education. Retrieved from ERIC Database. (ED437767).

47
EPILOGUE

Learning From Diverse Perspectives on Inclusive Instructional Design and Next Steps

Susie L. Gronseth

Across the chapters, the Universal Design for Learning (UDL) framework has been a central focus for many of the writers and was certainly central to the conception of this book, mentioned specifically in the book subtitle. Although the UDL framework is quite comprehensive and aligned to intentional inclusivity from the origination of a learning experience, the multiplicity of frameworks and perspectives that have emerged all over the world are recognized and embraced in this book. As part of the development of the book chapters, there were conversations between the editors and authors about the frameworks and terminology that align with their perspectives, making this a continual learning process for both sides. It expanded editors' understanding of what is happening around the world in the area of inclusive education and informed authors' understandings of how their initiatives might be connected to broader conversations and related work of others.

Figure 47.1 is a word cloud of the chapter abstracts that illustrates the scope of how the authors described their inclusive instructional design work. While *learning* held the central focus, *UDL* and its components were also prominent. Words associated with the implementation of inclusive instruction—*teachers, students, course, classroom,* and *use*—were also used frequently by the authors. Tools and formats for implementation, notably words such as *online* and *technology,* emerged as key themes. This chapter examines these themes more closely and suggests next steps for inclusive educators, advocates, and researchers.

Reading through the pages of this book, it is readily apparent that inclusive learning practices are being fueled in part by international policies, such as UNESCO's world declaration on education for all (1990), Salamanca statement on special education (1994), and policy guidelines for inclusion in education (2009). Country-specific legislation was also mentioned by many of the authors. For instance, Alvarez et al. (Chapter 7) chronicled Colombia's history of supportive

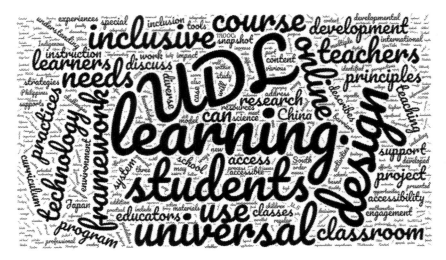

FIGURE 47.1 Word Cloud of Chapter Abstracts

government policies, including the most recent Decree 83/2015 that incorporated language about UDL—"Universal Design for Learning is a strategy that responds to diversity, whose goal is to maximize learning opportunities of all students, considering the broad spectrum of abilities, learning styles and preferences" (Ministerio de Educación Gobierno de Chile, 2015, p. 6). Israel's 1998 *Equal Rights for Persons with Disabilities Law* and related 2005 and 2013 amendments (as described by Bar and Shrieber in Chapter 37) mandate that "all public places and public services must be accessible to people of all disabilities," and this includes websites and digital resources for learning (Commission for Equal Rights of Persons with Disabilities, 2019, p. 14). Zhang and Zhao chronicled in Chapter 8 that in China, changes toward inclusion started in the 1980s with the issuance of *The Notification of Additional Teaching Guidelines for Full-Time Schools or Classes for the Mentally Disabled* (National Education Committee, 1988). China seems to be continuing in that direction, as indicated in the *People with Disabilities Educational Ordinance Act of 2017*—"Governments at all levels should gradually improve the ability of ordinary kindergartens and schools to receive students with disabilities, promote inclusive education, and ensure that disabled people enter ordinary kindergartens and schools to receive education" (Li, 2017).

Notably, the conceptualization and application of *inclusion* seems to vary significantly around the world. Views range from full inclusion of students with learning challenges or disabilities as part of general education programs to the provision of educational opportunities for all children to simply attend school and not be excluded because of their disabilities or socioeconomic status. This is not a static observation, though, as many countries are in the process of transitioning toward more inclusive instruction. Koreeda, for example, mentioned in

Chapter 14 that students with mild disabilities are being included in regular classes in Japan but that "the use of design flexibility to address varied needs of an entire class, as with the UD framework is not yet accepted." Lyner-Cleophas described South Africa's inclusive journey in Chapter 5:

> This transition shifts the focus away from diagnoses and remediation of deficits using specialist staff to a more holistic approach that envisions inclusive instructional design not just for students with learning barriers only but for all students. Curriculum differentiation is noted in [South African] education policy, and UDL offers an opportunity for curriculum differentiation.

Though the terms used to discuss these topics may differ around the world, there are numerous examples of how inclusive instructional design is presently being applied across teaching settings and geographic locations. Suwannawut, for instance, described in Chapter 2 her view from Thailand of how *inclusive design* parallels and diverges from *universal design*:

> Both universal design and inclusive design strive for similar goals and objectives—equal participation and social justice. However, they have different sets of assumptions, methods, and strategies to achieve those goals. Inclusive design is a broader paradigm of design that celebrates diversity and is inclusive of all users regardless of age, ability, gender, ethnicity, and economic circumstances.

Arndt and Luo reported in Chapter 31 that though few early childhood teachers surveyed in China are familiar with the UDL framework, they tend to be receptive to it, as meeting varied students' needs aligns well with Confucian philosophy. Further, many are implementing inclusive-type practices, such as supporting flexibility through varying the ways that their students are able to express their learning. Khanna's FACE program model in India (described in Chapter 9) brings together science and art in a holistic approach of multiple means of engagement and personal expression through healing relationships, creative consciousness, applicable knowledge, and sustainable livelihood. The Making Decisions about Instructional Supports and Adaptations model by Brusca-Vega and Trekles in the US offers UDL and assistive technology (AT) implementation guidance that takes into account learner tasks and demands, the learning environment, potential learning obstacles, adaptations, training and instructional support, and effectiveness (see Chapter 11). Such practices incorporate place-based cultural characteristics and philosophies that not only address needs of learners in that locale but when shared beyond country borders serve to enrich and broaden global conceptualizations of what constitutes inclusive instructional design.

Inclusive instructional practices also connect to other areas, such as social justice and equity, as Berhanu challenges us from Sweden in Chapter 3—"Issues of social justice, equity, and choice are central to the demands for inclusive education," and Lyner-Cleophas described in Chapter 5 that in South Africa, "education is a way to address the inequalities as a process." Expanding educational opportunities for Filipino learners is at the core of the Universal Access to Learning for Development (UAL4D) framework, which involves elements of web content accessibility, incorporates open educational resources (OERs), and supports mobile learning through massive open distance eLearning (MODeL) courses (see Bandalaria, Chapter 24). This is meaningful work, and it is encouraging that educators internationally are recognizing the importance of these global issues of social justice and equity and are applying them as drivers for the advancement of inclusive design and implementation practices in their own communities.

The importance of teacher training and professional development is stressed by many of the authors, as it is key for building educator capacity to incorporate inclusive practices as part of curriculum design and pedagogy. There are many different formats and approaches that have been developed in this area. For instance, Reynor described in Chapter 34 a UDL-focused action research project that teacher candidates in Ireland complete during the final year of study. The project leads the pre-service teachers to develop four lessons that are grounded in the UDL framework and then teach and reflect upon their implementation. Bar and Shrieber (Chapter 37) designed a two-hour collaborative activity using Lego building blocks that is part of a graduate course for educators in Israel. The activity prompts the educators to develop multiple means for representing instructions for building a Lego model. Cendros Araujo and Gadanidis detailed in Chapter 19 how collaborative mind mapping activities are being used in math education courses in Canada to support and model the UDL principles. Edge-Savage and Marotta (Chapter 38) have developed a blended learning professional development course in the US that involves instruction on UDL and assistive technologies, hands-on guided exploration of strategies and technologies, and professional learning network building through social media spaces. Art may also be a viable means for learning about and applying inclusive design, as Brand and DeRosa suggest in Chapter 46. By fusing arts education and pedagogy, pre-service and in-service teachers can discover new options for communicating content, supporting student engagement, and enabling learners to express their understandings.

The tools for inclusive learning around the world range from non-digital approaches to emerging technologies, software and web-based applications, and augmentative and alternative communication (AAC) devices. There is a notable ingenuity among inclusive learning advocates in which barriers are viewed not as impossibilities but as challenges for which solutions might be teacher-made, hand-crafted, and personalized. Working within the constraints of their contexts, educators and designers in different parts of the world are working to maximize the tools and resources that they have available. For instance, Lohmann, Owiny, and Boothe (Chapter 15) offered strategies for implementing UDL principles in math instruction that were derived from their experiences working in areas in which educational technology resources were limited. Khurana described in Chapter 13 how learning activities and experiences are creatively engineered as part of the school infrastructure in the Building as Learning Aid (BaLA) initiative in India. Hand-crafted solutions like the dot code technology described by Ikuta and Hisatsune in Chapter 20 are supporting multiple means of representation, access, and communication for learners with special needs in Japan and beyond. The original materials created with these tools "addres[s] the need for specialized assistive technologies in a manner that enables schoolteachers to create the supports for specific learner needs." Inclusive design ingenuity also fueled Anderson and Anderson (Chapter 22) to devise a wearable technology involving simple circuitry in a glove cover in order to provide greater visibility for users of mobility scooters.

When the application of UDL involves educational technologies, Bauder et al.'s UDL/SAMR (substitution-augmentation-modification-redefinition) technology integration model (Chapter 18) frames how technology use can support flexibility, provide supportive scaffolds for diverse learners, and re-envision education through capabilities of modern technologies. An example of re-envisioned education is the work of German researchers Menke, Beckmann, and Weber described in Chapter 39 that involves application of augmented and virtual reality tools within HVAC training curricula. Considering instructional applications of these emerging technologies in the light of UDL is worthwhile, as it can facilitate improvements to the overall robustness of a design to better meet the needs of all learners, as Menke and colleagues surmised:

> The interrelationship of AR/VR and UDL deserves heightened attention, as emerging technological innovations like AR and VR can otherwise easily lead to a loss of didactic achievements if the diverse needs and interests of learners are not adequately addressed.

In selecting chapters for this book, one of the greatest areas of interest by authors around the world is *online education*, with more proposed chapters on issues, tools, and strategies for supporting diverse learners in online settings than space available in this current volume. Online education seems to resonate with many in the inclusive learning community, as the online delivery medium can afford benefits of flexibility and expanded access to educational opportunities. Online instruction can be blended into face-to-face settings to offer self-paced, collaborative, and varied means of engagement and expressions of student learning, as Nieves, a middle school teacher in the US, described in Chapter 17. Online mobile technologies can provide affordances of "portability, social interactivity, context sensitivity, connectivity, and individuality," as illustrated through Boim-Shwartz and Cioban's online Israeli teacher professional development course (see Chapter 29). Education via online platforms can also enable international collaborations. Smith and De Arment exemplified this in Chapter 6 through their US-Jamaica online virtual classroom project. Online connections made through courses, professional networks, and classroom activities contribute to growth of inclusive instructional design and UDL through the ever evolving power of technology, as well as increased impacts on facilitating accessibility for *all*.

Online education, though, can present challenges for learners related to accessibility of digital materials and physical and time-based distances among learners and instructors. Proactively addressing learner variability as part of planning and design work (as recommended by Casarez, Hooks, Shipley, and Swafford in Chapter 4) not only promotes accessibility for specific learners with certain disabilities but generally improves the overall course design, providing more engaging and meaningful online learning experiences for all students. Best practices for creating accessible online course materials, such as those described by Bastedo and Swenson in Chapter 26, are important to adopt so that inaccessible digital materials do not create unnecessary barriers for online learners. Tools such as the auto-captioning feature of YouTube (as described by Rogers in Chapter 28) make it easier for designers to diversify content formats and support greater accessibility of multimedia online materials. Projects like the YourMOOC4all review system developed in UK/Spain (Iniesto, Rodrigo, and Hillaire—Chapter 25) are needed, as they enable learners to not only evaluate courses in regards to accessibility and application of UDL principles but access reviews of others in order to make future course selections. The reviews are helpful for course designers who can utilize the feedback to revise course design in subsequent iterations. Bridging the evaluation gap between designer/instructor and user experience is an area of great opportunity for continued development.

In sum, inclusive learning is complex, and there is understandably not a one-size-fits-all framework, approach, or tool that addresses all of the complexities inherent to varied learner needs, cultures, and context constraints. Further, application of inclusive practices is a moving target, as developing technologies change what is possible and introduce new barriers to be addressed. Challenges continue in the field to prove the impact, fidelity, and sustainability of inclusive instructional design models such as UDL (see Ferguson, Chapter 12; Edyburn, Chapter 44). However, there is great work happening globally in the area of inclusive instructional design, as exhibited by the collective efforts of the 85 contributors to this book. It is important that educators around the world continue to share their work by publishing formally and informally, as this provides opportunities for collaborative connections and knowledge building. Likewise, the inclusive learning community can greatly benefit through traversing physical and perceptual borders in order to expand awareness of voices and perspectives from around the world. In practical terms, this can involve reading international publications, attending professional learning events and conferences abroad, and utilizing social networking technologies to connect and collaborate with inclusive education colleagues globally. With the digital communication advances that now facilitate discussion and collaborative projects involving issues of shared interest, the challenges of educational inequity, exclusion, and injustice can be more rapidly addressed through the international sharing of ideas, resources, and solutions to support more widespread universal access through inclusive instructional design.

References

Commission for Equal Rights of Persons with Disabilities. (2019). *Equal rights for persons with disabilities law 5758–1998*. Retrieved from www.justice.gov.il/En/Units/CommissionEqualRightsPersonsDisabilities/Equal-Rights-For-Persons-With-Disabilities-Law/Pages/Equal-Rights-For-Persons-With-Disabilities-Law.aspx

Li, K. (2017). *People with disabilities educational ordinance act*. Retrieved from www.hbdpf.org.cn/xwzx/qgdt/162986.htm

Ministerio de Educación Gobierno de Chile. (2015). *Diversificación de la Enseñanza* (Decreto 83/2015). Retrieved from http://especial.mineduc.cl/wp-content/uploads/sites/31/2016/08/Decreto-83-2015.pdf

National Education Committee. (1988). The notification of additional teaching guidelines for full-time schools or classes for the mentally disabled. *People's Education*, (6).

UNESCO. (1990, March 5–9). *World declaration on education for all and framework for action to meet basic learning needs*. Adopted at World Conference on Education for All: Meeting Basic Learning Needs, Jomtien, Thailand. Paris, France: UNESCO.

UNESCO. (1994, June 7–10). *The Salamanca statement and framework for action on special education needs*. Adopted at World Conference on Special Education Needs: Access and Quality, Salamanca, Spain. Paris, France: UNESCO.

UNESCO. (2009). *Policy guidelines on inclusion in education*. Paris, France: UNESCO.

CONTRIBUTORS

A

Alicia Adlington is the Distance Programs Coordinator at Werklund School of Education. Alicia has worked in post-secondary education for over 10 years in a number of student engagement roles. Recent successes include developing and delivering sessions to help new graduate students acclimate themselves to the online learning environment.

Boris Alvarez, MBA, is director of the Fellow Group in Santiago, Chile, an institution focused on inclusive education and development of diverse teams across organizations. He has 11 years of experience working in clinical, management, and planning roles in hospital and university settings, as well as business development, and is a lecturer in inclusive education.

Kerry Armstrong has over 30 years of teaching experience in Canada. She produces work including articles, blogs, and presentations to implement the principles of UDL as a teacher and consultant since 2004.

Dr. Cindy L. Anderson is an Associate Professor in the College of Education at Roosevelt University, Chicago, IL, where she teaches technology, special education technology, and other courses. She has written and published extensively in the fields of special education technology and integrating technology into education.

Dr. Kevin M. Anderson is an adjunct professor for Michigan State University, Lansing, MI and retired school superintendent. He has written and published extensively in the fields of special education technology and integrating technology into education. He is a 2010 recipient of the Tech & Learning Leader of the Year award.

Janet Arndt, Ed.D. is director of the graduate program in education, associate professor of education, and licensure officer at Gordon College, Wenham, MA. She teaches in both undergraduate and graduate programs. Her research interests include transitions, learning needs of students with disabilities, the impact of social emotional competence on learning, family-school partnerships, and intentional teaching for young children.

Jo Axe, PhD, is professor in the School of Education and Technology at Royal Roads University. She also is a Chartered Professional Accountant/Certified General Accountant. Jo's teaching experience covers on-campus and online deliveries in both domestic and international programs. Current research interests include open educational practice, learning community development, and student engagement in online environments.

B

Melinda dela Peña Bandalaria, PhD, is professor at the University of the Philippines Open University (UPOU) and is actively involved in developing instructional materials, teaching, and doing research on open and distance eLearning. She led the pioneering work in the Philippines on MOOCs and is currently working on projects focusing on universal access to learning.

David Banes is a consultant and author in the use of technology to support those with a disability. Interested in disruptive innovation and the impact of emerging technology on products and services, he works with UNICEF and WHO, and is currently working on projects to promote access and interaction, mental health, and the developing AT ecosystem in the Middle East and Africa.

Amir Bar is an adjunct professor in the Kibbutzim College of Education, Technology and Art (Israel). He interned at the Center for Applied Special Technology (CAST) with David Rose and Anne Meyer. Amir is the founder of UCNLEARN, which designs and sells teaching aids for helping students with dyslexia improve their reading, spelling, and writing skills.

Kathleen Bastedo is an instructional designer at the Center for Distributed Learning (CDL) at the University of Central Florida (UCF). Her online teaching and learning research interests include accessibility to online materials for individuals with disabilities, simulations and training, and the cognitive theory of multimedia learning.

Debra K. Bauder, Ed.D., is associate professor of special education at University of Louisville, Kentucky, and in the field for over 40 years. Dr. Bauder provides training on technology/assistive technology and its use with individuals with disabilities and consults regarding UDL. She was a co-leader on Kentucky's UDL statewide project.

Jennifer Beckmann, M.Sc., is a research assistant at South Westphalia University of Applied Sciences in Soest, Germany, working on the design of AR/VR trainings and their evaluation for the HVAC industry in the ARSuL project, as well as the conceptual development and administration of online study programs at the department.

Kirk Behnke has an extensive professional background in assistive technology including augmentative communication. He develops and delivers professional development, technical assistance, and learning opportunities regarding assistive and accessible technologies, accessible educational materials and Universal Design for Learning (UDL) within the US and internationally.

Dr. Girma Berhanu is a professor in the Department of Education and Special Education at the University of Gothenberg, Göteborg, Sweden. His specialties include socio-cultural factors, including historical aspects and institutional frameworks, and research interests of race, ethnicity, and special education. Of particular interest to him are "group-based inequalities."

Shir Boim-Shwartz is a team leader at the online learning division of the Center for Educational Technology (CET) in Tel Aviv, Israel. Shir has a master's degree in Educational Technology and a bachelor's degree in Education, and has over 15 years of experience in E-learning.

Juliet Boone, a high school special education teacher in New York, is work-based learning certified and a Google certified educator, working to empower students to excel through best practices and instructional technology. She has worked at all levels of the educational system, and is a certified educational technology specialist.

Dr. Kathleen A. Boothe, Assistant Professor of Special Education and Program Coordinator at Southeastern Oklahoma State University, currently provides professional development for local school districts in the area of behavior and UDL. Dr. Boothe previously taught special education students at the elementary and secondary level.

Brenda Boreham has 35 years of classroom experience in Canada. She has presented workshops on literacy strategies and has written several resources for teachers and students.

Contributors **361**

Dr. Susan Trostle Brand is a Professor of Education and Social Justice at the University of Rhode Island, Kingston, Rhode Island. Dr. Brand is the author or editor of four textbooks and over 50 articles and book chapters. She has presented at over 150 conferences regionally, nationally, and internationally, and is a strong advocate for learner-centered, arts-integrated education at the public school and university levels.

Rita Brusca-Vega, Ed.D., is Associate Professor and Graduate Program Coordinator for Special Education at Purdue University Northwest, Indiana, USA. Her areas of expertise include working with students with intense needs, English learners with disabilities, and inclusive practices. She has been a teacher educator and consultant to schools for over 30 years.

C

Lesley Casarez, PhD, is the Program Director for Professional School Counseling at Angelo State University, where she teaches in a completely online program. Her research interests include access to online learning, technology, and counseling.

Rosa Cendros Araujo is currently a PhD candidate in the College of Education at Western University in Ontario, Canada. Her academic research cluster is curriculum studies and studies in applied linguistics.

Dr. Laura Chesson, an NSF Fellowship Recipient and Theodore Sizer Scholar, has worked as a teacher and administrator in rural, urban, and suburban districts for more than 20 years, following 10 years as project manager for IBM. A presenter at numerous national and regional conferences, she shares her work on creating innovative instructional technology environments and utilizing teacher leadership to accelerate the implementation of critical initiatives.

Dr. Elizabeth Childs is Associate Professor and Program Head for the MA in Learning and Technology at Royal Roads University, Victoria, British Columbia, Canada. She teaches in both blended and fully online environments. Her current research interests include open educational practices, flexible learning environments, fully online learning communities, and design thinking and maker research.

Eran Adi Cioban is a team leader at the online learning division of the Center for Educational Technology (CET) in Tel Aviv, Israel. Eran has a master's degree in Public Policy and a bachelor's degree in History, and has over seven years of experience in e-learning.

Katherine Cooper is a Cooperative Consultant with Greater Louisville Education Cooperative specializing in intellectual disabilities, autism, assistive technology/

UDL, and transition. She has earned her Master's Degree in Education from the University of Louisville, with an emphasis on assistive technology and UDL.

D

Elizabeth M. Dalton, PhD, is adjunct professor for the Communicative Disorders Department at the University of Rhode Island (specializing in AAC), senior consultant for Dalton Education Services International (DESI), and Director Emeritus of Development and Research, TechACCESS of RI. She studied UDL with CAST, Inc. during her post-doctoral work. Currently, she serves as co-chair of the UDL Special Interest Group, SITE.

Serra De Arment, PhD, is an assistant professor in the Department of Counseling and Special Education at Virginia Commonwealth University where her teaching and research focus on special educator quality and preparation for diverse and inclusive learning environments. She is the special education Curriculum Coordinator for the Richmond Teacher Residency program, a Virginia licensed elementary and special educator, and a National Board-Certified Exceptional Needs Specialist.

Dr. Maria De Freece Lawrence is a professor of science education at Rhode Island College in Providence. Her research interests include teacher preparation and professional development in science education and international issues in education.

Dr. Laurie DeRosa recently retired after a career as an arts educator for 35 years. In addition to teaching in the classroom, Dr. DeRosa taught at the college level preparing pre-service teachers to value the arts in education by learning to design and teach lessons using an interdisciplinary approach.

E

Jennifer Edge-Savage, MS, Ed.S., OTR/L, RYT, is an Assistive Technology Consultant and Professor in the field of Educational and Assistive Technology. She has been working in the field of AT and UDL for 20 years and is the recent Past President of the International Society for Technology in Education's (ISTE) Inclusive Learning Network.

Dave L. Edyburn, PhD, is Professor of Exceptional Education and Associate Dean for Research at the College of Community Innovation and Education, University of Central Florida (UCF). His research and teaching interests focus on the use of technology to enhance teaching, learning, and performance.

F

Dr. Britt Tatman Ferguson has provided education, staff development, and counseling for individuals from preschool through adulthood in a variety of settings. Currently she teaches online, is Program Director for the Moderate/Severe Credential program at National University, and has designed multiple online courses in her position.

G

Dr. George Gadanidis is professor in the Faculty of Education at Western University in Ontario, Canada. His research clusters in curriculum studies and studies in applied linguistics.

Susie L. Gronseth, PhD, is Clinical Associate Professor in Learning, Design, and Technology, College of Education, University of Houston. She teaches undergraduate and graduate courses in learning technologies, educational multimedia, teaching strategies, and instructional design. She specializes in UDL to address diverse learner needs in online, face-to-face, and blended contexts. Research interests include learning technologies to engage learners, varied ways of content representation, and differing opportunities to demonstrate knowledge and skills.

H

Jane Hanson, M.Ed., is a high school teacher who is involved in technology training, online learning, and course development. Her interests are instructional design, e-learning, and assisting online facilitators with their course design and implementation.

Lisa Harris, PhD, is associate professor in Core Education at Winthrop University in Rock Hill, SC, USA. She has worked with pre-service and in-service teachers to integrate technology into teaching for over 20 years. Her research interests include project-based learning, technology integration, and working with Professional Development Schools.

Garron Hillaire works at the Institute of Educational Technology, The Open University, Milton Keynes, United Kingdom and is PhD candidate by a Leverhulme Trust Doctoral Scholarship in Open World Learning based in The Open University researching emotional measurement in online discourse. As a member of the UDL Cadre for CAST.org, he assists CAST in scaling UDL implementations at all levels.

Yumi Hisatsune is a teacher at the Hokubu Elementary School, Nakatsu, Oita Prefecture, Japan. She graduated from Faculty of Education, Oita University. She has direct experience with disability due to previous serious illness, and by talking about her own experiences with having disabilities, she wants to help students have a dream and have hope.

David Hooks is a doctoral candidate and works as a STEM teacher at John Glenn Middle School. His research interests include technology integration, 21st century skills, STEM, and social issues.

I

Irma Iglesias is adviser to the Presidential Commission for Disability in Chile and specializes in issues of international perspectives and approaches to reduce barriers to learning, guaranteeing equity and quality teaching, with the Fellow Group L.A., Santiago, Chile.

Dr. Shigeru Ikuta is professor at Otsuma Women's University, Tokyo, Japan, having completed his doctoral work at Tohoku University, in Sendai, Japan. For more than 12 years, he has conducted school activities, including multimedia dot codes and eBooks with Media Overlays in support of students at special needs and general schools, with more than 200 teachers around the world.

Dr. Jeanne Carey Ingle is assistant professor at Bridgewater State University teaching classes in elementary education, education inequalities, and educational technology. She worked for many years as an elementary school teacher and continues to work with school districts and conduct research on using technology to improve student outcomes, closing achievement gaps, and using technologies to prepare pre-service teachers.

Francisco Iniesto works at the Institute of Educational Technology, The Open University, Milton Keynes, United Kingdom. He is a PhD candidate by a Leverhulme Trust Doctoral Scholarship in Open World Learning based in The Open University researching accessibility in MOOCs. Francisco's background is as a Computer Engineer from UAM with an M.Sc. in Educational Technology from UNED.

Vivian B. Intatano is an instructor at Raja Soliman Science & Technology High School, Manila, Philippines. She specializes in issues of effective teaching tools and emerging technologies.

J

Carol Johnson, PhD, is a Senior Lecturer (Online Learning and Educational Technologies) in the Melbourne Conservatorium of Music at Melbourne

University in Australia. She is involved in the research and study of online music pedagogy and professional development strategies for transitioning to teaching in the online environment.

K

Dr. Radhike Khanna has dedicated her every breath to uplifting and bettering the lives of mentally challenged individuals. Through her work in the education field with SPJ Sadhana School, Trusteeship at Om Creations Trust and Shraddha Charitable Trust, Dr. Khanna has constructed a more wholesome approach that nurtures and empowers these individuals into being gainfully employed.

Aashna Khurana (M.Ed.) is a trained Special Educator and is currently working as Assessment Associate at ASER Centre, Research Unit of Pratham Education Foundation. She adapts various existing educational assessment tools according to different disabilities and controls quality of implementation of various programs.

Dr. Kiyoji Koreeda is a professor at Toyo University in Japan. Dr. Koreeda received his doctoral degree from the United Graduate School of Education, Tokyo Gakugei University, Japan. His work focuses on educational support for students with various disabilities in Special Needs Education schools.

L

Yang (Flora) Liu, PhD, is a Learning and Instructional Design Specialist in the Faculty of Social Work at the University of Calgary. Her research interests are in game-based learning, instructional design, and computer-supported collaborative learning.

Jennifer Lock, PhD, is a Professor and the Associate Dean of Teaching and Learning in the Werklund School of Education at the University of Calgary. Her research interests are in e-learning, change and innovation in education, scholarship of teaching and learning in higher education, and makerspaces.

Dr. Marla J. Lohmann, Assistant Professor of Special Education at Colorado Christian University, currently volunteers as an informal consultant for a preschool teacher training program in Uganda. She previously taught Special Education students in the United States and served as a Guest Lecturer of Special Education at the University of Zambia for one semester.

Nili Luo, Ed.D. is Professor and Director of Early Childhood Education at Southwestern College in Winfield, KS and has nearly 30 years of teaching experience in multi-age group students' settings, including newborns to adult learners, in both China and the United States. Her research interests include early childhood curriculum design, assessment strategies, and parenting issues involving different cultural backgrounds.

Dr. Marcia Lyner-Cleophas is an educational psychologist and manages the Disability Unit at Stellenbosch University, Western Cape, South Africa. She works in higher education as a reflective practitioner in the field of disability inclusion, and previously worked at the Noluthando School for Deaf Learners and in high school. She is an active member of the Higher and Further Education Disability Services Association (HEDSA).

M

Terri Mack, Kay Kwee Kway Kwa, is a member of the Da'naxda'xw Awaetlala Nation. She has worked within Indigenous Education for 20 years and is now the CEO of Strong Nations Publishing, British Columbia, Canada.

Tsuge Masayoshi, PhD, is professor Division of Disability Sciences, Faculty of Human Sciences, University of Tsukuba, Japan.

Katharina Menke, M.A., studied Science Journalism and Interdisciplinary Media Studies. As a research assistant at South Westphalia University of Applied Sciences, she supports the conceptual development of online study programs at the department and works on how to create AR and VR trainings in the HVAC industry (project "ARSuL").

Mike Marotta, ATP, is a RESNA Certified Assistive Technology Professional, and the ISTE Inclusive Learning Network 2017 Outstanding Educator, who is a nationally and internally recognized speaker as well as a consultant providing direct services to individuals with all disabilities and school districts for almost 30 years.

Susan Molnar, MS.Ed., is an artist and educator, and worked as curriculum developer for ReadySC, a Division of the South Carolina Technical College System. She currently works for the North Carolina Department of Health and Human Services as a Content Training Developer for the NC FAST (North Carolina Families Accessing Services Through Technology) system as part of the NCDHHS IT division.

N

Shintaro Nagayama is a doctoral student in Disability Sciences, Graduate School of Comprehensive Human Sciences, University of Tsukuba, Japan.

Kathryn Nieves is a special education teacher at Sparta Middle School in Sparta Township Public Schools, New Jersey, USA. She is a Google Certified Trainer and uses technology to support and empower her students as they learn.

Katie Novak, Ed.D., is an internationally renowned education consultant as well as a practicing leader in education as an Assistant Superintendent of Schools at the Groton-Dunstable Regional School District in Massachusetts. She presents workshops both nationally and internationally focusing on implementation of Universal Design for Learning (UDL) and universally designed leadership.

O

Honami Okabe is studying in the Master's Program in Disability Science, Graduate School of Comprehensive Human Sciences, at University of Tsukuba in Ibaraki, Japan.

Dr. Ruby L. Owiny, is Assistant Professor of Education at Trinity International University, and also an associate with the international consulting company, 2 Teach LLC, which specializes in inclusive education. She served as volunteer consultant with Food for the Hungry, Inc. in Bolivia and Guatemala, providing trainings to teachers in rural and urban communities on literacy, mathematics, and behavior management.

P

Dr. Heather Pacheco-Guffrey is an Assistant Professor of Education specializing in STEM education training for pre- and in-service teachers. She studies issues of equity and representation in STEM education and develops technology-rich pedagogical strategies to support teaching and learning in science.

Kathryn Pole, PhD, is an associate professor of Curriculum and Instruction at The University of Texas at Arlington and is the coordinator of the Literacy Studies program, which includes a 100% online Master's Degree.

R

Ellen Reynor, PhD, is assistant professor in the School of Inclusive and Special Education in Dublin City University. She taught at the primary level, lectures in the B.Ed. and postgraduate inclusive and special education programs, and is currently chair of the M.Ed. in Dyslexia/SpLD. She is a member of the British Dyslexia Association and the Professional Association of Teachers of Students with Specific Learning Disability.

Covadonga Rodrigo, PhD, is professor of Computer Science, National University of Distance Education (UNED), Madrid, Spain. She is currently director of the Digital Inclusion UNED-Vodafone Foundation Research Chair.

Dr. Sandra Rogers is an instructional designer at UCLA in Los Angeles, CA. Her research interests include distance education, gaming, and second language acquisition.

S

Peggy Semingson, PhD, is an Associate Professor of Curriculum and Instruction at The University of Texas at Arlington and teaches 100% online in the area of literacy teacher education.

Gina Shipley is a doctoral candidate and an Instructor in the Department of Curriculum and Instruction at Angelo State University. Her research interests include online learning, social justice issues, and leadership in higher education.

Dr. Betty Shrieber is the head of the Educational Technology M.Ed. program in the Kibbutzim College of Education, Technology and Art (Israel). Her research area is in the field of Specific Learning Disabilities (SLD), ADHD, and Assistive Technology.

Thomas J. Simmons, PhD, is professor of education and human development at University of Louisville, Kentucky and has been a professional practicing in special education for over 35 years. He has been a teacher, professor, and rehabilitation counselor throughout this time.

Frances Smith, Ed.D., CVE, is an adjunct professor in the Graduate School of Education and Human Development at George Washington (GW) University and an independent consultant where her focus targets the importance of Universal Design for Learning in instruction, online design, and career assessment. She has been teaching a graduate course in Universal Design for Learning at GW since 2003 and was a postdoctoral UDL Fellow with CAST and Boston College in 2011–12.

Dr. Nantanoot Suwannawut works on the issues of inclusive education and access technologies for persons with disabilities and has served on several advisory committees, such as the Promotion of Information Access for Persons with Visual Impairments and Print Disability Project. Her areas of specialization are information accessibility, especially educational media production, and Human Computer Interaction (HCI).

Dallas Swafford is a doctoral candidate and works as the Director of Student Disability Services and an Adjunct Instructor in Curriculum and Instruction at

Angelo State University. Her research interests include accessibility of online course content, assistive technology, and leading the change toward accessibility.

Nancy Swenson has been an instructional designer at the University of Central Florida since 2000. Her online teaching and learning research interests include adult learning theory, accessibility of online courses, Universal Design for Learning, and quality of online courses.

T

Anastasia Trekles, PhD, is Clinical Associate Professor in Instructional Technology at Purdue University Northwest, Indiana, USA. Her specialty areas include assistive technology and web accessibility, and she has taught various courses at the undergraduate and graduate level for over 20 years.

Masayoshi Tsuge, PhD, is Professor in the Division of Disability Sciences, Faculty of Human Sciences, at the University of Tsukuba in Ibaraki, Japan.

V

Paola Andrea Vergara (Pampilioni) is professor at the College Polytechnic, Our Lady of the Presentation, Melipilla, Chile. She worked with the Chilean Ministry of Education to coordinate academic programs and teaching activities, and is currently with the Fellow Group LA.

W

Dr. Peter Weber is Professor at South Westphalia University of Applied Sciences in Soest, Germany, teaching computer science and e-business and serving as the head of the Competence Center E-Commerce (CCEC). Research interests include e-Business and e-Learning, and implications of technology-driven change in various industries, including education and retail.

Leanne Woodley is a Senior Education Consultant: Student Services at the Association of Independent Schools, NSW, Australia. She works collaboratively with teachers to support in the design of accessible learning and teaching, assessment experiences, and programs to address student variability in a range of educational settings.

Y

Lindsay Yearta, PhD, is assistant professor in Core Education at Winthrop University in Rock Hill, South Carolina teaching graduate and undergraduate courses in literacy and learning technologies. She is a former elementary school teacher and continues to work closely with kindergarten through grade 12 teachers. Research interests include digital literacies, critical literacy, and use of digital tools to meet the needs of each student in the classroom.

Z

Haoyue Zhang, M.Ed., is a doctoral student in the Learning, Design, and Technology program area at the University of Houston. Currently, Haoyue is teaching undergraduate courses by using Universal Design for Learning and flipped classroom.

George Zhao, PhD, is Assistant Professor of Instructional Technology in Woodring College of Education at Western Washington University. He specializes in educational technology and second language acquisition and is primarily interested in enhancing education within the affective domain through gamification and video production.

INDEX

Note: Numbers in **bold** indicate a table. Numbers in *italics* indicate a figure.

3D: navigation 327; printing 324, 327, **329**

A to Z Animals from Massachusetts *349*
abacus 123, *124*
ableism 36
access barriers 189–190; *see also* barriers
accessible education materials (AEM) 285, 289, **290**
accessible instructional materials 37, 185; assistive technology and 288
accessible online learning systems 17, 18, 20, 286; course content 209, 213, 356
Access to Learning: Assistive Technology and Accessible Instructional Materials 288
accommodations 62, **87**, 212, 328; exam 41; individual 65; reasonable 111; reducing the need for 31, 42–43
active ingredients 333, 338, 339–341; *see also* Edyburn, Dave L.
adaptations for improved performance 85, 89
Adapting the Barkhaa Series for Visually Challenged Children and other CWSN according to UDL 108
Adlington, Alicia xx, 250–256, 358
Advancement of Computing in Education (AACE) 10
affinity atmosphere 270
affordability 19, 188, 192, 294

affordances 23; educational 28, 225; of technology 255, 355; of virtual format 55
air tap 343, *344*
Al-Azawei, A. 37, 42
Alpabasa 174
Alvarez, Boris xviii, 59–66, 351, 358
Amazon: Kindle **147**; Echo 324
Amazon forest 248
American Fingerspelled Alphabet 21
American Sign Language 21
Americans with Disabilities Act (ADA) 5
Amyotrophic lateral sclerosis (ALS) 344
Anderson, Cindy L. xix, 179–181, 355, 358
Anderson, Kevin M. xix, 179–181, 355, 358–359
Angelo State University 30
apartheid 35
applied behavior analysis (ABA) 318
app-smashing 288
Armstrong, Kerry xix, 218–219, 358
Arndt, Janet xix, 233–241, 353, 359
Article 9 (UNCRPD) 38
Article 24 (UNCRPD) 38
artificial intelligence (AI) 197, 324, 325; 328, **329**; neural networks 343; in US education 198
Artiles, A. J. 28
assertive discipline 33, 334, *335*

assistive technology (AT) 3, 38, 353; and barriers to learning 171; common **301**; distribution 327; innovation 324; questions and results **290**; specialized 166; spreading the word 284–292, *286*; and UDL 329, 354, 355; in US classrooms 85–92, **87**; wearable 179–181
assistive technology (Ngram search term) 334, *336*, 337, *338*
Assistive Technology Toolkit 287, 289
assistive tools 72, 73, 289, 292, 355
Association of Higher Education and Disability (AHEAD) 259
at-risk youth 305
Attention Deficit Hyperactivity Disorder (ADHD) 91, 264, 269; in Japan 111–113
ATUDL (#) Twitter topic 286
augmentative and alternative communication (AAC) 171, 354
augmented reality (AR) 145–152, 215, **329**; future impact 324; trainings 294–303; and virtual reality 326–327
Augmented Reality Based Support for Learning in the HVAC Industry (ARSuL) 295–296, 298, 302–303
augmented virtuality (AV) 294, *295*
Australia 305–314
autism 325; *see also* Autism Spectrum Disorder; high functioning autism
Autism Spectrum Disorder (ASD) 77, 112, 113, 115, 118, 276; in Israel 276; Japan 269; *see also* Facing Autism through Communication with the Environment (FACE)
auto-captioning 325, 356; *see also* YouTube
avatar 289, **300**, 302, 303
average learner 63, 65
Axe, Jo xx, 215–216, 359

"back to basics" movement 333
Bandalaria *see* dela Peña Bandalaria
Banes, David xx, 323–329, 359
Bar, Amir xx, 283, 359
Barkhaa series 104–105, 108
barrier-free design 19
barriers 46, 60, 281, 305, 307; to access/accessibility 38, 187, 189–190, 191, 201; coexisting with 64–65; creating 201; to education 188; environmental 68; experiencing 258; inherent 341; language 190; learning 35, 39, 43, 71, 76–79, 264; minimized 120; overcoming/overthrowing 62, 63, 292;

potential **87**, 260, 312; poverty as 195; print 92; recognizing 263; reducing 128, 171, 194, 295, 303, 319, 328; removing or eliminating 95–97, 100, 101, 103, 105, 219, 268, 344; surmounting 78; to technology education 143
Bartholomew Consolidated School Corporation (BCSC) 323
Bastedo, Kathleen xix, 208–216, 356, 359
Bauder, Debra K. xix, 141–150, 355, 360
Beckmann, Jennifer xx, 294–303, 355, 360
behavioral problems 25, 270, 318, 319
behavior modification 78, **87**
Behnke, Kirk xx, 323–329, 360
bell-curve thinking 262
Berhanu, Girma xviii, 25–28, 353, 360
bilingual: curriculum 244; learning 120; lessons 248
blogs, blogging 41, 225, 228, 316
Bloom, Benjamin 8–10
Bloom's taxonomy of educational objectives 8–10, *8*; *see also* taxonomy of learning
Body Mass Index (BMI) 246
Boim-Shwartz, Shir xix, 224–225, 355, 360
Bolivia 120
Book Builder **51**, **53**, 55
Boone, Juliet xix, 182–184, 360
Boothe, Kathleen A. xviii, 120–129, 354, 360
Boreham, Brenda xix, 218–219, 360
Braille **87**, 105, 108, 211, 328
Brand, Susan Trostle xx, 346–349, 354, 361
British Columbia *see* Canada
Brusca-Vega, Rita xviii, 85–93, 353, 361
"buffet" approach to the classroom 98–101
Building as Learning Aid (BaLA) 106–108, *107*, 355
Business Process Outsourcing (BPO) 194, 195

caffeine 63
Canada 315, 339, 354
Carnegie Strategy Tutor 70
cartoons 21
cartography 115–117
Casarez, Lesley xviii, 30–31, 356, 361
Cendros Araujo, Rosa xix, 153–162, 354, 361
Center of Applied Special Technology (CAST) 3–4, 12, 14, 21, 244; Book Builder **51**; recommendations 68;

Index **373**

research/researchers at 47, 71, 111; UDL tools, development of 70, 73; website 50, 71, 306
Ceremonies in the Israeli-Jewish Culture 224
checkpoints (UDL) 3, 12, 14, 113–114, 116, 122, 340; application 213; categories 199; curricular guidelines 161; framework **300**, 302, 306, 311; mathematics lesson plan **128**
Chesson, Laura xviii, 81–82, 361
Childs, Elizabeth xx, 315–316, 361
Chile 59–66; chronology of policy towards inclusive education *61*
China: early childhood classrooms 233, 237–239; early childhood teachers 237–241, 353; educational technology 73–74; four stages of education 234–235; inclusion classrooms 236–237, 352; modern education 235–236; transformation of education in 72–74; UDL in 68–74
"China Education Modernization 2035" 240
China National Knowledge Infrastructure (CNKI) database 71
Chinese Journal of Special Education 71
Chinese Ministry of Education 70
Chinese philosophical traditions 233; *see also* Confucius, Confucianism
Chita-Tegmark, J. 48
choice 18, 28, 62, 64, 141, **219**, 284, 354; diversity of 105, 109; individual 27, 114, 116; instruction 173; of learning methods 73, 237; parental 27; pedagogical 260; smorgasbord or diet 98–101; students and learners 81, 82, 91, 157, 239, 288, **300**, 308; as a tool 97–98; user perception of 50
Cioban, Eran Adi xix, 224–225, 355, 361
citizenship 27
Civil Rights Act 5
class (socio-political) 25–28; *see also* gender; race
class differentiation 36
classroom 41, 42, 81, **177**, **247**; assistive technology, use of 287, 289, **290**; atmosphere 269–271; "buffet" approach to 98–99; computer-enhanced 56; content literacies in 229; disconnected 173–178; diversity in/of 64, 95, 260, 264; e-classroom 176, 177; educational technology, use of

284, 285; environment 118; experience 240; face-to-face 187; hydroponics 244; and images 153; inclusive 83–93, 104, 123, 166, 171; instruction 175, 176, 238; in Ireland 260; in Japan 269–271; Legos, use of 280–283; management 114; mathematics 120–129; mini-habitats 182; P–12 267; physical space of 105, 106, 107; pre-K–12 227, 244; smart speakers, use of 324; student engagement, maintaining 305; support methods 310; and technology 141–150, 323–329; traditional 17, 251; UDL activity in 275–277, 307; virtual 46–56, 356; *see also* China
classroom 270, 351; disconnected 175
classroom atmosphere 270
classroom environment 269; see also environment
class-wide social skill training (CSST) 318–319
coffee 63
colonization 35
Combined Activities for Maximized Learning (CAMaL) 105
Common Core Standards 100, 346
Communist revolution 233–234; *see also* China
competition (market) 27
computer-generated: experience 145; simulations 145, 326
computers: access to 52, 225; accessibility of 50, 89, 234; in the classroom 47, 121; dictation on 136; interaction with 88; lab **177**; literacy program 174; programming 183; in rural areas 71; in schools 173; screen 208; software incompatibility issues 74; and students 112; speech capabilities 276; use during tests 42
Conditions of Learning (Gagne) 8
Confucius, Confucianism 233–237, 240–241, 353
Contact Center Association of the Philippines (CCAP) 194
Convention on the Rights of Persons with Disabilities (CRPD) 60; *see also* UN Convention on the Rights of Persons with Disabilities
Cooper, Katherine M. xix, 141–150, 361–362
course 351; *see also* massive open online courses

course design strands 245, *245*
Crompton, H. 224
cross-curricular themes 315; *see also* curriculum
cross-linguistic understanding 244
Cummings, M. 343
Cummings, R. 332, 334, 337, 339
curriculum: adjustment 62; alignment 247, **247**; and artificial intelligence 198; arts-integrated 347–348, **347–348**; and assistive technology 284; barriers 63, 100; in China 234–237, 241; design framework 3, 9, 12; differentiation 39, 353; and disability 85–93; diversity 218; educational 17; face value acceptance of 346; flexible 21; guiding principles 40; inclusion 242–245, 251; mathematics **129**; and mind maps 154; multimodal 227; multisensory reading 135; one size fits all 31, 104, 259–260, 262; and online course content 208–216; pedagogy 354; primary school 264; reform 73, 347; resources 52; science 307, 312, 314; self-pacing 136; technology, use in/of **49**, 141–142, 174–175, 323; and Universal Design 41; and Universal Design for Learning 22, 42, 64, 71–72, 111, 146, 242–245, **247**, 323–324; visual-focused 227

Dalton, Elizabeth M. xvi–xxi, 1–14, 37, 76–79, 362
deafness in students 21, 96, 100, 276; *see also* hearing impairment
De Arment, Serra xviii, 46–56, 355–356, 362
Decree 83/2015 62; *see also* Chile
Decreto N° 100 60; *see also* Chile
deeper learning 237
deficits 259, 353; of learners 64, 65; learning 132; of design 65; remediation of 39
De Freece Lawrence, Maria xx, 242–249, 363
dela Peña Bandalaria, Melinda xix, 187–195, 359
demonstrative usage *114*
Department of Education of Groups of Special Needs (DEGSN)105, 108; *see also* India
Department of Higher Education and Training (DHET) 39–41
DeRosa, Laurie xx, 346–349, 354, 362
design-based research (DBR) 252, 256

developmental disabilities 270, 318; *see also* disabilities
devolution 27
Differentiated Classroom, The (Tomlinson) 9
differentiated instruction (DI) 9, 73, 98
digital: access, lack of 49; anchor charts 136; bulletin board 183; classroom 47; competencies 279; content 23, 30, 146, 276; content-creating 225; divide 190; era 37; file 213; formats 108; information 166; infrastructure 132; instructional design 276–278; instructional tools 56; materials 356; media 17, 22, 73; mind maps 153; mindset 315; repositories 17; resources 56, 227–229, 352; skill sets 74; spaces 48; stories **149**; technology 121, 250, **309**; texts 142, **147**, **300**; textbooks 108, 112, **147**; tools 142, 281, 323
digitized sources 40
dinner party analogy *see* Universal Design for Learning
disability, disabilities 3; abilities and 64; accessible online content for people with 208; awareness 41; categories 55; children with 108, 240, 284; cognitive 325; context-dependent xiv; developmental 182, 269–270, 318–319; discrimination based on 38; intellectual 69, 174, 276, 297; learners with 18, 31, 199, 328; mild 91, 353; mind mapping, benefits to persons with 162; persons with 188, 324; physical 189–190, 194, 258, 296; psycho-medical model of 259; and public policies 63; race, class, and gender, intersection with 25–28; rights of persons with 60, 112, 236, 238, 275, 352; schooling and 36, 77; severe 171, 276; social model of 25, 35, 42; students with 22, 37, 40, 50, 65, 70, 81, 85–93, 212, 339; support services 41; technology users with 17, 343; and telepresence robots 326; and universal design 19–23; and variability 65; views of 264; *see also* learning disabilities; special needs
disability scooter 179–180
disabled 20, 29, 64, 70, 259
disabling or enabling 25
discriminatory practices 36, 38, 234; prohibiting 4, 5; *see also* Non-Discrimination Law

disengagement 346; *see also* at-risk youth
district-based support teams (DBST) 38
diversified teaching 63
diverse, diversity 5; abilities 315; addressing 303; age 227; and artificial intelligence 325, 343–345; audiences 208; backgrounds 251, 315; blueprints 340; choices 109; in/of classrooms 64, 95, 237, 264; cultural 19, 48, **219**; curriculum 218, 341; economic 227; experiences 250; human 79; and inclusive design 18, 353; in India 103; interests 106; in Ireland 258; learners 23, 38, 40, 41, 52, 56, 62, 121, 175–177, **219**; learning 36–37, 91, 105, 112; needs 20, 31, 41, 71, 118, 141, 154, 161, 236; policies 352; in South Africa 35; students 38–39, 42, 43, 128, 259–260; and UDL 36, 72, 261–262, 277, 314; valuing 27
diversification 171, 192; of content 263, 356; of diets 248; educational design 14, 201; of methods 246; of pedagogical options 243
dot code content 164–165, **165**, 167–171, 355
drama 347, 348
Dreyer, L. 36

ecological relationships 183
Ecuador 242–249
Edge-Savage, Jennifer xx, 284–292, 354, 362
Education Act (Ireland) 258
Education Agenda *2030, the* 188
educational fad *see* fads in education
educational games 121, 123, **123**
educational reform: in Australia 305; in China 235–236; in Ireland 260; in Jamaica 46
educational technology 71–73, 150, 355; applications 182; in classrooms 284; skills 255; tools 146; *see also* assistive technology
educational technology (Ngram search term) 334, *336*, 337, *338*
educational universal design 269
education as a right 5, 38, 187, 236
Education for All Handicapped Children Act 5
Education for Persons with Special Educational Needs Act (EPSEN) 259
Education Resource Guide 219

Education Resource Information Center (ERIC) 70–71
Educause 42
Edulynx Corporation 194
Edyburn, Dave L. xx, 332–341, 339–340, 362
effectiveness 85, 90–92
"effectivity" 27
Egbert, J. 346
Eisner, E.W. 154
Elder, L. 332
eLearning 188, 198, 224; context 189–190; *see also* Massive Open Distance eLearning; Open Distance eLearning
elementary schools 62, 72; in Japan 269–271, 318–319; in the US 88, 288, 292, 348
emerging technologies and UDL 323–324, 327–328, **329**, 343–345
England 27
English language learner (ELL) 55, 81, 99, 132–133, 244, 287
environment 85, 88
ePals program 348
equal access 20, 30, 173, 259, 343
Equal Regular Education 69
Equal Rights for Persons with Disabilities Law 275, 352; *see also* Israel
equity: of access 4, 5, 315–316; audit 81; diversity, inclusion and 27; educational 48; and engagement 315–316; and equality 26, 103–109; in India 103–109; social 242; social justice and 353–354; in Sweden 28; *see also* inequity
eService management 193, 194
ethnic: groups 25; minorities 27; segregation 27
ethnicity 26, 60, 353
Every Student Succeeds Act (ESSA) 4–5, 14, 284
evidence-based strategies and practices 121, **122**, **309**, 340
evidence-informed practice 126, 252, 256
exclusion, exclusionism 36, 62, 194; and the digital divide 190
exit pathway 316
expanded access 30, 355
experiential project (EP) 245, *245*
EyeWriter 344, *345*

Facebook 288, 289, 325
face-to-face: classrooms 187, 276; courses 161, 288; delivery mode 157;

interactions 52; interviews 175; learning 155, 250, 285, 292; meetings 209, 287; settings 355
facial recognition technology 325
Facing Autism through Communication with the Environment (FACE) 76–79, 77, *78*, 353
fads in education 20, 332–334, *335*, 337–338, 340
Ferguson *see* Tatman Ferguson, Britt
Fernald, Grace 6
Fernald method 6–7
Filipino, Filipinos 190; learners 354; ODeL course offerings 189; school 177; teachers 173; workers 192; *see also* Philippines
fingerspelling 21
Frames of Mind (Gardner) 7
Free Art and Technology (FAT) 344
Fullan, M. 332
functionalist paradigm 19
functionality 143–144, 165–167, 326
furniture 88

Gadanidis, George xix, 153–162, 354, 363
Gagne, Robert 8–9
Gaible, E. 47
Gandhi (Mahatma) 76
Gardner, Howard 7, 347
gender 19, 25; bias 36; and ethnicity/race 26, 38; and inclusive design 353; parity 6; socioeconomic status and 25; and technology use 173, 244
Germany 295
Global Competitiveness Index 188
globalization 27
Global UDL Virtual Classroom project 46–56, **49**, *50*, **51**, **53**, *54*
Google Book project 333; Ngram 334, 337; Ngram Viewer 333, *335*, *336*; Trends 334–335, *337*, *338*
Graffiti Research Lab 344
Gronneberg, J. 41, 251–252
Gronseth, Susie L. xvi–xxi, 351–357, 363
Groton–Dunstable school district (USA) 81–82
group-oriented contingency (GOC) 318–319
Guatemala 120
Guidelines on the Use of Computer Laboratories in Teaching and Learning 173

handicapped 4, 77; *see also* disabled
Hanewald, R. 153
Hanson, Jane xx, 250–256, 363
Harris, Lisa xx, 267–268, 363
Harrison, Marc 39
hearing impairment 22, 31, **87**, 108, 188–189, 190, 221
heating, ventilation, and air conditioning industry (HVAC) 295–296, 298, 355
Hiebert, J. 48
Higher Education Act of 2008 340
Higher Education Authority Act 14
higher education institutions (HEIs) 259
Higher Education Law 21091 60; *see also* Chile
high-functioning autism (HFA) 111, 112
Hillaire, Garron xix, 197–206, 356, 363
Hilton, J. 142
Hisatsune, Yumi xix, 164–171, 355, 363
Hitchcock, C. 22, 71
home-stays 246
Hooks, David xviii, 30–31, 356, 364
how of learning 225, 254
How People Learn framework 49
human environment 269
hyperlinks 22, 23, 51, 55, **129**, 153
hypertext 22, 153

Iglesias, Irma xviii, 59–66, 364
Ikuta, Shigeru xix, 164–171, 355, 364
illuminated glove project 179–181
inclusion 27; laws around the world 5–7; US laws regarding 4–5
inclusive design 18–20; classroom 83; focus on design 19; frameworks of 23; learning 109; project 197–206; *see also* classrooms
inclusive education 37, 38; in China 70; fragmented approach 190; in Japan 269–271; in Ireland 258–264
inclusive instructional design 39, 62, 65, 181, 272, 285; approach 64; cases 273; diverse perspectives on 351–357; terms related to 334–338
inclusive learning (search term) 71
inclusive mathematics classroom 120–129
inclusive teaching and learning 20–23, 40; in China 69–71, 74; in Ireland 262; in Sweden 26; and technology 229; in the US 85–93, 229

Index 377

India 76–79, 353; differing learner needs in 103–104; inclusive initiatives 105–106; UDL practices in 103–109
Individuals with Disabilities Education Act (IDEA) 4–5, **290**
inequality 27, 38; education as a means to address 35, 36, 354; social 26, 173, 242
inequity 37, 81; educational 357; structural 345
information and communication technology (ICT) 47, 173, 187
information processing model of learning 96
Ingle, Jeanne Carey xviii, 132–133, 364
Iniesto, Francisco xix, 197–206, 356, 364
Initial Teacher Education (ITE) sector 259
instructional decisions 95, 267–268
instructional design 354; framework 14
Instructional Technology 132–133, **176**, 323; *see also* educational technology; information and communication technology (ICT)
Intatano, Vivian B. xix, 173–178, 364
Integrated Education for Disabled Children *(1976–77)* 103
integration 72, 171, 259; arts 346–347; of augmented reality (AR) 327; in classroom instruction 173; of digital and multimodal resources 227–229; of human rights and accessibility 39; of information and communication technology (ICT) 174, 177, 187, 355; of information 54; plan 85; programs 62; social 27, 38; technology 12, 41, 267, 288; of technology through UDL 141–150, 176, 323
Intelligence Reframed (Gardner) 7
interactive learning 236, 240; videos 186
intercultural competence (IC) 242–249, **247**
International Business Process Association of the Philippines' (IBPAP) 194
International Classification of Functioning, Disability and Health (ICF) 60
international service learning (ISL) 242
Internet Connectivity Project 174; *see also* Philippines
Internet of Things (IoT) 324–325
Ireland 258–264; The B. Ed. Research Project 261–262; mainstreams schools in 259; teacher education 260, 354; UDL in 259–261, *261*

Israel 275–283; disability law 352; educators/teachers 224–225, 354–355

Jamaica 46–56, 355
Japan 355; inclusive education system in 269–271, 353; UDL in 111–118
Japanese language 113–114, *114*
Johnson, Carole xx, 250–256, 364–365
Johnston, S. 39, 41, 251–252
justicia 242

Kanji *see* Japanese language
Kaufman Assessment Battery for Children (K-ABC) 115
Khanna, Radhike xviii, 76–79, 353, 365
Khurana, Aashna xviii, 103–109, 355, 365
Koehler, Matthew 10, *11*; *see also* TPACK
Korea 165
Koreeda, Kiyoji xviii, 111–118, 352–353, 365

Lachica, L. 173
Law N° 20,422 60; *see also* Chile
learning, teaching, and research model (LTRM) 315–316
learning disabilities (LD) 69, 89, 91–92, 111, 254, 269
Learning in Regular Classes 69
learning management system (LMS) 42, 208–213, 215, 228, 252–255
learning process 96, 96–97
learning-teaching model 198
Ledderhose Disease 179
Legos 275–283, 354
light-emitting diode (LED) 179–181; steps for constructing **180**, *180*
LilyPad technology 179–181
Linder, K. 221
Linking and Initiating a Network of Communication Through Synergy (LINCS) 79
Liu, Yang (Flora) xx, 250–256, 365
location-based technology 324–325
Lock, Jennifer xx, 250–256, 365
Lohmann, Marla J. xviii, 120–129, 354, 365
lone educators 288
low-tech 289; measures 40; solutions 120–129
Luo, Nili xix, 233–241, 353, 365–366
Lyner-Cleophas, Marcia xviii, 35–43, 353–354, 366

Mace, Ron 3, 12, 39
Mack, Terri xix, 218–219, 366
Madeline Hunter model 333
Maddux, C. D. 332, 334, 337, 339, 340
Making Decisions about Instructional Supports and Adaptations model 353
Making Decisions to Support All Students model 85, *86*, **87–88**, 92
manipulatives 123
Mao Zedong (Chairman) 234–235
Marotta, Mike xx, 284–292, 354, 366
Masayoshi *see* Tsuge
Massive Open Distance eLearning (MODeL) courses 191, 192–193, 354
massive open online courses (MOOCs) 192–195; reviews 197–206; *see also* YourMOOC4all
mastery learning 9–10
Mathematics Glossary 70
Math ML 70
Mavundla, S. 37
Menke, Katharina xx, 294–303, 355, 366
mind maps 153–162, *156*, *158*, *159*, 354
Mindmeister 154, 155, 157
Mindomo 154, 155, 157, 160
Ministry of Education, Culture, Sports, Science, and Technology (MEXT) (Japan) 269
mixed reality (MR) 294
mobile learning 215, 224, 354; applications (apps) 281
Modern Special Education 71
Molnar, Susan xx, 343–345, 366
Morris, A. 48
multiculturalism 27
multiliteracies 153
multimedia 17, 21, 73, *291*, **301**; content 294; formats 303; online materials 356; representations 302; tools 288, 291; tutorials 286
multiple intelligences 7–8, 347
Multiple Means of Action and Expression, Engagement, and Representation 225; and the arts **348**, 354; and augmented reality 297; in Chile 62; in China 237; and disability 89; and FACE 77, 353; instructional modules **51**, **53**; in Israel 224–225; in Jamaica 48; in Japan 166, 355; in Massachusetts 81; and Massive Open Online Courses (MOOCs) 199, **203–205**; and mathematical strategy **122**; and mind maps 154, 160; and online programs 135–136, 251; UDL,

core principles of 3–4, 7, 12, 40, 68, 96–97, 99, 251–252; and teacher candidates 267–268; and technology 323, **329**; in the United States 81, 85, 182–184, 221–222, 243–244; in the virtual classroom 55; "We Are All Connected" Series **219**; *see also* SAMR
Multisensory Instruction (MI) 6–7
Multisensory Reading 135–136
Museo Ethnohistorico de Artesannias del Ecuador Mindalae 243
Myanmar 165

Nagayama, Shintaro xx, 318–319, 366
National Commission on Special Needs in Education and Training (NCSNET) 36, 38
National Committee on Education Support Services (NCESS) 36
National Council for Educational Research and Training (NCERT) 105
National Curriculum Framework 2005 107; *see also* India
National Service of Disability 60; *see also* Chile
National Technology Act 14
National Technology Plan 340
National Universal Design for Learning (UDL) Summit 47
networked learning 315
neuroscience 39, 59, 96, 153; cognitive 261; research 3, 12, 262; theory 22
new grammar 333
new mathematics 333
New South Wales Standards Authority (NESA) Science Syllabus 307, 311, 314; *see also* Australia
Ng, W. 153
Ngram *see* Google Book project
Nieves, Kathryn xviii, 135–136, 355, 367
NMC 2018 Horizon Report 47
No Child Left Behind 346
Non-Discrimination Law 20609 60; *see also* Chile
Non-Governmental Organizations (NGOs) 174, 175
nonverbal communication 170
Notification of Additional Teaching Guidelines for Full-Time Schools or Classes for the Mentally Disabled, The 352
Novak, Katie xviii, 81–82, 367
novice 99, 255; mistakes of 101

object technology 248
occupational therapist (OT) 287
Okabe, Honami xx, 269–271, 367
Oman 165
one-size-fits-all approach 104, 262, 264, 294, 356
online learning 10, 17–23, 135; accessible 20–23; asynchronous 135–136; community 48, **51**, 54; content 276, 283; courses 41–42, 208–216; distance education 187–194; graduate orientation program 250–256; growth of 47; modules 49; programs 30; and UDL 135–136; web design principles 50; *see also* massive online open courses
Ontario Software Acquisition Program Advisory Committee (OSAPAC) 160
Open Distance eLearning (ODeL) 188, 189, 193
Open Distance Learning Act 188
open education (Ngram search term) 334, *335*, *337*
open educational environments 315–316
open educational resources (OER) 30, 47, **191**, 316, 354; course materials as 191; *see also* Massive Open Distance eLearning
openness 315; five Rs 316
otherness 26
outcome-based education 333
overcoming fear and barriers 292
Owiny, Ruby L. xviii, 120–129, 354, 367

Pacheco-Guffrey, Heather xviii, 132–133, 367
painting and pictures 91, 99, 100, 108, 115–117, 145; book task 312; puzzles 248
Pedagogical Content Knowledge (PCK) 10, *11*
Pedagogical Knowledge (PK) *11*
pedagogical practices 23, 30, 111
peer tutoring 123–124
pendulum syndrome 332
People with Disabilities Educational Ordinance Act of 2017 70, 252; *see also* China
personalization 315
personalized learning (Ngram search term) 334, *336*, *337*, *338*, 340
Persons with Disability (PWDs) 194
Philippines 173–178; universal access case study 187–195
Pole, Kathryn xix, 227–229, 367

Pond Keepers project 182–184, *184*
Post-School Education and Training (PSET) sector 37, 39, 41
potential obstacles 85, 89
Pratham's Instructional Framework 104–106
process orientation 18–19
professional learning networks (PLNs) 229, 289, **290**
programmed learning (Ngram search term) 333, 334, *335*, *337*
project-based learning 126–127, **127**
Project DI (Diversity and Inclusion) 194
Puentedura, Ruben R. 11–12, 142, *143*

Qatar xvi
QR codes **148**, 183, *184*, 281
quality education 120, 188, 260
Quality Indicators for Assistive Technology (QIAT) 285, 288, 289, 292
Quan, Tony *see* Tempt1
Quito 242, 243, 246; *see also* Ecuador

race 5, 25–28, 38, 60, 344; *see also* ethnicity; gender
racial segregation 36
Read with Me 70
reality therapy 333
Reality–Virtuality Continuum 294, *295*
reasonable accommodations *see* accommodations
recognition network 21, 22, 254, 295
Rehabilitation Act 31
Republic Act 10650 (Philippines) 188
Reynor, Ellen xx, 258–264, 354, 367
right brain–left brain instruction 333
Right to Education Act (RTE) 2009 103
Rights of Persons with Disabilities Act 2016 103
robotics and drones 325–326, 328, **329**
Rodrigo, Covadonga xix, 197–206, 356, 368
Rodrigo, M.T. 173
Roe, M. 346
Rogers, Sandra A. xix, 221–222, 368
role-play 40
Rose, David xiv–xv, 39, 48, 71, 104, 275–276, 295
Rouse, M. 325
rural: Bolivia 120; China 71, 234; educators 56; India 104, 105; Jamaica 46, 49, 51; Quito 242; schools 263; United States 72, 81
rural–urban divide 36

Salamanca Statement and Framework for Action on Special Needs Education 5, 25, 258, 351
SAMR model 11–12, 141–150, **147–149**
Sarva Shiksha Abhiyan 2001 103
Saudi Arabia 165
school for all 26
school-based support teams (SBST) 38
science, engineering, and art (SEA) 245, *245*
Science, Technology, Engineering, Art, Math (STEAM) 346
Science, Technology, Engineering, and Math (STEM) 346
Screening, Identification, Assessment and Support (SIAS) 38
segregation 35; *see also* South Africa
Semingson, Peggy xix, 227–229, 368
Sensitizing Attitudes for Normalizing Tendencies and Offsetting Latent Adult Non-acceptance of Autism (SANTOOLAN) 79
Shipley, Gina xviii, 30–31, 356, 368
Shrieber, Betty xx, 275–283, 352, 354, 368
Si, se puede (Yes, it can be done) 242
sign language 21, 105, 108, 201
Simmons, Thomas J. xix, 141–150, 368
Smartboard 239–240
Smith, Frances xviii, 46–56, 355, 368
social: class 26; biophysical- 60; cues 91; demands **87**; emancipation 18; integration 27; justice 20, 35, 43; media 198, 285–289, **290**, 292, 327, 354; model 36, 42; responsibility 168, 187; skills 116, 168; welfare 27, 28
social-emotional learning (SEL) 244, 245, *245*
social skill training (SST) 318
South Africa 35–43, 353
South African Constitution 35, 38
Spain 5, 356
spatial-visual intelligence 7, **347**, **348**
special education: in Chile 62; in China 69; students 135, 171; support 120; in Sweden 25–28; teachers 73, 91, 93, 166, 276, 287
special educational needs (SEN) 111, 113, 118, 258, 259, 319
Special Education Promotion Plan (2014–2016) 70; *see also* China
specially-abled students 76
special needs 72, 89, 105, 108
special needs education (SNE) 38, 269

special support service inventory 111
speech-language pathologist (SLP) 287
Spreading the Word about AT and UDL 285–292
standardization 27
stereotypes 20, 26
Stevens, R. 95
storytelling 146, 347
Strategic Disability Framework on the Post-School Education and Training System 39
Strategic Intervention Materials (SIM) 176
strategic network 254
Student, Environment, Task, Tools (SETT) 285, 288, 289, 292
Student Disability Services 31
students in a class 269
subject-based teaching 269
substitution-augmentation-modification-redefinition (SAMR) 11–12, 141–150, **147–149**, 355
Support Needs Assessment (SNA) structures 38
surface learning 237
Sustainable Development Goals (SDGs) 120, 242; SDG#4 188
Suwannawut, Nantanoot xviii, 17–23, 353, 368
Swafford, Dallas xviii, 30–31, 356, 368
Sweden 25–28, 353
Swenson, Nancy xix, 208–216, 356, 369

Tagore, Rabindranath 104
Tan, C. 237
target population 18
tasks and demands 85, 88
Tatman Ferguson, Britt xviii, 95–101, 356, 363
taxonomy of learning 8–9
teacher: education 260; learning 284–292; professional development 72–73, 354; training 36, 41, 46, 85, **88**, 90, 95, 174, 347; programs 268
teacher candidates (TC) 155, 157, 158, 160
teaching and learning 96
Teaching at the Right Level (TaRL) 105
teaching-learning program design 107
teaching machines 334, *335*
teaching philosophy: in China 72, 74, 241
teaching practices 115–118
Teaching with Technology **177**
Technological Content Knowledge (TCK) 10, *11*

Technological Knowledge (TK) *11*
Technological Pedagogical Content
  Knowledge (TPACK) 10–12, *11*,
  267–268
Technological Pedagogical Knowledge
  (TPK) 10, *11*
telematics 17
Tempt1 (Tempt One) 344, *345*
text-to-speech 41
Thailand 21, 353
Thwaite (The Honorable Reverend) 48
Tomlinson, Carol 9
Torii, M. 271
TPACK *see* Technological Pedagogical
  Content Knowledge
training and instructional support 85, 90
Trekles, Anastasia xviii, 85–93, 353, 369
Tsuge, Masayoshi xx, 269–271,
  318–319, 366
Twenty Eleven 50
Twitter 229, 286, 287, 289; Tweetdeck 288

UAL4D Framework 188, 190, **191**,
  195, 354
UDL: Tools and Strategies for ALL
  Students 286–292
UNESCO 5, 6, 120, 187, 188
Unilab Foundation 194
United Arab Emirates 165
United Farm Workers 242
United Nations Convention on the Rights
  of Persons with Disabilities (UNCRPD)
  38, 39, 103, 187
United Nations Sustainable Development
  Goals 242
United States Rehabilitation Act 4
United States 6, 71, 165; case study
  221–222; Center for Applied Special
  Technology (CAST) 111; education
  reform 346; and individualized
  education programs 284; Latina/o
  communities 242; mental map 145;
  online course offerings 251; special
  education centers 90; teachers 165
universal access (UA) 37
Universal Access to Learning for
  Development (UAL4D) framework 188,
  190–195, 354
universal design (UD) 37, 39–40; definition
  of 18, 103; and policy in South Africa
  35–43; *see also* inclusive design
universal design for learning
  (query term) 334

Universal Design for Learning (UDL) 37;
  authentic 64; Book Builder 55; in China
  68–74; corpus 338–339; decaffeinated
  59–66; design-based integration
  251–252; and differentiated instruction
  98; dinner party analogy 98; emergent
  tech and 343–345; as framework for
  instructional decisions 64, 267–268;
  Guidelines 70; implementation 42;
  importance of 97–98; instruction
  modules **51**, **53**; interventions 339–340;
  in Japan 111–118; and learner diversity
  40–42; Progression Rubric 82; situated
  74; research base 338–340; Studio 70;
  Toolkit 70; understanding 95–96; and
  variability 65; web-based resources
  129; *see also* checkpoints; diverse,
  diversity; Global UDL Virtual Classroom
  project; inclusive instructional design;
  integration
universal design for learning (Ngram
  search term) 334, *336*, 337, *338*
Universal Design for Learning Educators
  Checklist 306
Universal Design for Learning Guidelines
  2.2 122, 244
Universal Design for Learning (UDL)
  Learning Communities 65
Universal Design for Learning: Theory and
  Practice (Meyer, Rose, and Gordon) 14
Universal Design for Learning Virtual
  Classroom 46–56
University of the Philippines Open
  University (UPOU) 188, 190; UPOU
  Networks 191
uPar 292
user-centered design 295, 297, 344

variability 35–36, 37, 161; learner 48, 56,
  63, 65, 103, 255, 292; student 41, 47, 81
variation in learning 103
Vergara, Paola Andrea xviii, 59–66, 369
video-conference 52, 54
videos 22, 31, 82, 133, 142, **147**, **148**, 153,
  255; Alpabasa 174; blog 225; captioned
  40, 41, **149**, 212; clips 55, 91, 240,
  308; games *126*; and hypertext 153;
  internet 99; lectures 221–222; and mind
  map 155; and Mindmeister 157; as
  multimedia/multimodal 191, 213, 215,
  227, 228; as open educational resources
  136, 191, **203**; producing 276–282, **278**;
  sharing 73–74

virtual environments (VE) 17, 294, 326
virtual reality (VR) 145, **149**, 324, 355; and augmented reality 215, 294–303, 326–327
Vision 2030 Jamaica National Development Plan 46
visual: aids 116; artifacts 228; arts 347; chunking *125*; disabilities 19; displays **87**; icon 166; impairment 22, 23, 108, 188, 190, 199, 276, 323, 325; learning methods 7; memory 117; mind maps 153, 161; models 121, **122**, 124–125; presentations 114; representations 52, *54*, 141, 153–154, 280; resources **309**; stimuli 115; symbols 225; and verbal information 112
Visual-Auditory-Kinesthetic-Tactile (VAKT) 6–7
visualization 154, 161–162, 299
visual-spatial multiple intelligences **348**
vocational training 36, 175, 176, 188, 297

Walt Disney World 180–181
Walton, E. 36
wearable technology 326; *see also* assistive technology; augmented reality
"We Are All Connected" series 218–219, **219**

Web Content Accessibility Guidelines (WCAG 2.1) 191, **191**, 199, 208, 213
Weber, Peter xx, 294–303, 355, 369
webinars 40, 227, 228, 287, 288
what of learning 225, 254
whiteboard **128**, 144, **147**, 169, 239
White Paper 6 36–37
why of learning 225, 253
Woodley, Leanne xx, 305–314, 369
Wordpress 49–50, 52
word problems 125–126, **126**
workplace 295, 315, 324
World Wide Web Consortium (W3C) 191, 199, 208, 209, 215

Yearta, Lindsay xx, 267–268, 369
Youku 74
YourMOOC4all review system 198–206, *202*, **203–205**, 356
YouTube 40, 73–74, 262, 281; automated captioning tool 221–222, *222*, 325, 326; captioning manager **142**; videos 176, 212, 228, 279

Zambia 120, 121
Zhang, Haoyue xviii, 68–74, 352, 370
Zhao, George xviii, 68–74, 352, 370

Printed in the United States
by Baker & Taylor Publisher Services